Communications in Computer and Information Science 343

Juan Manuel Dodero   Manuel Palomo-Duarte
Pythagoras Karampiperis (Eds.)

Metadata
and Semantics Research

6th Research Conference, MTSR 2012
Cádiz, Spain, November 28-30, 2012
Proceedings

 Springer

Volume Editors

Juan Manuel Dodero
University of Cádiz, Spain
E-mail: juanma.dodero@uca.es

Manuel Palomo-Duarte
University of Cádiz, Spain
E-mail: manuel.palomo@uca.es

Pythagoras Karampiperis
National Center for Scientific Research "Demokritos"
Athens, Greece
E-mail: pythk@iit.demokritos.gr

ISSN 1865-0929   e-ISSN 1865-0937
ISBN 978-3-642-35232-4   e-ISBN 978-3-642-35233-1
DOI 10.1007/978-3-642-35233-1
Springer Heidelberg Dordrecht London New York

Library of Congress Control Number: Applied for

CR Subject Classification (1998): H.3.4-7, I.2.4, H.2.8, I.7.1, I.7.4, H.4.1-3, H.5.3-4, I.2.6

Typesetting: Camera-ready by author, data conversion by Scientific Publishing Services, Chennai, India

Printed on acid-free paper

Springer is part of Springer Science+Business Media (www.springer.com)

Preface

Metadata and semantics are undoubtedly one of the cornerstones of the Web and its future applications. The wide range of possibilities to enhance the current Web using metadata and ontologies moves many researchers and enterprises worldwide to study how to create and use conceptual, theoretical, and methodological frameworks to offer innovative computational solutions in that direction. Further, metadata in its several forms can be considered the fabric of a new concept of digital library, which spans across systems, and the efforts of the European Union on the creation of the Europeana digital library are a prominent example of this emergent idea. Now the concept of "linked data" has become a key driver of innovation that promises a reorganization of metadata to allow for direct linking between collections, avoiding information silos and enabling a new range of applications that are able to benefit from direct interlinking between resources.

In accordance with the principles of the original Metadata and Semantics Research Conference (MTSR) event in 2005 and following the steps of its successors MTSR 2007 (Corfu, Greece), MTSR 2009 (Milan, Italy), MTSR 2010 (Alcalá de Henares, Spain), and MTSR 2011 (Izmir, Turkey), MTSR 2012 was conceived as a meeting point for researchers in the field to discuss specialized results as general contributions to the state of the art. The conference attempts to gather a truly multi-disciplinary audience, with research papers coming from different IT-related fields such as information science and computing (in all its areas, including information systems), but also from any application-specific areas.

The conference as in previous years was organized in a general/main track and several others: a track on Metadata and Semantics for Open Access Repositories; Research Information Systems and Infrastructures; a second on Metadata and Semantics for Cultural Collections and Applications and finally one on Metadata and Semantics for Agriculture, Food and Environment. All the papers underwent a thorough and rigorous peer-review process. The review and selection this year was highly competitive to guarantee that only papers containing substantial novel research results of relevance for the international R&D audience were accepted for publication. Only 23 of 85 submissions were accepted as full papers, representing around a 27% of the total. Other papers covering interesting and insightful results in special tracks or project/experience reports were accepted, totalling 33 accepted contributions.

This proceedings book collects the papers presented at the MTSR 2012 event, which was held in the University of Cádiz, Spain. We express our sincere thanks to the university officers and the local organizers for their professional and hard work, which made the event a reality. Also, we would like to mention the important support of several sponsors, including the Software Process Improvement research unit, the Open Source and Free Knowledge Office of the University of Cádiz, the Technology and Sustainability Research Institute in Spain, and

Agro-Know Technologies in Greece. Further, the Open Discovery Space Project (http://opendiscoveryspace.eu/) funded by the European ICT PSP program provided support for the organization and co-located a visionary workshop on the adoption of e-learning resources in Spanish schools during the days close to the conference dates, allowing for the creation of synergies between conference attendants and project partners' representatives.

The conference this year invited two extraordinary keynote speakers, Mathieu D'Aquin and Alessio Malizia, who increased the quality of the conference and contributed with discussions on the latest advances in the field. The conference organization is grateful for their willingness to participate.

We would like to finish by thanking all the people that made possible the conference: members of the Program Committees (Track Committees included), the Steering Committee, and the Organizing Committees (both general and local).

September 2012   Juan Manuel Dodero
                                           Manuel Palomo-Duarte
                                          Pythagoras Karampiperis

Organization

Program Chairs

Dodero, Juan Manuel (Chair)	University of Cádiz, Spain
Karampiperis, Pythagoras (Chair)	NCSR Demokritos, Greece

Organization Chairs

Dodero, Juan Manuel (Chair)	University of Cádiz, Spain
Palomo-Duarte, Manuel	University of Cádiz, Spain
Ruiz-Rube, Iván	University of Cádiz, Spain
Stoitsis, Giannis	Agro-Know Technologies, Greece

Conference Steering Committee

Sicilia, Miguel-Angel	University of Alcalá, Spain
Manouselis, Nikos	Agro-Know Technologies, Greece
Sartori, Fabio	Università degli Studi di Milano-Bicocca, Italy

Local Organizing Committee

Balderas Alberico, Antonio	University of Cádiz, Spain
Mota Macías, José Miguel	University of Cádiz, Spain
Palomo Duarte, Manuel	University of Cádiz, Spain
Ruiz Carreira, Mercedes	University of Cádiz, Spain
Ruiz-Rube, Iván	University of Cádiz, Spain
Tocino García, José Tomás	University of Cádiz, Spain

Program Committee

Altun, Arif	Hacettepe University, Turkey
Anido Rifón, Luis	Universidad de Vigo, Spain
Athanasiadis, Ioannis N.	Democritus University of Thrace, Greece
Bartol, Tomaž	University of Ljubljana, Slovenia
Budin, Gerhard	University of Vienna, Austria
Chebotko, Artem	University of Texas - Pan American, USA
Colomo-Palacios, Ricardo	Universidad Carlos III de Madrid, Spain
Corchuelo, Rafael	University of Seville, Spain
Costopoulou, Constantina	Agricultural University of Athens, Greece
Cunningham, Sally Jo	Waikato University, New Zealand

Dallas, Costis	Panteion University, Greece
Derobio, Antonella	Università degli Studi di Padova, Italy
Dogdu, Erdogan	Teknoloji ve Ekonomi University, Turkey
Garoufallou, Emmanouel	Technological Educational Institute of Thessaloniki, Greece
Gergatsoulis, Manolis	Ionian University, Greece
Gradmann, Stefan	Humboldt-Universität zu Berlin, Germany
Houssos, Nikos	National Documentation Centre, Greece
Iglesias, Carlos A.	Universidad Politécnica de Madrid, Spain
Kaltenböck, Martin	Semantic Web Company, Austria
Kanellopoulos, Dimitris	University of Patras, Greece
Kop, Christian	University of Klagenfurt, Austria
Labra Gayo, José Emilio	University of Oviedo, Spain
Moen, William	University of North Texas, USA
Ochoa, Xavier	Escuela Superior Politécnica del Litoral, Ecuador
Palavitsinis, Nikos	Greek Research and Technology Network, Greece
Palmonari, Matteo	University of Milano-Bicocca, Italy
Poulos, Marios	Ionian University, Greece
Sánchez-Alonso, Salvador	University of Alcalá, Spain
Senkul, Pınar	Middle East Technical University, Turkey
Sgouropoulou, Cleo	Technological Educational Institute of Athens, Greece
Sugimoto, Shigeo	University of Tsukuba, Japan
Summann, Friedrich	Universität Bielefend, Germany
Ünalır, Murat Osman	Ege University, Turkey
Tudhope, Douglas	University of Glamorgan, UK
Zarraonandia, Telmo	Universidad Carlos III de Madrid, Spain

Track on Open Access Repositories, Research Information Systems and Infrastructures

Special Track Chairs

Subirats, Imma	Food and Agriculture Organization of the United Nations, Italy
Houssos, Nikos	National Documentation Centre, Greece

Program Committee

Castelli, Donatella	Italian National Research Council, Italy
Carr, Les	University of Southampton, UK
Dunshire, Gordon	University of Strathclyde, UK
Giaretta, David	Science and Technology Facilities Council, UK
Ioannidis, Yannis	University of Athens, Greece

Jack, Kris   Mendeley, UK
Jeffery, Keith   Science and Technology Facilities Council, UK
Jörg, Brigitte   German Research Centre for Artificial
                                  Intelligence, Germany
Krichel, Thomas   Long Island University, USA
Luzi, Daniela   Italian National Research Council, Italy
Manghi, Paolo   Italian National Research Council, Italy
Manola, Natalia   University of Athens, Greece
Manouselis, Nikos   Agro-Know Technologies, Greece
Matthews, Brian   Science and Technology Facilities Council, UK
Plexousakis, Dimitris   University of Crete, Greece
De Robbio, Antonella   University of Padova, Italy
Rodrigues, Eloy   University of Minho, Portugal
Schöpfel, Joachim   University of Lille, France
Stathopoulos, Panagiotis   National Documentation Centre, Greece
Tzitzikas, Yannis   University of Crete and ICS-FORTH, Greece
Wittenburg, Peter   Max Planck Institute for Psycholinguistics,
                                  The Netherlands
Zeng, Marcia   Kent State University, USA

Track on Metadata and Semantics for Cultural Collections and Applications

Special Track Chairs

Gergatsoulis, Manolis   Ionian University, Greece
Meghini, Carlo   Consiglio Nazionale delle Richerche, Italy
Papatheodorou, Christos   Ionian University, Greece

Program Committee

Christodoulakis, Stavros   Technical University of Crete, Greece
Dallas, Costis   Panteion University, Greece
Davies, Rob   MDR Partners, UK
Dekkers, Makx   Independent consultant, Spain
Ferro, Nicola   University of Padua, Italy
Isaac, Antoine   Vrije Universiteit Amsterdam, The Netherlands
Lourdi, Irene   University of Athens, Greece
Manouselis, Nikos   Agro-Know Technologies, Greece
Ore, Christian-Emile   University of Oslo, Norway
Roberts, Dave   Natural History Museum, UK
Sfakakis, Michalis   National Documentation Centre, Greece
Tudhope, Douglas   University of Glamorgan, UK

Track on Metadata and Semantics for Agriculture, Food and Environment

Program Chairs

Athanasiadis, Ioannis N.	Democritus University of Thrace, Greece
Manouselis, Nikos	Agro-Know Technologies, Greece
Keizer, Johannes	Food and Agriculture Organization of the United Nations, Italy

Program Committee

Antoniou, Grigoris	University of Crete, Greece
Beck, Howard	University of Florida, USA
Brewster, Christopher	Aston University, UK
Caracciolo, Caterina	Food and Agriculture Organization of the United Nations, Italy
Carlson, Jack	Colorado State University, USA
Donnelly, Kathryn	Norwegian Institute of Food, Fisheries and Aquaculture Research, Norway
Dowding, Ed	Sustaination, UK
Houssos, Nikos	National Documentation Center, Greece
Jaiswal, Pankaj	Oregon State University, USA
Keet, Maria	University of KwaZulu-Natal, South Africa
Konstantopoulos, Stasinos	NCSR Demokritos, Greece
Le Hénaff, Diane	INRA, France
Martini, Daniel	Association for Technology and Structures in Agriculture, Germany
Nesic, Sasa	IDSIA, Switzerland
Penev, Lyubomir	Pensoft Publishers, Bulgaria
Protonotarios, Vassilis	Agro-Know Tecnologies, Greece
Roberts, Dave	The Natural History Museum, UK
Rizzoli, Andrea Emilio	Istituto Dalle Molle di Studi sull'Intelligenza Artificiale, Switzerland
San Gil, Iñigo	University of New Mexico, USA
Sánchez-Alonso, Salvador	University of Alcalá, Spain
Stellato, Armando	University of Rome Tor Vergata, Italy
Verhelst, Lieke	Alterra – Wageningen UR, The Netherlands
Vignare, Karen	Michigan State University, USA
Subirats, Imma	Food and Agriculture Organization of the United Nations, Italy

Table of Contents

Track on Metadata & Semantics for Open Access Repositories, Research Information Systems & Infrastructures

Track on Metadata & Semantics for Cultural Collections & Applications

Track on Metadata and Semantics for Agriculture, Food and Environment

Semantic Geodemography and Urban Interoperability*

Joaquín Borrego-Díaz, Antonia M. Chávez-González, Mónica A. Martín-Pérez, and José A. Zamora-Aguilera

Dept. of Computer Science and Artificial Intelligence - University of Seville, Avda. Reina Mercedes s/n. 41012 Seville, Spain

Abstract. Nowadays there exists an increasing interest on the use of the information collected by cities coming from different resources as data with dynamic nature like the one provided by sensor networks, as static data associated to the socio-technical system that the city performs. As well as the Semantic Sensor Web allows the standardization of data, it is essential to give an appropriate dealing to geo-demographic data. In this paper, an approach to the semantization of the geo-demographic information is presented, with the aim of achieving interoperability within other systems of the *geospatial cyberinfrastructure*. Furthermore, fundamental aspects of the creation of ontologies by starting from socio-demographical systems are discussed and the process is illustrated with a case study.

1 Introduction

Today, flows of information produced and extracted from cities are becoming increasingly interesting. The integration of these data for the improvement of processes and services is one of the mainstays on which the concept of *smartcity* is based. Data sources range from sensors to other with a more statical nature such as the ones provided by national census and other administrative and commercial databases or social and demographical surveys [4]. For an accurate combination of data we need semantic-level systems of operability. Although there exist initiatives such as *Semantic Sensor Web*, in the case of socio-technical systems (the ones which deal with socologic, demographic and cultural data) it has not been advanced so much as in that of the former. To provide metadata (and mainly ontologies) for geodemographic representation is essential to design innovative products, processes or services by semantic interoperability of two kinds of systems:

- Systems for Urban Computing: *Urban Computing* is a branch of Pervasive Computing that investigates urban settings and everyday lifestyles. A lot

---

* Partially supported by TIN2009-09492 project (Spanish Ministry of Science and Innovation), cofinanced with FEDER founds, and *Proyecto de excelencia* TIC-6064 *Conceptos emergentes en sistemas complejos. Aplicaciones en entornos urbanos y en complejidad cultural* financed by *Junta de Andalucía*.

J.M. Dodero, M. Palomo-Duarte, P. Karampiperis (Eds.): MTSR 2012, CCIS 343, pp. 1–12, 2012.

of information to develop pervasive applications for urban environments is often already available, even if scattered and not integrated: maps, points of interest, user locations, traffic, pollution, events are just a few examples of the digitalized information which we can access on the Web [8].

- *Geodemographic information systems* represent a kind of business tool for interpreting data that consists mainly of a demographic database, digitized maps, and software. Data are captured on the computer, updated, maintained and organized for effective use and manipulation. Locational and spatial variations of population features are analyzed. Although primary goal is marketing, such systems are widely used for several applications [7].

The achievement of a trustworthy semantic interoperability among both kind of systems is essential to the design of semantic sociotechnical systems which combine both kinds of information. Particularly in smartcities projects, because it would allow the design of taylored services and processes to specific neighborhoods or urban spaces. The interoperability will make easier the management and valuation of the socioeconomical consequences of regions. Thus, new methodologies should be designed for urban spaces and these methodologies represent an opportunity to take into positions in new cities growing at a fast pace in emerging regions [10].

The aim of this paper is to present an approach to the semantization of geodemographic information from the point of view of the Semantic Web framework (described in Sect. 2). The design of socio-geodemographic ontologies is the precious step to carry out the semantic interoperability between urban computing and geodemographic information systems associated to cities or regions (Sect. 3). Also we discuss the fundamental features of the transformation from geodemographic information to an ontology (Sect. 4), by showing the ideas with a case study (Sect. 5). Meta-descriptions of digital resources are represented, and the gap between sociodemographic characterizations and formal descriptions are shown. The paper ends with our conclusions about the approach as well as their relationships with other ontology-based solutions.

2   Semantic Web and (Urban) Ciberinfrastructure

The Semantic Web (SW) aims to extend the current WWW realm to trustworthy process the information by means the metadata representation, which is enriched (transformed in Knowledge) by means the use of its misunderstanding interpretation provided by ontologies. As an extension of the actual Web, the implementation of the WS must overcome big obstacles [3] from the point of view of the knowledge representation and reasoning. Its layer structure (RDF/ RDF(S)/ OWL/ Ontologies) sets several abstraction levels in which ontologies play a key role. The interest for applying typical WS techniques, as the ontologies are, comes from got the results, to a certain extent, by means of automatic reasoning, what grants them trust. WS technologies extend to important fields such as the *Semantic Sensor Web* [19] or the management of *Linked Data*.

Other aspect to bear in mind when considering the use of ontologies for urban surveys, is the analysis of the *geospatial ciberinfrastucture (GCI)* that the city enjoys. A ciberinfrastructure (CI) combines data sources, computing platforms and services together to provide people information and computing tools in an information-driven world. Geospatial ciberinfrastructure adopts intrinsic principles and geospatial information to support processing abilities such as geospatial analysis and geospatial decision [23]. GCI analysis is essencial, not only for the establishment of a research and development agenda in the city, but to capture its intrinsic features and the influence and relationship between the city and physical, social and geographical elements of urban framework. Having in mind that the integration of every systems conforming a GCI is not feasible in practice, a GCI provides, by means of ontologies, a common semantic framework to enable semantic interoperability and shared understanding. In this context, a case of special interest is the one of the location based service, PDAs and iPhones, due to the increasing number of mobile devices, the further introduction of sensors and Geographical Information Systems (GIS) available devices.

Ontologies can play a key role to deal with and streamline the information that the city owns, by means of GCI and getting interoperability for heterogeneous urban information systems [13]. Nevertheless, the process of construction of ontologies for urban development or city management, faces the gap between pragmatic heterogeneity concerned with urban concepts and the difficulty about formalizing concepts within a technological framework like WS is (besides the representation in OWL-like standards). As an example, the concept "residence" of an individual is crucial, and its formalization should -in geodemographics- include features on the social role that the residence stamps [6]. There are other urban concepts for which not only there is not a precise definition but, in any case, the limits of a definition are fuzzy and, thus, capable to lead to inconsistencies.

Therefore, geodemographics should be included like one of the systems belonging to the GCI, thus information will be cut across within geospatial domain (social, environmental, etc.) by other GCI systems. The evolution of GCI will produce platforms where data are collected, analyzed and used by communities and, besides, the specialization and adaption of results to different sociodemographic realities provides the infrastructure with an added value.

3   Geodemographies as Knowledge Augmented Spaces

Geodemography deals with the study of the information about complex social realities which are the reason for emerging phenomena arising in cities and sensor-based information is not able to represent. The origins of geodemographics date from 19th century but the development of a software specifically designed to facilitate the design of classification systems to sort out people and places is which motivates the growth in social scientific interest in these classifications. That is how geodemographics play a key role in the analysis of the relation between places and society [6]. The relevance of the modernization of information processing and representation lies in the fact of it facilitates the study of networks, neighborhoods and communities making possible to analyze how these elements are perceived by citizen and which methods are more appropriate for understanding and promoting them.

Although cities are complex systems in which a number of (physical, social, virtual, etc.) networks interweave and connect, and are based on scalability and urban-morphology principles [5], the social dimension linked to spaces strongly determines the rest of networks. The existence of a semantic geodemographics will facilitate the interoperability among the different systems at a semantic level. In that context, to make use of a geodemographical layer provides management systems the capability of connecting real-time extracted data with social, demographical and economical features leading to a suitable decision making with the best information and a better diagnosis. GCI can use this kind of information (with static nature) to advice and obtain connections between the behavior of the city (and residents) and the social framework of a concrete zone.

The opportunity of encourage the sustainability of sociotechnical systems is especially interesting. These systems are concerned with society, organizations, individuals, their behavior and the technological infrastructure that they use. Smartcities have become global sociotechnical systems, including the sustainability issue. Large and long-lived impacts on sustainability will require enabling, encouraging, and sustaining changes in behavior -on the part of individuals, organizations, and nation-states over the long term. Informatic technologies, and in particular real-time information and tools, can better equip individuals and organizations to make daily, ongoing, and significant changes in response to a constantly evolving set of circumstances [15]. For example, spatial formalizations are empirically linked to multiscale transport systems and a range of urban socioeconomic consequences in different urban cultures worldwide [18]. Therefore, sociogeodemography aids to understand the transport as a global phenomena of communities. It is worth to notice the opportunity of encourage the social benefits of connecting, by means open data, people who share the same neighborhoods or practices, reducing gas emissions, power consumption, as well as keeping citizen informed about local events [1].

Nevertheless, *Local* term can be controversial, although it is aimed that the information locate sectors and zones with a special interest. This term includes spatial categories such as "community", "neighborhoods" or area. With respect to physical place, it refers to the physical support of local communities. But it is possible that it refers to communities that persist in an area or a time [12]. Effectively, places and identities have gone hand in hand but social assignment of identities is a complex task created through practices of consumption across a range of spaces which are key in defining who we are.

4   Semantizing Geodemographies

From Urban Informatics' point of view, sociogeodemographic ontologies provides support for both metadata and interoperability in several levels of information ecosystem in the city (see Fig. 1). It allows to enhance information (metadata) from sensors with information about the population of the area, for example. Also provides information about the urban features associated to geodemographic indices. In this way the city model provided by the information can be enriched with knowledge that allows to argument decisions which influences city behavior.

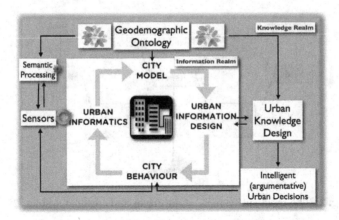

Fig. 1. Knowledge from the ontology to the urban information ecosystem

Intended use: The first step is to limit and specify the intended use of the ontology. As we commented, and thinking on smartcities, our aim is to fit together that information within the information flows of the city for providing it with quality from the social point of view. Of course, this goal must consider that the GCI is a *middleware* among different information sources and it integrates several functions. Therefore, the ontology has to reflect and standardize the socio-demographical information available to build systems for combining this information, in such a way that GCI provides us with (both spatial and digital) knowledge, etc. To suppose that the ontology is useful for other kind of tasks would mean that its scope of application would be unstable, fuzzy and therefore not usable. For example, to consider demographical geo-located sectors as communities de facto does not imply to consider virtual communities or the ones built under other criteria. In that case, social heterogeneity performed by semantic geo-demographics can be different from the one that the pre-existent GCI considers.

Requirements: Mainly two requirements have to be considered:

- **Ontology must facilitate the high level information fusion** that allows future social changes. The recollection of new information from residents is necessary to update the sociotechnical systems within GCI. On the one hand, a process for building formal ontologies to provide a conceptual framework for higher level fusion processing is necessary [14],. On the other hand, there are approaches [9] addressing issues related to the capability of generating and integrating user-generated information into the GCI, to be reused and shared. In [9] authors present semiautomatic mechanisms to augment the availability of user-generated information, improving the visibility of geospatial resources.

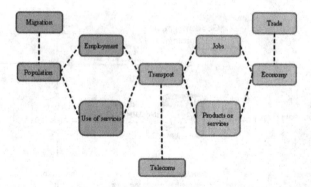

Fig. 2. The main subsystems of an urban and regional system [22]

- **Ontology must provide knowledge about (and for) Urban Systems**:
  Main urban subsystems (Fig. 2, extracted from [22]) depend from information that can be provided by geodemographic systems. Knowledge provided
  by geodemographic metadata aids to refine and analyze the modelization of
  such subsystems. The figure shows the elements in broad terms—the population and the economy as a framework with the addition of activities, interactions and infrastructure—all by location: people reside, work, shop and
  use services at a variety of locations. Indeed, representing spatial interaction
  is a key underpinning for many urban and regional models [22].

5   Extracting an Ontology. An Example

At this point, we face the matter of building an ontology from sociodemographi-
cal data. It is worth to remark that geodemographics systems can be considered
under three points of view: as datasets apt to be treated statistically, as systems
to be interpreted by especialistas and, also as a semiformal representation of a
geodemographic conceptualization. The last one is the sound one to be considered for building an ontology, although above two considerations have to be taken
in account. To illustrate the results of that process, we present some features of
the ontology that we have extracted from Mosaic. Mosaic comprises a range of
geodemographic segmentation systems which, by mean of statistical techniques
of classification, leads to classify individuals into groups (subdivided into more
specific profile types) under qualitative and quantitative criterion. Mosaic products have been created by Experian Group, and some of them are, for example,
Mosaic UK, Mosaic Public Sector, Mosaic Global and Mosaic Commercial. Each
one is oriented to a business type. The design of these tools includes the use of
geographic information systems and software for database management. Mosaic
Global is a tool used in marketing to get the segmentation of consumers focused
to the analysis and assessment on customer research: prospective, recruitment
and loyalty. Groups are defined by attending to demographic and socio-economic
features such as age, ethnicity, level of affluence and accommodation among

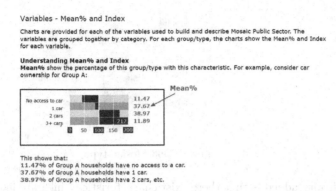

Variables - Mean% and Index

Charts are provided for each of the variables used to build and describe Mosaic Public Sector. The variables are grouped together by category. For each group/type, the charts show the Mean% and Index for each variable.

Understanding Mean% and Index
Mean% show the percentage of this group/type with this characteristic. For example, consider car ownership for Group A:

This shows that:
11.47% of Group A households have no access to a car.
37.67% of Group A households have 1 car.
38.97% of Group A households have 2 cars, etc.

Fig. 3. Explaining Mosaic charts

others. These characteristics are, in general, similar for a large proportion of the population in a concrete zone.

The online Mosaic Interactive guide brings the consumer visual classification and descriptive and statistical information backed up by more detailed information in the eHandbook. It offers quick synopsis for describing groups and types, their features and behavior as well as graphics used to build groups (see Fig. 3).

There exist other segmentation systems as CAMEO (UK) and ACORN (UK). ACORN and Mosaic provide detailed descriptions of a range of sociodemographic environments, explaining the reasons and the scope of each one. From the ontological point of view, they are *ideal types* in which documentation explicit information is not included [6]. They are archetypes which can be explained by statistical data (interpreted by expert scientist), but they do not fully characterize each class. Finally, we must also take into account that original definitions in Mosaic present difficulties to transform them into metadata: variance across individuals into a class, variance of requirements for belonging to the class or lack of critical requirements [21].

5.1   The Semantic Gap between Semantics and Geodemographics

In the case of Mosaic, it uses about 400 data variables, 11 groups and 61 types. From the point of view of its utility, there are some strengths: it make feasible to carry out interventions and services in a more specific way, to locate social marketing and identify social inequalities. Several limitations are the following: lack of transparency in methods for compiling and processing data (considering the statistical robustness of results performed by the tool as well as the ecological side of this issue) [11]. For example, the proportion of the average with respect to a characteristic often do not match with the description of the group. It is very frequent, in particular with data such as net income of the family, one of the most significant features of certain groups and types. It is usual to find cases, in principle, featured by earning high (or very high) incomes, but percentages for them match with low incomes, as it occurs in type O63 (see Fig. 4).

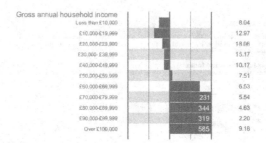

Fig. 4. Incomes in O63 Mosaic type

Other difficulty added is that there exist characteristics which are likely critical for the identification of groups (following their description), but these features have not been included in the definition because of sufficient statistical data have not been provided. This is what occurs, for example, with the (urban, rural, etc.) neighborhoods, the size of houses or tax rates. In other cases, even having enough statistical data, they look like void data, as the number of holidays. Finally, the information brought by the description is conflicting. As an example, we can cite the type O63. The age in this type is given by means of two ranges in the same document: 35-45 y 25-55 years. Other example can be found in type O61: on the one hand, we have "Well paid professional couples, often with children, choosing to live in diverse urban areas rather than the suburbs", and on the other hand, couples without children still (what matches with data).

These circumstances have made hard the classification and identification of the set of classes of the ontology, because many of the properties could not be included or have been included with low percentages. Further, we have to add the fact of several classes have been defined as conjunction of a range of properties and, therefore, the percentage of individuals belonging to these classes (fulfilling the properties) can be significantly reduced.

5.2   Methodology

The methodology to build the ontology consists of three stages (see Fig. 6):

1. Analysis of the geodemographic system:
   - Analysis of geodemographic types used by the system
   - Analysis of geodemographic data
   - Analysis of expert's interpretation of geodemographic
2. Interpretation
   - Interpretation of types as (demographic) classes
   - Interpretation of data as (object or data) properties on classes
   - Interpretation of segmentation
3. Ontology engineering
   - *Middle-out* method for hierarchy construction
   - Axiomatization (actually necessary conditions) of classes by means the characterization of (object or data) properties
   - Interpretation of segmentation in axioms

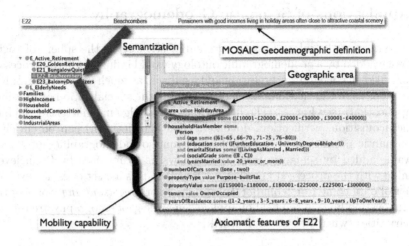

Fig. 5. Semantization of a Mosaic geodemographic class

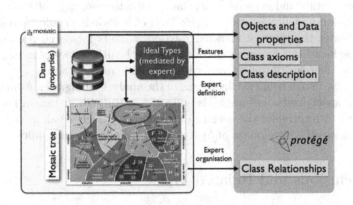

Fig. 6. Semantization of a geodemographic class

In each step the difficulties above commented have been faced. In general, there is a distance (separate by sociodemographics experts) between data presented in Mosaic and the description of every type, which is used to characterize (recognize) each class. From the point of view of the use of Mosaic in GCI, translated to an ontology, the definitions have to be profiled under weaker requisites but maintaining the richness of the information. For example, the class E22, as we show in Fig. 5, is described by including among the fundamental features, those ones which lead us to combine the information with mobility aspects, geodemographic zone, etc. Thus, that *axioms* can provide valuable information for the systems of the GCI. This option is the one we have choose by semantizing data and it provide us with a set of axioms (all of them are conditions or requisites for belonging to the class) which can be selected to get information about the Mosaic type we use (see Fig. 6).

6   Applications of Semantic Geodemography

In the context of the information ecosystem of a smarcity, the sphere of social knowledge added by a geodemographic ontology would influence all the processes of informational collect, interpretation and feedback, as much in the Urban Informatics scope as in the city management by leading the specialization of decisions and applications (see Fig. 1). The life cycle of knowledge in smartcities (including the acquisition, verification, documentation and decision) can be enriched with semantic processing of data, not only from sociodemographic ontologies. The value added by semantic technology allows us to mediate by (high level) reasoning with the processed knowledge. Of course, this aspect does not exclude the fact of data come from collaborative practices or *crowdsourcing*. Some of the main innovation lines in the field of applied semantic geodemography are related to smart cities (with their social features):

- Combined use with urban planning/landscape systems (as for example [16]). This combination facilitates knowledge to decide urban interventions. In emergent cities and regions which faces with the problem of their ground and developing [10], the reuse of this kind of knowledge could be possible.
- It facilitates the birth of knowledge-based markets for social products and services: location for new community centers, health service planning. It can estimate their social impact according available metadata.
- To increase urban resilience by means of the analysis of digital information [4] and the specialization of methods and process through metadata reasoning.
- It allows to interrelate the social dimension of distinct urban models [13]
- It facilitates the developing of *hyperlocal* social o community apps.

7   Conclusions and Related Work

In this paper we sketch the main lines of geodemographic ontology design and engineering. We also have pointed out the limitations, from Knowledge Engineering, to the develop of geodemographic systems. However, the opportunity and potential benefits of its application made the enterprise both interesting and necessary: ontologies provides knowledge to GCI. In general, geodemographic ontologies and metadata can enrich several urban subsystems (see Fig. 7 where a subset of properties of MOSAIC semantization are linked as knowledge source in the modelization of some urban subsystems).

There exist a number of works with aim to interrelate social and physical structure in cities and regions. Geodemographic ontologies have to be aligned with other semantic tools which shape geographic concepts as for example he Semantic Framework of the Universal Ontology of Geographical Space (UOGS) [17], mainly to a sound use of *location similarity* [17] concept in geodemographic field. In [2] introduces the *variograms* to determine binary similarities and their application on spatial data would allow the qualitative spatial reasoning with geodemographic zones.

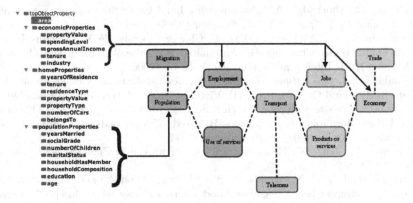

Fig. 7. Geodemographic knowledge for Urban Systems

With respect to urban ontologies, it is interesting to consider the relationship with *TownTology*[1] (see also [20]. Towntology project aims to develop ontologies for urban civil engineering, thus a geodemographic ontology can enhance the social dimension of the system, as well as to estimate the impact on the community of the urban intervention. The aligning of both ontologies is, however, problematic because there exist a gap among two disciplines and urbanist have to design ontologies which allow co-exploit metadata and knowledge.

There exist other geodemographic systems, as for example CAMEO[2], OAC[3] by ONS/University of Leeds, ACORN[4] or CLOUD CLIENT[5] which can be semantized as well. In fact, the semantic interoperability among such systems is an interesting future research line.

Lastly, it is interesting to face the challenge of the revision of geodemographic ontologies. Urban ontologies have to be adaptive in some features because several urban subsystems have a dynamic nature [20]. Geodemography is static in essence, but its relationship with the urban dynamics can motivate ontology revision. The refinement (or reshaping) of demographic concepts can produce incoherences that ontology engineer can not explain. Thus, intelligent interfaces for ontology repairing have to be designed for this specific case which encompasses metadata and high level (rough) definitions.

References

1. Smarter Neighborhoods Smarter City. Solutions for a More Sustainable New York. Siemens Report, http://www.usa.siemens.com/sustainable-cities/

---

[1] http://www.towntology.net/

[2] http://www.callcredit.co.uk/products-and-services/
consumer-marketing-data-and-segmentation/cameo-classifications/cameo-uk

[3] http://areaclassification.org.uk/getting-started/
getting-started-what-is-the-output-area-classification/

[4] http://www.caci.co.uk/acorn-classification.aspx

[5] http://cloud-client.co.uk/

2. Ahlqvist, O., Shortridge, A.: Characterizing Land Cover Structure with Semantic Variograms. In: [17], pp. 401–415. Springer (2006)
3. Alonso-Jiménez, J.A., Borrego-Díaz, J., Chávez-González, A.M., Martín-Mateos, F.J.: Foundational Challenges in Automated Semantic Web Data and Ontology Cleaning. IEEE Intelligent Systems 21(1), 42–52 (2006)
4. Aranda-Corral, G.A., Blanco-Escudero, A., Borrego-Díaz, J., Gomar-Acosta, M.: Data-in-the-cloud City. In: Proc. 7th Virtual Cities and Territories, Lisboa (2011)
5. Batty, M.: Cities as Complex Systems: Scaling, Interaction, Networks, Dynamics and Urban Morphologies. In: Meyers, R.A. (ed.) Encyclopedia of Complexity and Systems Science, pp. 1041–1070. Springer (2012)
6. Burrows, R., Gane, N.: Geodemographics, Software and Class. Sociology 40(5), 793–812 (2006)
7. Burrows, R., Ellison, N., Woods, B.: Neighbourhoods on the net: The nature and impact of internet-based neighbourhood information systems. Joseph Rowntree Foundation (2005)
8. Della Valle, E., Celino, I., Dell'Aglio, D.: The Experience of Realizing a Semantic Web Urban Computing Application. Transactions in GIS 14(2), 163–181 (2010)
9. Díaz, L., Granell, C., Gould, M., Huerta, J.: Managing user-generated information in geospatial cyberinfrastructures. Fut. Gen. Comp. Syst. 27, 304–314 (2011)
10. Dobbs, R., Remes, J., Manyika, J., Roxburgh, C., Smit, S., Schaer, F.: Urban world: Cities and the rise of the consuming class. Report of McKinsey Global Institute (June 2012)
11. Dougan, S.: Using Mosaic en Islington,
http://obesity.thehealthwell.info/node/26781
12. Ellison, N., Burrows, R.: New Spaces of (Dis)engagement? Social Politics, Urban Technologies and the Rezoning of the City. Housing Studies 22(3), 295–312 (2007)
13. Falquet, G., Métral, C., Teller, J., Tweed, C. (eds.): Ontologies in Urban Development Projects. Springer (2011)
14. Little, E.G., Rogova, G.L.: Designing ontologies for higher level fusion. Information Fusion 10, 70–82 (2009)
15. Millett, L.I., Estrin, D.L. (eds.): Computing Research for Sustainability. The National Academies Press (2012)
16. Montenegro, N., Gomes, J.C., Urbano, P., Duarte, J.P.: A Land Use Planning Ontology: LBCS. Future Internet 4, 65–82 (2012)
17. Riedl, A., Kainz, W., Elmes, G.A. (eds.): Progress in Spatial Data Handling. Springer (2006)
18. Schumacher, P.: Parametricism. In: Leach, N. (ed.) Digital Cities, Architectural Design, pp. 14–45 (July/August 2009)
19. Sheth, A., Henson, C., Sahoo, S.S.: Semantic Sensor Web. IEEE Internet Computing 12(4), 78–83 (2008)
20. Teller, J., Cutting-Decelle, A.-F., Billen, R. (eds.): Future of Urban Ontologies. Proc. Final Conference of the COST Action C21 – Towntology: Urban Ontologies for an Improved Communication in Urban Development Projects (March 2009)
21. Ure, J., Procter, R., Lin, Y., Hartswood, M., Ho, K.: Aligning Technical and Human Infrastructures in the Semantic Web: a socio-technical perspectiven. In: 3rd Int. Conf. on e-Social Science, Michigan, USA (2007)
22. Wilson, A.: The Science of Cities and Regions. Springer Briefs in Geography. Springer (2012)
23. Yang, C., Raskin, R., Goodchild, M., Gahegan, M.: Geospatial Cyberinfrastructure: Past, Present and Future. Computers, Environment and Urban Systems 34, 264–277 (2010)

Providing LOD-Based Functionality in Digital Libraries

Ioannis Papadakis and Konstantinos Kyprianos

Ionian University, Dept. of Archives and Library Science
Ioannou Theotoki 72, Corfu, 49100, Greece
papadakis@ionio.gr, k.kyprianos@gmail.com

Abstract. Libraries and other memory institutions have wasted no time in realizing that linked data technologies provide the necessary means to solve important interoperability issues that have been plaguing the community for decades. Despite the wide availability of cultural heritage information as linked open data – LOD, there seems to be a lack of LOD services that are targeted towards the end-user. In this paper, a LOD-powered, subject-based browsing service is proposed, capable of integrating resources from diverse repositories. More specifically, the proposed work describes a service that is built on top of a DSpace-based digital library of thesis and dissertations that not only exposes its topical information (i.e. subject headings) to the wider linked data community, but also manages to provide its end-users with additional relevant resources originating from a remote repository (i.e. New York Times – NYT articles database). The proposed service has been accordingly evaluated through a user survey.

Keywords: Linked Data, SKOS, SPARQL, Subject Headings, User Survey.

1   Introduction

Nowadays, an ever-increasing amount of semantic cultural heritage information is provided as linked open data – LOD [2]. Stakeholders of memory institutions and especially libraries have soon realized that the adoption of LOD technologies will not only aid in solving important interoperability issues that have been plaguing the community for decades [10], but also would provide the necessary infrastructure for the creation of new, value-added services. Such services will be capable of integrating semantic information that exists within traditional institutional repositories such as Online Public Access Catalog – OPAC systems with third-party information such as picture and video archives, or knowledge bases like DBpedia[1].

A very important type of semantic information that exists within memory institutions is the topical information of the underlying resources. Memory institutions and especially libraries have exhibited throughout the years remarkable consistency in creating and accordingly consuming topical information [10] within their repositories, conforming to widely accepted standards and practices. The adoption of linked data

---

[1] DBpedia. http://dbpedia.org/ Date accessed: 12/07/2012.

J.M. Dodero, M. Palomo-Duarte, P. Karampiperis (Eds.): MTSR 2012, CCIS 343, pp. 13–24, 2012.
© Springer-Verlag Berlin Heidelberg 2012

technologies such as LOD triplestores and their corresponding SPARQL endpoints from major data providers of cultural heritage institutions is a major step towards the provision of highly interoperable institutional repositories.

Despite the wide availability of such technologies, there seems to be a lack of LOD services that are targeted towards the end-user. Memory institutions are mainly concerned in transforming and exposing their topical information as linked data, without paying the necessary attention to the usability and usefulness of the services that are based on linked data.

In this paper, a LOD-powered subject-browsing service is proposed that is built upon a digital library of thesis and dissertations. The proposed service not only exposes its' topical information to the wider linked data community, but also manages to provide relevant resources originating from remote repositories (i.e. New York Times – NYT articles) through the alignment of such information in a transparent for the end-user way. The proposed service has been accordingly evaluated through a user survey.

The remainder of this paper is structured as follows. The next section presents the current status of linked data in memory institutions. In section 3, the proposed LOD-based service with its corresponding architecture and structure is outlined. Section 4 presents the results of a user survey analysis that has been conducted. Finally, section 5 concludes the paper and points directions for future work.

2   The Linked Data Movement in Memory Institutions

Nowadays, many libraries and other memory institutions publish information as linked data. In the following lines an overview of the corresponding literature is presented.

During the past century, Library of Congress Subject Headings - LCSH dominated the library domain as the de facto controlled vocabulary for assigning subject descriptors to resources [11]. Thus, the fact that since 2008, LCSH are also published as LOD[2] [3] is indicative of the intentions of the library domain concerning the adoption of linked data. Following the steps of LCSH, RAMEAU, the French approach in subject headings cataloging are also available as linked data[3] [13]. Another key player of the library community that made an effort to expose information on the Web as linked data is the Dewey Decimal Classification – DDC System [14]. In a similar manner, the Finnish Ontology Library Service ONKI[4] is another case of linked data employment in libraries. Moreover, the Semantic Computing – SeCo Research Group has many ongoing projects related to the linked data community, like the National Semantic Web Ontology Project (FinnONTO) [9]. The national swedish library created the LIBRIS[5] system [5] as an effort to incorporate LOD technologies within the Swedish library sector. In 2008, the entire LIBRIS catalog was published as linked data, rendering it as the first union catalog ever participating in the LOD-cloud[6] as a whole.

---

[2] LCSH. http://id.loc.gov Date accessed: 12/07/2012.
[3] RAMEAU / SKOS. www.cs.vu.nl/STITCH/rameau/ Date accessed: 12/07/2012.
[4] ONKI. http://onki.fi/en/browser/ Date accessed: 12/07/2012.
[5] Libris. http://libris.kb.se/ Date accessed: 12/07/2012.
[6] Lod-cloud. http://lod-cloud.net Date accessed: 12/07/2012.

It is worth mentioning that all the above attempts in publishing library linked data on the Web are based on the Simple Knowledge Organization System – SKOS [12]. Finally, the importance of the linked data movement to the cultural heritage community could not go unnoticed from Europeana [15]. Thus, data.europeana.eu[7] is part of Europeana's ongoing effort of making its metadata available as linked data.

Another class of linked data approaches within memory institutions concerns thesauri and their corresponding subject descriptors. Along these lines, the STW Thesaurus for Economics[8] [16], the Agricultural Thesaurus and Glossary – ATG[9] and AGROVOC LOD[10] are indicative examples of LOD-ready thesauri providing their data as dereferenceable URIs.

The rest of this section presents LOD services that not only publish their information as linked data, but also consume linked data provided by third parties.

The first service presented is the Polythematic Structured Subject Heading[11] – PSH [6]. PSH is a bilingual (i.e. Czech-English) tool to organize and search for documents by subject. End-users of PSH manipulate an elegant, interactive GUI in order to browse through the subject headings of the underlying LOD triplestore by taking advantage of their syndetic structure [4], providing also links to DBpedia and/or LCSH.

Another LOD service that takes a further step from just publishing linked data for the cultural heritage community is the EuropeanaConnect Media Annotation Prototype [17]. According to the authors of [17], end-users are able to interact with an annotation mechanism on top of Europeana's digital assets that exposes annotations as linked data.

To sum up, it is evident that the key players of the cultural heritage community seem to have realized the importance and the benefits of linked data and have started to endorse LOD services. However, meaningful integrated linked data applications for the end-users are still hard to find on the Web.

3   Proposed Work

In this paper, a LOD-powered, subject-based browsing service[12] is presented, capable of integrating resources originating both from the DSpace[13]-based digital library of thesis and dissertations at the University of Piraeus in Greece[14] and the NYT[15] articles

---

[7] Europeana LOD. http://version1.europeana.eu/web/lod/
     Date accessed: 12/07/2012.
[8] STW Thesaurus for Economics. http://zbw.eu/stw Date accessed: 12/07/2012.
[9] Agricultural Library Thesaurus. agclass.nal.usda.gov/agt.shtml Date accessed: 12/07/2012.
[10] AGROVOC. http://aims.fao.org/standards/agrovoc/about
     Date accessed: 12/07/2012.
[11] PSH. http://psh.ntkcz.cz/skos/home/html/en Date accessed: 12/07/2012.
[12] Subject-based service. http://neel.cs.unipi.gr/entry/
     Date accessed: 10/07/2012.
[13] DSpace software. http://www.dspace.org Date accessed: 12/07/2012.
[14] Digital library. http://digilib.lib.unipi.gr/dspace/ Date accessed: 10/07/2012.
[15] The New York Times. http://www.nytimes.com/ Date accessed: 12/07/2012.

database. The DSpace-based digital library refers to a DSpace installation containing around 4.380 theses and dissertations on economics, business, management, informatics, maritime studies and banking of post graduate students and around 3.500 bilingual (English-Greek) subject headings describing the collection. The resources of the underlying digital library are assigned specific subject headings that are integrated with the subject headings of the NYT indexing vocabulary through an alignment algorithm that will be presented later in this paper and accordingly stored as linked data in a corresponding LOD triplestore.

The service manages not only to expose subject headings as linked data, but also succeeds in providing its end-users with additional resources coming from a remote repository (i.e. NYT database) through the employment of the NYT api tool[16]. The augmenting of such information is achieved in a transparent way for the end-user.

3.1   Architecture

As illustrated in Figure 1, the proposed service relies on a LOD repository consisting of aligned subject headings deriving from the underlying DSpace-based digital library and the NYT. Such subjects constitute an ontology, which is based on the SKOS specifications.

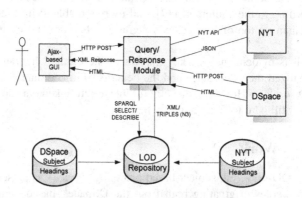

Fig. 1. The overall system architecture

End-users interact with the underlying LOD repository through a simultaneously bilingual, Ajax-based GUI. The GUI provides the opportunity to end-users to search for subjects or to browse them in order to locate relevant thesis and dissertations as well as NYT articles.

The information flow among the components of the proposed architecture is facilitated through an accordingly designed Query/Response Module that is implemented in Python. Thus, in the event of a user interaction, an HTTP POST request is issued and accordingly served by the Module in order to provide adequate XML/html responses that are ultimately handled by the Ajax-based GUI.

---

[16] NYT api. http://prototype.nytimes.com/gst/apitool/
Date accessed: 12/07/2012.

More specifically, in order to satisfy a request from the GUI, the Query/Response Module addresses a SPARQL query to the corresponding endpoint of the underlying LOD repository[17], which, in turn, replies with a SPARQL xml result. As stated earlier, the LOD repository consists of the aligned subject headings of the underlying digital library and the NYT. If the corresponding response contains a subject heading from DSpace, then the Query/Response Module creates another query that is addressed to the DSpace digital library as a HTTP POST request. If the corresponding response contains a subject heading that also belongs to NYT, then the Query/Response Module additionally creates an HTTP GET request to the NYT's api tool. The responses from DSpace and NYT are provided as plain html and json respectively.

3.2   Cool URIs in Subject-Based Browsing Services

As stated in [1], a basic requirement of participating in the linked data movement is to use dereferenceable URIs. Thus, every single subject heading of the proposed service corresponds to a dereferenceable URI. The majority of the subject headings that exist within the LOD repository belong to the LCSH system and are accordingly identified (e.g. http://id.loc.gov/authorities/subjects/sh94002414).

Moreover, for the needs of the digital library's subject-based indexing, additional subject headings have been created and accordingly assigned a new URI. These URIs belong to the local namespace of the service (i.e. http://id.lib.unipi.gr/authorities/subjects/) and are dereferenced through the local SPARQL endpoint.

3.3   Linked Data Based on SKOS

For the needs of the proposed service, it was decided to adopt the SKOS specifications in order to create a LOD repository consisting of subject headings that belong to the NYT namespace, LCSH namespace and the locally defined one.

More specifically, according to the SKOS specifications, subject headings are modeled as concepts [7], and they are hierarchically organized according to their syndetic structure [4], as this hierarchy is explicitly defined by the LCSH[18].

Table 1 summarizes the employment of the SKOS terminology in order to model the relations between different concepts of the underlying LOD repository:

Table 1. Employment of SKOS terminology

Subject Headings	SKOS terminology
Broader Term	skos:broader
Narrower Term	skos:narrower
Related Term	skos:related
Use	skos:prefLabel
Use For	skos:altLabel
-	skos:exactMatch
-	skos:closeMatch

---

[17] Proposed service's SPARQL endpoint. http://neel.cs.unipi.gr/endpoint/ Date accessed: 27/07/2012.

[18] LCSH. http://authorities.loc.gov Date accessed: 12/09/2012.

3.4   Alignment Process

In order to align the subject headings deriving from the local digital library and the ones deriving from NYT, it was decided to employ the mapping ontology algorithm that was presented in [8]. According to this algorithm, two terms are considered equivalent if they are exactly the same. In this case, the SKOS terminology that is used to declare such relationship is <skos:exactMatch>.

Furthermore, there are several cases in which two subject headings are considered as partially equivalent:

- One subject heading may be in plural and the other in singular (e.g "Bankrupt-cies" in NYT and "Bankruptcy" in DSpace)
- Suffix variation: some terms may be different with the use of some extra charac-ters (e.g. "Iraq war (2003-)" in NYT and "Iraq war, 2003-" in DSpace)
- One subject heading may have another word order (e.g. "Colleges and Universi-ties" in NYT and "Universities and colleges" in DSpace)
- One subject heading may correspond to a synthetic term and vice versa (e.g. "Advertising and marketing" in NYT and "Advertising" and "Marketing" in DSpace).

The SKOS terminology that is used to declare such relationships is <skos:closeMatch>.

After applying this algorithm, a total of 207 subject headings were found in both NYT and LCSH (i.e. 111 'closematch' and 96 'exactmatch'). The criteria underpin-ning partial equivalence between NYT and LCSH are based on per-case empirical rules that have been posed by experienced librarians. Quantification of such criteria has proved to be difficult to impose due to the inherent fuzziness of spoken languages. Thus, the proposed algorithm is partially based on human intervention.

In the next section, the GUI of the proposed service is demonstrated.

3.5   Ajax-Powered GUI

End-users interact with the LOD-powered service through an accordingly developed, Ajax-based GUI. The GUI builds upon its previous version, which is presented in [4]. More specifically, the GUI consists of the following components: a) the autosuggest input box, b) the subject-based browsing system, c) the DSpace and NYT search results.

a) Auto-suggest input box

End-users are initially prompted to express their information needs in Greek and/or English (depending on the language choice) into an auto-suggest input box (see figure 2). The input box reacts to user's typing by suggesting subject headings. Such a com-ponent acts as an entrypoint to the service and helps end-users verbalize their infor-mation needs.

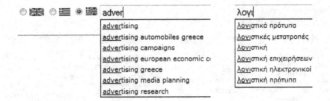

Fig. 2. Auto-suggest bilingual functionality in English and in Greek

b) Subject-based browsing system

Upon selection of a suggestion, a box representing the subject heading is sketched below the auto-suggest input box (see figure 3). The bilingual version of the box is comprised of the authorized English label of the subject heading together with the corresponding Greek translation and the variant terms of the selected subject heading in English and Greek respectively. End-users are able to dynamically exclude one of the two languages from the GUI by selecting the appropriate flag that is shown in figure 2.

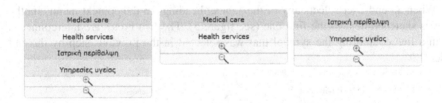

Fig. 3. Sketched box for "Medical care" in both languages, English and Greek

Beneath the labels there are two metaphors in yellow background that correspond to the 'zoom in' (+) and 'zoom out' (−) functionality of the service. The (+) and (−) signs retrieve the narrower and broader terms of the subject heading respectively. Thus, upon selection of any of these two metaphors, a context menu next to the sign is sketched containing the corresponding subjects.

If the end-user selects a subject heading consisting of a subdivision, the box contains, apart from (+) and (−), a new relation that is named after the subdivision of the previously selected subject heading (i.e. 'Standards' in figure 4). Upon selection of the relation, the context menu that is accordingly sketched contains subject headings that share this subdivision. Such functionality refers to the extended syndetic structure as described in [4]. If there are several subject headings in the sketched box that share the same subdivisions apart from the one that was selected in the previous step (e.g. 'greece' in figure 4), these are grouped together and presented as a separate folder, named by the common subdivision (see the 'breadcrumb' of the context menu in figure 4).

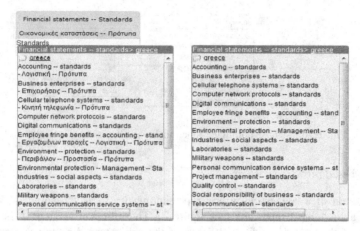

Fig. 4. The subject heading "Financial statements -- standards" and its corresponding 'standards' subject headings in both languages and in English only

End-users may access the subject headings within a folder by clicking on that folder. In that case, the breadcrumb navigation bar on top of the context menu shows the user's path to the current location.

When an end-user selects any of the subject headings in the context menu, another box is sketched next to the first one (see figure 5). The two boxes are interconnected with a line containing the symbol that was selected in the previous step by the end-user.

Fig. 5. The subject headings "Advertising" and "Publicity" are associated with the "NT" relation

c) DSpace – NYT search results

When a subject heading from the context menu is selected, a query containing the specific subject is dispatched to the underlying OPAC and a list of the corresponding resources is presented to the end-users. If a selected heading is associated with an equivalent or partially equivalent NYT subject heading, then another query is dispatched to the NYT articles' database and a list of the corresponding articles is presented to the end-users as a new tab next to the list of the DSpace' s results, ranked by their popularity. Finally, end-users are able to click on a search result in order to navigate to the specific resource, or, reformulate their query (using the auto-suggest functionality or the sketched boxes).

The next section evaluates the proposed service through an accordingly designed user survey analysis. The evaluation focuses in the functionality and effectiveness of the proposed service. On the contrary, the added value of the additional information (i.e. NYT articles) that is fetched from the service is not evaluated. As far as linked data is concerned, the contribution of this paper resides in the methodology of integrating diverse datasets, not in the quality of the datasets per se.

4 Evaluation

Following the steps of Borlund [19] who supported the idea that the evaluation of an Interactive Information Retrieval - IIR system involves the "simulated work task situation", we concluded that the evaluation process of the proposed service should consist of a user survey employing real search task scenarios and adequately designed questionnaires. More specifically, the goals of the specific evaluation process were threefold: i) to determine the value of using the proposed service as a way of learning the collection with respect to the users' specific information needs, ii) to evaluate the user satisfaction regarding the proposed service and iii) to evaluate its overall performance and efficiency.

The survey was carried out at the University of Piraeus' library during July 2012. Nineteen participants were recruited. The whole process lasted approx. 10 minutes for each participant and consisted of 4 phases, organized as follows:

1. A pre-task questionnaire[19], to capture the participants' experiences, background and demographics.
2. System training, during which the participants became accustomed with the functionality of the system.
3. Search task scenarios. The participants were asked to carry out 4 search task scenarios of increasing difficulty with the proposed service. The first two were verbalized in English and the other two in Greek. The tasks were the following: Try to find relevant information about a) "Stress management", b) "Computer network protocols", c) "Economic matters" related to "Greece" and the "European Union" and d) "Regression analysis[20]".
4. A post-task questionnaire, to capture the participants' thoughts and overall impression about the proposed service.

The following section presents the results of the evaluation process.

4.1 Pre-task Questionnaire Analysis

According to the pre-task questionnaire, 6 out of 19 participants were undergraduate students, 2 were postgraduate students, 2 were PhD candidates and 4 were university staff. The remaining 5 participants had no direct relation to the University of Piraeus.

---

[19] The pre- and post- task questionnaires and the results of the survey can be accessed at: https://docs.google.com/open?id=0B-zgNdHCG27DSEY5R1dybGRVdkE

[20] The third and fourth task were given in Greek: c) "Οικονομικά θέματα" σχετικά με την "Ελλάδα" και την "Ευρωπαϊκή Ένωση" and d) "Ανάλυση παλινδρόμησης".

All the participants agreed that they had medium to high experience in searching and browsing for information on the web. Moreover, 13 of the participants had visited the library's digital library at least one time before. Finally, 18 out of 19 participants stated that they prefer to employ both English and Greek language when searching and browsing for information on the web.

4.2   Post-Task Questionnaire Analysis

According to the responses of the participants to the post-task questionnaire, 90% found the proposed service very easy or easy to use. Furthermore, 85% of the participants agreed that the autosuggest search box helped them in satisfying their information needs. Slightly smaller (i.e. 68%) was the percentage of the participants that stated that the overall GUI helped them in satisfying their information needs. The decrease in user satisfaction from the autosuggest box to the overall GUI could be attributed to the fact that nowadays, autosuggest functionality has become an integral part of many web sites. Thus, web users are accustomed to such functionality. On the other hand, some of the metaphors of the proposed service are not so popular on the web and, consequently, could have raised the difficulty in handling the service, thus affecting the overall user satisfaction.

Also, 79% of the participants agreed that the proposed service assisted them in concluding the corresponding search session fast.

As far as the bilinguality of the proposed service is concerned, 73% of the participants agreed or strongly agreed that the simultaneously bilingual interface (English – Greek) helped them in finding all the relevant information within the underlying collection. This could be attributed to the fact that the proposed service simultaneously addresses one query for each version of the subject (i.e. Greek – English, Use – Use For) and merges the corresponding results in a single list. On the contrary, the traditional DSpace system requires different queries in order to get all the relevant results. For example, searching for "regression analysis" within the traditional DSpace yields 7 results and its' Greek translation (i.e. "Ανάλυση παλινδρόμησης") yields the remaining 10 of the 17 that would have been retrieved in the case the proposed service was employed.

Regarding the understandability of the proposed service, the participants were asked whether training was necessary in order to use the service effectively. About half of the participants needed training before using the service. The percentage is even higher among people that did not have any familiarity with DSpace. Having also in mind the aforementioned moderate results about user satisfaction of the provided GUI, it can be safely concluded that the provided GUI is not as straightforward as it should be.

Finally, in order to find the overall impression of the participants about the proposed service, we asked them to tell us whether they would use the proposed service again in order to fulfill their future information needs. According to their responses, 74% of the participants agreed to use the proposed service again. This leads to the conclusion that the efficiency of the proposed service dominated over its rather steep learning curve.

5   Conclusions and Future Work

In this paper, a LOD-powered subject browsing service is presented, capable of integrating resources from two diverse repositories, namely the digital library of thesis and dissertations at the University of Piraeus in Greece and the NYT articles. The integration was performed through the alignment of their corresponding subject headings. The alignment wouldn't be possible if the subject headings of each repository were not available as linked data.

Furthermore, the proposed service utilizes an innovative subject browsing system that, with minor modifications, is applicable to any SKOS-based instance data[21] [18] (e.g. other digital libraries). A key feature of such a system is the fact that it manages to hide system-specific terminology from the end-user.

Another key aspect of the proposed service is the simultaneous bilingual GUI. End-users are able to see the original subject headings as defined by the corresponding authority (in this case, Library of Congress) and their translations at the same time. This is particularly important for services that are addressed to people speaking another language than the one that is used to describe the resources of the underlying assets. There are cases where end-users are familiar with the original version of the subject heading and other cases where end-users are familiar with the translated one. The proposed simultaneous bilingual GUI treats both cases uniformly without requiring explicit interaction from the end-user.

Future work will be targeted towards the application of same principles that govern the proposed service to other digital libraries in Greece with similar content. Then, the ultimate goal will be to create a federated digital library of thesis and dissertations consisting of member digital libraries that communicate with each other through the employment of linked data technologies.

References

1. Bizer, C., Heath, T., Berners-Lee, T.: Linked Data - The Story So Far. Int. J. Semantic Web Inf. Syst. 5(3), 1–22 (2009)
2. Berners-Lee, T.: Linked Data - Design Issues (2006),
   http://www.w3.org/DesignIssues/LinkedData.html
   (date accessed: November 28, 2011)
3. Summers, E., Isaac, A., Redding, C., Krech, D.: LCSH, SKOS and linked data. In: Proceedings of the 2008 International Conference on Dublin Core and Metadata Applications (DCMI 2008). Dublin Core Metadata Initiative, pp. 25–33 (2008)
4. Papadakis, I., Stefanidakis, M., Kyprianos, K., Mavropodi, R.: Subject-based Information Retrieval within Digital Libraries Employing LCSHs. Dlib Magazine 15(9/10) (2009),
   http://www.dlib.org/dlib/september09/
   papadakis/09papadakis.html, doi:10.1045/september2009-papadakis

---

[21] Software concerning this service will be available through the Project's website: http://swrg.ionio.gr Date accessed: 12/07/2012.

5. Söderbäck, A., Malmsten, M.: LIBRIS - Linked Library Data. Nodalities: the Magazine of the Semantic Web 5(11/12) (2008), http://www.talis.com/nodalities, http://www.talis.com/nodalities/pdf/nodalities_issue5.pdf (date accessed: November 28, 2011)

6. Mynarz, J., Kozuchova, K., Kamradkova, K.: Polythematic Structured Subject Heading System & Creative Commons (2009), http://www.techlib.cz/files/download/id/649/psh-cc.pdf

7. Isaac, A., Summers, E.: SKOS Simple Knowledge Organization System Primer. W3C Group Note (2009), http://www.w3.org/TR/skos-primer/

8. Papadakis, I., Kyprianos, K.: Merging Controlled Vocabularies for More Efficient Subject-based Search. International Journal of Knowledge Management -IJKM 7(3), 74–90 (2011)

9. Hyvönen, E., Viljanen, K., Tuominen, J., Seppälä, K.: Building a National Semantic Web Ontology and Ontology Service Infrastructure –The FinnONTO Approach. In: Bechhofer, S., Hauswirth, M., Hoffmann, J., Koubarakis, M. (eds.) ESWC 2008. LNCS, vol. 5021, pp. 95–109. Springer, Heidelberg (2008), http://www.seco.tkk.fi/publications/2008/ hyvonen-et-al-building-2008.pdf

10. Paepcke, A., Chang, C.K., Winograd, T., Garcia-Molina, H.: Interoperability for digital libraries worldwide. Commun. ACM 41(4), 33–42 (1998), doi:10.1145/273035.273044

11. Stone, A.T.: The LCSH Century: A Brief History of the Library of Congress Subject Headings, and Introduction to the Centennial Essays. Cataloging and Classification Quarterly 29(pt. 1/2), 1–16 (2000) ISSN: 0163-9374

12. Miles, A., Perez-Aguera, J.R.: SKOS: Simple knowledge organisation for the web. Cataloging & Classification Quarterly 43(3-4), 69–84 (2007), doi:10.1300/J104v43n03_04

13. van der Meij, L., Isaac, A., Zinn, C.: A Web-Based Repository Service for Vocabularies and Alignments in the Cultural Heritage Domain. In: Aroyo, L., Antoniou, G., Hyvönen, E., ten Teije, A., Stuckenschmidt, H., Cabral, L., Tudorache, T. (eds.) ESWC 2010, Part I. LNCS, vol. 6088, pp. 394–409. Springer, Heidelberg (2010)

14. Markey, K.: Searching and browsing the Dewey Decimal Classification in an online catalog. Cataloging and Classification Quarterly 7(3), 37–68 (1987)

15. Purday, J.: Think culture: Europeana.eu from concept to construction. The Electronic Library 27(6), 919–937 (2009)

16. Neubert, J.: Bringing the "Thesaurus for Economics" on to the Web of Linked Data. In: Workshop at the WWW 2009 Conference on Linked Data on the Web (LDOW), Madrid, Spain, April 20 (2009)

17. Haslhofer, B., Momeni, E., Gay, M., Simon, R.: Augmenting Europeana Content with Linked Data Resources. In: 6th International Conference on Semantic Systems. ACM, Graz (2010)

18. Papadakis, I., Stefanidakis, M.: Visualizing ontologies on the web. In: New Directions in Intelligent Interactive Multimedia. SCI, vol. 142, pp. 303–312. Springer (2008) ISBN: 978-3-540-68126-7

19. Borlund, P.: The IIR Evaluation Model: a Framework for Evaluation of Interactive Information Retrieval Systems. Information Research 8(3) (2003)

SSONDE: Semantic Similarity on LiNked Data Entities

Riccardo Albertoni[1,2] and Monica De Martino[2]

[1] OEG-DIA,
Facultad de Informática Universidad Politécnica de Madrid,
Boadilla del Monte, Madrid, Spain
ralbertoni@fi.upm.es
[2] CNR-IMATI,
Via De Marini, 6 – Torre di Francia - 16149 Genova, Italy
demartino@ge.imati.cnr.it

Abstract. The paper illustrates SSONDE, a framework to assess semantic similarity on linked data entities. It describes the framework architecture, its design assumptions and its configuration functionalities. SSONDE relies on an instance similarity in which asymmetricity and context dependence are specifically conceived to compare linked data resources according to their metadata. Two different applications to consume linked datasets are illustrated showing SSONDE as a building block technology to sift linked data resources.

Keywords: Instance Similarity, Linked Data, Metadata Analysis.

1   Introduction

Linked data provides a promising framework to encode, publish and share metadata of resources in scientific and industrial domains. Significant factors are enabling linked data as the ideal place where to share metadata: (i) linked data relies on light-weighed ontologies, which are encoded in Resource Description Framework (RDF) and can be exploited to provide ontology driven metadata. Such a kind of metadata takes advantage of the Open Word Assumption, enabling the adoption of domain specialized and independently developed metadata vocabularies which are pivotal to document resources produced in complex and loosely coupled pipelines; (ii) linked data is consistent with the current web architecture. It is not proposing a brand new platform replacing the existing technologies. It relies on content negotiation exploiting the standard HTTP protocol, so that, linked data solutions can be layered on existing domain-specific metadata architecture; (iii) linked data comprises a mature stack of frameworks to expose and manage metadata (e.g., D2R [1]), to retrieve non-authoritative RDF fragments published around the web (e.g., Sindice [2]), to consolidate metadata exposed in independently-provided datasets (e.g., SILK [3]), to search and navigate retrieved RDF fragments according to the entity oriented paradigm (e.g., SIGMA [4]), to query RDF fragments by appropriate query language (i.e., SPARQL), to store, manipulate and reason on these fragments once there are retrieved (e.g., Sesame, Virtuoso, Jena).

J.M. Dodero, M. Palomo-Duarte, P. Karampiperis (Eds.): MTSR 2012, CCIS 343, pp. 25–36, 2012.
© Springer-Verlag Berlin Heidelberg 2012

As a consequence of these enabling factors, linked data is adopted by data producers such as European Environment Agency, US and some EU Governs, whose first ambition is to share (meta) data making their processes more effective and transparent. Such as an increasing interest and involvement of data providers surely represents a genuine witness of the web of data success, but in a longer perspective, there will be a compelling need for frameworks supporting earlier linked data consumers in their decision making processes.

In this paper, we introduce SSONDE, a framework which enables a detailed comparison, ranking and selection of linked data resources through the analysis of their RDF ontology driven metadata. SSONDE implements the instance semantic similarity we presented in [5] under a linked data settings. SSONDE's similarity is especially designed to support in resource selection, namely the process stakeholders engage to choose a set of resources suitable for a given analysis purpose: (i) it deploys an *asymmetric* similarity assessment to emphasize containments between resource features, containment makes explicit information about *gains* and *losses* the stakeholders get adopting a resource in place of another; (ii) it relies on an explicit formalization of *contexts* to tailor the similarity assessment with respect to specific user-defined selection goals.

The crucial contribution of this paper is the SSONDE's JAVA open source framework, which is freely available for third parties usages. SSONDE pushes our instance similarity as a handy tool to analyze entities whose metadata are exposed as linked data. It has been designed to fit in the application layer of the *Crawling Architectural Pattern*, a linked data architectural pattern known as suitable for implementing applications on top of an open, growing set of sources [6]. SSONDE has been demonstrated in two scenarios related to the analysis of environmental and researcher metadata. Both the applications are introduced and in particular the latter is discussed in more details.

The paper is organized as follows: Section 2 introduces the SSONDE framework, describing the design assumptions, framework's components and configuration; Section 3 presents two concrete scenarios in which SSONDE has been deployed analyzing RDF metadata exposed in real linked data datasets; Section 4 discusses instance similarity's related works; Section 5 provides conclusions and future works.

2   Framework Description

SSONDE moves our context depended and asymmetric instance similarity [5] from locally stored ontology driven repositories to a settings compatible with the linked data assumptions. In order to success in this transition, SSONDE

- extends the notion of context presented in [5], making explicit the reference to namespaces, so that, it is possible to exploit properties from distinct RDF schemas in the context formalization;
- deactivates the modules computing the similarity among instances on the bases of their class hierarchies, so that, poor structured hierarchies adopted in the current linked data do not negatively affect the similarity results;

- makes the similarity assessment independent from the existence of a least upper bound (*lub*), so that, instances from distinct class hierarchy can be compared;
- revises the similarity underneath data model, assuming the adoption of the RDF model and accessing data by SPARQL instead of by Protégé API, so that, consolidated RDF framework can be exploit dealing with crawled linked data.

SSONDE is an open source framework developed in JAVA and Jena. It is conceived as a command-line tool that can be configured through a JSON file and it can be downloaded[1], used and modified for free under the GNU GPL license.

SSONDE is designed coherently to *Crawling Architectural Pattern* [6]: RDF datasets are assumed to be crawled, cleaned, integrated and locally stored exploiting framework explicitly suited for that purpose (e.g., LDIF [7]). This pattern has been selected mainly for two reasons: (i) vocabulary mapping and entity consolidation deserve to be dealt with dedicated frameworks since they strongly affect the correctness of similarity assessment; (ii) on the fly dereferencing of large sets of entities is a slow process which is even quite inefficient in term of bandwidth. Especially when SSONDE explores thousands of entities belonging to few datasets, the construction of local stores built up by exploiting RDF dumps is preferable. In case RDF dump are not available for a dataset, LDSpider [8] and Jena Fuseki can be deployed to crawl and store linked data in local RDF stores.

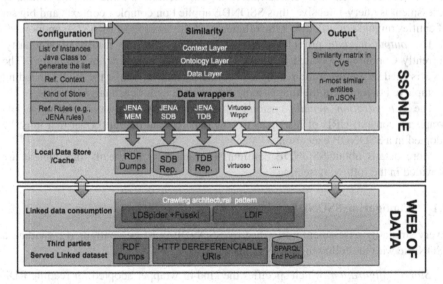

Fig. 1. Components of the semantic similarity framework SSONDE

The framework can be described in terms of different modules (see Fig. 1).

The *similarity module* deploys the semantic similarity algorithm. It is structured in: (i) a *context layer*, which provides the formalism to parameterize the similarity assessment by specifying criteria induced by application contexts. Criteria are

---

[1] Source code can be downloaded at http://purl.oclc.org/NET/SSONDE

specified in terms of features and operations to be applied comparing those features. The features correspond to RDF properties, which can be data properties or object properties depending on whether their values are RDF literals or instances themselves, whilst operations are functions determining how to compare the selected RDF properties; (ii) an *ontology layer* which interprets the criteria induced by the application context and compares instances related by the object properties involved in the context criteria; (iii) a *data layer* which provides similarity functions for data types and is activated by the ontology layer when data properties are involved in the context criteria. Given two resources x, y the similarity value sim(x,y) ranges between 0 and 1. The asymmetry of semantic similarity is designed to highlight the containment among resource features, which is particularly useful to interpret the resource dependencies: (i) if sim(x,y)=1 and sim(y,x)=1 then x and y have the same features; (ii) if sim(x,y)=1 and sim(y,x)<1 then the feature of x are contained in the features of y but the vice versa doesn't hold; in any case, sim(x,y) is proportional to the percentage of features that x shares with y.

The *data wrapper* module enables the access to different kinds of stores. Currently, in-memory stores as well as Jena SDB and Jena TDB stores are supported. Further RDF stores (e.g., Virtuoso, Sesame) can be included by re-implementing the OntologyModel Java Interface. Analogously, a direct access to SPARQL end points can be provided even in federated-like form, but keeping in mind that the similarity assessment is query-intensive, thus SSONDE applied on complex contexts and big set of entities might seriously affect the efficiency of the less robust SPARQL endpoints.

The *output module* provides different encodings for the results of similarity, currently Common Separated Value (CVS) and JSON encoding are supported. The CVS is used to represent the results as a similarity matrix, whilst the JSON encoding is employed to represent the first N-most similar entities for each target entities.

The *configuration module* customizes the similarity assessment defining data wrappers, context, URIs of resources to be compared and output format that must be adopted in a SSONDE execution.

More details about SSONDE configuration and how to specify the context are provided in the following section.

2.1   Configuring SSONDE

Every similarity assessment performed by SSONDE must be configured providing a JSON file with the following JSON Objects:

- *StoreConfiguration*, which specifies the kind of wrapper adopted for reading RDF data, and all information related to wrapper configuration. For example, it is possible to specify the directory of store; a list of Jena rules if the wrapper provides a Jena reasoner; some URLs referring at additional RDF documents that must be dereferenced and included in the RDF data collection;
- *ContextConfiguration*, which specifies the context to be applied in the similarity assessment. Currently, it is a path referring to a text file in which the context formalization is encoded in an in-house format, but we are considering to encode context in JSON as well;

- *InstanceConfiguration*, which specifies on which instances' URIs the similarity must be worked out. A list of the URIs or a reference to a JAVA class generating on-the-fly the list of URIs can be provided. The latter option is useful when the list of instances to be compared is large and can be generated by querying the wrapped repository. In that case, the JAVA class must implement the ListOfInputInstances interface and the abstract method ArrayList getListOfInstanceURIs();
- *OutputConfiguration*, which specifies where and how the semantic similarity results must be written. Two options are supported: (i) similarity matrix encoded as a CVS file; (ii) a JSON file, in which for each of the instances included in the analysis, the similarity values with their n-most similar instances are reported.

Example 1: A JSON Configuration File
The following example shows a JSON configuration file in which SSONDE reads triples from a TDB store (i.e., CNRR/data/), it dereferences a RDF schema, (i.e., "http://www.w3.org/2004/02/skos/core#"), and it assesses the similarity according to the context formalization specified in "CNRR/CCRIPubIntCoa.ctx". The similarity is worked out on resources returned by a JAVA procedure (i.e., "application.Data CNRIt.GetResearcherIMATIplusCoauthor"), and results are written as a similarity matrix encoded in the CVS file (i.e., "CNRR/CCRIPubIntCoa.res.cvs").

```
{ "StoreConfiguration":{
     "KindOfStore":"JENATDB",
     "RDFDocumentURIs":[
        "http://www.w3.org/2004/02/skos/core#"
     ],
     "TDBDirectory":"CNRR/data/"
  },
  "ContextConfiguration":{
     "ContextFilePath":" CNRR/CCRIPubIntCoa.ctx"
  },
  "InstanceConfiguration":{
     "InstanceURIsClass":"application.dataCNRIt.
GetResearcherIMATIplusCoauthor"
  },
  "OutputConfiguration":{
     "KindOfOutput":"CVSFile",
     "FilePath":" CNRR/CCRIPubIntCoa.res.cvs"}}
```

Further details pertaining to SSONDE configuration are discussed in the framework documentation. After preparing the configuration file is always advisable to validate its syntactical correctness by using one of the JSON checking services[2].

---

[2] e.g., JSON Formatter & Validator http://jsonformatter.curiousconcept.com

2.2   How to Specify a Context

In the real world, the same bunch of linked data resources can be analyzed having in mind quite different target applications, so it is very important to put in place flexible mechanisms for fine-grain customizations. In SSONDE, this kind of flexibility is provided by specifying a context for each similarity assessment. Users specify the application context indicating the resource features and operations to be considered in the similarity assessment. Resource features correspond to RDF properties, and the operations can be *Count*, *Inter* and *Simil*, which compare property values respectively according to their cardinality, their intersection and their recursive similarity. Contexts are defined as text files according to the format introduced in [5] with minor modification to consider the namespaces deriving from the adoption of multiples RDF/OWL vocabularies:

```
PREFIX namespaceA: <urlA>
PREFIX namespaceB: <urlB>
[owl:Thing]->{
 {(namespaceA:attribute1,operationForAttribute1),…
  …(namespaceB:attributeN, operationForAttributeN)},
 {(namespaceA:relation1,operationForRelation1),…
  …(namespaceB:relationM, operationForRelationM)}}
```

In particular, when the operation *Simil* is applied to properties whose values are RDF literals (e.g., strings, numbers) then the values are compared considering data type similarity functions served by the *data layer*; when *Simil* is applied to properties whose values are resources themselves (aka, object properties), values are compared recursively by following the criteria specified in the context for that recursion. So, in the case the operation *Simil* is selected, i.e., (xxx:yyy, *Simil*) occurs in one of the previous pairs, the context must include what criteria to apply when the object property xxx:yyy is reached. That is done by adding the recursive path [owl:Thing, xxx:yyy]   and listing its criteria as shown in the following excerpt:

```
[owl:Thing, xxx:yyy]->{
{(namespaceA:attribute1, operationForAttribute1),…
…(namespaceA:attributeN, operationForAttributeN)},
{(namespaceB:relation1, operationForRelation1),…,(
namespaceB:relationM, operationForRelationM)}}
```

Example 2: Context 1 " Researcher's Comparison"
This example shows a context specification defined to compare linked data resources representing researchers. It compares researchers considering the publications they share (via *pub:autoreCNRDi* property) and similarities in their research interests (via *dc:subject* property). The similarity on research interests is worked out "recursively", assuming two topics are as similar as they share *skos:broader* topics.

```
PREFIX skos: <http://www.w3.org/2004/02/skos/core#>
PREFIX owl: <http://www.w3.org/2002/07/owl#>
```

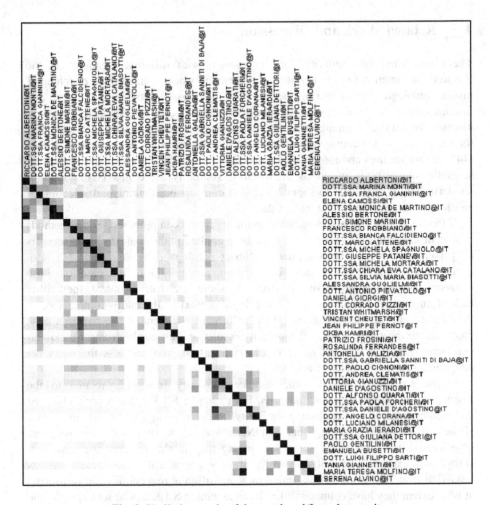

Fig. 2. Similarity matrix of data retrieved from data.cnr.it

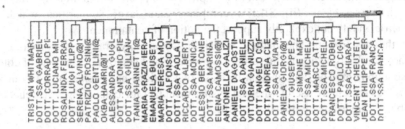

Fig. 3. Cluster analysis of data retrieved from data.cnr.it

4   Related Work and Discussion

The term "semantic similarity" has been used with different meanings in the literature. It sometimes refers to ontology alignment, where it enables the matching of distinct ontologies by comparing the names of the classes, attributes, relations, and instances [11]. Semantic similarity can also refer to concept similarity where it assesses the similarity among terms by considering their distinguishing features [12], their encoding in lexicographic databases [13], their encoding in conceptual spaces [14], mixing features and information theoretic approach [15]. In SSONDE, however, semantic similarity is meant as an instance similarity since this is the kind of similarity which is pivotal to support detailed comparison, ranking and selection of entities that are exposed in the web of data.

Different methods to assess instance similarity have been proposed. Some methods rely on description logics [16]; some have been applied in the context of web services [17]; some others have been applied to cluster ontology driven metadata [18, 19]. Surprisingly, none of these methods supports recognition in the case of those instances, albeit different, have effectively the same informative content: they either lack of an explicit formalization of the role of context in the entity comparison, or they fail identifying and measuring if the informative content of one overlaps or is contained in the other. Thus, the similarity results are not easily driven by explicit parameterizations or are not interpretable in terms of gain and loss the users get adopting a resource in place of another.

In the context of linked data, instance similarity is usually related to the discovering of interlinks among datasets. For example, SILK [3] is a very advanced and well-engineered tool exploiting similarity for determining *owl:sameAs* interlinks. However, it is worth noting that SSONDE and SILK deal with two different objectives: SILK compares resources assuming they might represent the same real entity, and exploits similarity to verify if they are actually the same, whereas SSONDE compares resources assuming they are different real entities and measuring at what extent they have commonalities. Even assuming SILK can be set to pursue the SSONDE's goals, (i) SILK's formalization of context relies on Link Specification Language (Silk-LSL) which doesn't explicitly support the notion of recursive similarity assessment; (ii) SILK's combines data layer similarities which are symmetric and do not explicitly support the notion of containment.

At the best of our knowledge, SSONDE is the only framework providing an instance similarity which is linked data compatible and deploys the notions of context and containment. The combination of these two notions has been shown in our past research as extremely useful when analysing metadata for comparing researchers [5], 3D objects, environment linked data [10].

5   Conclusions and Future Work

This paper illustrates SSONDE, an open source framework supporting in the comparison of linked data resources. SSONDE is implemented in accordance to the crawling architectural pattern, and it pushes our instance similarity as a ready-to-go tool for the analysis of linked data. SSONDE is demonstrated in two applications where metadata is analysed to enable domain experts in their decision-making processes.

Future extensions will consider new measures especially suited for geo-referenced entities, the provision of interfaces sifting entities according to their similarity (e.g., by exploiting existing visualization frameworks such as Exibit, Google visualization and JavaScript InfoVis Toolkit to support in complex information searches [20]), and the adoption of MapReduce paradigm to parallelize the similarity assessment.

Acknowledgements. Part of this research activity has been performed within the project Nature-SDIplus is co-funded by the Community Programme eContentplus ECP-2007-GEO-317007. Albertoni's contribution to this work was carried out during the tenure of an ERCIM "Alain Bensoussan" Fellowship Programme. This Programme is supported by the Marie Curie Co-funding of Regional, National and International Programmes (COFUND) of the European Commission".

References

1. Bizer, C., Cyganiak, R.: D2R Server – Publishing Relational Databases on the Semantic Web. Poster at the 5th International Semantic Web Conference, Athens, USA (2006)
2. Oren, E., Delbru, R., Catasta, M., Cyganiak, R., Stenzhorn, H., Tummarello, G.: Sindice.com: a document-oriented lookup index for open linked data. International Journal of Metadata Semantics and Ontologies 3, 37 (2008)
3. Volz, J., Bizer, C., Gaedke, M., Kobilarov, G.: Discovering and Maintaining Links on the Web of Data. In: Bernstein, A., Karger, D.R., Heath, T., Feigenbaum, L., Maynard, D., Motta, E., Thirunarayan, K. (eds.) ISWC 2009. LNCS, vol. 5823, pp. 650–665. Springer, Heidelberg (2009)
4. Tummarello, G., Cyganiak, R., Catasta, M., Danielczyk, S., Delbru, R., Decker, S.: Sigma: Live views on the Web of Data. Web Semantics: Science, Services and Agents on the World Wide Web 8, 8–17 (2010)
5. Albertoni, R., De Martino, M.: Asymmetric and Context-Dependent Semantic Similarity among Ontology Instances. In: Spaccapietra, S. (ed.) Journal on Data Semantics X. LNCS, vol. 4900, pp. 1–30. Springer, Heidelberg (2008)
6. Heath, T., Bizer, C.: Linked Data: Evolving the Web into a Global Data Space. Synthesis Lectures on the Semantic Web: Theory and Technology 1, 1–136 (2011)
7. Schultz, A., Matteini, A., Isele, R., Mendes, P.N., Bizer, C., Becker, C.: LDIF - A Framework for Large-Scale Linked Data Integration. In: 21st International World Wide Web Conference (WWW 2012), Developers Track, Lyon, France (2012)
8. Isele, R., Umbrich, J., Bizer, C., Harth, A.: LDspider: An open-source crawling framework for the Web of Linked Data. In: Proceedings of 9th International Semantic Web Conference (ISWC 2010) Posters and Demos, pp. 6–9 (2010)
9. Baldassarre, C., Daga, E., Gangemi, A., Gliozzo, A., Salvati, A., Troiani, G.: Semantic Scout: Making Sense of Organizational Knowledge. In: Cimiano, P., Pinto, H.S. (eds.) EKAW 2010. LNCS, vol. 6317, pp. 272–286. Springer, Heidelberg (2010)

10. Albertoni, R., De Martino, M.: Semantic Technology to Exploit Digital Content Exposed as Linked Data. In: Cunningham, P., Cunningham, M. (eds.) eChallenges e-2011. IIMC International Information Management Corporation, pp. 1–8 (2011) ISBN: 978-1-905824-27-4
11. Euzenat, J., Shvaiko, P.: Ontology matching. Springer (2007)
12. Janowicz, K., Keßler, C., Schwarz, M., Wilkes, M., Panov, I., Espeter, M., Bäumer, B.: Algorithm, Implementation and Application of the SIM-DL Similarity Server. In: Fonseca, F., Rodríguez, M.A., Levashkin, S. (eds.) GeoS 2007. LNCS, vol. 4853, pp. 128–145. Springer, Heidelberg (2007)
13. Rada, R., Mili, H., Bicknell, E., Blettner, M.: Development and application of a metric on semantic nets. IEEE Transactions on Systems Man and Cybernetics 19, 17–30 (1989)
14. Schwering, A.: Hybrid Model for Semantic Similarity Measurement. In: Meersman, R., Tari, Z. (eds.) OTM 2005. LNCS, vol. 3761, pp. 1449–1465. Springer, Heidelberg (2005)
15. Pirró, G., Euzenat, J.: A Feature and Information Theoretic Framework for Semantic Similarity and Relatedness. In: Patel-Schneider, P.F., Pan, Y., Hitzler, P., Mika, P., Zhang, L., Pan, J.Z., Horrocks, I., Glimm, B. (eds.) ISWC 2010, Part I. LNCS, vol. 6496, pp. 615–630. Springer, Heidelberg (2010)
16. d'Amato, C., Fanizzi, N., Esposito, F.: A dissimilarity measure for ALC concept descriptions. In: Proceedings of the 2006 ACM Symposium on Applied Computing, SAC 2006, pp. 1695–1699. ACM Press (2006)
17. Hau, J., Lee, W., Darlington, J.: A Semantic Similarity Measure for Semantic Web Services. In: Web Service Semantics Workshop at WWW (2005)
18. Maedche, A., Zacharias, V.: Clustering Ontology-Based Metadata in the Semantic Web. In: Elomaa, T., Mannila, H., Toivonen, H. (eds.) PKDD 2002. LNCS (LNAI), vol. 2431, pp. 348–360. Springer, Heidelberg (2002)
19. Grimnes, G.A., Edwards, P., Preece, A.D.: Instance Based Clustering of Semantic Web Resources. In: Bechhofer, S., Hauswirth, M., Hoffmann, J., Koubarakis, M. (eds.) ESWC 2008. LNCS, vol. 5021, pp. 303–317. Springer, Heidelberg (2008)
20. Albertoni, R., Bertone, A., De Martino, M.: Information Search: The Challenge of Integrating Information Visualization and Semantic Web. In: 16th International Workshop on Database and Expert Systems Applications, DEXA 2005, pp. 529–533. IEEE Computer Society (2005)

Creating a LO Metadata Profile for Distance Learning: An Ontological Approach

George Nikolopoulos, Aikaterini Kalou, Christos Pierrakeas, and Achilles Kameas

Educational Content, Methodology
and Technology Laboratory (e-CoMeT Lab)
Hellenic Open University (HOU)
Patras, Greece
{nikolopoulos,kalou,pierrakeas,kameas}@eap.gr

Abstract. The importance of Learning Objects (LOs) in the learning process - especially in the case of distance education - has been underlined significantly in the literature. The ability of administrating LOs in terms of accessibility, reusability and interoperability seems to be ensured by adopting an appropriate metadata schema which fully and adequately describes them. Several metadata standards have been developed such as DC (Dublin Core) and IEEE-LOM. In the context of our work, we explore them and conclude that none of these standards does completely meet the requirements of distance learning material. Therefore, we propose a new metadata schema that is actually an application profile of the widely adopted IEEE LOM and has special orientation in distance education. We also enrich this subset with some additional attributes that represent concepts like learning outcomes. Then, we create an ontological representation of this new educational schema with a view to improving the potential of LOs' discovery and retrieval within an intelligent e-learning system.

1   Introduction

Metadata are structured information used to describe the features of a resource (digital or not), thus making easier its management and retrieval. According to the definition in [2], metadata are "machine-readable information about electronic resources or other things". A set of metadata elements combined so as to serve a specific purpose, constitute a metadata schema. The great importance of metadata lies in the fact that the "meta"-information they convey is machine readable, therefore interoperability among applications can be achieved.

In the case of educational recourses, the set of metadata used to describe their characteristics, needs to be able to capture their educational and pedagogical aspects. Therefore, apart from *author, title* or *type* – fields that are common in all metadata schemas - an educational metadata schema should also include information regarding the resource's particular learning type, its intended end users, the educational context and many more.

Learning objects (LOs) are a kind of educational resources and constitute a novel approach in organizing the educational material. They have been widely used for the

J.M. Dodero, M. Palomo-Duarte, P. Karampiperis (Eds.): MTSR 2012, CCIS 343, pp. 37–48, 2012.

creation of web educational content by many modern e-learning systems, such as Learning Management Systems or Learning Content Management Systems [13]. What we lack though, is a metadata schema for the proper characterization of learning objects, and especially for learning objects that are designed to serve the scope of a distance learning course. Existing metadata schemas, as described in literature, are not adequate enough to express all aspects of distance education, and the necessity for a new metadata schema arises.

Having realized this need, we propose a metadata schema with special orientation in education and particularly in the characterization of distance learning material. After reviewing existing approaches for describing educational resources, in section 2, our educational metadata schema is extensively presented in section 3. Its ontology transformation is given in section 4, where the need to adopt such a representation technique for a metadata schema is also outlined. Conclusions follow, in section 5.

2   Existing Metadata for LOs

Generally speaking, metadata standards are defined as schemas, developed by an organization or institution so as to cover their needs to the best possible extent. The use of a single metadata standard is not a recommended solution, since each application has its special features. Alternatively, the use of application profiles is suggested. According to [7], an application profile is *"an aggregation of metadata elements selected from one or more different schemas and combined into a new compound schema"*.

The IEEE Learning Technology Standards Committee (LTSC) has developed a standard for the description of learning material and learning resources, known as IEEE Learning Object Metadata (IEEE LOM) [8]. LOM is without doubt a widespread standard for educational metadata and focuses mainly on the description of LOs. It includes more than 60 elements classified into 9 categories, each one of them containing metadata for various aspects of a LO, including its technical characteristics and rights, as well as educational and instructional features.

On the other hand, the Dublin Core Metadata Initiative was developed by organizations so as to aid the sharing of web resources and has no particular focus in education. Its initial schema, the Dublin Core Metadata Element Set (DCMES) [3] known as Dublin Core, consists of 15 elements. A second version, the Qualified Dublin Core (QDC) [4], comes to extend the previous schema, by importing 7 new elements. At the same time, QDC includes a group of qualifiers specifying the semantics of the elements in such a way so that they may be useful in resource discovery.

The ARIADNE[1] profile intended to describe learning material used in secondary and post-secondary education in order to solve two major problems: a) the indexing of LOs (i.e., the creation of the metadata by persons) and b) the exploitation of metadata by users looking for relevant pedagogical material (which should be as easy and efficient as possible). The current version of ARIADNE is an IEEE LOM profile and is fully compatible with the LOM specification.

---

[1] http://www.ariadne.ac.uk/

Moreover, the IMS LRM[2] is a set of specifications for learning resources, developed by the global organization Instructional Management System (IMS). It includes elements useful for the description of learning resources, while the specifications address issues like content packaging, question and test interoperability, learning design and simple sequencing. IMS LRM adopts all the categories and elements of the LOM standard.

Two more LOM application profiles, that were created so as to describe resources locally, are CanCore[3] (Canadian Core) and UK LOM Core[4]. CanCore, used mainly in Canada, simplifies LOM maximizing at the same time interoperability between different projects. UK LOM Core, designed for United Kingdom educational system, intends to provide guidelines to those who desire to create, use and apply metadata.

GEM[5] (Gateway to Educational Materials) is a RDF metadata vocabulary, designed for the description of educational resources. It includes all DCMI elements with new properties focused on education. GEM has also created controlled vocabularies including catalogs for the level of end users, evaluation methods and tools and the types of resources. GEM Consortium has access to GemCat, a tool which generates metadata in a format consistent with the GEM standard.

Finally, the Sharable Content Object Reference Model[6] (SCORM) is a reference model which controls how the learning content is organized, described and linked with Learning Management Systems. The CAM (Content Aggregation Model) is the one of the three specifications that handles and adopts the IEEE LOM schema. However, SCORM allows the extension of LOM, thus enabling organizations to add new elements and enhance the existing controlled vocabularies.

3   Educational Metadata Schema for the Hellenic Open University

There is not one metadata standard appropriate to fulfill the requirements and needs of every application. Some standards focus on technical metadata, other on educational metadata while some other on more specialized elements. When an institution or organization needs a standard in order to characterize, retrieve or archive its resources, it uses an existing schema enriched with other elements or creates a new one.

To build our schema, we took into account several criteria and the needs of an institution, such as the Hellenic Open University which is specialized in lifelong and distance education. An eligible, flexible and functional schema is required so as to characterize a large amount of learning material. Moreover, the metadata elements to be integrated into the proposed schema, should meet the requirements of other structures that manage LOs, like institutional libraries. So, since institutional libraries are usually based on a cataloging standard, it is necessary for our proposed schema to

---

[2] http://www.imsglobal.org/metadata/
[3] http://cancore.athabascau.ca/en/
[4] http://zope.cetis.ac.uk/profiles/uklomcore
[5] http://www.learningcommons.org/educators/library/gem.php
[6] http://www.adlnet.gov/capabilities/scorm/scorm-2004-4th

describe, at least, some common characteristics like title, description, format and creation date of a LO.

Our proposed schema is actually an application profile of IEEE LOM but with a particular orientation in distance learning material. The IEEE LOM was chosen as a basis for creating the profile due to its wide acceptance in the academic environment and its extensive usage by institutional repositories. The profile adopts the majority of IEEE LOM's elements, augmenting them with some additional attributes in order to represent concepts commonly used in distance education, like learning outcomes. The proposed schema is rich enough, so that it can effectively describe all aspects of a LO (educational, technical, etc.), but not exceedingly analytic as to become difficult to use.

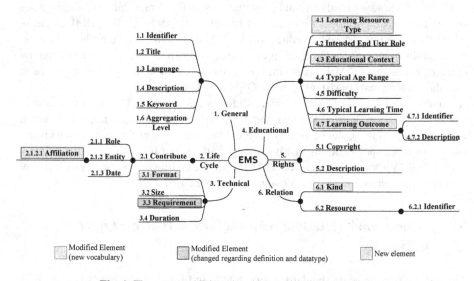

Fig. 1. The proposed Educational Metadata Schema (EMS)

Fig. 1 summarizes the elements of which the proposed metadata schema consists. Apart from those that have been directly taken from IEEE LOM (those not marked with a specific color in Fig. 1) and are considered to come with equivalent semantics, three additional types have been included. The first type concerns elements which have differences in the value space of their controlled vocabulary compared to their counterparts in the IEEE LOM schema. More specifically, for those elements we have modified the predefined set of values that they can accept in an attempt to meet a LO's specific characteristics. The second type includes elements that come with modifications in their definition and data type, while the third one regards new entries in the proposed schema.

The elements of our proposed metadata schema that come with modifications in the value space of their controlled vocabulary are three in total: 1) *Format* of the *Technical* category, 2) the *Learning Resource Type* of the *Educational* category and 3) *Kind* of the *Relation* category.

As far as the *Format* element is concerned, we have defined a new set of allowable values which appears in Table 1. The given set is based on IANA MIME types[7], given in IEEE LOM, but is oriented for the characterization of distance learning material and particularly for LOs that are going to be utilized by an adaptive learning system. The set in Table 1 emerged after studying the characteristics of the educational material that is already used by the Hellenic Open University (HOU) and seems to be quite broad in order to cover a wide range of technical data types.

Table 1. Possible values of the *Format* element (i.e. technical data types of the resource)

Proposed Value Space			
Text	document hypertext	Streaming Media	audio recording animation self-running presentation webcast video
Image	Photo Map Graph Image presentation	Application	interactive software hypermedia application wiki presentation

Learning Resource Type is another element with substantial modifications regarding its controlled vocabulary compared to the one in the IEEE LOM schema. The main problem with the corresponding IEEE LOM element is that apart from the values which express educational information (e.g. *Exercise, Problem Statement, Simulation*) it also contains values that refer to technical information (e.g. *Diagram, Figure, Graph*). Moreover, some important types of LOs such as *Example, Serious Game, Case Study* or *Project* are absent.

To this end, we define a completely new list of acceptable values that reflects the most common types of educational material used within distance education courses and incorporates only information about the instructional perspective of a resource. This list of values is, to a certain degree, based on the content object types provided by the ALOCOM generic content model[8]. The complete list of the learning types we propose is presented in Table 2.

Another important modification concerns the *Kind* element that belongs to the *Relation* category. In this element, the controlled vocabulary, used as its value space, expresses the various kinds of relationships among LOs. So, apart from the existing relationship *has part* and its inverse one *is part of* we make provision for two additional types of relationships:

1) *supports* and its inverse *is supported by* attempts to correlate a "supportive" LO that contains complementary or prerequisite knowledge, with one that has a key role in the learning process (a "core" LO).

---

[7] http://www.iana.org/assignments/media-types/index.html
[8] http://kuleuven.academia.edu/ErikDuval/Papers/1227319/ ALOCOM_a_generic_content_model_for_learning_objects

2) *is alternative type* relationship correlates two or more LOs that are exactly the same in their educational content and differ only in their technical format. This is a highly significant relationship especially if the objective is to provide personalized learning depending on the preferences of each learner.

Table 2. Possible values of the *Learning Resource Type* element

Proposed Value Space		
1. **Guidelines**	9. **Activity**	11. **Self-Assessment**
2. **Presentation**	– Case Study	– Multiple Choice Questions
3. **Demonstration**	– Problem Solving	– Open Type Question
4. **Lecture**	– Text Composition	– Problem Statement
5. **Definition-**	– Question	12. **Experiment**
Principle-Law	10. **Simulation**	13. **Serious Game**
6. **Narrative Text**	– Interactive	14. **Exercise**
7. **Analogy**	– Non Interactive	– Multiple Choice Questions
8. **Example**		– Open Type Question
		– Problem Statement
		15. **Project**

The only element that has been adopted with different definition and data type is *Requirement*. In the context of our metadata schema, the *Requirement* element is used to describe any software or hardware requirements which are necessary in order to use a LO. Its data type has been altered to *LangString*. Thus, its completion simply requires writing statements like *"This LO requires the use of Adobe Acrobat Reader. Version newer than 6.xx"*. On the other hand, the original IEEE LOM element needs much more, so this modification simplifies the process of describing the requirements of a LO to a great extent.

Finally, we have augmented our schema with some new elements that were necessary in order to represent concepts commonly used in distance education. We added the sub-element *Affiliation*, as shown in Fig. 1, which determines the status of the entity that has contributed to the creation and development of the LO. The *Learning Outcome* element, placed under the *Educational* category, expresses the correlation of a LO with one or more learning outcomes. In particular, for each learning outcome that a LO satisfies, one needs to give its natural language statement, via the *Description* element, as well as to assign to it an identifier (*Identifier:Entry* and *Identifier:Catalog*), according to a specific identification system. The *Educational Context* element now implies the actual context where the learning process takes place, and can accept values like "distance education", "face to face learning" and "blended learning". This is a key element in terms that it gives information about the mode of learning for which the particular object is appropriate.

4   An ontological approach

In what follows, we first outline the reason for using an ontology for representing our proposed metadata schema. We then explain in details the structure of the deployed ontology.

4.1   Why We Need an Ontology

The elements of any educational metadata schema should be managed in any available format e.g. SQL tables, text files, HTML meta-tags and so on [11]. Such a technical realization of the abstract model in a specific format is called a *binding*. As it is known, for IEEE LOM, XML and RDF bindings are defined. The usage of XML for the LO metadata expression facilitates the indexing process and the retrieval of annotated learning resources. However, this format seems to be not sufficient enough to address the limitation of text-based searching, since XML does not provide the meaning of the described structures. The Resource Description Framework[9] (RDF) attempts to overcome the problem by adding semantics to each metadata element of any schema. The description of LOM elements via RDF facilitates their integration into e-learning systems which nowadays are dominated by Semantic Web technologies and especially by the notion of ontology.

Even though RDF is intended for representing knowledge, it lacks reasoning abilities; RDF does not support making inferences or deductions. Therefore, a much more expressive framework is required, so that metadata can be meaningfully encoded. Ontologies, expressed in OWL (the most widely-used ontology language) are the pillar of Semantic Web and provide the ability to represent any domain of interest in a more structured way. The ontological expression of LO metadata converts them into machine-understandable information. Moreover, metadata that are represented by ontological models in OWL, are enhanced with richer properties.

In general, a survey of the literature on the usage of ontologies in web-based education returns a great number of systems that embed ontological models in their implementation [1]. These ontological models can reflect many various aspects of an e-learning system, such as student profiles and knowledge domains. The integration of LOs components to such systems requires a more semantically enriched representation [5]. Therefore, many research groups have attempted to annotate semantically the LO metadata. Some representative examples are ALOCOM, SCORM, OntoLo, Edu-Bank, ACM CCS, etc.

4.2   The LO Ontology

In this subsection, we describe the deployed ontology that represents our proposed application profile. In order to build this ontology, we followed a widely-adopted

---

[9] http://www.w3.org/TR/rdf-primer/

methodology, proposed in [12]. For its formal representation, we used OWL 2 - the most recent version of the Web Ontology Language - whereas for creating and managing our ontology, we used the Protégé editor.

The notion of LO is reflected in the *LearningObject* class. The elements of the *General* category are represented by the corresponding datatype properties, such as *title, language, description,* and *aggregation level*. In particular, the *aggregation level* is an integer datatype property that can take values from 1 to 4. The *language* property can be filled with any of the known language identifiers, like *"en"* for English or *"el"* for Greek.

The *Contribute* element of the *Life Cycle* category is captured by the *Contributor* class and the corresponding elements are represented by datatype properties, such as *contributeDate, affiliation* and *contributorRole*. *ContributorRole* is an enumerated datatype property that can be filled with the values *publisher, creator, reviewer* or any other similar concepts, expressing allowable roles in the life cycle of a LO. Instances of the class *Contributor* are linked to any instance of the class *LearningObject* via the object property *contributor*.

The *Format* category consists of the following four elements: *Text, Image, Streaming Media* and *Application*. Each of them is captured as a subclass of the *Format* class. This hierarchical structure is shown in Fig. 2. The controlled vocabulary, expressing allowable values for each element in the *Format* category, are represented as instances of the corresponding classes (see Table 1 – the second column involves the instances). The remaining elements in this category, expressing the physical size, software or hardware requirements or time duration for streaming media, are described by the datatype properties *size, requirement* and *duration*, respectively.

Fig. 2. The class hierarchy of the ontology

The *Learning Resource Type* element that specifies the different educational types of LOs is captured by the *LearningResourceType* class. This element is associated with a predefined list of terms, represented as instances in the ontology. However, these terms can be further refined and hence they have been placed as sub-classes of the main *LearningResourceType* class. The ontological structure of the *Learning Resource Type* element is indicated in Fig. 3.

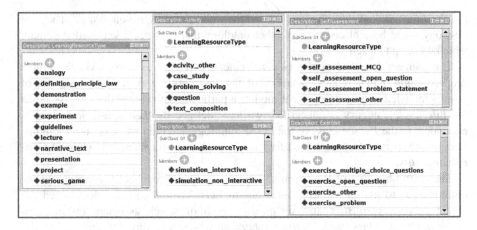

Fig. 3. The *Learning Resource Type* category in the ontology

The remaining elements of the proposed metadata schema, belonging to the *Education* category and expressing concepts like the intended end users, the instructional context, the age range of end users, as well as difficulty and average learning time, are captured by the corresponding datatype properties.

The datatype property *rights* has been defined in order to capture the copyright data that apply for a LO. Finally, the potential relationships among LOs, appearing as members of the *Relation* category, are represented as object properties in our ontology linking two instances of the *LearningObject* class. These object properties have been placed as sub-properties of the main property *isRelatedtoMA*, as shown in Fig. 4.

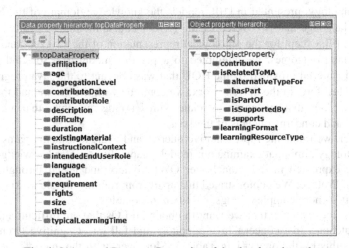

Fig. 4. Object and Datatype Properties of the developed ontology

There are also some additional elements coming from various categories of the metadata profile that could be represented in the ontology, only after importing some other supporting ontologies. Such ontologies are the *LearningOutcome ontology* presented in

[9], the *Java ontology* described in [10] and the well-known FOAF ontology[10]. The Java ontology could be replaced by any other ontology that captures a knowledge domain which we want to teach.

The element *keyword* of the *General* category can be expressed via the object property *subject* that relates instances of the *LearningObject* class to instances of classes included in an ontology that models a particular knowledge domain. As far as the *Life Cycle* category is concerned, we have defined the *LearningObject* class as equivalent to the *Person* class of the FOAF ontology and then we make use of the built-in object properties *foaf:name* and *foaf:surname* so as to formulate the element *Contribute:Entity*.

The main objective of the combination of *LearningObject* and *LearningOutcome* ontologies is to assign learning outcomes to LOs. To this end, we determined the object properties *satisfies* and *satisfiesInd*, both of which associate instances of *LearningObject* class with *LearningOutcome* instances, directly and indirectly, respectively. The latter is going to be used in implicit inferences. The indirect correlation of LOs can be only elaborated by restriction rules and by exploiting existing reasoning mechanisms. As a consequence, we have defined the following rule, expressed in the Semantic Web Rule Language (SWRL): *"IF (x is-a LearningObject) AND (y is-a LearningObject) AND (p is-a LearningOutcome) AND (y satisfies p) AND (x complements y) THEN (x satisfiesInd p)"*. With this rule, it can be inferred that a LO satisfies a learning outcome indirectly, if this LO is supportive for another one, created in order to serve the aforesaid learning outcome.

4.3   Evaluating Some Example Queries

The Java ontology, presented in [10], models the knowledge domain of the Java programming language that is covered by the HOU's course module of 'Software Engineering'. In [9], except for the ontological representation of the structure and taxonomy of learning outcomes, we attempted to apply this model to a selected piece of educational material provided by the HOU that was relevant to the Java programming language. Therefore, in the current work, we continue with the design and the implementation of LOs that are going to relate with learning outcomes that are already constructed and concern concepts of the Java.

Moreover, we ran some representative queries and evaluated them against the populated ontology aiming at examine our model's capability to infer knowledge. These queries are expressed in the Manchester OWL Syntax and tested through the DL query tab of Protégé. We demonstrated that apart from running simple lookup queries, we can request more complex things, based on this ontology.

Consider, for example, that we want to obtain all LOs that are difficult and satisfy learning outcomes that concern Java operators and fall into Cognitive Domain. We can express this by the query#1 in Table 3. Moreover, with the query#2 we can retrieve those LOs that their learning resource type is narrative text. Finally, with query#3, we can retrieve all LOs that satisfy in anyway those learning outcomes that are relevant to Java operators.

---

[10] http://xmlns.com/foaf/spec/

Table 3. Some Example Queries in Manchester OWL Syntax

#	Query
1	**satisfies** some (subject some **Operator** and domain value **CognitiveDomain**) and **difficulty** value **'difficult'**
2	**learningResourceType** value **narrative_text**
3	**satisfies** some (subject some **Operator**) and **satisfiesInd** some (subject some **Operator**)

Of course similar requests can be made for different domain subjects, different levels of knowledge and any kind of relationship modeled in the ontology as a property. All these semantic queries are actually examples of competency questions for the proposed ontology. Competency questions are a commonly used technique for evaluating such formalisms [6].

5   Conclusions

Having realized the need to effectively characterize the educational material that serves the needs of a course delivered from distance, we propose a metadata schema with educational perspective and particular orientation in distance learning. The aim of the proposed schema is to provide a complete element set for the characterization of LOs or of any other kind of educational material, intended to be exploited by e-learning systems and applications.

Our educational metadata schema is actually a profile of the widely known IEEE LOM. It adopts the majority of LOM's elements, it modifies some other or even augments it with additional elements representing concepts that are common in distance education. Learning outcomes are, for example, such concepts and any LO is constructed with the view to serve a specific learning outcome. Our schema is rich enough, so that it can effectively describe both educational and technical aspects of a LO, but not exceedingly analytic so as to become difficult in use.

As a next step, we tried to model our schema as an ontology. Ontologies come with many applications in the field of education and their usage for representing the structure of a LO could end up to the development of advanced, intelligent applications. The ontological representation of our educational metadata schema was accomplished by appropriately "translating" its structural elements to classes, properties and instances in the ontology.

The proposed work comes to address the drawbacks that come up by the usage of a cataloging standard and the deficiency of the current metadata schema in the Hellenic Open University. Furthermore, the expression of the presented schema in an ontology language makes more feasible the integration of the HOU's infrastructures into semantic-aware e-learning systems.

Our future work is focused on the development of an ontology-based e-learning system for the HOU that is going to offer personalized learning from distance. The resulted learning object metadata ontology can be easily combined with other ontologies, modeling other notions in distance education. The importance of such an ontological representation lies in its possible exploitation by systems that can handle semantics and thus understand the role of each single piece of educational material.

Furthermore, we are going to design tools and methods able to create reusable LOs in accordance with the proposed metadata schema. Our major goal is to provide HOU's students with advanced, personalized services for efficiently handling and disseminating educational material.

Acknowledgments. This research described in this paper has been co-financed by the European Union (European Social Fund – ESF) and Greek National Funds through the Operational Program "Education and Lifelong Learning" of the National Strategic Reference Framework (NSRF) (Funding Program: "HOU").

References

1. Al-Khalifa, H.S., Hugh, D.: The Evolution of Metadata from Standards to Semantics in E-Learning Applications. In: Proceedings of Seventh Conf. Hypertext and Hypermedia, Hypertext 2006 (2006)
2. Berners-Lee, T.: Web architecture: Metadata. Retrieved from World Wide Web Consortium, W3C (1997), http://www.w3.org
3. DCMI: Dublin Core Metadata Element Set, version 1.1. DCMI Recommendation (2008), http://www.dublincore.org/documents/dces/
4. DCMI: DCMI Metadata Terms. DCMI Recommendation (2008), http://dublincore.org/documents/dcmi-terms/
5. Gaević, D., Jovanović, J., Devedžić, V.: Ontologies for Reusing Learning Object Content. . In: Proceedings of the 5th IEEE International Conference on Advanced Learning Technologies (3th International Workshop on Applications of Semantic Web Technologies for e-Learning), Kaohsiung, Taiwan, pp. 650–654 (2005)
6. Grüninger, M., Fox, M.S.: Methodology for the design and evaluation of ontologies. In: IJCAI 1995 Workshop on Basic Ontological Issues in Knowledge Sharing (1995)
7. Heery, R., Patel, M.: Application profiles: mixing and matching metadata schemas. Ariadne (25) (2000)
8. Hodgins, W., Duval, E.: Draft Standard for Learning Object Metadata. Institute of Electrical and Electronics Engineers, Inc. (2002), http://ltsc.ieee.org/wg12/files/ LOM_1484_12_1_v1_Final_Draft.pdf
9. Kalou, A., Solomou, G., Pierrakeas, C., Kameas, A.: An Ontology Model for Building, Classifying and Using Learning Outcomes. In: International Conference on Advanced Learning Technologies, Rome (2012)
10. Kouneli, A., Solomou, G., Pierrakeas, C., Kameas, A.: Modeling the Knowledge Domain of the Java Programming Language as an Ontology. In: Popescu, E., Li, Q., Klamma, R., Leung, H., Specht, M. (eds.) ICWL 2012. LNCS, vol. 7558, pp. 152–159. Springer, Heidelberg (2012)
11. Nilsson, M., Palmér, M., Brase, J.: The LOM RDF binding - principles and implementation. In: 3rd Annual Ariadne Conference. Katholieke Universiteit Leuven, Belgium (2003)
12. Noy, N., McGuiness, D.: Ontology Development 101: A Guide to Creating Your First Ontology. Stanford Knowledge Systems Laboratory Technical Report KSL-01-05 (2001)
13. Schreurs, J., Al-Zoubi, A.Y.: Converting Content to Reusable Learning Objects Adaptable to User Preferences and Infrastructure. In: Bastiaens, T., Carliner, S. (eds.) Proceedings of World Conference on E-Learning in Corporate, Government, Healthcare, and Higher Education 2007, pp. 6537–6544. AACE, Chesapeake (2007)

On the Search for Intrinsic Quality Metrics of Learning Objects

Cristian Cechinel[1], Sandro da Silva Camargo[1], Salvador Sánchez-Alonso[2], and Miguel-Ángel Sicilia[2]

[1] Computer Engineering Course
Federal University of Pampa, Caixa Postal 07
96400-970, Bagé (RS), Brazil
contato@cristiancechinel.pro.br, camargo.sandro@gmail.com
[2] Information Engineering Research Unit
Computer Science Dept., University of Alcalá
Ctra. Barcelona km. 33.6 – 28871 Alcalá de Henares (Madrid), Spain
{salvador.sanchez,msicilia}@uah.es

Abstract. Assessing quality of learning resources is a difficult and complex task that often revolve around multiple and different aspects that must be observed. In order to evaluate quality, it is necessary to consider the particular spectrum of users and the particular set of criteria used by these users to value the resources. Existing approaches for assessing LOs quality are normally based on broadly interpreted dimensions that can be subject of divergence among different evaluators. The present work identifies lower-level and easily quantifiable measures of learning objects that are associated to quality with the aim of providing a common and free from ambiguities ground for LO quality assessment.

Keywords: Learning objects, Quality Metrics, Intrinsic Features.

1 Introduction

Assessing quality of learning resources is a difficult and complex task that often revolve around multiple and different aspects that must be observed. In fact, the very definition of quality is not straightforward. Vargo, Nesbit, Belfer & Archambault (2003) state that, even though LO evaluation can be considered a relatively new field, it has roots with an extensive body of prior work on the evaluation of instructional software. As stated by Bethard, Wetzer, Butcher, Martin & Sumner (2009) quality is contextual and it will depend on *"the alignment between the user constituency being served, the educational setting where deployed, and the intended purpose of the resource"*. Vuorikari et al. (2008) highlights that existing evaluation approaches could be differentiated based on the process they focus. Among others, they mentioned two characteristic examples of approaches, those which focus on the process of creating resources, and those who focus on ready resources and their evaluation.

J.M. Dodero, M. Palomo-Duarte, P. Karampiperis (Eds.): MTSR 2012, CCIS 343, pp. 49–60, 2012.
© Springer-Verlag Berlin Heidelberg 2012

According to Williams (2000), what a LO ought to be is related to the perspectives of different opinions of those who are the actual users of the resource. So, in order to evaluate quality, it is necessary to consider the particular spectrum of users and the particular set of criteria used by these users to value the resource. Each type of evaluation should consider who are the people who care about the LO (the audience of the LO), and what do they care or have interest about. The people who care about the LO could be, for instance, students, teachers, instructional designers, an organization, among others. These audiences can have different understandings and expectations about the LO, and thus can use distinct criteria and values to judge the quality of the LO (for instance, reusability, quality of the metadata, the instructional approach, among others). According to (Williams, 2000), the combination of these information would then define how should one conduct the process of evaluation of a LO. Besides Williams (2000), other authors have also claimed that concerns about quality normally focus on different criteria. For instance, in the context of digital libraries, Custard & Sumner (2005) stated that the main issues related to quality are: Accuracy of content, Appropriateness to Intended Audience, Effective Design, and Completeness of Metadata Documentation. In the specific field of learning multimedia resources, the so far most recognized instrument for quantitatively measuring quality, the Learning Object Review Instrument (LORI) (Nesbit, Belfer, & Leacock, 2003), approaches quality evaluation of *"ready for use"* LOs according to nine different criteria (Content quality, Learning goal alignment, Feedback and adaptation, Presentation design, Interaction usability, Accessibility, Reusability, Standards compliance) which are rated in a 1 to 5 Likert scale. Even though Leacock & Nesbit (2007) provide structural and theoretical foundations for assessing and understanding these many aspects of LORI that involve quality, they still are all broadly interpreted dimensions that can be subject of divergence from different evaluators. Moreover, different evaluators can also give more importance to one specific dimension than to the others.

An alternative solution for such subjectivity is trying to identify lower level measures of LOs that are related to some of these quality dimensions and that are easily quantifiable and consequently free from ambiguities and misinterpretations. Examples of such strategy can be already observed to assess quality of learning object metadata (Ochoa, 2008) and more recently to estimate and measure learning objects reusability (Sanz-Rodriguez, Dodero, & Sánchez-Alonso, 2010). Moreover, Cechinel, Sánchez-Alonso, and García-Barriocanal (2011) have encountered statistical associations between quality and several intrinsic features of LOs stored on the MERLOT[1] repository and have initially developed Linear Discriminant Analysis (LDA) models for automated quality assessment of LOs based on such metrics. The generated models were able to classify resources belonging to the *Simulation* ∩ *Science & Technology* subset between *good* and *not-good* with 72.16% of accuracy, and between *good* and *poor* with 91.49% of accuracy. On another round of experiments, (Cechinel, 2012; Cechinel, Sánchez-Alonso, Sicilia, & Amador, 2011) also identified associations between intrinsic features of LOs and their quality and

---

[1] www.merlot.org

have used such metrics for the creation of models for automated quality assessment through the use of data mining classification algorithms. In all these works, the authors claimed that the different metrics associate to quality depending on their category of discipline (Arts, Business, Science and Technology, etc) and their type (Simulation, Animation, Tutorial, Collection, etc) and the perspective of quality considered (whether the quality impression was given by the community of users or the experts).

The present paper expands the previous works developed by (Cechinel, 2012); Cechinel, Sánchez-Alonso, and García-Barriocanal (2011); (Cechinel, Sánchez-Alonso, Sicilia, et al., 2011) by using a slightly different approach. On the previous works, the authors explored the creation of statistical profiles of highly-rated learning objects by contrasting information from *good* and *not-good* resources and then used these profiles to generate models for quality assessment. In the present work we first generate the models for automated quality assessment by using data mining classification algorithms (decision trees) and then extracted from these models the most important metrics associated to quality for the studied subsets. Moreover, in the previous works, the authors worked with a sample of learning objects covering approximately 20% of the repository and studied from 1 to 3 subsets of MERLOT, whilst here we worked with a higher collection of resources and studied a total of 21 distinct subsets of MERLOT (intersections between category of discipline and material type). At last, the present study is finally focused on the search of intrinsic quality metrics that can be used as a basis for the further development of learning resources, whilst the previous works were focused on the development of models for automated quality assessment of learning resources.

The reminder of this work is structured as follows: Section 2 describes existing research related to the search of intrinsic quality metrics in learning objects (and in adjacent fields). Section 3 explains the methodology followed on the study, and section 4 shows the metrics found for some specific subsets of MERLOT as well as an initial discussion about these preliminary findings. Finally, section 6 presents the final remarks and possible directions for future work.

2   Learning Objects Quality versus Intrinsic Measures

Besides the work of (Cechinel, 2012; Cechinel, Sánchez-Alonso, & García-Barriocanal, 2011; Cechinel, Sánchez-Alonso, Sicilia, et al., 2011) there are some works in adjacent fields where evidences between intrinsic features of resources and their quality were found. For instance, Custard & Sumner (2005) created a support vector machine model to assess the quality of resources inside an Educational Digital Library by using intrinsic measures such as the Number of Links and the Number of Words. Blumenstock (2008) have found that the Number of Words in Wikipedia is associated with the quality of the articles, and Stvilia, Twidale, Smith, & Gasser (2005) were able to automatically discriminate high quality articles inside a Community-Based Encyclopedia using intrinsic metrics such as the Number of Internal and External Links, the Number of Words, and the Number of Images. At last, in the field of usability, Ivory and Hearst (2002) have found that good websites contain (for instance) more words and links than the regular and bad ones.

Our approach is initially related exclusively to those aspects of learning objects that are displayed to the users and that are normally associated to the dimensions of presentation design and interaction usability (included in LORI (Nesbit et al., 2003) and the dimension of information quality (normally mentioned in the context of educational digital libraries). Precisely, the references for quality assurance used in here are the ratings given by the peer-reviewers (experts) of the repository.

3   Method

The method followed on this study was the creation of models for automated quality assessment of learning objects based on the intrinsic features of the resources and represented through decision trees. Once the models are generated, we selected the best ones to take an in-depth look and to identify which are the most important intrinsic features used by them in the process of quality assessment. Such features are considered here as possible quality metrics that should be further taken into account during the development of learning objects.

3.1   Data Collection

A database was collected from MERLOT through the use of a crawler (Fernández, 2011) that systematically traversed the pages and collected information related to 35 metrics of the resources. As MERLOT repository is mainly formed by learning resources in the form of websites, we evaluated intrinsic metrics that are supposed to appear in such technical type of material (i.e., link measures, text measures, graphic measures and site architecture measures). The 34 metrics collected for this study (see Table 1) are the same as used by (Cechinel, Sánchez-Alonso, & García-Barriocanal, 2011) and some of them have also been mentioned in other works which tackled the problem of assessing quality of resources (previously presented on section 2).

Table 1. Metrics collected for the study

Class of Measure	Metric
Link Measures	Number of Links, Number of Unique[a] Links, Number of Internal Links[b], Number of Unique Internal Links, Number of External Links, Number of Unique External Links
Text Measures	Number of Words, Number of words that are links[c]
Graphic, Interactive and Multimedia Measures	Number of Images, Total Size of the Images (in bytes), Number of Scripts, Number of Applets, Number of Audio Files, Number of Video Files, Number of Multimedia Files
Site Architecture Measures	Size of the Page (in bytes), Number of Files for downloading, Total Number of Pages

[a] The term Unique stands for "non-repeated"
[b] The term internal refers to those links which are located at some directory below the root site
[c] For these metrics the average was not computed or does not exist

As resources in MERLOT vary considerably in size, a limit of 2 levels of depth was established for the crawler, i.e., metrics were computed for the root node (level 0 - the home-page of the resource), as well as for the pages linked by the root node (level 1), and for the pages linked by the pages of the level 1 (level 2). As it is shown in table 1, some of the metrics refer to the total sum of the occurrences of a given attribute considering the whole resource, and other metrics refer to the average of this sum considering the number of the pages computed. For instance, an object composed by 3 pages and containing a total of 30 images, will have a total number of images of 30, and an average number of images equals to 10 (30/3). Information of a total of 20,582 learning resources was collected. From this amount, only 2,076 were peer-reviewed, and 5 of them did not have metadata regarding the category of discipline or the type of material and were disregarded. Table 2 presents the frequency of the remaining 2,071 materials for each dataset formed by the intersection of category of discipline and material type.

Table 2. Frequency of materials for each dataset formed by the intersection of category of discipline and material type

Material Type/Discipline	Arts	Business	Education	Humanities
Animation	4	23	21	16
Case Study	0	3	23	16
Collection	8	52	56	43
Drill and Practice	2	23	13	28
Learning Material	5	0	0	0
Learning Object Repository	0	0	1	0
Lecture/Presentation	6	42	38	48
Online Course	0	0	1	0
Other Resource	0	0	0	0
Professional Paper	0	0	0	0
Quiz/Test		14	10	4
Reference Material	6	83	40	51
Simulation	57	63	40	78
Tutorial	6	76	73	93
Workshop and Training Material	0	0	0	0
Total	94	379	316	377

Material Type/Discipline	Mathematics and Statistics	Science & Technology	Social Sciences	Total
Animation	8	22	4	98
Case Study	3	3	2	50
Collection	50	80	15	304
Drill and Practice	19	37	5	127
Learning Material	0	13	0	18
Learning Object Repository	4	1	3	9
Lecture/Presentation	13	32	20	199
Online Course	0	1	0	2
Other Resource	0	2	0	2
Professional Paper	0	1	0	1
Quiz/Test	11	23	1	63
Reference Material	68	102	6	356
Simulation	40	150	18	446
Tutorial	48	86	11	393
Workshop and Training Material	0	0	3	3
Total	264	553	88	2071

Considering that many subsets are formed by very small amount of resources, we restrained our experiment to just a few of them. Precisely, we worked with 21 subsets formed by the following types of material: *Collection*, *Reference Material*, *Simulation* and *Tutorial*, and that had 40 resources or more[2] (gray hashed in table 2). In total, we worked with information of 1,429 learning resources which represent 69% of the total collected data.

3.2   Generation of Models for Automated Quality Assessment

Classes of quality for each subset were created using the terciles of the ratings given by the peer-reviewers. Resources with ratings below the first tercile were classified as *poor*, resources with ratings equal or higher the first tercile and lower than the second tercile were classified as *average*, and resources with ratings equal or higher the second tercile were classified as *good*. The classes of quality *average* and *poor* were then joined in another class called *not-good*.

The classes of quality were then used as the output reference for generating and testing models for automated quality assessment of the resources through the use of Decision Trees which are models are commonly used in data mining. Their goal is to examine input variables and to induce a tree which will be used to predict the value of a target variable. In the resulting tree, each interior node corresponds to one of the input variables; and each leaf node represents a value of a target variable given the values of input variables. As decisions trees are easy to understand and interpret (the resulting rules are easily explained), they allow us to evaluate the most important intrinsic features of learning objects required to build the models, which are considered here to be associated to quality.

The experiments were conducted with Matlab (MATLAB, 2010) and using CART (Classification and Regression Trees) classification algorithm (Breiman, Friedman, Stone, & Olshen, 1984). CART algorithm builds a classification tree by recursively splitting the variable space based on impurity of each input variable in order to determine the split until termination condition is met (Santhanam & Sundaram, 2010). In order to estimate the performance of our predictive model we have used the Leave-One-Out cross-validation technique. So, we have partitioned our data in three complementary subsets: training, validation and testing. Considering n the size of the sample, the size of each subset can be defined as follows: training = $((n-1)*0.85)$, validation = $((n-1)*0.15)$ and, testing = (1). With the purpose of reduce variability; we have repeated the experiments n times and the final results are the average of all repetitions (Kohavi, 1995).

Table 3 presents the average results achieved for each subset ordered by Accuracy.

---

[2] The difficulties for training, validating and testing predictive models for subsets with less than 40 resources would be more severe.

Table 3. Results achieved by the decision trees models

Filename	Accuracy	Sensitivity	Specificity	Kappa	MAE	Nodes
Math & Statistics ∩ Tutorial	0.88	0.81	0.91	0.72	0.13	7
Humanities ∩ Simulation	0.73	0.53	0.85	0.41	0.27	13
Math & Statistics ∩ Reference Mat.	0.72	0.78	0.68	0.44	0.28	17
Humanities ∩ Tutorial	0.67	0.62	0.70	0.32	0.33	24
Arts ∩ Simulation	0.65	0.53	0.71	0.23	0.35	11
Education ∩ Collection	0.61	0.55	0.64	0.18	0.39	16
Humanities ∩ Collection	0.60	0.70	0.52	0.22	0.40	9
Business ∩ Simulation	0.60	0.43	0.69	0.12	0.40	17
Business ∩ Reference Material	0.59	0.41	0.71	0.11	0.41	21
Business ∩ Collection	0.56	0.64	0.50	0.13	0.44	11
Math & Statistics ∩ Simulation	0.55	0.35	0.70	0.05	0.45	8
Science & Tech. ∩ Simulation	0.53	0.35	0.66	0.01	0.47	40
Science & Tech. ∩ Collection	0.46	0.21	0.61	-0.19	0.54	24
Education ∩ Tutorial	0.45	0.24	0.59	-0.17	0.55	19
Science & Tech. ∩ Tutorial	0.44	0.26	0.55	-0.19	0.56	18
Math & Statistics ∩ Collection	0.42	0.29	0.52	-0.20	0.58	12
Humanities ∩ Reference Material	0.41	0.35	0.46	-0.19	0.59	14
Business ∩ Tutorial	0.41	0.31	0.48	-0.21	0.59	20
Education ∩ Simulation	0.40	0.36	0.42	-0.20	0.60	12
Science & Tech. ∩ Reference Mat.	0.23	0.50	0.15	-0.20	0.77	29

In Table 3, *Accuracy* stands for the overall accuracy of the models; *Sensitivity* is related to the ability of the model to correctly identify *good* resources (*true positives*),; *Specicity* stands for the accuracy of the model to correctly classify *not-good* resource (*true negatives*). Moreover, *Kappa* is a coefficient that varies from -1 to 1 and indicates the overall agreement between the observed and the expected data (where 1 means total agreement); MAE represents the mean absolute error, and *Nodes* indicates the number of nodes included in the given model.

As it can be seen in the Table, the models presented different results depending on the given subset. The best results were found for the subset *Math. Statistics ∩ Tutorial* which achieved 0.88 of overall accuracy and a MAE of 0.13, followed by *Humanities ∩ Simulation* with an overall accuracy of 0.73 and a MAE of 0.27, and *Math & Statistics ∩ Reference Material* with an overall accuracy of 0.72 and a MAE of 0.28. The models tend to have higher accuracies to correctly classify *not-good* resources (higher *specificity*) than to classify *good* resources (*sensitivity*). Figure 1 helps to visualize this.

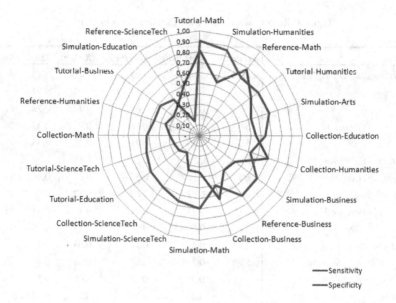

Fig. 1. Sensitivity versus Specificity of the models

Considering that it was not possible to generate good models for all studied subsets, we selected the seven best models of table 3 (gray-hashed) for an in-depth look. All these seven models presented a minimum overall accuracy of 0.60, and minimums *sensitivity* and *specificity* of 0.50.

4   Results and Discussion

Table 4 presents the most important metrics for each one of the previous selected subsets together with their percentage of importance[3]. As it can be seen in the table, quality in some subsets can be "explained" by just a few metrics. For instance, for the subset *Math & Statistics ∩ Tutorial*, the most important metrics are the *Size of the page* and the *Number of Images* and just these two metrics together represent 96.83% of the importance of the model. Moreover, for the *Humanities ∩ Collection* the 4 following metrics represent together 92.7% of the importance of the model: *Average Number of Internal Links, Average Number of Words, Average Number of Unique External Links*, and *Number of Audio Files*. On the other hand, the quality of the rest of the subsets is explained by a higher number of metrics (from 5 to 8 metrics). For instance, for the *Humanities ∩ Tutorial* subset, the most important metrics are: *Size of the page, Average Number of Scripts, Number of External Links, Average Number of Unique Internal Links, Number of Words, Number of words that are links, Number of Links* and *Average Number of Images*, and they represent together 89.34% of the importance of the model.

---

[3] We restricted the metrics to those with a percentage of importance higher or equal to 5%.

Table 4. Importance of the metrics for the selected subsets

Math & Statistics ∩ Tutorial		Humanities ∩ Simulation	
Metrics	*Importance*	*Metrics*	*Importance*
Size of the page	61,13%	Average Size of the Images	41,32%
Number of Images	35,70%	Number of Scripts	16,68%
Math & Statistics ∩ Reference Material		Average Number of External Links	14,75%
Metrics	*Importance*	Number of Internal Links	11,16%
Average Number of Words	28,71%	Average Number of Links	6,67%
Total Number of Pages	16,74%	Size of the Images	5,04%
Number of Links	16,44%	*Humanities ∩ Tutorial*	
Average Size of the Images	12,35%	*Metrics*	*Importance*
Size of the Images	9,12%	Size of the page	24,80%
Average size of the page	8,16%	Average Number of Scripts	15,16%
Number of words that are links	6,88%	Number of External Links	14,99%
Arts ∩ Simulation		Average Number of Unique Internal Links	8,42%
Metrics	*Importance*	Number of Words	8,40%
Number of Words	28,53%	Number of words that are links	6,78%
Average Number of Unique External Links	26,84%	Number of Links	5,43%
Average Number of Images	15,01%	Average Number of Images	5,36%
Size of the page	10,60%	*Education ∩ Collection*	
Number of Links	10,51%	*Metrics*	*Importance*
Humanities ∩ Collection		Number of Unique External Links	19,41%
Metrics	*Importance*	Size of the page	17,96%
Average Number of Internal Links	43,23%	Number of External Links	12,52%
Average Number of Words	36,31%	Average Number of Links	11,94%
Average Number of Unique External Links	6,79%	Average Number of Unique Internal Links	11,28%
Number of Audio Files	6,37%	Number of Video files	8,76%
		Number of Words	8,70%

Some of the metrics appear more than two times in the studied models and could be considered the most important for the context of the present work. This is the case of:

1. *Size of the Page* - included in 4 models: *Arts ∩ Simulation, Education ∩ Collection, Math & Statistics ∩ Tutorial* and *Humanities ∩ Tutorial*),
2. *Number of Words* - included in 3 models: *Arts ∩ Simulation, Education ∩ Collection* and *Humanities ∩ Tutorial*); and
3. *Number of Links* (included in 3 models: *Arts ∩ Simulation, Humanities ∩ Tutorial* and *Math & Statistics ∩ Reference Material*).

Although there is no metric that can be considered important in all studied subsets, it is possible to group the metrics according to the classes presented in table 1 (*Link*

Measures, Text Measures, Graphic, Interactive and Multimedia Measures and *Site Architecture Measures*) and to observe some sort of tendencies in some specific cases. In table 5 we present the percentages related to the number of times that each class of metric appears in the model of each subset.

Table 5. Percentage of appearance of the classes of metrics in the models of each subset

Subset	Graphic, Interactive and Multimedia	Link	Site Architecture	Text
Arts ∩ Simulation	20.0%	40.0%	20.0%	20.0%
Education ∩ Collection	0.0%	57.1%	28.6%	14.3%
Humanities ∩ Collection	25.0%	50.0%	0.0%	25.0%
Humanities ∩ Simulation	50.0%	50.0%	0.0%	0.0%
Humanities ∩ Tutorial	25.0%	37.5%	12.5%	25.0%
Math & Statistics ∩ Reference Material	28.6%	14.3%	28.6%	28.6%
Math & Statistics ∩ Tutorial	50.0%	0.0%	50.0%	0.0%

As it is shown in table 5, there is a prevalence of some classes of metrics for some specific subsets. For instance, 57.1% of the metrics used in the model of quality generated for the *Education ∩ Collection* subset belong to the class *Link Measures*. The class *Link Measures* also appear as the most prevalent to represent the model of quality of the *Humanities ∩ Collection* with 50% of the metrics. The quality model of *Humanities ∩ Simulation* is represented by 50% of *Graphic, Interactive and Multimedia* metrics and 50% by *Link Measures*, and the quality model of *Math & Statistics ∩ Tutorial* is represented by 50% of *Graphic, Interactive and Multimedia* metrics and 50% by *Site Architecture Measures*. The models generated for the subsets *Arts ∩ Simulation, Humanities ∩ Tutorial* and *Math & Statistics ∩ Reference Material* presented a more distributed percentage of the metrics along the different classes.

5   Final Remarks

Evaluating quality of learning objects is a difficult task that normally involves several distinct aspects and different stakeholders, and the existing learning object evaluation methods and frameworks are not free from ambiguities. There is a clear need for searching metrics of learning objects that can help in the process of measuring and assessing their quality in a more objective way. The present work describes the first results of a methodology that allows identifying lower-level measures of learning objects that are associated to quality. In this work, 34 intrinsic features of learning objects catalogued in the MERLOT repository were crawled and used in the construction of models for automated quality assessment. As the models were built through the use of decision trees, it was possible to establish the percentage of importance of these metrics and to identify which are the most important features of learning objects that are associated to quality in the specific studied subsets. For instance, we observed that *Link Measures* are the most prevalent quality metrics for resources of *Education ∩ Collection*, and that Link *Measures* and *Graphic,*

Interactive and Multimedia Measures are the most prevalent for resources of *Humanities ∩ Simulation*. Moreover, *Graphic, Interactive and Multimedia Measures* and *Site Architecture Measures* are the only used to classify quality of *Mathematics & Statistics ∩ Tutorial* materials. From the used metrics, it was also possible to observe that *Size of the Page, Number of Words*, and *Number of Links* were the most included in the studied models.

These are important findings that can further help to establish a common ground of lower-level quality measures of learning objects that can be considered during the development of such materials. Future work will explore the threshold values of these metrics for *good* and *not-good* resources, and will include other possible metrics that are still not implemented in the crawler (e.g., readability measures such as Fog-Index).

Acknowledgments. The work presented here has been funded by the European Commission through the project IGUAL (www.igualproject.org) – Innovation for Equality in Latin American University (code DCIALA/19.09.01/10/21526/245-315/ALFAHI (2010)123) of the ALFA III Programme, and by Spanish Ministry of Science and Innovation through project MAVSEL: Mining, data analysis and visualization based in social aspects of e-learning (code TIN2010-21715-C02-01).

References

Bethard, S., Wetzer, P., Butcher, K., Martin, J.H., Sumner, T.: Automatically characterizing resource quality for educational digital libraries. Paper Presented at the Proceedings of the 9th ACM/IEEE-CS Joint Conference on Digital Libraries, Austin, TX, USA (2009)

Breiman, L., Friedman, J., Stone, C.D., Olshen, R.A.: Classification and Regression Trees, 1st edn. (1984)

Cechinel, C.: Empirical Foundations for Automated Quality Assessment of Learning Objects inside Repositories (Ph.D. Doctoral Thesis), University of Alcalá, Alcalá de Henares (2012)

Cechinel, C., Sánchez-Alonso, S., García-Barriocanal, E.: Statistical profiles of highly-rated learning objects. Computers & Education 57(1), 1255–1269 (2011), doi:10.1016/j.compedu.2011.01.012

Cechinel, C., Sánchez-Alonso, S., Sicilia, M.-Á., Amador, C.V.: Evaluating Models for Automated Quality Assessment of Learning Objects inside Repositories. Paper Presented at the 6th Latin American Conference on Learning Objects and Technology Enhanced Learning – LACLO 2011, Montevideo, Uruguay (2011),
http://laclo2011.seciu.edu.uy/publicacion/laclo/
laclo2011_submission_14.pdf

Custard, M., Sumner, T.: Using Machine Learning to Support Quality Judgments. D-Lib Magazine 11(10) (2005)

Fernández, M.R.: Métricas en repositorios de objetos de aprendizaje (Bachelor Final Project), University of Alcalá, Alcalá de Henares, Spain (2011)

Ivory, M.Y., Hearst, M.A.: Statistical profiles of highly-rated web sites. Paper Presented at the Proceedings of the SIGCHI Conference on Human Factors in Computing Systems: Changing Our World, Changing Ourselves, Minneapolis, Minnesota, USA (2002)

Kohavi, R.: A Study of Cross-Validation and Bootstrap for Accuracy Estimation and Model Selection. Paper Presented at the IJCAI (1995)

Leacock, T.L., Nesbit, J.C.: A Framework for Evaluating the Quality of Multimedia Learning Resources. Educational Technology & Society 10(2), 44–59 (2007)

MATLAB, version 7.10.0. The MathWorks Inc., Natick (2010)

Nesbit, J.C., Belfer, K., Leacock, T.: Learning object review instrument (LORI). E-learning research and assessment network (2003), http://www.elera.net/eLera/Home/Articles/LORI%20manual (retrieved)

Ochoa, X.: Learnometrics: Metrics for learning objects (Ph.D. Doctoral Thesis), KatholiekeUniversity Leuven, Leuven (2008), https://lirias.kuleuven.be/bitstream/1979/1891/2/ThesisFinal.pdf (retrieved)

Santhanam, T., Sundaram, S.: Application of CART Algorithm in Blood Donors Classification. Journal of Computer Science 6(5), 548–552 (2010), doi:10.3844/jcssp.2010.548.552

Sanz-Rodriguez, J., Dodero, J., Sánchez-Alonso, S.: Metrics-based evaluation of learning object reusability. Software Quality Journal, 1–20 (2010), doi:10.1007/s11219-010-9108-5

Vargo, J., Nesbit, J.C., Belfer, K., Archambault, A.: Learning Object Evaluation: Computer-Mediated Collaboration and Inter-Rater Reliability. International Journal of Computers and Applications 25(3), 1–8 (2003)

Vuorikari, R., Manouselis, N., Duval, E.: Using Metadata for Storing, Sharing and Reusing Evaluations for Social Recommendations: the Case of Learning Resources. In: Social Information Retrieval Systems: Emerging Technologies and Applications for Searching the Web Effectively, pp. 87–107. Idea Group Publishing, Hershey (2008)

Williams, D.D.: Evaluation of learning objects and instruction using learning objects (2000), http://reusability.org/read/chapters/williams.doc (retrieved)

State of the Art on Methodologies for the Development of a Metadata Application Profile

Mariana Curado Malta and Ana Alice Baptista

Algoritmi Center, University of Minho
mariana.malta@algoritmi.uminho.pt, analice@dsi.uminho.pt

Abstract. This article presents the state of the art on methodologies for the development of a metadata application profile. For this purpose we have performed searches in scientific on-line databases and made other efforts such as global searches on the Web and calls on the mailing lists of the metadata communities to find articles and Web pages about metadata application profiles development and metadata best practices or methodologies. These searches produced 21 items of which 9 have information on how the metadata application profiles were developed. As a result of this analysis we have found small formulas or private recipes for very particular phases of the process, but none is described in detail. We have also found guidelines that were too global and not sufficiently detailed for the metadata application profile development. As far as we could determine, there is no comprehensive methodological support for the metadata application profile development.

1 Introduction

This article reports part of a Semantic Web related research project that deals with a framework of semantic interoperability among the world community of social and solidarity economy web based information systems. In this project it has been identified the need to develop a metadata application profile (AP) in order to achieve such interoperability [Malta and Baptista, 2012]. An application profile is a technique used to adapt to the specific needs of a certain community [Lynch, 1997]. It uses data elements from different metadata schemes and puts them together with local developments in order to adjust to a particular community [Heery and Patel, 2000]. According to the Semantic Web Activity Webpage (2012) "The Semantic Web provides a common framework that allows data to be shared and reused across application, enterprise, and community boundaries" [W3C, 2012]. In this cross-boundaries context, the development of AP is expected to be a complex task that needs an adequate methodological support. By methodology we mean a body of operations to reach a goal. A methodology shows how to operationalize defined steps. To find the adequate methodological support to develop an AP, we have performed a literature review. We carried out searches in on-line scientific databases. Then, to complement the literature review, we have performed wider searches on Google search engine[1] and sent calls

---

[1] http://www.google.com - accessed in 19 July 2012.

J.M. Dodero, M. Palomo-Duarte, P. Karampiperis (Eds.): MTSR 2012, CCIS 343, pp. 61–73, 2012.

to some mailing lists of the metadata cummunity. We have found small formulas or private recipes for very particular phases of the process of development of an AP, but none is described in detail. We have also found guidelines that were too global and not sufficiently detailed for the AP development.

This article is organized in 5 sections. In Section 2 we explore the concept of an application profile in order to define the limits of our work. Section 3 presents the work methodology. Section 4 reports the findings and analyses these findings. Finally, closing conclusions and future work are drawn in section 5.

2   Application Profile

Any standard was always a basis for the implementation of profiles (even before the existence of the Internet). A good example was the community Z39.50[2] which created profiles to refine the standard options [Baker et al., 2001]. An application profile was based on a standard, and it was a technique that helped a certain community to refine the standard to their needs [Lynch, 1997]. Later, with the Semantic Web, and with the advent of the RDF[3] syntax, programmers had the technology for the combination of individual elements of a variety of different metadata schemes. It was an open gate to the possibility of choosing the most appropriate elements to describe resources [Heery and Patel, 2000]. Heery and Patel (2000) define an application profile as consisting of: "Data elements drawn from one or more namespaces schemas combined together by implementors and optimised for a particular local application" [Heery and Patel, 2000]. In 2008 Baker, Nilsson and Johnston define an application profile (DCAP - Dublin Core Application Profile) as: "A document (or set of documents) that specifies and describes the metadata used in a particular application" [Baker et al., 2008].

Dublin Core Metadata Initiative[4] (DCMI) specifies the rules to implement a DCAP in its recomendation "Singapore Framework for Dublin Core Application Profiles" (see [Baker et al., 2008]). This document is a synopsis of all the research done among the metadata community until that date. It is a very important document since it defines a framework to implement semantic interoperability[5] among different communities of practice.

For the sake of our work, when we refer to a metadata application profile (AP), we refer to metadata profile implementations that meet either the definitions of Lynh (1997), Heery and Patel (2000) or Baker et al. (2008).

---

[2] http://www.loc.gov/z3950/agency/ - accessed in 1.12.2011.

[3] A standard model for Web data interchange [W3C, 2010] - see
http://www.w3.org/TR/rdf-concepts - accessed in 10 July 2012.

[4] See http://www.dublincore.org - accessed in 19 July 2012.

[5] Semantic interoperability focuses on meaningful exchanges of information, i.e. the information has the same interpretation (or very closely) by both the sender and the receiving systems.

3   Methodology

In order to develop our work we have devided the searches in two parts: Part I - Identification and analysis of the existing development of AP; Part II - Identification and analysis of the existing methodologies used for the development of AP.

We carried out general searches and then more refined searches in on-line databases. The databases used were: *Google Scholar*[6], *ISI Web of Knowledge*[7], *Networked Digital Library of Thesis and Dissertations*[8], Scopus[9] and Oaister[10]. The searches were made in English, French, Spanish and Portuguese for Part I and in English for Part II; and in the fields 'title of the article' and 'body of the article'.

In the first phase of the searches we chose a set of articles. In the second phase, we analyzed the references of the articles chosen in the first phase, new articles where chosen due to the relevance of their title and later by the relevance of their summary. This process was iterative in what new articles were concerned, ending when articles referenced to each other. In the third phase of the searches we looked for articles citing the articles of the first phase. New articles were selected according to the same rules of the second phase.

Concerning **Part I** the keywords used for the searches were: Metadata Application Profile, Dublin Core Application Profile, Metadata Element Set, Metadata Scheme, and Metadata vocabulary.

Concerning **Part II** the keywords used for the searches were: Application Profile Methodologies, Application Profile and Methodologies, Dublin Core Application Profile Methodologies, Dublin Core Application Profile and Methodologies, Metadata and Methologies.

After the literature review, we have made efforts to find more metadata application profiles through: (i) Google[11] searches with the same terms defined in the literature review; (ii) Information received by email after sending an email to the "General" DCMI mailing list [12] with an information request on AP development; (iii) Information received on the "Architecture" DCMI mailing-list[13].

Finally we analysed every item (text document or webpage) that came out of the searches. The methodology was as follows:

1. Every item to be analised was printed out and numbered;
2. A word processing document was created: the matrix document;
3. A new line was introduced in the matrix document with a reference (number defined in phase 1) to the new item being analysed;

---

[6] http://scholar.google.com - accessed in 10.07.2012.
[7] http://www.isiWebofknowledge.com - accessed in 10.07.2012.
[8] http://www.ndltd.org/serviceproviders/scirus-etd-search   -   accessed   in 10.07.2012.
[9] http://www.scopus.com - accessed in 10.07.2012.
[10] http://oaister.worldcat.org - accessed in 10.07.2012.
[11] http://www.google.com - accessed in 19 July 2012.
[12] dc-general@jiscmail.ac.uk
[13] dc-architecture@jiscmail.ac.uk

4. Every time there was important information to keep in the item analysed, it was copied to the matrix document, with a reference to the source page number (if it was an article; no number was kept if it was a web page). This phase finished every time there was no more important information to keep in the analysed item;
5. The process went back to step 3 until there was no more items to be analysed.

We have organised the items in 3 different categories:

- scientific articles, technical documents, manuals which refer explicitly to methodologies for the development of AP or methodologies concerning metadata applications or best practices. We will call them *Manuals*.
- a set of scientific articles that systematise information related to specific areas or even more horizontal areas. We mean articles that report the state of the art of AP of a specific domain, or analyse a certain characteristic on the AP development in a general domain basis. We will call them *Methodological articles*.
- finally, a set of scientific articles that report the development of AP. These articles include sections that refer to "ways of doing" or "recipes" for specific moments of the AP development. We will call them *Profile articles*.

4   Results

We analysed each of the items in the light of: (i) the steps: we call it *steps*; (ii) how these steps are executed: we call it *how*. We have set a scale of coverage range for the AP in what the "how" is concerned - we call it *coverage*. Basically, when the item defines the "how", we want to measure what part of the whole AP development this "how" covers: 1 - Partially covered; 2 - Moderately covered; 3 - Totally covered. When there is no "how", the coverage is defined as "n/d".

Bellow you can read the results found on each category.

4.1   Manuals

- **Chen and Chen (2005)**: The Metadata Lifecycle Model is a model to systematize the metadata working procedure in digital libraries [Chen and Chen, 2005]. It has 4 stages:
  1. Requirement Assessment and Content Analysis:
     - Acquisition of Metadata Base Needs;
     - Review of Relevant Metadata Standards and Projects ;
     - Investigation of Deep Metadata Needs;
     - Identification of Strategies for the Metadata Schemes and Achieving Interoperability with Well-known Metadata Standards.
  2. System Requirement Specification;
     - Preparation of the Metadata Requirement Specification;
     - Evaluation of Metadata Systems.

3. Metadata System;
   - Preparation of Best Practice Guidance;
   - Development of the Metadata System .
4. Service and Evaluation
   - Maintenance of Metadata Service ;
   - Evaluation of Metadata Performance.

Steps: Yes; How: No; Coverage: n/d

- **BSI (2005)**: Makes recommendations about data models for any organisation creating application profiles of international metadata standards, for use in the domain of teaching and learning [BSI, 2005]. Focuses on the two standards: Dublin Core Metadata Element Set and IEEE LOM.

Steps: Yes; How: No; Coverage: n/d

- **IMS Global Learning Consortium (2005a) (2005b)** : Developed by IMS Global Learning Consortium, specify the steps for developing an AP. Part 1 focuses on issues that are related to the management process and methodology. Second part is purely technical. Part 1 has an "Outline of a Process for Creating an Application Profile" section which presents, in a very global way, the steps for the development of an AP in the domain of learning objects. Bellow we summarize the most important steps:

1. Feasibility and Risk Analysis: to identify the stakeholders; to determine the size of the community market;
2. Capturing the Requirements: to identify the specific requirements of the community that is going to use the AP;
3. Project Group Guidelines: generic guidelines on how to develop the AP, using tools like scenarios and case studies, and also some group techniques.

Also has a defined set of rules for the AP development to be found in the next group of documents. These rules have to do with compliance issues with the base schemas used on AP.

Steps: Yes; How: Yes; Coverage: 1

- **CWA (2006)**: Created in 2006 by the European Committee for standardisation. It is a guide for the development of AP in the area of e-learning. Shows the major guidelines, giving examples on how to define the metadata elements of the AP: advises on the creation of a matrix having the data elements as lines and the properties of the data elements as columns. The major guidelines are:

1. Definition of the own requirements;
2. Selection of the data elements;
3. Definition of the obligation of data elements;
4. Definition of the value space;
5. Definition of the relationship and dependency;
6. Definition of the data type profiling;
7. Definition of the technical binding.

Steps: Yes; How: Yes; Coverage: 1

- **Baker et al. (2008)**: The Singapore framework defines what a DCAP is and presents the rules for its development:

1. Definition of the functional requirements (mandatory);
2. Definition of the domain model (mandatory);
3. Description Set Profile (mandatory);
4. Usage guidelines (optional);
5. Encoding syntax guidelines (optional).

Steps: Yes; How: No; Coverage: n/d

4.2   Methodological Articles

– **Duval et al. (2002)**: presents practices of metadata, one of them being the use of AP. It shows rules and key issues. Summary of the manual CWA (2006).
  Steps: No; How: No; Coverage: n/d
– **Friesen et al. (2002)** : presents a set of topics that are important for the implementation of AP in the domain of learning objects. Uses as examples two AP (TLF and CanCore). Advise on some techniques: the use of a good data model, the use of good practice examples, the use of standard base schemes, the use of incremental actions in order to achieve the final goal of interoperability.
  Steps: Yes; How: No;Coverage: 1
– **Currie et al. (2002)**: Provides a method for making "interoperability visible". The approach is to aggregate all elements of the different metadata resources colections, "consider the processes thatcould be used to rationalise the aggregated set of elements and then show how the agencies might work together to harmonise the resulting application profile. This process is referred to as ARH – HA!: visualise the processes of aggregate, rationalise, and harmonise in order to be motivated to harmonise commonly-owned, distributed, heterogenous metadata collections" [Currie et al., 2002, p. 179].
  Steps: No; How: Yes;Coverage: 1
– **EESV (2012)** : The European project ISA, which has recently developed the AP "ADMS", makes available in its documentation a document dedicated to the methodology of the management of a cross-cultural and geographically distributed group that builds the AP. But it does not show any information concerning the methodology for the AP development.
  Steps: No; How: Yes; Coverage: 1

4.3   Profile Articles

– **DCMI (nd)**: Proposes the use of scenarios for their AP development.//
  Steps: No; How: Yes; Coverage: 1
– **Onyancha et al. (2001)**: Reports the development of the AP "AGRIS", in the agriculture domain. It has a reference to the methodology used [Onyancha et al., 2001, pag. 7]:
  1. Development of a conceptual map of the different types of information resources used in the AGRIS project portal;

2. Remodelling of the project data model to meet current information needs (such as description of Web pages and databases);
3. Evaluation of standards and common resource description practices;
4. Mapping of currently used elements to the available element pool from the standards ;
5. Proposing the unavailable elements and schemes to be included in the AP;
6. Binding.

Steps: No; How: No; Coverage: n/d

- **Agostinho et al. (2004)**: Shows the first steps on the development of the AP "LOMAP" in the learning objects domain. Some methodological steps, they are:
  1. To perform an AP literature review on AP of the same application domain;
  2. To choose a base metadata schema as the starting point;
  3. To apply the elements of the base schema to a set of resources in order to understand the strengths and weaknesses of these elements, and to remove the issues that can arise from this application.
  4. To analyse the results of the previous step;
  5. To apply an existing application profile to a sample of learning objects;
  6. To analyze the results of the previous step;
  7. To develop the AP based on the previous steps.

Steps: Yes; How: Yes; Coverage: 1

- **de La Passadiere and Jarraud (2004)**: Reports the development of the French AP "ManUel", in the learning objects domain. The guidelines are based on the study of user needs and community of practice of the AP. The guidelines are [de La Passadière and Jarraud, 2004, pag. 10]:
  1. To study the needs: consulting the different user communities; studying the standards;
  2. To develop a solution: define the adopted principles; justify the choices made;
  3. To develop the AP.

Steps: Yes; How: No; Coverage: n/d

- **Marzal García-Quismondo et al. (2006)**: Reports the development of the Spanish AP "MIMETA", in the learning objects domain. The reported methodology is based on both documents Agostinho et al. (2004) and Chen and Chen (2005) [Marzal García-Quismondo et al., 2006, pag. 553]:
  1. A literature review on educational metadata and analysis of the major standards and specifications developed in the field of educational technologies;
  2. An analysis of the main educational digital library projects;
  3. Development of an AP with the main identified standards: to choose initially the more generic elements, then to choose the more detailed elements.

Steps: Yes; How: No; Coverage: n/d

– **Wilson et al. (2007)**: Reports the development of the AP "MAP", in the libraries domain. It refers that the approach to the AP was influenced by BSI (2005) [Wilson et al., 2007, pag. 7]:
  1. Gather requirements;
  2. Identify appropriate schemes;
  3. Select data elements;
  4. Specify rules for data elements;
  5. Review against other requirements;
  6. Finalise draft;
  7. Create crosswalks;
  8. Scope requirements for XML Binding;
  9. Develop a maintenance plan.

  Steps: Yes; How: No; Coverage: n/d

– **Buonazia and Masci (2007)**: Reports the development of the AP "PICO" under the scope of the "Cultura Italia" project , in the cultural heritage domain. Has a whole section about the methodology used in PICO development. We summarise [Buonazia and Masci, 2007, pag. 394]:
  1. users and domain analysis;
  2. definition of user scenarios and user cases;
  3. overall architecture design;
  4. content analysis;
  5. analysis of the state of the art on descriptive metadata standards;
  6. design of the metadata scheme;

  The methodology has more steps but they are not related to the AP development.

  Steps: Yes; How: Yes; Coverage: 1

– **Eadie (2008)**: Reports that a working group has been launched composed by people from different backgrounds related to the AP application domain. It also refers that when the project is completed there is the intention to broaden the discussion to a wider consultant group. The workplan is presented:
  1. Draft development of the functional requirements;
  2. Draft development of the Entity-Relationship diagram and the set of attributes;
  3. Draft development of the AP;
  4. Group discussion;
  5. AP refinement with the information coming from group discussions;
  6. Development of simple catalogue guides for AP use;
  7. Work presentation to the community;
  8. Development of acceptance plans for the community.

  Steps: Yes; How: Yes; Coverage: 1

– **Salokhe et al. (2008)**: Reports the development of the AP Organization, in the domain of Agriculture. The methodology used for its development was [Salokhe et al., 2008, pag. 3]:
  1. Project definition, its goal and context;

2. Existing metadata standards assessment and creation of metadata scheme;
3. Comparison of each defined element with the ISO11179 standard elements;
4. XML binding development;
5. Real data testing with the binding defined in the previous item;
6. Guidelines development;

Steps: Yes; How: No; Coverage: n/d

- **Bountouri et al. (2009)**: Reports the development of the "PSI" AP, in the domain of Public Service Information. It has one section for presentation of the implementation methodology of the AP. It broadly presents [Bountouri et al., 2009, pag.4]:
  1. Comparison of every metadata standard with "DC" and Addition of extra properties and sub-properties;
  2. Semantic resolution and harmonisation of properties and sub-properties;
  3. Specification of the "PSI" AP.

  Steps: Yes;How: No; Coverage: n/d

- **Palavitsinis et al. (2009)**: Reports the development of the "Organic.Edunet" AP, in the domain of agriculture learning resources. In the section "generic process for an AP development", refers the generic steps used for its development, as follows:
  1. Definition of the "Organic.Edunet" requirements;
  2. Selection of IEEE LOM ;
  3. Semantic refinement (so as to serve better the needs of the Organic.Edunet);
  4. Specification of the constraints and the domains of the elements;
  5. Specification of the element relationships and dependencies;
  6. Introdution of new elements to respond to specific needs;
  7. AP completion (which includes binding and technological issues of how metadata is obtained, created and stored).

  Steps: Yes; How: No;Coverage: n/d

- **Zschocke et al. (2009)**: Reports the development of the "CIGAR" AP, in the domain of learning objects. It is targeted at distributed and multi-language community. Reports a revision of different AP IEEE LOM based to identify the mandatory IEEE LOM elements used in the AP implementation of other organisations. This helped to understand better the elements sub-set which are normally used to describe the basic learning objects caracteristics and their influence in the development of the "CIGAR" AP. Due to the international destributed nature of the community, the multi-language support was considered essential [Zschocke et al., 2009, pag. 16]. **Steps: Yes; How: Yes; Coverage: 1**

4.4 Analysis

From the 21 analised items only 9 have information on how to develop an AP, but they were all scaled as "partially covered" in what the AP development coverage is concerned. Baker et al. (2008) is the most comprehensive document concerning the development of an AP, but it doesn't actually explain in detail how to develop it. This document is the climax of a process of development of stored knowledge, coming from Heery and Patel (2000) and Duval et al. (2002), through IMS Global Learning Consortium (2005a) and IMS Global Learning Consortium (2005b), ending in CWA (2006). We came across a few guidelines or "hows" in specific parts of the development process which are interesting and should be kept for future work. But these guidelines, specially in the documents catalogued as "Profile articles", are too centered in a particular domain. These guidelines are presented in table 1.

Table 1. Important guidelines found on the analysis to be kept for future work

Items	What
[Allinson and Powell, 2006] [Eadie, 2008]	Workgroups composed by people of different profiles
[de La Passadière and Jarraud, 2004]	The support in the AP development of workgroups within the target community
[Chen and Chen, 2005], [BSI, 2005], [IMS Global Learning Consortium, 2005a] [CWA, 2006], [Baker et al., 2008], [de La Passadière and Jarraud, 2004] and [Eadie, 2008]	The need for a requirement analysis, however in none of these documents can we find any form of development procedure
[Chen and Chen, 2005], [BSI, 2005], [Onyancha et al., 2001], [Agostinho et al., 2004], [Marzal García-Quismondo et al., 2006], [Buonazia and Masci, 2007] and [Salokhe et al., 2008]	The need for a state of the art development of the AP and metadata standard schemes. The documents further refer that a state of the art can be accomplished through: (i) a literature review ([Agostinho et al., 2004], [Marzal García-Quismondo et al., 2006]);(ii) project study ([Marzal García-Quismondo et al., 2006] and [Buonazia and Masci, 2007]); (iii) standards evaluation and study of common practices ([Onyancha et al., 2001])
[Agostinho et al., 2004] and [Marzal García-Quismondo et al., 2006]	The need for choice of one or more base metadata schemes as a starting point.
	The need for metadata elements specification is defined in all documents, in fact the core of the AP development. There is no reference to how this should be undertaken. However there are a few guidelines:
[IMS Global Learning Consortium, 2005a], [Friesen et al., 2002], [DCMI, nd] and [Buonazia and Masci, 2007]	Through scenario building and case construction.
[Agostinho et al., 2004]	Through the application of the chosen base metadata scheme elements to a set of resources. This work is done in two steps: (i) element application to a resource sample and respective subsequent analysis; (ii) answer to a set of questions and respective subsequent analysis.
[Marzal García-Quismondo et al., 2006]	Through the choice of element of: (i) generic caracteristics of the base schemes; (ii) specific caracteristics of the base schemes.
[Baker et al., 2008], [Onyancha et al., 2001], [Eadie, 2008]	The need to prepare a data model is refered in many documents. This model, in the case of Baker et al. (2008), can be expressed only through text or using a more formal approach, as UML; in the case of Eadie (2008) the diagram entity-relationship is used.
[CWA, 2006]	For the definition of the metadata elements, they sugest the creation of a matrix having the data elements as lines and the properties of the data elements as columns.

5 Conclusions and Future Work

We have made the state of the art on the methodologies used for a metadata application profile (AP) development. The study consisted of a literature review and other efforts to find scientific articles, manuals, reports, documents or webpages about AP development methodologies, metadata best practices methodologies, AP or AP development. We have found small formulas or private recipes for very particular phases of the process, but none is described in detail. We have also found global guidelines that were not sufficiently detailed for the AP development. As far as we could determine, there is no comprehensive methodological support for the metadata AP development. In a cross-boundaries context, as it is the context of the Semantic Web, the development of AP is expected to be a complex task that needs an adequate methodological support. The metadata community would benefit from a detailed cross-domain methodology. It is our aim to contribute to the definition of a comprehensive methodological support for the development of an AP. For the short-term future work, we plan to finalize the study on AP and report to the metadata community our findings under two axis: (i) Identification and analysis of the existing metadata application profiles; (ii) Temporal evolution of the AP. AP are specific kinds of data models; it is reasonable to think that the already well established methodologies for the development of data models in the scope of software engineering can be useful, as a basis, to the AP development. Therefore, our next goal will be to study in detail the more representative methodologies for the development of data models in the context of the software engineering and, then, analyse and combine them with the specific needs of AP, especially in what regards global interoperability concerns.

Acknowledgement. Sponsored by Fundação para a Ciência e Tecnologia - Projecto Estratégico do Centro Algoritmi - Ref.: FCOMP-01-0124-FEDER-022674.

References

[Agostinho et al., 2004] Agostinho, S., Bennett, S., Lockyer, L., Harper, B.: Developing a learning object metadata application profile based on lom suitable for the australian higher education context. Australasian Journal of Educational Technology 20(2), 191–208 (2004)

[Allinson and Powell, 2006] Allinson, J., Powell, A. (2006). Swap application profile, http://www.ukoln.ac.uk/repositories/digirep/index/SWAP (accessed in July 1, 2012)

[Baker et al., 2001] Baker, T., Dekkers, M., Heery, R., Patel, M., Salokhe, G.: What terms does your metadata use? application profiles as machine-understandable narratives. Journal of Digital Information 2(2), 10 (2001)

[Baker et al., 2008] Baker, T., Nilsson, M., Johnston, P.: The singapore framework for dublin core application profiles (2008), http://dublincore.org/documents/singapore-framework/ (accessed in June 26, 2011)

[Bountouri et al., 2009] Bountouri, L., Papatheodorou, C., Soulikias, V., Stratis, M.: Metadata interoperability in public sector information. Journal of Information Science 35(2), 204–231 (2009)

[BSI, 2005] BSI, BS 8419-1:2005 Interoperability between metadata systems used for learning, education and training. Code of practice for the development of application profiles. BSI (2005)

[Buonazia and Masci, 2007] Buonazia, I., Masci, M.: Il pico application profile. un dublin core application profile per il portale della cultura italiana (2007)

[Chen and Chen, 2005] Chen, Y., Chen, S.: Metadata lifecycle model and metadata interoperability. In: 5th International Conference on Conception of Library and Information Science (2005)

[Currie et al., 2002] Currie, M., Geileskey, M., Nevile, L., Woodman, R.: Visualising interoperability: Arh, aggregation, rationalisation and harmonisation. In: Proceedings of the 2002 International Conference on Dublin Core and Metadata Applications: Metadata for e-communities: Supporting Diversity and Convergence. Dublin Core Metadata Initiative, pp. 177–183 (2002)

[CWA, 2006] CWA, Guidelines and support for building application profiles in e-learning (CEN Workshop Agreement, CWA 15555:2006 E). CEN, European Committee for Standardization (2006),
ftp://ftp.cenorm.be/PUBLIC/CWAs/e-Europe/
WS-LT/cwa15555-00-2006-Jun.pdf (accessed in July 2, 2012)

[DCMI, nd] DCMI (n/d). Dublin core education application profile (working draft of v0.4), https://docs.google.com/Doc?id=dn8z3gs_38cgwkvv (accessed in July 2, 2012)

[de La Passadière and Jarraud, 2004] de La Passadière, B., Jarraud, P.: Manuel, a lom application profile for c@mpusciences. Sciences et Technologies de l Information et de la Communication pour l Éducation et la Formation 11 (2004)

[Duval et al., 2002] Duval, E., Hodgins, W., Sutton, S., Weibel, S.: Metadata principles and practicalities. D-lib Magazine 8(4), 16 (2002)

[Eadie, 2008] Eadie, M.: Towards an application profile for images. Ariadne 55 (2008)

[EESV, 2012] EESV, P. E. S.: Process and methodology for core vocabularies. Technical report, Interoperability solutions for European Public Administrators (2012)

[Friesen et al., 2002] Friesen, N., Mason, J., Ward, N.: Building educational metadata application profiles. In: Proceedings of the International Conference on Dublin Core and Metadata for e-Communities, pp. 63–69 (2002)

[Heery and Patel, 2000] Heery, R., Patel, M.: Application profiles: mixing and matching metadata schemas. Ariadne 25, 27–31 (2000)

[IMS Global Learning Consortium, 2005a] IMS Global Learning Consortium, I: IMS Application Profile Guidelines: Part 1 - Management Overview. IMS Global Learning Consortium, Inc., version 1 edition (2005a)

[IMS Global Learning Consortium, 2005b] IMS Global Learning Consortium, I: IMS Application Profile Guidelines: Part 2 - Technical Manual. IMS Global Learning Consortium, Inc., version 1.0 edition (2005b)

[Lynch, 1997] Lynch, C.A.: The z39.50 information retrieval standard - part i: A strategic view of its past, present and future. D-Lib Magazine (1997)

[Malta and Baptista, 2012] Malta, M., Baptista, A.: Social and solidarity economy web information systems: State of the art. In: Vidal, A., Torres, T. (eds.) Social e-Entreprise: Value Creation through ICT, ch. 1. IGI Global (in press, 2012)

[Marzal García-Quismondo et al., 2006] Marzal García-Quismondo, M., Calzada Prado, J., Cuevas Cerveró, A.: Desarrollo de un esquema de metadatos para la descripción de recursos educativos: el perfil de aplicación mimeta. Revista Española de Documentación Científica 29(4), 551–571 (2006)

[Onyancha et al., 2001] Onyancha, I., Keizer, J., Katz, S.: A dublin core application profile in the agricultural domain. In: International Conference on Dublin Core and Metadata Applications, p. 185 (2001)

[Palavitsinis et al., 2009] Palavitsinis, N., Manouselis, N., Sanchez Alonso, S.: Evaluation of a Metadata Application Profile for Learning Resources on Organic Agriculture. In: Sartori, F., Sicilia, M.Á., Manouselis, N. (eds.) MTSR 2009. CCIS, vol. 46, pp. 270–281. Springer, Heidelberg (2009)

[Salokhe et al., 2008] Salokhe, G., Pesce, V., Liesthout, J.: Organization metadata application profile. Technical report, FAO (2008)

[W3C, 2010] W3C, Rdf - w3c standards (2010), http://www.w3.org/RDF/ (accessed in January 14, 2012)

[W3C, 2012] W3C, W3c semantic web activity (2012), http://www.w3.org/2001/sw/ (accessed July 30, 2012)

[Wilson et al., 2007] Wilson, K., Billington, L., Moir, S., Carpenter, S.: Development of a metadata application profile at the state library of new south wales. Library Papers, 4 (2007)

[Zschocke et al., 2009] Zschocke, T., Beniest, J., Paisley, C., Najjar, J.: The lom application profile for agricultural learning resources of the cgiar. International Journal of Metadata, Semantics and Ontologies 4(1), 13–23 (2009)

Festivalization of the City Support: A Case Study

Mizar Luca Federici[1], Andrea Gorrini[2], Lorenza Manenti[3], and Fabio Sartori[3]

[1] CROWDYXITY s.r.l. - Crowd Dynamics and Complexity
Via Ventura 3, 20134 - Milano, Italy
m.federici@crowdyxity.com
[2] INFORMATION SOCIETY Ph.D. Program
University of Milan-Bicocca
Via Bicocca degli Arcimboldi 8, 20126 - Milano, Italy
a.gorrini@campus.unimib.it
[3] CSAI - Complex Systems and Artificial Intelligence Research Center
University of Milan - Bicocca
viale Sarca, 336, 20126 - Milano, Italy
{gorrini,manenti,sartori}@disco.unimib.it

Abstract. Supporting festivalization involves the analysis of events and crowd taking part in them. The definitions of "events" and "crowds" are still representing a controversial issue that has been tackled by different disciplines like Sociology, Philosophy and Computer Science. We have recently developed an ontology of events taking advantage of results and perspectives already present in literature and in available resources like DBpedia. The main innovation of our approach is the integration of an ontology of events with an ontology of crowds (developed with reference to Canetti's theory). Starting from a conceptual framework a complete ontology has been implemented in Protègè to create a versatile tool to profile crowds taking part in big events. This paper mainly focuses on a real case study of event, a rock concert, with the aim to support all the people involved (i.e. organizers, security and audience) in configuring similar situations.

1 Introduction

Festivalization is one of the processes of the recreational turn in European cities. Festivals can be defined as musical, operatic or theatrical events, taking place every year, at the same place and at approximately the same time. The concept has been extended to incorporate the question of events[...] More generally, the attempt to create what are called events is more and more important, and is seen by promoters as one way to generate profit or to play with the image of the city [1].

The organization of big events[1] (such as trade exhibition, musical, artistic and cultural festivals) is becoming a consolidated urban policy to promote and refurbish urban areas (in particular dismissed industrial areas).These kinds of intervention are aimed at enhancing the city potentiality, catalyzing investments, improving urban services, creating a sense of belonging of citizens to the city [2]. The scarcely predictable impact of

---

[1] Properly named as "festivalization of the city".

J.M. Dodero, M. Palomo-Duarte, P. Karampiperis (Eds.): MTSR 2012, CCIS 343, pp. 74–82, 2012.
© Springer-Verlag Berlin Heidelberg 2012

the extraordinary touristic flows during the event will make difficult for organizers and authorities to plan and manage the events. In particular, large cities have to be prepared to avoid disruption, and to guarantee accessibility and security. The participants to these kinds of events are said *urban crowds*.

Festivals integrate people and establish inner-communities; they induce commonly shared experiences and encourage an atmosphere of fun, pleasure and excitement. In this way festivals facilitate the processes of transferring pleasant experiences onto other subjects, places or phenomena related to them (i.e. onto a city). Festivals act as an urban image device [3]: An ontology that combines events and crowds offers the possibility to collect, systematize and correlate knowledge on these important phenomena that will require a great attention in the immediate future. With this work we want to propose a computational framework for crowd profiling and simulation, in order to support decision makers, designers and organizers of big events.

The definition of *event* is still an open question, as well as is how it should be considered in the systematization of an ontology. In Philosophy, *realists* consider that events are real things and that they should be considered to belong to the same class of objects. On the other side, *non-realists* neglect that events can provide a fixed framework of reference for an ontology that could give account of our practices of definition. Moreover, while objects are said to exist in clear temporal and spatial boundaries, events instead can be said to occur, or to take place, but their boundaries of existence are not clearly defined. The dichotomy events versus objects is not the only possible one and philosophical positions about that are several (see [4]).

Many ontologies [5] [6] [7] and frameworks like SUMO [8] and OpenCyc[2] have been developed to represent events. The main idea behind these attempts is to consider events as concrete experiences (i.e. *objects*) spatially and temporally located in the world: in our opinion, the event classification is strictly related to a kind of crowd that participates it. In other words, no definition of event is possible if it cannot be verified by a group of people sharing a given set of attributes at a given time and space.

No agreement can be also found in literature about what a *crowd* is, because of the difficulty in empirical investigation of the phenomenon [9]. Early interest in studying crowd started in the late 19th century and was mainly inspired by riots and revolutions. Gustave Le Bon [10] defined crowd behaviour as irrational and a potential threat to society. Far from this perspective, the Social Identity Model [11] states that being in a crowd does not leads to a loss of control of individual behaviour, but rather to an increase of behaviours in accordance to the group norms. In our framework, we refer to the definition and theory of crowds elaborated by Elias Canetti [12], a very detailed classification of crowds according to criteria such as *attitude to grow*, attributes of *density* and *equality* and the *nature of the goal* people belonging to it wish to reach by grouping themselves. Canetti was able to identify a variety of crowds, and he categorized them in pairs of opposite: *open* and *closed*, *stagnating* and *rhythmic*, *quick* and *slow*. Canetti introduced the term "discharge" to describe the cause of the assembling of the crowd: *discharge* is a mechanism through which individuals become crowd, where individual differences are dropped.

---

[2] www.opencyc.org

The rest of the paper is organized as follows: in section 2 a full description of our event ontology, from the technical point of view, will follow. At last in section 3, we will show a case study related to an urban crowd at a musical event. Final remarks and conclusions will be presented in section 4.

2   The Implementation of the Event Ontology

Starting from literature, we introduced the definition of an event as *a structured entity, spatial-temporally defined*. We enlarge this basic definition in order to consider aspects that are primary elements in the development of a computational model for crowd profiling and simulation, that is the target of this ontology.

The main conceptual elements have been already described in the past (see [13]): in this paper, the focus is on the how the implementation of this ontology has been possible starting from them. The basic elements we considered were:

- *Event*: a structured spatial-temporally entity, participated by person, and characterized by script;

- *Place*: spatial extension of an event;
  - *Venue*: the space in which the event take place;
  - *Entrance*: the gates which permit persons to access the venue;
  - *Exit*: the gates which allows persons to leave the venue;
  - *Utility*: necessary objects to support the spatial structure of the event;

- *Duration*: temporal duration of an event;
  - *Inflow*: starting time of the event;
  - *Involvement*: execution time of the event;
  - *Downflow*: ending time of the event;

- *Person*: the participants to the event;
  - *Staff*: the responsibles of the management the event;
  - *Security*: the responsibles of the security of the event;
  - *Artist*: the responsibles of the performance of the event;

- *Script*: procedural structure that characterizes an event;

- *Discharge*: the product of the performance, able to assemble people within a crowd;

- *Crowd*: a gathering of people, standing in close proximity at a specific location to observe a specific event, who feel united by a common social identity.

The aim of the development is to adequate the proposed event ontology to the existing works in literature. For this reason, we adopted the concepts of *Place* and *Person*

Table 1. Metadata representation of properties and datatypes for Event Ontology. Note that *p1* is the prefix for DBpedia ontology.

Label	Domain	Range	Comment
location	*Event*	*p1:Place*	relates an event to its spatial location
playingTime	*Event*	*Duration*	relates an event to its temporal duration
belongTo	*Utility*	*p1:Place*	relates an utility to its spatial position
isPartecipatedBy	*Event*	*p1:Person*	relates an event to involved people
isComposedOf	*Event*	*Event*	relates an event to its sub-events
isCharacterizedBy	*Event*	*Script*	relates an event to its script
produce	*Script*	*Discharge*	relates a script to the discharge produced
perform	*p1:Person*	*Script*	relates a person to the performed script
motivation	*p1:Person*	*Discharge*	relates a person to the experienced discharge
create	*Discharge*	*Crowd*	relates a discharge to the created crowd
motivationLevel	*p1:Person*	*xsd:integer*	level of motivation in participating to a discharge
intensity	*Script*	*xsd:integer*	level of intensity of the performed script
role	*p1:Person*	*xsd:String*	role of a person respect to the event

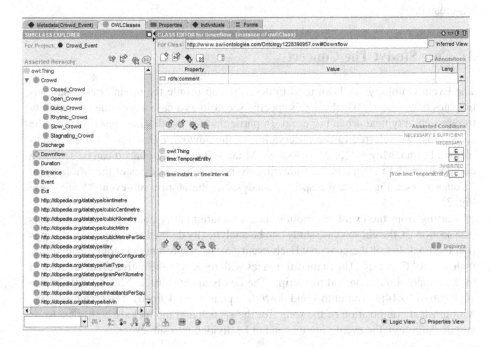

Fig. 1. An overview on the implementation of Ontology of Event in Protègè

as they were defined in DBpedia Ontology[3]. The concepts of *Inflow*, *Involvement*, *Downflow* are modelled by means of the OWL-Time ontology[4]. See [14] for details about an ontology for the representation of crowd concepts has been developed in the past. Starting from these assumptions, the implementation of our Event Ontology in Protègè has been organized into two main phases:

- Loading of existing ontologies: in order to extend previous results found in literature, the first step in the development was focused on the identification of basic corroborated ontologies. We imported in Protègè the version 3.6 of DBpedia Ontology, and the latest version of OWL-Time Ontology. Moreover, in order to exploit the previous work of conceptualization of the theories on crowd, we imported the Canetti's Crowd Ontology;
- Classes, properties and data-types definition: the second phase is devoted to the implementation of the innovative aspects of this Ontology of Events. An overview on the metadata description of properties and data-types are presented in Table 1, in which label, domain, range such as a textual definition of these elements are shown.

In Fig. 1 a screenshot where several classes of the ontology developed in Protègè is depicted: we chose to use the version 3.4 of the platform for its user-friendly interface and the integration with Jambalaya[5] plugin to visualize the knowledge bases the user has created.

3   Case Study: The Concert

The Event Ontology has been used to describe and profile the urban crowd that participates to a concert. We chose this specific scenario as a case study, due to its ability to represent a typical urban big event. In particular, for the detailed description of the case study, we referred to the observation of the *Jovanotti Ora Tour*[6], at the Mediolanum Forum, May 11th, 2011 - Assago, Milano (Italy). This concert can be seen as a composition of 15 songs: in the following we propose the analysis of the whole event *"Concert"* (see Fig. 2), and a specific analysis of the atomic sub-event *"Song"* (see Fig. 3).

Starting from the event description as a structured entity composed of sub-events (see section 2), the chosen case study can be analytically defined as a sequence of songs (i.e. the track list of the concert). Each event *"Song"* represent the atomic part of the main event *"Concert"*. The main differences with respect to the native event are related to the temporal duration and the script. The involvement starts at May 11, 2012 from 10:10pm to 10:14pm (no inflow and downflow phases are defined). The script overlaps with musical composition of the song, for the speech and the melody both. Due to its atomic definition, the event *"Song"* can not be divided into sub-event.

---

[3] http://dbpedia.org/ontology/
[4] http://www.w3.org/TR/owl-time/
[5] http://www.thechiselgroup.org/jambalaya
[6] http://www.soleluna.com/

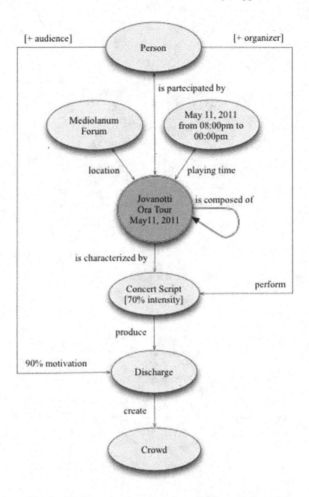

Fig. 2. A schematic representation of the event *Concert*

The main goal of the Ontology is building up rules to allow the instantiation of *Discharges*: as introduced above, the discharge can be generated when people actively takes part in an event. In the concert case study, we could identify two kinds of discharges: the *local* one due to a song sub–event and the *global* one due to the whole concert. While the global discharge can be obtained as a mean of the local ones, the local discharge is more difficult to detect, since the concert is generally divided into more involving and less involving sequences by the artist and his/her staff, according to the script he/she wishes to perform. For these reason, there are many songs during a concert where the audience motivation level and the intensity of the artist performance are at a very low level, and the discharge is not created. If and only if a discharge is generated, the link to the crowd ontology is activated, with the analysis of the kind of crowd that is originated

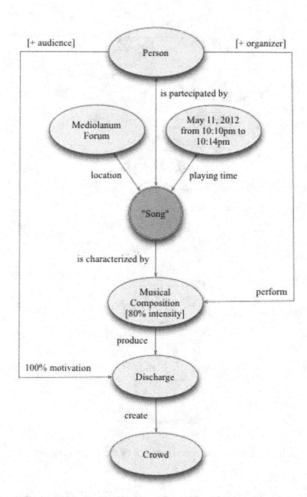

Fig. 3. A schematic representation of the sub-event *"Song"*

from it. According to [14], three kinds of crowds have been identified in the case study: closed, due to the location of the concert, quick and rhythmic due to the nature of the event. Figure 4 show the Protègè interface that allow to generate a Discharge instance according to specific rules.

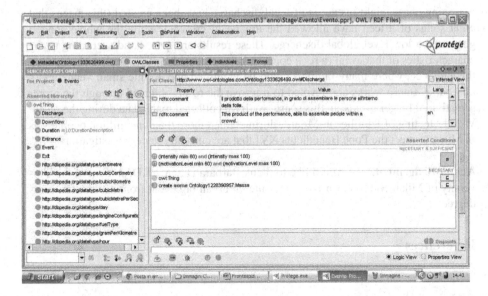

Fig. 4. The interface for the the generation of a Discharge from the intensity and motivation levels: the devoted rule is shown, as well as the activation of Crowd ontology in case of discharge

4   Conclusions and Future Works

Being able to represent events and crowds participating them is a very important research topic. Municipalities are very interested in understanding how urban crowds appear and disappear, due to the dangerous situation that can possibly arise. Tools like an ontology creating a link between an event and the crowd involving in it can be very useful to analyze why and how people aggregate into a crowd, as well as to identify possible causes of troubles or danger for the community. The work presented in this paper is aimed at supporting decision makers, designers and organizers in the managing of big events, by means of a computational framework for crowd profiling and simulation. The knowledge of crowd profiles could be a useful contribution for a successful management of each phase of an event. We refer in particular to the best practices related to ensure security during the event. To achieve this objective we have illustrated a synthetic theoretical discussion about events and crowds.

The implementation of this framework in the Protègè platform was developed thanks to the integration with existing ontologies such as DBpedia and OWL-Time. The innovative perspective of this work is based on the relationship between events and crowd: this fusion offers the possibility to collect and systematize knowledge, data, and information on big event that will require a great attention in the immediate future.

The case study shown in the paper is encouraging in this sense: the rock concert is a very good sample of how crowds dynamically vary during an event. Moreover, the clear division of a concert into sub–events (i.e. the songs) has allowed us to positively evaluate the general idea behind our approach, that is the existence of two kinds of discharges in the analysis of events and crows participating them. At the end of the reasoning phase, eight instances of local discharge have been created (this means that eight songs of fifteen have allowed the arising of crowds), while the whole concert generated a low level global discharge. These results are quite good according to the characteristics of that event (a rock concert with a relatively small number of people in the audience, where many families could be identified and a quite small venue area). Of course, future works are devoted to improve the result obtained through the representation of bigger events: in this sense, we have collected many data during the recent World Meeting of Families in Milan[7], during which more than one million people was in Milan to meet the Pope Benedictus XVI that are currently under investigation.

Acknowledgement. We would like to thank Barbara Diana, Ph.D. student of the University of Milan-Bicocca, for the contribute on urban big event from her master thesis degree.

References

1. Stock, M.: European cities: Towards a recreational turn? Studies in Culture, Polity and Identities 7(1) (2007)
2. Krantz, M., Schätzl, L.: Marketing the city. European Cities in Competition, 468–491 (1997)
3. Karpinska-Krakowiac, M.: Festivalization of the city. contemporary examples. Urban People Magazine 11(2) (2009)
4. Casati, R., Varzi, A.: Fifty years of events: An annotated bibliography 1947 to 1997. Philosophy Documentation Center, Bowling Green, OH (1997)
5. Gangemi, A., Guarino, N., Masolo, C., Oltramari, A., Schneider, L.: Sweetening Ontologies with DOLCE. In: Gómez-Pérez, A., Benjamins, V.R. (eds.) EKAW 2002. LNCS (LNAI), vol. 2473, pp. 166–181. Springer, Heidelberg (2002)
6. Mühl, G., Fiege, L., Pietzuch, P.R.: Distributed event-based systems. Springer (2006)
7. Kaneiwa, K., Iwazume, M., Fukuda, K.: An Upper Ontology for Event Classifications and Relations. In: Orgun, M.A., Thornton, J. (eds.) AI 2007. LNCS (LNAI), vol. 4830, pp. 394–403. Springer, Heidelberg (2007)
8. Niles, I., Pease, A.: Towards a standard upper ontology. In: FOIS, pp. 2–9 (2001)
9. Adamatzky, A.: Dynamics of crowd-minds: Patterns of irrationality in emotions, beliefs and actions. World Scientific Pub. Co. Inc. (2005)
10. Le Bon, G.: The crowd (1895), New York, Viking (1960)
11. Reicher, S.: The psychology of crowd dynamics. Blackwell Handbook of Social Psychology: Group Processes, 182–208 (2001)
12. Canetti, E., Stewart, C.: Crowds and power. Farrar, Straus and Giroux (1984)
13. Federici, M.L., Gorrini, A., Manenti, L., Sartori, F.: A proposal of an event ontology for urban crowd profiling. In: Bajec, M., Eder, J. (eds.) CAiSE Workshops. LNBIP, vol. 112, pp. 97–104. Springer (2012)
14. Bandini, S., Manenti, L., Manzoni, S., Sartori, F.: A knowledge-based approach to crowd classification. In: Peacock, R.D., Kuligowski, E.D., Averill, J.D. (eds.) Pedestrian and Evacuation Dynamics, pp. 515–525. Springer, US (2011)

---

[7] http://www.family2012.com/index.php?l=en

A Prototype Metadata-Driven Decision Support Tool for Scholarly Literature Reviews

Emmanouel Garoufallou[2], Dimitris Rousidis[1], and Panos Balatsoukas[3]

[1] University of Alcala, Madrid, Spain
drousid@gmail.com
[2] Alexander Technological Educational Institute of Thessaloniki, Macedonia, Greece
mgarou@libd.teithe.gr
[3] University of Manchester, United Kingdom
panagiotis.balatsoukas@manchester.ac.uk

Abstract. The aim of this paper is to present the main components of a novel metadata-driven decision support tool for scholarly literature reviews, called PANDORA. The purpose of the tool is to make use of data mining, as a means of identifying semantic similarities between scholarly articles and creating visual models of their relationship. The implementation of user-defined metadata is an important predicate of the tool's design. As opposed to standard information retrieval tools that treat all metadata equally, the present tool allows users to assign degrees of importance to a selected set of metadata, thus producing a more personalised view of users' needs. The paper concludes with a summary of the next steps involved in the design and evaluation of the tool.

Keywords: Metadata, Decision support systems, Information seeking.

1 Introduction

Recent studies have shown that the growth of scholarly output is rising exponentially. For example, [1] calculated that the number of published peer-reviewed journal articles per year was approximately 2.5 million and concluded that this amount will increase significantly in the next few years. Given this wealth of scholarly output, the identification of the most relevant information becomes a very demanding task, both in terms of time and effort spent by the researcher. Although modern search engine technologies can support the search for relevant information, there is still a debate on whether these systems can meet users' decision making needs during the information seeking process (e.g. [2], give a review).

PANDORA is a novel decision support tool for the retrieval and analysis of scholarly output (such as journal papers, conference presentations and e-books) that aims to address the aforementioned limitations. The proposed tool makes use of metadata, data mining and information visualisation techniques as a means of augmenting the decision making abilities of scholars' and university students' when searching for relevant scholarly information. In particular, the proposed tool helps users to identify whether an article is of interest by comparing it with one or more articles selected by

J.M. Dodero, M. Palomo-Duarte, P. Karampiperis (Eds.): MTSR 2012, CCIS 343, pp. 83–88, 2012.
© Springer-Verlag Berlin Heidelberg 2012

the user. This comparison is based on a set of user-defined qualitative criteria (such as article titles, abstracts, keywords, citations, author affiliation details and even methods used). Although similar attempts have been documented by researchers in the fields of citation mining and relevance feedback research (e.g. [3-4]), the present study goes a step further by including an exhaustive list of user-centred criteria for measuring similarity between articles. These are documented in the form of a relational metadata schema with associated values defined for each metadata element.

In addition to the results of the similarity comparisons, that filter out non relevant scholarly output, the user of the system should be able to create visual models of the relationship between scholarly publications, such as, changes in research topics across a period of time for a specific journal or set of journals, or, changes in the similarity of the research conducted between two or more researchers. Therefore, the proposed tool is not limited to the identification of relevant articles, but also aims at improving the understanding of the context of a complex research environment.

1.1   Aim and Objectives

The aim of this paper is to present the main components of PANDORA. In particular, the specific objectives are: 1. to summarise the main technical characteristics of the tool; and 2. to explain the metadata workflow used in PANDORA.

2   Description of the Main Technical Characteristics of PANDORA

PANDORA is based on Java programming code. It is initially developed as a desktop application using Microsoft Windows. However, once the software is completed, it will be tested on different platforms, such as Linux and Mac OS X to ensure that the program is working correctly across different operational systems. Also, it is on our future plans to embed the tool on a website, or use it as a plug in tool to already existing web-based information retrieval systems (such as institutional repositories and academic digital libraries). The purpose of this section is to provide a step-by-step walkthrough of the tools' main characteristics. These are:

⋏ *Uploading and conversion of files.* Initially a file (i.e. a journal article) will be fed into the tool. All files irrespectively of their original extension format (e.g. .doc, .odt, .pdf) are automatically converted into the .xml format. By uploading a file the system is programmed to compare it with all articles held in a person's hard disc (in the case of personal information management system), or an institutional repository (in the case of institution wide systems). Also, the program can target all articles of a web-based open access journal title if requested by the user. To date, due to copyright restrictions and information governance issues the tool has been focused only on open access journal articles in the area of Information Science and Information Systems research. The user of PANDORA can initiate either a *one to many* or a *many to many* comparison. In the case of *one to many* comparisons only one article is fed into the tool by the user and the tool compares it to a specified pool of articles. However, the user can upload more than one articles to compare (i.e. *many to many*).

⊿ *Creation of database tables*. Having uploaded and converted an article, the next step is the creation of database tables for each uploaded file. The number and type of tables is based on a set of pre-determined metadata (Table 1). As well as to the use of metadata, the tool is able to fragment the abstract or the main body of the article, or both, parse them and create new tables with all the words and the number of their appearance in the article. This is particularly useful in cases where keywords are not available as a separate field in the article. Finally, because the objective of this tool is to permit comparisons based on metadata that contain values related to methodological characteristics of journal articles, separate tables are created that document the methods reported on an article (e.g. *Survey, Interview*, or *Experiment*).

⊿ *Selection and assignment of weights to metadata for similarity measurement* (this is explained in detail in section 3.3).

⊿ *Data mining*. After creating the tables at least two files have to be processed by the tool so sufficient records to be available for applying the data mining algorithms. Classification and clustering analysis will be performed and the data mining algorithms will be selected. The software provides an adequate variety of data mining techniques and algorithms for the user to choose from (currently three options are available: k-means, CART and kNN). Using the data mining function a user should be able to visualise the complex article relationships and build models that present various types of trends, such as the progress, across time, of the work of one or more scientists and/or institutions, as well as the identification of areas of emerging research interest.

Table 1. List of metadata

Article Metadata	Citation metadata
Article Title (String)	Number of references *(Integer)*
Article's scientific field (String)	Transformation *(Yes/No)*
Article format-extension (String)	Cited author(s) *(String)*
Open Access *(Yes/No)*	Cited source *(String, title of the Journal)*
Year published (integer)	Year published *(Integer)*
Outdated *(Distance from current year)*	Cited title(s) *(String)*
Online *(Yes/No)*	URL *(Yes/No, String)*
Author metadata	Access date *(Yes / No, integer)*
Number of Authors *(Integer)*	Length of article *(Integer, number of pages)*
Author(s) names *(String)*	
Author(s) Ranking *(h-index, if available)*	**Main body metadata**
Author(s) Employer *(String, name of affiliation)*	Parsing for keywords *(Yes/No)*
Keyword metadata	Text fragmentation *(Yes/No)*
Keywords exist on Article *(Yes/No)*	Methods used *(Interviews=Yes/No,*
Keyword manual input *(Yes/No)*	*Questionnaires=Y/N, Experiments=Y/N, User*
Keyword auto-search *(Yes/No)*	*studies=Y/N, Focus groups=Y/N,*
Abstract metadata	*Observations=Y/N; Action research*
Abstract available *(Yes/No)*	*=Y/N,Ethnography=Y/N; Survey=Y/N, Case*
Parsing for keywords *(Yes/No)*	*studies=Y/N). Data (Figures = Yes/No, Tables*
Text fragmentation *(Yes/No)*	*= Yes/No, Codes = Yes/No, Equations = Y/N).*

3   Metadata Workflow Used in PANDORA

Figure 1 presents the metadata workflow used to support the development and implementation of metadata for the needs of this project.

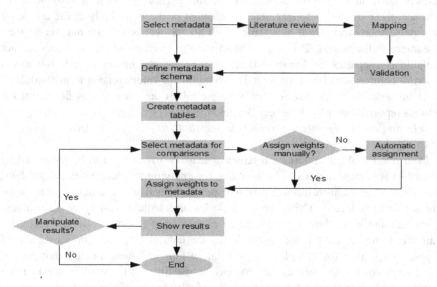

Fig. 1. PANDORA's metadata workflow

3.1   Selection, Mapping, Validation and Definition Process

The *selection* of metadata elements was based on a literature review in the field of Information Seeking behaviour research. In particular, the review was focused on work documenting the criteria people tend to apply when searching and evaluating scholarly output. Examples of such criteria include: *Topicality* (i.e. Keywords, subject headings, Abstracts), *Quality* (i.e. details about the author, author's affiliation or author's reputation), *Tangibility* (i.e. presence of an appendix, tables, figures, program codes, or raw datasets); *Validity* (i.e. related to the methods used for data collection and analysis), *Availability*, *Document characteristics* (e.g. version or language of the article), and finally, *Relationship with other sources* (i.e. use of citations). These criteria were transformed into corresponding metadata elements through a *mapping* process. This process involved the mapping of all identified criteria to already existing metadata elements (for example, existing metadata elements were identified in mainstream standards, such as the Dublin Core and the IEEE Learning Object Metadata). Also, new metadata elements were created for those criteria where no matches with the contents of already existing metadata standards exist. Each selected metadata element was accompanied by a corresponding value (Table 1). The resulted list of metadata was presented for *validation* to academic librarians and scholars of the Technological Institute of Thessaloniki, Greece. Finally, having specified a basic set of metadata elements, the next step was to *define* an XML-based metadata schema. This schema was used as a template for the creation of database tables.

3.2   Creation of Metadata Database Tables

Each database table contains information about a specific metadata element. Metadata elements are relational because tables can be associated, thus inheriting data held among different metadata elements. This relational association is achieved through the use of attributes that are common across the various metadata tables. For example, an AUTHOR ID attribute could be used in order to associate an AUTHOR table with two ARTICLE TITLE tables. In this manner, the final output of the relational tables could be thought of as a semantic web of a scholarly universe (in the case of this project this universe is limited to articles fed into PANDORA for comparison).

3.3   Use of Metadata for Setting Similarity Comparisons

As opposed to standard information retrieval tools that treat all metadata equally, the present tool allows users to assign degrees of importance to selected metadata, thus producing a more personalised view of the results during the literature review process. Therefore, the actual output of the data mining algorithm depends on user defined input. This decision was made because both scholars and university students tend to exhibit dynamic decision making behaviour during the evaluation of the relevance of scholarly output. This dynamic behaviour, which is characterised by changes in the way users tend to apply metadata in order to search for and evaluate information, is common in cases where information seekers experience cognitive shifts [2]. In order to address this dynamic behaviour, the tool provides users the opportunity to select the most important metadata elements and assign weights to them (Figure 2).

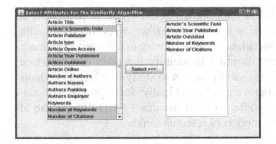 

Fig. 2. Selecting and adding weights to metadata elements

The process of assigning weights to selected metadata elements can be completed manually, or automatically. In the case of manual assignment of weights a user is prompted to assess the importance of a selected metadata element using decimals between 0 and 1. For automatic assignment of weights, scores are computed by the tool using equation 1. However, research is in progress in order to experiment with different types of weight measures. Weights are embedded to a standard cosine similarity measure (equation 2), the product of which is used to identify groups of articles that are similar to users' needs and translate the records of the tables within the database into vector scores that are appropriate for the data mining clustering. Due to the short length of this paper a more detailed description of the similarity measure and data mining algorithm will be presented in follow up publications.

$$W_i = \log \frac{N}{X_{ij}} \qquad (1)$$

Where, W = Weight score; N = No. of articles used in the comparison; X = No. of all articles (j) sharing a common metadata value (e.g. publication date or keyword) with a source article (i).

$$sim_{(i,j)} = \frac{I \cdot J}{|I||J|} \qquad (2)$$

3.4   Use of Metadata to Manipulate Results

Two types of results are presented in the result section: 1. a ranked list of all articles that are similar to the one(s) used for initiating the comparison; and 2. a visual representation of the result set (for example, based on k-means clustering, CART or kNN). The user has the option of manipulating the results. This is achieved by modifying metadata specifications. For example, the assigned metadata weights can be modified, or additional metadata elements can be selected for inclusion in the similarity comparisons. Furthermore, the user has the option to combine metadata in order to build visual models that represent trends in scholarly research, e.g. a user may choose the AUTHOR'S NAME and PUBLICATION DATE metadata in order to model changes in the publication history of one or more authors across time.

4   Conclusions

Research is in progress to improve and develop further PANDORA. In particular, in terms of system design the project team is focused on further experimentation with different similarity algorithms and metadata weights. In terms of user experience research, a usability test is in progress in order to identify the main user interface problems. An important objective of the usability test is to study how users (students and scholars) select metadata and assign weights to it. Finally, focus groups with students and researchers are scheduled in order to elicit use cases related to the use of metadata for the development of visual models of research trends.

References

1. Gargouri, Y., Hajjem, C., Lariviere, V., Gingras, Y., Brody, T., Carr, L., Harnad, S.: Self-Selected or Mandated, Open Access Increases Citation Impact for Higher Quality Research. Plos One 5(10) (2010),
   http://www.plosone.org/article/info:doi/10.1371/
   journal.pone.0013636
2. Balatsoukas, P., Morris, A., O'Brien, A.: An evaluation framework of user interaction with metadata. Journal of Information Science 35(3), 321–339 (2009)
3. Kostoff, R., del Río, J., Humenik, J., García, E., Ramírez, A.: Citation Mining: Integrating Text Mining and Bibliometrics for Research User Profiling. Journal of the American Society for Information Science and Technology 52(13), 1148–1156 (2001)
4. Thelwall, M., Sud, P.: A comparison of methods for collecting web citation data for academic organisation. J. of the Am. Soc. for Info. Sci. and Tech. 62(8), 1488–1497 (2011)

Linking Folksonomies to Knowledge Organization Systems

Jakob Voß

Verbundzentrale des GBV, VZG
voss@gbv.de

Abstract. This paper demonstrates enrichment of set-model folksonomies with hierarchical links and mappings to other knowledge
organization systems. The process is exemplified with social tagging
practice in Wikipedia and in Stack Exchange. The extended folksonomies are created by crowdsourcing tag names and descriptions to
translate them to linked data in SKOS.

Keywords: social tagging, mapping, linked data, SKOS, crowdsourcing,
digital libraries (cs.DL), information retrieval (cs.IR).

1 Introduction

With the rise of social software and web applications, social tagging has become
a popular method to organize collections. Tagging is a process where keywords
(tags) are manually assigned to a resource for retrieval. In contrast to traditional
subject indexing, keywords are generally chosen freely by users and shared in a
community. Many forms and applications of social tagging exist and are subject
to research [4]. The outcome of activities in a tagging system is called a folksonomy. This paper first summarizes basic properties of social tagging with Stack
Exchange and Wikipedia as two popular instances of set-model folksonomies.
These systems are then compared to knowledge organization systems and the
enrichment with hierarchical links and mappings to other systems via crowdsourcing is demonstrated.

2 Social Tagging and Folksonomies

No common definition of social tagging and folksonomies exists among authors
and disciplines. As terms like social tagging, social indexing, and collaborative
tagging are used interchangeably, tagging can be defined as manual indexing on
the Web [14]. The specific type of a tagging system depends on several parameters [4,8,14]. In particular, tagging properties include:

- **source of resources:** which can either be supplied by the tagging system
  or created/collected by its users

J.M. Dodero, M. Palomo-Duarte, P. Karampiperis (Eds.): MTSR 2012, CCIS 343, pp. 89–97, 2012.

- **tagging rights:** who is allowed to assign and modify tags?
- **tagging support:** for instance recommendations and visible tag descriptions
- **tag aggregation:** set-model where all users collectively tag a resource or bag-model where each user individually tags a resource.
- **tag management:** restrictions on which tags to use, methods of creation and description of tags independent from the action of tagging, etc.
- **tag connectivity:** hierarchical and other relationships between tags

Most research on tagging systems focuses on bag-model tag aggregation. This means that each resource can be tagged multiple times and every user can choose his individual set of tags to describe the resource. Folksonomies in bag-model tagging systems emerge as implicit consensus from large numbers of tagging events. Several approaches exist to derive folksonomies from tagging data by statistical analysis, including tag connectivity [1,5,7,10,11,12]. With Set-model tag aggregation in contrast there is only one common set of tags for each resource. Hence, the folksonomy is more directly given as snapshot of community consensus. Folksonomies expressed in set-model tagging systems can be defined as dynamic knowledge organization systems created by communities of distributed volunteers. Two popular instances are presented in the following with tags in Stack Exchange and categories in Wikipedia.

2.1   Tags in Stack Exchange

Stack Exchange is a growing network of question & answers communities with Stack Overflow as first and most prominent instance.[1] All content is licensed under Creative Commons Attribution Share Alike license (CC BY-SA) and accessible via a public API. Since Stack Overflow was launched in 2008, the Stack Exchange network has grown to almost 90 sites with 2 million users, 5 million questions, and 9 million answers (as of autum 2012). Since 2010 there is some academic research about Stack Exchange and the data that is provided by Stack Exchange sites.[2] Most of this research is focused on factors of success, quality and motivation and similar aspects of crowdsourcing. The tagging system of each community has not been analyzed yet. In Stack Exchange sites up to five tags are assigned to each question by its author. Reuse of existing tags is encouraged by typeahead suggestions and by limiting creation of new tags to experienced members of the community. Users with some reputation can also modify the tag-set of any question.[3] Each tag can be defined with a short tag excerpt and a more detailed tag description, both editable in a wiki. Hierarchical links between

---

[1] See http://stackexchange.com and http://stackoverflow.com.

[2] See http://meta.stackoverflow.com/questions/134495 for a bibliography.

[3] Editing rights in Stack Exchange are controlled by an elaborated system of reputation points. In Stack Overflow 500 points are required for retagging and 1500 for creating tags. In beta sites levels are 200 and 150 respectively.

tags are not supported on purpose.[4] Figure 1 shows the extended info page of a tag with its tag excerpt and tag description.

2.2 Categories in Wikipedia

In Wikipedia articles are tagged by so called categories, which can be assigned and modified together with the normal content of an article.[5] Categories are used for knowledge organization and for quality management, for instance to flag articles that lack references. Each category is described with a wiki page of its own. Category pages can be assigned to other categories, resulting in a directed graph of categories. The category system of Wikipedia is a thesaurus with similar structural and statistical properties like other social tagging and knowledge organization systems [16]. In addition to categories, most articles in Wikipedia can be used as concepts for knowledge organization. Wikipedia articles and categories translated to SKOS/RDF are provided by DBPedia project [2], including mappings from articles to authority files [15].[6]

3   Knowledge Organization Systems

Knowledge organization systems include systems such as classifications, taxonomies, thesauri, and authority files [6,13]. Each system defines a set of concepts that are used for the creation of metadata in digital libraries. Depending on context and community, knowledge organization systems are also known as controlled vocabularies, terminologies, and ontologies. An important topic in the research on networked knowledge organization systems (NKOS) is semantic interoperability of multiple systems via mappings and cross-concordances. or alignments. As defined by Mayr and Petras in the KoMoHe project [9], cross-concordances consist of manually created, directed relations between controlled terms of two knowledge organization systems. Mapping relations include equivalence, hierarchy, and association, possibly extended by a degree of confidence. To express and exchange mappings between knowledge organization systems, a common model of all connected systems is required. The most prominent model by now is the Resource Discovery Framework (RDF) in general and the Simple Knowledge Organization System (SKOS) in particular, covering the most common types of thesauri, authority files, and mappings. For instances of vocabularies and mappings published in SKOS/RDF see AGROVOC [3], TheSOZ [18], and the Library of Congress Subject Headings (LCSH). In SKOS/RDF each concept is identified by an URI and concepts are linked with a predefined set of RDF properties (table 1). Synonyms can be combined as multiple labels of one concept.

---

[4] See `http://meta.stackoverflow.com/questions/tagged/tag-hierarchy` for discussion of the decision against tag (mono)hierarchies.
[5] See `http://en.wikipedia.org/wiki/Wikipedia:Categorization`.
[6] Available at `http://dbpedia.org`.

Table 1. Relations between concepts in the SKOS model

concept relation	mapping relation	purpose
skos:broader	skos:broadMatch	direct hierarchical link (up)
skos:narrower	skos:narrowMatch	direct hierarchical link (down)
skos:related	skos:relatedMatch	associative link
	skos:closeMatch	equivalence link with low confidence
	skos:exactMatch	equivalence link with high confidence

The relations skos:broader/broaderMatch and skos:narrower/narrowMatch are inverse respectively, the other relations are symmetric, and skos:exactMatch is transitive. More elaborated models of cross-concordances allow for non-symmetrical and single-to-multiple mapping relations. [9,12]. The SKOSified terminologies presented in this paper make use of th relations skos:broader, skos:narrower, skos:related, and skos:closeMatch (to avoid transitive mappings). Hierarchical mappings will be added later.

4 From Folksonomies to Knowledge Organization Systems

A set-model based folksonomy is continuously modified and extended by members of a community. The volunteers make use of tagging not to create a reusable folksonomy but as tool for knowledge organization within their project. Because of the open and dynamic nature of the projects, nobody is responsible for the full tagging terminology. This makes centralized approaches to enrich the folksonomy difficult. For this reason additional mapping and linking can best be managed within the tagging system. If enrichment is also done by the community, it can be crowdsourced together with the folkosonomy. Two methods of seamless integration are presented below.

4.1 Links from Tag Names

The first method to link a folksonomy with a knowledge organization system is used at the Stack Exchange site about theoretical computer science.[7] In this community some tags follow the syntax "xx.name" where "xx" is part of a notation from the classification of the Computing Research Repository (CoRR)[8]

---

[7] http://cstheory.stackexchange.com

[8] The Computing Research Repository (http://arxiv.org/corr) is part of the arXiv repository.

and "name" is a descriptive name. For instance the tag "lo.logic" refers to
the category "Logic in Computer Science" with CoRR notation "cs.LO". Some
CoRR categories have no tag at cstheory.stackexchange and for some categories
multiple tags exists. Based on this tag naming rules, a formal SKOS mapping
can be derived with 1-to-1 close/exact matches and 1-to-n narrower/broader
matches:

```
[ skos:notation "LO";
  skos:prefLabel "Logic in Computer Science"@en ]
  skos:closeMatch <http://cstheory.stackexchange.com/tags/lo.logic> .

[ skos:notation  "DS" ;
  skos:prefLabel "Data Structures and Algorithms"@en ]
  skos:narrowMatch
    <http://cstheory.stackexchange.com/tags/ds.algorithms> ,
    <http://cstheory.stackexchange.com/tags/ds.data-structures> .
```

To illustrate the use of this mapping, a simple statistical analysis was conducted.
The total number of computer science papers archived at arXiv.org in 2011 for
each CoRR category was compared to the number of question tagged with corresponding tags. Appendic A lists the 16 CoRR categories with at least 10 related questions and the number of papers per question. One can see that there
are more research papers in artificial intelligence, computer vision and pattern
recognition, and information theory compared to more questions in computational complexity, algorithms and data structures, computational geometry, and
programming languages.

4.2   Links from Tag Descriptions

Both Stack Exchange and Wikipedia have a wiki page for each tag, which can
be edited independently from the act of tagging single questions or articles.
This form of tag management can be used to express more elaborated types of
links between the folksonomy and other knowledge organization systems. Participation in this enrichment, however, is lower than tagging activity because tag
descriptions are less visible members of the communities. Figure 1 shows the tag
description of tag ils.[9]

The wiki contains HTML links to other tags and links that make use of
concepts from other knowledge organization systems (Wikipedia, LCSH, JITA
classification, and GND authority file) to get related resources. These links can
be harvested via Stack Exchange API and translated to semantic relationships
in SKOS. The translation between HTML links in the tag description and
URIs in the linked system must be configured for each. For instance a link to
Wikipedia is translated to DBPedia and a link to a Worldcat search by LCSH is

---

[9] Available at http://libraries.stackexchange.com/tags/ils/info.

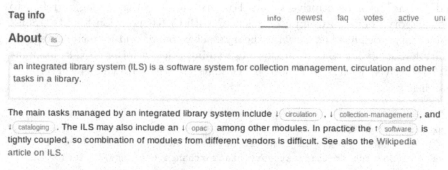

Fig. 1. Tag description with hierarchical links and mapping

translated to an URI at `http://id.loc.gov`. This results in the following concept in SKOS/RDF:[10]

```
<http://libraries.stackexchange.com/tags/ils> a skos:Concept ;
  skos:prefLabel "ils"@en ;
  skos:scopeNote "an integrated library system (ILS) is a software
    system for collection management, circulation and other tasks
    in a library."@en ;
  skos:broader
    <http://libraries.stackexchange.com/tags/software> ;
  skos:narrower
    <http://libraries.stackexchange.com/tags/circulation> ,
    <http://libraries.stackexchange.com/tags/collection-management> ,
    <http://libraries.stackexchange.com/tags/cataloging> ,
    <http://libraries.stackexchange.com/tags/opac> ;
  skos:closeMatch
    <http://dbpedia.org/resource/Integrated_library_system> ,
    <http://id.loc.gov/authorities/subjects/sh95003216> , # LCSH
    <http://eprints.rclis.org/handle/10760/3775> ,       # JITA
    <http://d-nb.info/gnd/4583297-3> .                   # GND
```

A similar method has been applied experimentally in German Wikipedia to link categories with other knowledge organization systems. Figure 2 shows the category description of category "Hörspiel" (radio play). An infobox is used to show links to corresponding concepts in Regensburger Verbundklassifikation (RVK), Dewey Decimal System (DDC), and GND authority file.

---

[10] Scripts to download/transform links are available at
   `https://github.com/nichtich/se2skos`

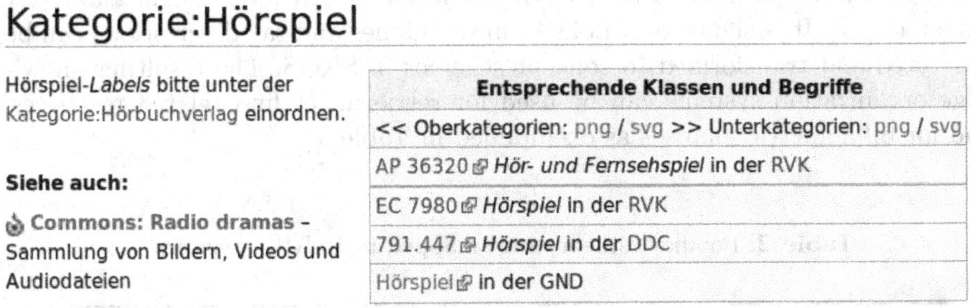

Kategorie:Hörspiel

Hörspiel-*Labels* bitte unter der Kategorie:Hörbuchverlag einordnen.

Siehe auch:

🔊 **Commons: Radio dramas** – Sammlung von Bildern, Videos und Audiodateien

Entsprechende Klassen und Begriffe
<< Oberkategorien: png / svg >> Unterkategorien: png / svg
AP 36320 🖉 *Hör- und Fernsehspiel* in der RVK
EC 7980 🖉 *Hörspiel* in der RVK
791.447 🖉 *Hörspiel* in der DDC
Hörspiel 🖉 in der GND

Fig. 2. Category description with mappings to other knowledge organization systems

Translation of these links to mappings in SKOS is based on the template syntax of MediaWiki. If multiple links are specified to the same system, as RVK in the example, the relation skos:narrowMatch is used instead of skos:closeMatch. The translation results in the following RDF statements (hierarchical and associative relations between categories are omitted because they are already included in DBPedia):

```
<http://de.dbpedia.org/resource/Kategorie:H%C3%B6rspiel>
  a skos:Concept ; skos:prefLabel "Hörspiel"@de ;
  skos:narrowMatch
    <http://data.bib.uni-mannheim.de/data/rvk/AP_36320> , # RVK
    <http://data.bib.uni-mannheim.de/data/rvk/EC_7980> ;  # RVK
  skos:closeMatch
    <http://dewey.info/class/791.447/> , # DDC
    <http://d-nb.info/gnd/4025435-5> .  # GND
```

Adoption of category descriptions enriched with mappings in Wikipedia is still low because category pages are less visible to Wikipedia users and because creation of a mapping requires knowledge of the linked knowledge organization system. A special mapping tool may boost, such as the tool that was used to match biographic articles in German Wikipedia and GND authority files [15].

5   Summary and Discussion

Two instances of folksonomies with set-model tag aggregation have been presented with tags in Stack Exchange and categories in Wikipedia. In contrast to bag-model tagging systems, enriched folksonomies cannot be calculated but one must explicitly express links and mappings to other knowledge organization systems. Tag names and tag descriptions can be used to express these additional connections. Curation of links and mappings by the social tagging community depends on visibility (tagging support) and ease of tagging. Simple equivalence links, which make up 45% of typical mapping relations [9] are easier to manage. These mapping can also be provided in simplified form, such as BEACON files which are also used to map GND authority records, Wikipedia and other resources [17]. It is shown how links from tag names and tag descriptions can be harvested and transformed to concept schemes in SKOS. The resulting knowledge organization systems can be used for retrieval, to find related resources, and for bibliometric analysis as exemplified in Table 2.

Table 2. Popular cstheory tags mapped to CoRR categories

category	papers	questions	relation	tags
cs.AI	788	42	18.76	ai.artificial-intel
cs.CC	421	931	0.45	cc.complexity-theory
cs.CG	225	133	1.69	cg.comp-geom
cs.CR	485	143	3.39	cr.crypto-security
cs.CV	384	11	34.91	cv.computer-vision
cs.DB	244	29	8.41	db.databases
cs.DC	450	93	4.84	dc.parallel-comp, dc.distributed-comp
cs.DS	800	915	0.87	ds.algorithms, ds.data-structures
cs.FL	194	150	1.29	fl.formal-languages
cs.GT	324	34	9.53	gt.game-theory
cs.IT	1692	41	41.27	it.information-theory
cs.LG	464	53	8.75	lg.learning
cs.LO	567	151	3.75	lg.logic
cs.NA	137	15	9.13	na.numerical-analysis
cs.NE	150	23	6.52	ne.neural-evol
cs.PL	242	122	1.98	pl.programming-languages

References

[1] Barla, M., Bieliková, M.: On Deriving Tagsonomies: Keyword Relations Coming from Crowd. In: Nguyen, N.T., Kowalczyk, R., Chen, S.-M. (eds.) ICCCI 2009. LNCS, vol. 5796, pp. 309–320. Springer, Heidelberg (2009)

[2] Christian Bizer, C., Lehmann, J., Kobilarov, G., Auer, S., Becker, C., Cyganiak, R., Hellmann, S.: DBpedia – A Crystallization Point for the Web of Data. Journal of Web Semantics: Science, Services and Agents on the World Wide Web 7, 154–165 (2009)

[3] Caracciolo, C., Morshed, A., Stellato, A., Johannsen, G., Jaques, Y., Keizer, J.: Thesaurus Maintenance, Alignment and Publication as Linked Data: The AGROOVOC Use Case. In: García-Barriocanal, E., Cebeci, Z., Okur, M.C., Öztürk, A. (eds.) MTSR 2011. CCIS, vol. 240, pp. 489–499. Springer, Heidelberg (2011)

[4] Gupta, M., Li, R., Yin, Z., Han, J.: An Overview of Social Tagging and Applications. In: Aggarwal, C. (ed.) Social Network Data Analytics, pp. 447–497. Springer (2011)

[5] Heymann, P., Garcia-Molina, H.: Collaborative creation of communal hierarchical taxonomies in social tagging systems. Technical report, Stanford University (2006)

[6] Hodge, G.: Systems of knowledge organization for digital libraries (2000)

[7] Lin, H., Davis, J., Zhou, Y.: An Integrated Approach to Extracting Ontological Structures from Folksonomies. In: Aroyo, L., Traverso, P., Ciravegna, F., Cimiano, P., Heath, T., Hyvönen, E., Mizoguchi, R., Oren, E., Sabou, M., Simperl, E. (eds.) ESWC 2009. LNCS, vol. 5554, pp. 654–668. Springer, Heidelberg (2009)

[8] Marlow, C., Davis, M., Boyd, D.: HT06, tagging paper, taxonomy, Flickr, academic article, ToRead. In: Proceedings of Hypertext 2006 (2006)

[9] Mayr, P., Petras, V.: Cross-concordances: Terminology mapping and its effectiveness for information retrieval. In: 74th IFLA World Library and Information Congress (2008)

[10] Moosavi, A., Li, T., Lakshmanan, L.V.S., Pottinger, R.: ONTECTAS: Bridging the Gap between Collaborative Tagging Systems and Structured Data. In: Mouratidis, H., Rolland, C. (eds.) CAiSE 2011. LNCS, vol. 6741, pp. 436–451. Springer, Heidelberg (2011)

[11] Solskinnsbakk, G., Gulla, J.A.: A Hybrid Approach to Constructing Tag Hierarchies. In: Meersman, R., Dillon, T., Herrero, P. (eds.) OTM 2010, Part II. LNCS, vol. 6427, pp. 975–982. Springer, Heidelberg (2010)

[12] Specia, L., Motta, E.: Integrating Folksonomies with the Semantic Web. In: Franconi, E., Kifer, M., May, W. (eds.) ESWC 2007. LNCS, vol. 4519, pp. 624–639. Springer, Heidelberg (2007)

[13] Tudhope, D., Koch, T.: New Applications of Knowledge Organization Systems: introduction to a special issue. Journal of Digital Information, 4 (2006)

[14] Voss, J.: Tagging, Folksonomy & Co-Renaissance of Manual Indexing? (2007)

[15] Voss, J.: Wikipedia als Teil einer freien bibliothekarischen Informationsinfrastruktur. In: Lülfing, D. (ed.) 95. Deutscher Bibliothekartag, pp. 63–74. Klostermann (2007)

[16] Voss, J.: Collaborative thesaurus tagging the Wikipedia way (2006)

[17] Voss, J., Schindler, M., Thiele, C.: Link server aggregation with BEACON. In: International Symposium for Information Science (2011)

[18] Zapilko, B., Schaible, J., Mayr, P., Mathiak, B.: TheSoz: A SKOS Representation of the Thesaurus for the Social Sciences. Journal of Semantic Web (to appear, 2012)

Semi-automated Application Profile Generation for Research Data Assets[*]

João Rocha da Silva[1], Cristina Ribeiro[2], and João Correia Lopes[2]

[1] Faculdade de Engenharia da Universidade do Porto/INESC TEC, Portugal
[2] DEI — Faculdade de Engenharia da Universidade do Porto / INESC TEC, Portugal
{pro11004,mcr,jlopes}@fe.up.pt

Abstract. Selecting the right set of descriptors for the annotation of a specific dataset can be a hard problem in research data management. Considering a dataset in an arbitrary domain, an application profile is complex to build because of the abundance of metadata standards, ontologies and other descriptor sources available for different domains. We propose to partially automate the process of data description by generating application profile recommendations based on a research data asset knowledge base. Our approach builds on existing technologies for exploring linked data and results in a process which can be tightly coupled with the research workflow, giving researchers more control over the description of their data. Preliminary experiments show that we can build on state-of-the-art technologies for search indexes, graph databases and triple stores to explore existing sources of linked data for our profile generation.

1 Introduction

Research data assets are very diverse, creating the need for a myriad of metadata descriptors adequate for each research domain. However, this diversity of metadata specifications makes the description of the datasets increasingly complex for researchers. While frequently unaware of the intricate complexities of data curation, they are a critical part of the data management workflow since they are both producers and consumers of research data [16]. Also, they are among the most benefited stakeholders in this process since it has been shown that linking properly described base data to research papers can lead to an increase in paper citation rate [20]. Current approaches at research data management usually call for a data curator [17,15], which is normally an expert on data management but not necessarily knowledgeable about the specific research topic of the data assets and, while this approach successfully yields high-quality curated data, considerable effort is required in this process [21]. Also, this curator-researcher interaction can only be carried out at specific moments throughout the research

[*] Supported by Ph.D. grant SFRH/BD/77092/2011, provided by the FCT (Fundação para a Ciência e Tecnologia).

workflow—in most cases at very late stages—while it should be carried out continuously, starting as early as possible [11].

In this paper, we propose a semi-automated data asset description model to make dataset description easier for researchers, acting as an automated assistant throughout the data curation process. The benefits include an off-load on data curators, while enabling the data management process to start earlier in the research activity schedule. Bringing data management to an earlier stage of the process may help researchers since annotated datasets are easier to share with similar research groups, reducing the traditional exchange of emails or other direct contacts whenever data exchange is necessary, for example. Our work aims at semi-automatically selecting the most appropriate metadata descriptors for a specific dataset. Recent developments in the field of the semantic web, linked data and graph databases make it technically viable to take the topology of a fairly large knowledge base (or a subset thereof) into account when making the suggestions; we will discuss some of these possibilities.

2   Linking Research Data Assets

Linked data aims to establish connections between uniquely identified resources using unambiguous descriptors. Our current goal is to take advantage of the characteristics of linked data to recommend a set of descriptors that a researcher can use to annotate a specific dataset, without having to study complex domain-specific metadata standards. If we instead allow researchers more freedom to describe their datasets at an early stage (albeit roughly) and have a curator perform a validation step later, more datasets may actually enter the management process. Ad-hoc or duplicate metadata descriptor may be a problem, because it is unrealistic to believe that researchers would possess detailed knowledge about all descriptors in their domain, but we expect to mitigate this issue through our approach.

We regard all the datasets managed by a repository as part of a graph in which a dataset is a vertex, and the edges are the metadata descriptors (this model bears much resemblance to existing linked data knowledge bases, such as DBpedia). There have been recent moves towards transparent linking of resources through instances of properties taken from existing *semantic metadata* standards [1]. Semantic metadata consists in metadata descriptors that carry very specific semantics [8], something that is especially valuable for describing research datasets due to the specificity and diversity of notions involved in the research activities that make up the context of data production.

Figure 1 shows an example of a small subset of this "dataset knowledge base" containing 4 datasets. One is from the domain of chemistry (shown as ⬭), and three are from the domain of gravitational field analysis (shown as ⬔). This example highlights the inherent ambiguity between terms in these domains. Gravimetric analysis (in the chemistry domain) is sometimes referred to as *gravimetry*, and defined as " the quantitative measurement of an analyte by weighing a pure, solid form of the analyte."[19]. *Gravimetry* is a term which

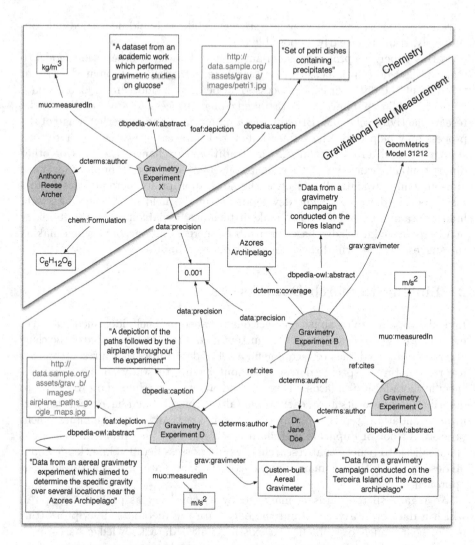

Fig. 1. A set of interconnected research datasets

is also used in gravitational field analysis and measurement as "the measurement and analysis of the Earth's gravity field and its space and time variations" [4]. When searching for datasets by specifying a textual query, a system using pure text indexing might return all the datasets shown in the figure (albeit with different ranking scores). This creates the need to take into account other factors for disambiguating the concepts and contribute to the score, such as the topology of the local knowledge base subset in the *vicinity* of those datasets. The knowledge base depicted in Figure 1 uses 10 existing or purpose-created descriptors (or properties, in ontology vocabulary) from 5 different ontologies, shown in Table 1.

Table 1. Overview on the metadata descriptors used in the knowledge base depicted in Figure 1

Descriptor	Source ontology	Meaning
chem:formulation	A purpose-built ontology for chemical experiments	The chemical formulation of the composition analysed in a chemical experiment
dcterms:creator	Dublin Core RDF Schema	"An entity primarily responsible for making the resource" [5]
dbpedia-owl:abstract / dbpedia:caption	DBpedia ontology	A short textual description of the resource / The caption of the image depicting the resource (indicated by the foaf:depiction property instance)
muo:measuredIn	Measurement Units Ontology[18]	"The unit used in the measurement of a particular quality value"
data:precision	A purpose-built ontology for specifying numerical parameters	The numerical precision of a measurement of a particular value
foaf:depiction	Friend Of A Friend Vocabulary Specification	"The depiction property is a relationship between a thing and an Image that depicts it." [3]
grav:gravimeter	A purpose-built ontology for gravitational field intensity measurement experiments	The identification of the gravimeter (device) used for the measurement of the intensity of a magnetic field
dcterms:coverage	Dublin Core RDF Schema [5]	"The spatial or temporal topic of the resource, the spatial applicability of the resource, or the jurisdiction under which the resource is relevant."
ref:cites	A purpose-built ontology for dataset cross-referencing	"The subject resource makes a partial/whole reference to the object resource"

3 Semi-automated Application Profile Generation

Our goal is to explore diverse linked data sources and use the links between resources or *property instances* to select a set of properties considered more relevant for the annotation of a target research dataset. Figure 2 illustrates this challenge—the new dataset is the circle, which needs to be connected to the rest of the knowledge base via a set of property instances, shown as the dashed arrows. The ends of each arrow (highlighted by the question mark) are to be filled in by the researcher with either literals (in the case of datatype properties) or other resources in the knowledge base (e.g. datasets that are related to the one being added). The selection is intended as a recommendation: a descriptor may not be filled in by a researcher if he/she does not agree with the suggestion.

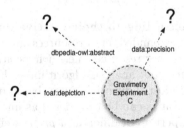

Fig. 2. A new dataset being added to the dataset knowledge, and its recommended properties

Link prediction is defined in social network analysis as "the task of inferring links in a graph G_{t+1} based on the observation of a graph G_t." [14], and is aimed at predicting relationships between people within a network [13] over time. Current link prediction approaches can combine nodes' content (*aggregated features*) [9] with *topological features* [10,6,14].

We approach property recommendation as a sequence of the following four steps, the first of which relies on a large textual index to narrow down the exploration to a subgraph, and the others explore the topology and content of the subgraph to provide a set of recommended properties:

1. **Setting the scope of the base data used in the recommendation**
   Performing an analysis over the whole graph at runtime is technically inviable, so a subset of the knowledge base must be selected to serve as the basis for the recommendation. This sub-setting operation can be performed based on a series of *keywords* explicitly collected from the researcher or obtained from any indirect process. The keywords are ran as a query against a free-text index built over the datatype properties (string literals) of the resources. The most highly-ranked resources are likely to be relevant in the user's research domain, and will therefore constitute the initial sub-graph over which the next steps in this process can operate.

2. **Expanding the connections between the nodes within the selected scope**
   The selection on the first step is based on the textual content of the resources on the graph's vertexes. Complementary information comes from the graph topology, and we can expand connections on the subgraph to enrich it through the properties connecting the resources in the graph. This may bring into focus resources which are not directly linked via textual connections and may also reduce the number of disconnected graphs obtained from the search results. A challenge for this approach is, however, selecting the most effective depth of expansion—all connections by 1, 2 or more levels may be expanded, depending on the available processing power, for example. A more selective alternative is to expand only those connections between the resources that possess the highest hub/authority values within each increasingly large subgraph (using the hub/authority definition of the HITS algorithm [12]).

3. **Scoring the nodes according to their relative importance**
   The third step takes the expanded set of resources and scores them according to their connections to other resources, i.e. their position in the knowledge base's topology. Existing link analysis algorithm such as HITS or PageRank can determine the most influential nodes, based on their inbound and outbound connections. Links can be considered as unqualified, giving equal weights to different properties, or different *a priori* weights can be provided according to the features of the resource and property on each link.

4. **Scoring the properties that relate the nodes according to their importance**
   After knowing which are the most prominent nodes contained in the subgraph of results, we may take their inbound and outbound properties and calculate their scores by combining the frequency with which they appear within the result subgraph, as well as the hub/authority value of the resources that they connect.

3.1 Experimental Work

Our approach relies on a large knowledge base, containing a diverse set of resources connected by instances of many different properties. Since building a research data asset knowledge base using linked data is very time-consuming, we have decided to perform some experiments using data from DBpedia, an existing linked data knowledge base. Bizer et. al. specified the DBpedia project as a community-driven initiative designed to extract information from Wikipedia and make the information publicly available on the Web [2]. DBpedia offers several datasets that specify sets of resources and links between those resources, using concepts taken from ontologies such as FOAF (Friend of a Friend) [3], FreeBase [7] or DBpedia's own ontology. The information is generic, and thus not specifically targeted at interconnecting research datasets. The structure of the knowledge base is similar however, making these datasets an interesting workbench for initial experimentation of our approach.

The knowledge base is separated into several datasets usable on their own, but that can be combined to provide additional knowledge and connections between resources. For example, there is a dataset which contains all the *extended abstracts* of the resources present in the knowledge base, which is the text portion that is normally found in the initial section of a resource's corresponding Wikipedia page. We have used this dataset in our small experiment since it contains a sizeable amount of running text. To establish the links between the resources, we have also included the *page links* dataset, which contains the representation of all the links between resources in Wikipedia.

Our prototype currently offers two search modes: a *simple* search mode scores resources according to their extended abstracts' and URI's textual content using the Apache Lucene library, and a *propagated* search, where the scores of resources within the results list that are connected via wikipedia links are boosted. The boosting is performed by simply adding the score of all *neighbours* multiplied by 0.5 (an arbitrarily selected "dampening" parameter) to the score of the resource itself. The boosting is symmetric, meaning that if resources A and $\{B_0,..B_n\}$ are contained in the results list and there is a link between A and $B_i : i \in 0..n$, regardless of the link's direction,

$$score_{propagated}(A) = score_{simple}(A) + 0.5 * \sum_{i=0}^{n} score_{simple}(B_i), \text{ and}$$

$$score_{propagated}(B) = score_{simple}(B) + 0.5 * \sum_{i=0}^{n} score_{simple}(A_i)$$

The contribution of each of the "neighbours" to the final score of the resource is shown in the results list. At the present time, the application provides a basic ranking system for the resources (steps 1 to 3 the process outlined above), and is a first step in selecting the most appropriate technology stack for building a system that incorporates all four steps.

Figure 3 highlights the last step in the four-step recommendation process. We can see the impact on the ranking of adding a simple topological signal, which

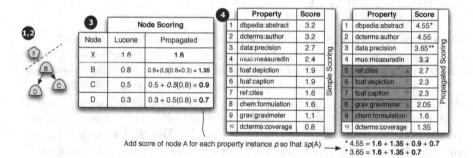

Fig. 3. Ranking the properties in the query results subgraph

is the existence of a property connecting two resources. In step 4 of the figure (and also of our method), the properties are ranked and the top-n properties are presented to the end-user. For a knowledge base G, two resources A and B and a property $P \in G$, the propagated score of P is calculated as $score_{propagated}(P) = \sum score_{propagated}(A)$, for all p such that p is an instance of property P and $p(A) = B$.

We have also written a multi-threaded loader program that adds the dataset triples to the knowledge base and indexes each resource's extended abstract; it scales rather well, until it becomes bound by I/O speed. Knowledge base triples are currently stored in a fully de-normalized PostgreSQL database with only three tables to make querying as fast as possible, but it has become clear from our experiments that a different solution will have to be used, because the system becomes very slow (even on indexed text columns) due to the large number of vertexes (3.550.567, 2.66GB uncompressed) and even more due to the huge number of edges (145.877.010, 36.68GB uncompressed, wikipedia page links only). To cope with this kind of numbers we are currently experimenting with OrientDB and Jena, which are open-source storage layers especially designed to handle very large numbers of triples. A long-standing solution, Neo4j, was left out because it is made available under a rather restrictive Commercial/GPL license instead of the Open Source License Apache 2.0, which is less usage-restrictive.

4   Conclusions and Future Work

In this paper we have presented our goal of partially automating the selection of metadata profiles for the description of research datasets. By linking research data assets in a graph-like knowledge base, we can gather evidence of the importance of candidate descriptors from their use.

The proposed approach uses the contents of each node in the graph as well as its topology to perform a ranking of the properties within the knowledge base using state-of-the art link analysis algorithms, in order to rank and suggest properties that are considered adequate for the description of a dataset from a specific domain.

A small prototype for performing basic manipulation over a subset of DBpedia, a linked data knowledge base, has been built. It provides a first insight on the complexities of handling the massive amounts of information contained in these triple-based knowledge bases, as well as a preliminary study for the implementation of our proposed four stage recommendation model. Future work perspectives include an iterative development of the prototype to turn it into a testbed for gathering feedback from real users on the quality of recommendations—using generic resources at first and then real research data assets from existing research groups at U.Porto.

References

1. Al-Khalifa, H.S., Davis, H.C.: The evolution of metadata from standards to semantics in E-learning applications. In: Proceedings of the Seventeenth Conference on Hypertext and Hypermedia - HYPERTEXT 2006, p. 69 (2006)
2. Bizer, C., Lehmann, J., Kobilarov, G., Auer, S., Becker, C., Cyganiak, R., Hellmann, S.: DBpedia - A crystallization point for the Web of Data. Web Semantics: Science, Services and Agents on the World Wide Web 7(3), 154–165 (2009)
3. Brickley, D., Miller, L.: FOAF Vocabulary Specification 0.98 (2010)
4. Calais, E.: Gravity and the figure of the Earth (2012),
   http://web.ics.purdue.edu/~ecalais/teaching/eas450/Gravity1.pdf
5. Dublin Core Metadata Initiative. DCMI Metadata Terms (2012),
   http://dublincore.org/documents/dcmi-terms/#terms-creator
6. Fire, M., Tenenboim, L., Lesser, O., Puzis, R., Rokach, L., Elovici, Y.: Link Prediction in Social Networks Using Computationally Efficient Topological Features. In: 2011 IEEE Third Int'l Conference on Privacy, Security, Risk and Trust and 2011 IEEE Third Int'l Conference on Social Computing, pp. 73–80 (October 2011)
7. Google Freebase. Freebase Documentation (2012),
   http://wiki.freebase.com/wiki/Main_Page
8. Haase, K.: Context for semantic metadata. In: Proceedings of the 12th Annual ACM International, pp. 204–211 (2004)
9. Hasan, M.A., Chaoji, V., Salem, S.: Link prediction using supervised learning. In: SDM 2006: Workshop on Link (2006)
10. Huang, Z.: Link Prediction Based on Graph Topology: The Predictive Value of the Generalized Clustering Coefficient (2006)
11. Jones, S., Ross, S., Ruusalepp, R.: Data Audit Framework Methodology (2009)
12. Kleinberg, J.M.: Authoritative Sources in a Hyperlinked Environment. Journal of the ACM (JACM) 46(5), 604–632 (1999)
13. LibenNowell, D.: The link prediction problem for social networks. In: CIKM 2003 Proceedings of the Twelfth International Conference on Information and Knowledge Management, pp. 556–559 (November 2004)
14. Lichtenwalter, R.N., Dame, N., Chawla, N.V.: Vertex Collocation Profiles: Subgraph Counting for Link Analysis and Prediction (1019), 1019–1028 (2012)
15. Lyon, L.: Dealing with Data: Roles, Rights, Responsibilities and Relationships. Technical report (2007)
16. Martinez-Uribe, L., Macdonald, S.: User Engagement in Research Data Curation. In: Agosti, M., Borbinha, J., Kapidakis, S., Papatheodorou, C., Tsakonas, G. (eds.) ECDL 2009. LNCS, vol. 5714, pp. 309–314. Springer, Heidelberg (2009)

17. P. A. A. i. D. Media. Digital preservation strategies. Workbook on Digital Private Papers, pp. 222–246 (2008)
18. Morfeo Project. Measurement Units Ontology (2008),
    http://forge.morfeo-project.org/wiki_en/index.php/
    Units_of_measurement_ontology
19. Oracle ThinkQuest. Information Internet: Chemistry Gravimetry (2012),
    http://library.thinkquest.org/10679/chemistry/gravimet.html
20. Piwowar, H.A., Day, R.B., Fridsma, D.S.: Sharing detailed research data is associated with increased citation rate. PLoS One 2(3) (2007)
21. Treloar, A., Wilkinson, R.: Rethinking Metadata Creation and Management in a Data-Driven Research World. In: 2008 IEEE Fourth International Conference on eScience, pp. 782–789 (December 2008)

The Use of Metadata Objects in the Analysis and Representation of Clinical Knowledge

Panos Balatsoukas, Richard Williams, Emma Carruthers,
John Ainsworth, and Iain Buchan

Northwest Institute for Bio-Health Informatics, University of Manchester, United Kingdom
{panagiotis.balatsoukas,Richard.Williams2,Emma.Carruthers,
John.Ainsworth,Buchan}@manchester.ac.uk

Abstract. The aim of this paper is to present the use of metadata in a novel clinical decision-making tool, called COCPIT. The purpose of the tool is to make use of interactive care pathways in order to analyse and represent information stored in patients' health records. The implementation of re-usable metadata objects is an important predicate of the system's specification both for the design of visual care pathways and the statistical representation of clinical knowledge. The paper concludes with a summary of the next steps involved in the design and evaluation of metadata for COCPIT.

Keywords: Metadata, Health Informatics, Semantics, Decision support.

1   Introduction

This paper is focused on the application of metadata for the development of a novel clinical decision-support software, called COCPIT. COCPIT makes use of re-usable *interactive care pathways* in order to analyse and represent clinical information related to patients' care. An *interactive care pathway* can be defined as the digital infrastructure and run-time environment where people (normally healthcare professionals) can create, edit, share and analyse *care pathways* interactively [1]. In particular, *care pathways* define a chronological sequence of steps, mostly commonly diagnostic or treatment, to be followed in providing care for a patient [2]. For example, from initial admission to a hospital, to diagnosis and treatment. A care pathway may branch as a result of a diagnostic result and it may be cyclic where repetition of a sequence of steps is required for the maintenance of a health state. There will typically be many paths through a care pathway, and each patient will follow one path. Care pathways are used to aid clinical decision-making, as they effectively implement (national) clinical guidelines [3] for use within the National Health Service (NHS). Care pathways also help to ensure quality standards are met and to reduce variation in practice. For example, when matched against individual patient health records, care pathways can show variations and missed opportunities in the provision of treatment and care for individual patients or a group of patients. Specifically, the purpose of the COCPIT tool is two-fold: Firstly, to facilitate easy creation and development of interactive care pathways that take into account already

J.M. Dodero, M. Palomo-Duarte, P. Karampiperis (Eds.): MTSR 2012, CCIS 343, pp. 107–112, 2012.
© Springer-Verlag Berlin Heidelberg 2012

existing NHS guidelines (or variations of these guidelines in order to meet local needs). Secondly, to provide users the opportunity to represent statistical information about patients' care through interaction with the contents of a care pathway. This type of statistical information may include descriptive statistics, such as the number of unique patients receiving a specific treatment or diagnosis for their disease at a specific point in time. Also, statistical output can be further manipulated by the user, for example, by clustering the results according to patient demographic data (such as ethnicity, age or gender), or, according to selected risk factors (such as smoking, hypertension or stress). Also, the COCPIT tool can calculate the time it takes for a patient to get transferred between stages of a care pathway (for example, from a diagnostic result to a specific type of treatment), or the length of stay in a specific sub-path of a care pathway. Finally, as well as to descriptive statistics the COCPIT tool can perform complex statistical analysis, such as Cox Proportional-Hazards tests and Kaplan-Meier Survival curves, or perform analysis of variance tests in order to identify variations between expected and actual care delivered to patients.

1.1   Aim and Objectives

The aim of this paper is to describe the role of metadata for the analysis and representation of clinical knowledge in COCPIT. In particular, the objectives are: to introduce a novel object-oriented metadata specification for building visual interactive care pathways; and, to describe how these specifications can be used in order to represent clinical information held in distributed patient healthcare records.

2   Metadata for Building Interactive Care Pathways

An interactive care pathway is represented visually as a flowchart consisting of nodes and edges (Figure 1). Each node represents an event (i.e. a stage where something happens to the patient, for example in terms of treatment or diagnosis), while edges (i.e. the arrows) show the path that a patient should follow within a given care pathway. For example, before a *Thrombolysis* treatment is administered to a patient with suspected stroke, a patient should have a *Screen Test Positive* and a *CT scan*. Both events (i.e. nodes) and arrows (i.e. edges) are defined by metadata objects.

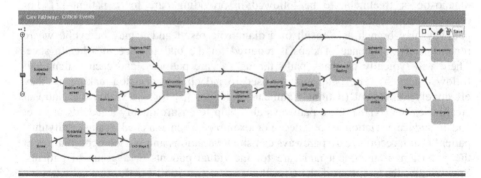

Fig. 1. An Interactive care pathway

A metadata object contains a set of metadata elements with corresponding values that provide enough context to a given event, or an edge (Table 1). An important characteristic of this context is that it controls the relationship between events. For example, by using appropriate metadata a user can specify what criteria a patient should meet in order to get transferred from a diagnostic event A (e.g. CT scan) to another diagnostic event B (e.g. Malnutrition screening).

Table 1. Metadata specification for events in a care pathway

First level	Second level	Third level	Fourth level
<Title/>			
<Description/>			
<Clinical_code/>	<Code_id/>		
	<Clinical_value/>	<Minimum/>	
		<Maximum/>	
		<Definition/>	
<Validity_criteria/>	<Clinical_code/>	<Code_id/>	
		<Clinical_value/>	<Minimum/>
			<Maximum/>
			<Definition/>
		<Occurrence/>	<Minimum/>
			<Maximum/>
		<Time/>	<Minimum/>
			<Maximum/>
			<Definition/>

Table 1 shows four levels of metadata granularity following a parent-child relationship. Usually values are assigned to leaf metadata elements, where granularity ends. In particular, the metadata elements used for documenting an event are:

⌖ the *Title* of the event (e.g. CT of head). The use of this element is optional;

⌖ the *Description* of the event (a user can add details and make comments about the specific event). The use of this element is optional;

⌖ the *Clinical code* of the event. Each event is assigned to a unique clinical code (<Code_id/>). The use of this element is mandatory and the user is not allowed to input a random code. Instead, a code, which contains alphanumeric characters (e.g. GFH20!), should be selected from a controlled vocabulary of terms, called SNOMED. This vocabulary is maintained by the UK NHS and contains a list of medical terms related to specific types of diseases, diagnostic tests and treatments. Each vocabulary term is associated to a unique code. This is important for supporting the semantic interoperability between care pathways generated by different primary and secondary care authorities as well as because these codes are used by clinicians in individual health records in order to document the care provided to patients. In addition to clinical codes a user is prompted to define the context of a given event further by inputting values (Clinical_value/>). Each clinical code may have a <Minimum/> and/or a <Maximum/> value as well as further information about the unit or the type of the specified value (<Definition/>). For example, an event in a care pathway related to the *prescription of statins* (for patients diagnosed with a stroke) could possibly take a value between 100 and 150 mg/dl, where 100 is the <minimum/> value, 150 is the <maximum/> value, and finally the unit of prescription, i.e. mg/dl, is documented using the <Definition/> element. Finally, as opposed to the <Code_id/> element, the use of which is mandatory, the <Clinical_value/> element and associated sub-elements are specified for optional use.

⨯ The *Validity criteria* of the event. The scope of this metadata element is to set conditions according to which a specific patient can progress from event A to event B. This rule may apply when the results from a previous node (or nodes) determine the course of the patient. For example, if patients are prescribed statins, then they should previously have been diagnosed with high cholesterol. In this hypothetical example, in order for a patient to progress to the node (i.e event): *prescription of statins*, she should have satisfied first the condition of being diagnosed with high cholesterol (e.g. cholesterol reading > 4mmol/L). In order to present this information in a metadata object a user needs to identify the clinical code (<Code_id/>) for Cholesterol (e.g. AGBCD") and populate the sub-elements of the <Clinical_value/> element with <Minimum/> and <Maximum/> values as well as with an appropriate unit for the <Definition/> element. In addition, the user may use the <Occurrence/> and <Time/> elements. Using the <Occurrence/> metadata element, a user can specify the number of times a specific clinical code should occur before deciding whether a patient should progress towards the next step of the care pathway. For example, in the case of cholesterol readings, the <Occurrence/> metadata element could contain information about the number of times a patient should have been diagnosed with a specific cholesterol reading before proceeding to the next event which could be the prescription of a lipid-lowering medication. Like in the case of the <Clinical_value/> metadata element, occurrence can be expressed using the leaf sub-elements <Minimum/> and<Maximum/>. The <Time/> element can be used by a clinician in order to define how long will it take for a user to get transferred from event A to event B. The Minimum and maximum time is expressed using integers, while the <Definition/> metadata element is used to contextualise the values (e.g. minutes, hours, days, weeks, months, or years). The use of the <Validity_criteria/> metadata is optional. However, when a decision is made to use this element, it is required by the user to provide a correct <Code_id/> sub-element.

2.1   Building Compound Metadata Statements

In addition to the population of metadata elements with values a user has the option of using Boolean expression (AND, OR, NOT) in order to create more complex metadata statements. The use of Boolean operators is available in the case of the <Clinical_code/> and <Validity_criteria/> metadata elements. For example, by using the Boolean operator AND in the case of the <Validity_ criteria/> metadata element, a user should be able to express compound conditions that a patient should meet in order to get transferred from an event A to an event B. As it is shown in Figure 2, in order for a patient to be assigned to the event number four (clinical code: 333000) the following two conditions must apply from the departing nodes: ACR > 60ml AND eGFR<60ml). Finally, Figure 3 shows the User Interface of the Metadata editor.

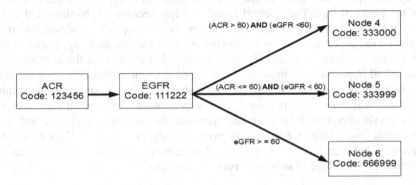

Fig. 2. Example of a compound metadata statement

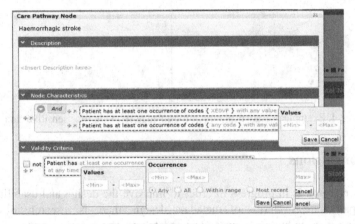

Fig. 3. Metadata object editor

3   Knowledge Representation from Patient Healthcare Records

This section explains how events and edges in a care pathway can be used in order to analyse and represent information held in patients' healthcare records. When a clinical code in a patient's health record matches the code used in the metadata object of an event it is said to enter the event. This is the reason why the <Code_id/> sub-element is always defined for mandatory use. Therefore, a single event in a care pathway may count all patients who's personal electronic health records indicate that they experienced this event. When a clinical code is assigned to a given event through the metadata object specification, the COCPIT tool's matching algorithm scans the patient record database(s) (accessible through the data management framework of COCPIT) for matches with clinical codes assigned to already existing patient health records. The use of standard clinical codes supports semantic interoperability between the events and the information provided in the patient's individual health records. The presentation of the statistical output is based on 2-dimensional graphs, such as bar-charts, pies and histograms. Normally these are used to represent descriptive statistics such as the number of unique, or total, patient visits to a specific event. In order to display this type of data the user needs only to select an event (i.e a node) or an edge from the care pathway. The selected event, or edge, becomes highlighted and stands out from the remaining elements of the care pathway, thus making it easy for users to retain a sense of orientation while navigating across a care pathway. Statistics may be displayed for more than one event concurrently. For example, if the user selects an event, called *Hypertension diagnosed* , and a second event, called *Thrombolysis,* from the care pathway, the results displayed should show the percentage and/or the number of patients who had been diagnosed with hypertension the moment they received Thrombolysis treatment. Edges can communicate statistical information as well such as the mean time it takes for patients to move from event A to event B, or patient life expectancy between events (Figure 4). Furthermore, statistical analysis can be performed for user-defined subsets of patient population.

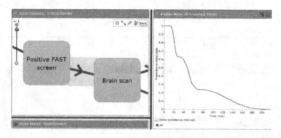

Fig. 4. Example of statistical output for an edge showing time sensitive data

4   Conclusions

Currently, research is in progress in order to improve the design and usability of the tool. In particular, in terms of metadata design, there is research in progress investigating into the human aspects of metadata use. For example, a usability test is currently examining how users of the COCPIT tool interact with the metadata editor (Figure 3). Also, focus groups are scheduled in order to examine the views of health professionals about how the existing metadata elements of COCPIT can be semantically improved in order to meet different user needs.

References

1. Ainsworth, J., Buchan, I.: E-labs and work objects: towards digital health economies. In: Communications Infrastructure, Systems and Applications, pp. 205–216. Springer, Berlin (2009)
2. Campbell, A., Hotchkiss, R., Bradshaw, N., Porteous, M.: Integrated care pathways. British Medical Journal 316(7125), 133–137 (1998)
3. Map of Medicine (2012), http://www.mapofmedicine.com/ (retrieved June 08, 2012)

An Ontology Based Data Collection Service
to Support eGov Service Design

Muriel Foulonneau and Younes Djaghloul

Tudor Research Centre,
29, av. John F. Kennedy
L-1855 Luxembourg, Luxembourg
{muriel.foulonneau,younes.djaghloul}@tudor.lu

Abstract. In the past few years, the eGovernment sector has engaged into the
use of semantic representations for data models and datasets, in particular with
the open government data movement and the creation of initiatives to share
semantic resources (JoinUp portal) and create core vocabularies (e.g., Core
Business). In the scope of the EU SPOCS project to implement a cross border
service infrastructure, a semantic layer allows exchanging documents to support
procedures related to the service directive. It highlighted the necessity to collect
data from public administrations on the procedures and documents but also on
the equivalence of documents issued by foreign countries. The implementation
of a data collection system based on ontologies raises challenges in relation
with the generation of questions from ontologies as well as the annotation and
update of the ontology to create and validate the data collected. In order to
address these challenges, we are implementing a mechanism to generate
questions and trace the information over a question answer process with an
annotation framework based on the W3C Open annotation model.

Keywords: ontology annotation, question generation, ontology evolution,
eGovernment dataset.

1 Introduction

The European eGovernment sector has engaged into the use of semantic
representations for data models and datasets, with the support in particular of the
European Commission ISA programme (Interoperability Solutions for European
Public Administrations[1]). Semantic models are more and more important as public
administrations share data models (e.g., JoinUp portal[2]) and datasets (Open
Government Data movement).

However important, datasets that describe eGovernment systems or provide
equivalence information between resources are expensive to create when they do not
already exist. They are rarely made available in semantic formats (RDF, RDFS,

---

[1] http://ec.europa.eu/isa/
[2] http://joinup.ec.europa.eu/

J.M. Dodero, M. Palomo-Duarte, P. Karampiperis (Eds.): MTSR 2012, CCIS 343, pp. 113–120, 2012.
© Springer-Verlag Berlin Heidelberg 2012

OWL). Moreover, the collection of data from the administrations remains a challenge because of the lack of availability of agents and the distribution of relevant data across different organisations and datasets. However, in certain types of applications, a large number of equivalences can be inferred. For instance document types can be assumed to be equivalent, either because they belong to the same hierarchical structure (birth certificates, even from a different country), or because of legal constraints (e.g., European driving licences). We are implementing a system that generates forms from semantic models in order to complete a dataset of equivalences between document types. The use of ontology-based mechanisms aims to support the reconciliation of information coming from different sources, as well as improve the equivalence management process, thanks to inferences associated with the semantic infrastructure (OWL language and reasoners).

In this paper, we describe the process to collect data from a semantic model, as well as the ontologies used for the domain model and its annotation. We then propose mechanisms to enhance the data collection process.

2   The Interoperability Layer of the eGov Documents Infrastructure

In the context of the EU service directive, the creation and provision of a service across boundaries should be facilitated, despite the heterogeneous local organisations, the variety of procedures, and the multilingual issues. The SPOCS project is dedicated to the transfer of documents across EU countries. It has developed processes in order to facilitate the provision of documents issued in any European countries to administrations of any other European countries. This should enable a person for instance to set up a company in another country or to expand a business from one country to another, through a procedure which requires documents from his home country as well as any country where the company is already active. The project has therefore built an infrastructure of services to allow PSCs (Points of Single Contact) in each country to verify the documents transferred from another country.

A first semantic layer was created to support the discovery and syndication of services as well as to embed documents into a metadata package [1]. A second set of semantic services was created with the provision of enhanced semantic features in the user interface and the use of Open Data on documents and procedures related to the implementation of the EU services directive. In this context, a particularly important service is dedicated to the verification of equivalences between documents provided to administrations. Indeed, administrative procedures usually require documents, whose name and sometimes existence depends on the country. In order to verify that a document is indeed accepted for another document, it is necessary to define document equivalences, encode them and make them available through a service.

3   A Document Equivalence Model

We define the equivalence between two document types as the acceptance of a document type as a replacement for another document type. We propose to use an ontology to represent the equivalence of document types (Figure 1). For example, a birth certificate would be an instance of the class *Document type*. A document (i.e., instance of Document) has a type *birth certificate*. Then a Portuguese birth certificate, potentially of a particular model, can have an equivalence with a Luxembourgish birth certificate. The Equivalence is represented as a class because two types of conditions can impact this equivalence: the context of a particular procedure and the addition of an attribute, such as a certification or an official translation.

We could not use the OWL Equivalent Class mechanism or even the SKOS mapping properties[3], such as *skos:broadMatch* because 1) the equivalence should be contextual in certain cases and 2) the equivalence is not a symmetric property. Indeed if the Luxembourgish government accepts a Portuguese document *Dp1* in replacement of the Luxembourgish document *Dl1* in the scope of the Luxembourgish procedure *Pl1*, it does not bind the Portuguese government in the equivalent procedure *Pp1* to accept *Dl1* as a replacement for *Dp1*.

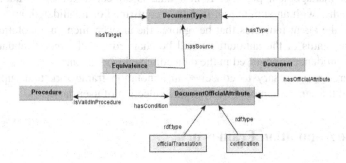

Fig. 1. Ontology for Document Equivalence

A document equivalence could be deduced from either the legislation (which requires modeling the legislation itself), or the definition of a hierarchical structure of documents (i.e., a Portuguese passport is a passport and a Luxembourgish passport is also a passport), or through an ad hoc relation created by administrative agents to guarantee the acceptance of a document in the scope of another one.

Modeling the overall legislation can help determine some of the equivalences. We are investigating the modeling of legislation through the Carneades software [2]. It was however considered by the administration that the completeness of rules should be ensured through the direct collection of data with administrative agents in the various public bodies, since not all documents are administrative documents. We are therefore building mechanisms to collect equivalences between documents.

4   The Design of an Infrastructure for Collecting Data on Equivalences

The system aims to generate questions from the semantic model in order to annotate the original model, add, remove or replace data.

---

[3] http://www.w3.org/TR/skos-reference/#mapping

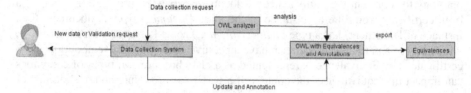

Fig. 2. Mechanism to collect information from administrative agents

Document types and their equivalences are analyzed (OWL analyzer) to identify 1) missing information or 2) information to validate. A data collection request is then sent to the Data Collection System, which issues a corresponding question to the administrative agent.

An annotation mechanism is needed in order to trace all actions and support the equivalence management process. If new data is collected, then it is added to the model, together with an annotation. If data is confirmed or invalidated, an annotation is added. If the agent indicates that he ignores the answer, then an annotation is also created. The status of the annotations will be changed and the model updated when sufficient confidence is acquired in the data collected from agents.

It is therefore necessary to conceive an annotation framework that supports the evolution of the semantic model through the collection of user data.

5   The Annotation Framework

The annotation model in the Data Collection Service that is being implemented in the scope of the project must support the annotation of a semantic model in order to trace an action (addition, confirmation, removal, replacement) and its description (author, date) in a question answer context. We therefore investigated solutions for the annotation of resources.

5.1   The Open Annotation Model

Annotations of semantic models (e.g., RDF graphs) have gained attention together with the increasing necessity to trace the transformation of data and therefore add provenance information to triples or graphs (W3C Provenance model[4]), thus the interest in the standardization of named graphs [3]. However these frameworks do not provide a comprehensive set of user actions on the graph.

User annotation frameworks have proliferated since the W3C Annotea framework[5], in particular to support scholarly work (e.g., [4], [5]) and the provision of user generated content on digital resources [6] [7].

The recent Annotation ontology [8] defines a set of concepts to reconcile the biomedical ontologies with the scientific documents through user annotations for

---

[4] http://www.w3.org/TR/prov-dm/
[5] http://www.w3.org/2001/Annotea/

instance. The framework however envisions a wider applicability, although mainly in the scholarly environment. The Open Annotation Collaboration provides a "Web and Resource-centric interoperable annotation environment" to support scholarly work by enabling annotations across server boundaries [9]. The OAC was initially centered on humanities approaches to scholarly annotations.

The recently created W3C Open Annotation Community[6] aims to integrate the Annotation ontology and the Open Annotation Collaboration framework into a generic data model for annotating digital resources, the Open Annotation Core Data Model, released in 2012[7]. It defines a resource of type *annotation* with a *target* (what is being annotated) and a *body* (i.e., the content of the annotation).

5.2   The Implementation of the Data Collection Annotation Model

We implemented this mechanism for the annotation of the Equivalence ontology model in order to support the annotation of the equivalence between two document types. It contains the Open Annotation namespace (*oa*), the SPOCS namespace for the Equivalence model (*sam*) that will be annotated, as well as a specific Data Collection Annotation namespace (*dca*).

Since we base our work on the Open Annotation Data Model, the *Annotation* used in the Data Collection Service (Figure 3) is defined as a subclass of the *Annotation* class defined in the Open Annotation model. An annotation has an instance of the *Equivalence* class as *target*.

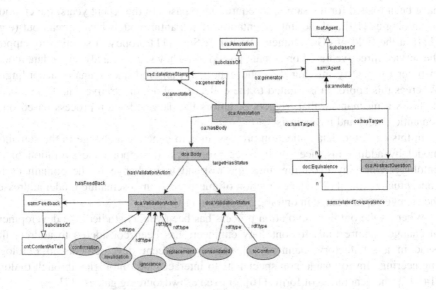

Fig. 3. The Data Collection Annotation model

---

[6] http://www.w3.org/community/openannotation/
[7] http://www.openannotation.org/spec/core/

Figure 3 presents the adaptation of the model to support the addition of properties at the level of both the annotation and the body.

An annotation can be created either by a human *Agent* or by the system, potentially as the result of the application of an inference rule.

In the context of an equivalence that needs to be confirmed, the action of the *Agent* is logged in the form of an annotation. In the original Open Annotation Core Data Model, the annotation body is not defined as a class in order to allow any type of resource to be either the target or the body of an annotation. We however created a specific *Body* class and defined associated properties. The body of the annotation contains a validation action, i.e., a confirmation, an invalidation, a replacement, or a statement of ignorance/incompetence. This is displayed as an agreement, a disagreement or a "do not know" statement. A possibility to propose an alternative option will be implemented in the future to enable a replacement mechanism.

As a result of one or more validation processes, the equivalence can be confirmed, invalidated or have a "To Confirm" status, meaning that the OWL analyzer component will select these equivalences for proposing them in the context of the validation process.

6   Related Work

Data can be collected through a variety of strategies, including online forms, generated questions or dialogs, or implicit tracks left by users (e.g., these documents have been loaded for the same procedure in the past). In the recent years, the creation of ontologies [10] and the implementation of semantic models have spread out (e.g., [11]) in the field of eGovernment. Weber & Sure [11] propose a solution to support the service directive based on semantic services. They suggest analyzing a data model in order to identify missing data and generate a tailored questionnaire accordingly. Whereas this approach is limited to the collection of administrative data from a user, it shows a mechanism that triggers or tailors the data collection process based on a semantic model and its analysis.

In this case, the data collection process aims to generate a change in the semantic model by adding instances or instance properties. It supports the evolution of an ontology. Ontology evolution aims to "respond to a change in the domain or its conceptualization" [12]. The extraction of questions from a semantic model addresses the change capture stage in ontology evolution [13].

Whereas the ontology evolution process has been widely studied, the development of change capture tools for ontology engineers has been considered to address the issue in a satisfactory manner [12]. However, recent developments in ontology engineering aim to enable non specialists to interact with ontologies through dialogs [14][15], the generation of forms [16], or even crowdsourcing games [17].

The data collection based on semantic models raises a number of key issues in relation with the quality of the collected data [18], the use of inference mechanisms, the process of question creation [19], and the collaborative evolution of the semantic model, including the consolidation of potentially conflicting perspectives.

7 Conclusion and Future Work

In this work, we describe a data collection service based on ontologies and the associated annotation framework to support the data collection process. A first version of the data collection service, based on the annotation model presented in section 4 was implemented. It allows supporting the generation of questions and the update of a semantic model.

Our future work will focus on the evaluation of the proposed mechanisms to optimize the data collection process. The ontology-based data collection approach needs to be assessed according to both its acceptance by the agents themselves as well as quantitative performance metrics. Indeed it will be necessary to measure how much effort is required from agents through an ontology based data collection service in comparison with a system that would not be optimized, i.e., which would request all the data.

Furthermore, data collection is needed in many other cases, in particular the acceptability of degrees and diplomas. This requires setting up an overall infrastructure, including governance mechanisms to ensure the validity of the data collected and the mix between official sources, i.e., equivalences deduced from the legislation and rules defined by administrations.

Acknowledgments. The work reported in this paper was partially supported by the European project ICT PSP SPOCS. The authors would like to acknowledge the contribution of the COST Action IS1004. www.webdatanet.eu.

References

1. Papadakis, A., Rantos, K., Stasis, A.: Promoting e-Gov Services: e-Document Interoperability Across EU. In: 2011 15th Panhellenic Conference on Informatics (PCI), pp. 304–308 (2011)
2. Gordon, T.F.: Combining Rules and Ontologies with Carneades. In: Proceedings of the 5th International RuleML2011@BRF Challenge, Fort Lauderdale, Florida, USA, November 3-5 (2011)
3. Carroll, J.J., Bizer, C., Hayes, P., Stickler, P.: Named Graphs, Provenance and Trust. In: Proceedings of the 14th International Conference on World Wide Web, pp. 613–622 (2005)
4. Zhao, J., Goble, C., Greenwood, M., Wroe, C., Stevens, R.: Annotating, Linking and Browsing Provenance Logs for e-Science. In: Proc. of the Workshop on Semantic Web Technologies for Searching and Retrieving Scientific Data, pp. 158–176 (2003)
5. Bradley, J.: Pliny: A Model for Digital Support of Scholarship. Journal of Digital Information 9 (2008)
6. Chavez, R., Cole, T.W., Dunn, J., Foulonneau, M., Habing, T.G., Parod, W.: DLF-Aquifer Asset Actions Experiment. D-Lib Magazine 12 (2006)
7. Haslhofer, B., Jochum, W., King, R., Sadilek, C., Schellner, K.: The LEMO Annotation Framework: Weaving Multimedia Annotations with the Web. International Journal on Digital Libraries 10, 15–32 (2009)

8. Ciccarese, P., Ocana, M., Garcia Castro, L., Das, S., Clark, T.: An Open Annotation Ontology for Science on Web 3.0. Journal of Biomedical Semantics 2 (2011)
9. Hunter, J., Cole, T.W., Sanderson, R., Van de Sompel, H.: The open annotation collaboration: A data model to support sharing and interoperability of scholarly annotations. In: Pierazzo, E. (ed.) Digital Humanities 2010: Conference Abstracts. Digital Humanities 2010, London, United Kingdom, July 7-10, pp. 175–178 (2010)
10. Orthofer, G., Wimmer, M.: An ontology for eGovernment: Linking the scientific model with concrete projects. In: Proceedings of the Workshop on The Semantic Web Meets eGovernment within the AAAI Spring Symposium Series at Stanford University, p. 3 (2006)
11. Weber, I., Sure, Y.: Towards an Implementation of the EU Services Directive with Semantic Web Services. In: Abramowicz, W. (ed.) Business Information Systems. LNBIP, vol. 21, pp. 217–227. Springer, Heidelberg (2009)
12. Flouris, G., Manakanatas, D., Kondylakis, H., Plexousakis, D., Antoniou, G.: Ontology change: Classification and survey. Knowl. Eng. Rev. 23(2), 117–152 (2008)
13. Stojanovic, L., Maedche, A., Motik, B., Stojanovic, N.: User-Driven Ontology Evolution Management. In: Gómez-Pérez, A., Benjamins, V.R. (eds.) EKAW 2002. LNCS (LNAI), vol. 2473, pp. 285–300. Springer, Heidelberg (2002)
14. Dimitrova, V., Denaux, R., Hart, G., Dolbear, C., Holt, I., Cohn, A.G.: Involving Domain Experts in Authoring OWL Ontologies. In: Sheth, A.P., Staab, S., Dean, M., Paolucci, M., Maynard, D., Finin, T., Thirunarayan, K. (eds.) ISWC 2008. LNCS, vol. 5318, pp. 1–16. Springer, Heidelberg (2008)
15. Costetchi, E., Ras, E.: From informal to formal knowledge representation using QAF triad. Paper Presented at the Workshop Interagir Avec Des Représentations Formelles at the IHM, Conference, Sophia Antipolis, France (2011)
16. Tao, C., Embley, D.W., Liddle, S.W.: FOCIH: Form-Based Ontology Creation and Information Harvesting. In: Laender, A.H.F., Castano, S., Dayal, U., Casati, F., de Oliveira, J.P.M. (eds.) ER 2009. LNCS, vol. 5829, pp. 346–359. Springer, Heidelberg (2009)
17. Thaler, S., Siorpaes, K., Simperl, E.: SpotThe-Link: A Game for Ontology Alignment. In: Proceedings of the 6th Conference for Professional Knowledge Management, WM 2011 (2011)
18. Gligorov, R., Baltussen, L.B., van Ossenbruggen, J., Aroyo, L., Brinkerink, M., Oomen, J., van Ees, A.: Towards Integration of End-User Tags with Professional Annotations. In: Proceedings of the WebSci 2010, April 26, Raleigh, NC, US (2010)
19. Foulonneau, M.: Generating Educational Assessment Items from Linked Open Data: The Case of DBpedia. In: García-Castro, R., Fensel, D., Antoniou, G. (eds.) ESWC 2011. LNCS, vol. 7117, pp. 16–27. Springer, Heidelberg (2012)

Towards the Development of a Knowledge Base for Realizing User-Friendly Data Mining

Roberto Espinosa[1], Diego García-Saiz[2], Jose Jacobo Zubcoff[3],
Jose-Norberto Mazón[3], and Marta Zorrilla[2]

[1] WaKe research, University of Matanzas "Camilo Cienfuegos", Cuba
roberto.espinosa@umcc.cu
[2] University of Cantabria, Spain
{diego.garcias,marta.zorrilla}@unican.es
[3] WaKe research, University of Alicante, Spain
jose.zubcoff@ua.es, jnmazon@dlsi.ua.es

Abstract. Initiatives as open data, make available more and more data to everybody, thus fostering new techniques for enabling non-expert users to analyse data in an easier manner. Data mining techniques allow acquiring knowledge from available data but it requires a high level of expertise in both preparing data sets and selecting the right mining algorithm. This paper is a first step towards a user-friendly data mining approach in which a knowledge base is created with the aim of guiding non-expert users in obtaining reliable knowledge from data sources.

1 Introduction

Knowledge Discovery in Databases (KDD) is a complex process aiming at extracting knowledge patterns from large data sets. Successfully applying data mining techniques requires a high level of expertise in both preparing data sets and selecting the right mining algorithm [11]. Consequently, the KDD process requires the know-how of an expert in order to obtain reliable and useful knowledge in the resulting patterns. Interestingly, the advent of the open data movement enables non-expert users to access more and more data. This scenario fosters new techniques for discovering knowledge in a friendly manner and without mastering concepts and data mining techniques. A definition of user-friendly data mining applications is suggested in [9] where data mining is considered as a automated process in which all steps are interactively controlled by the user, at the same time that useful information is not lost. To realize this process, we envision that four factors must be addressed in user-friendly data mining: (i) contextualizing data mining and figuring out initial non-expert user requirements; (ii) considering quality of data sources and how it affects data mining results; (iii) facilitating the use of data mining algorithms (e.g., by using parameter-less algorithms); and (iv) providing an easy-to-interpret and visual-appealing output for knowledge patterns.

In this paper, our focus is on dealing with quality in data sources, since it requires significantly more manual effort than the data mining task itself [5].

J.M. Dodero, M. Palomo-Duarte, P. Karampiperis (Eds.): MTSR 2012, CCIS 343, pp. 121–126, 2012.
© Springer-Verlag Berlin Heidelberg 2012

Our preliminary step in this direction consists of describing a knowledge base as a useful resource for acquiring results of experiments (described by means of scientific workflows) in which the behavior of data mining algorithms is studied in presence of one or several data quality criteria. Our knowledge base consists of a set of models (conformed to a metamodel for data mining experiments) and it can be used as a resource by non-expert data miners in order to select the best algorithm to apply regarding the quality of data sources [10]. It is worth noting that our knowledge base can be used (i) directly, by non-expert data miners that have certain expertise in data management; or (ii) indirectly, by using a kind of "recommender" that query the knowledge base to guide non-expert data miners by suggesting the best algorithm to be applied to the data.

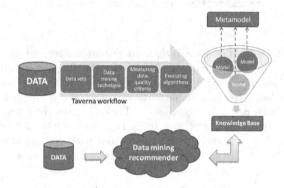

Fig. 1. Overview of our approach for building a knowledge base

Our running example is based on the educational data mining community in which several data can be shared by educators, thus being considered as an open data scenario. Importantly, data mining is being profusely used [13] in the educational context as consequence of the rapid expansion of the use of technologies in supporting learning, not only in established institutional contexts and platforms, but also in the emerging landscape of free, open, social learning online. Although there are tools as ElWM [15] which help instructors to analyse their virtual courses, a knowledge base as proposed here will become a crucial resource for designing a recommender that help instructors (as non-expert data miners) in applying the right data mining algorithm on their data sets and to extract conclusions oriented to improving the teaching-learning process.

2   Related Work

As our knowledge base, there are several approaches for keeping knowledge related to data mining activities. OntoDM [12] proposes a general ontology for data mining, while DAMON (DAta Mining ONtology) [2] is a taxonomy that offers domain experts a way to look up tasks, methods and software tools given a certain goal. KDDONTO [3] aims at discovering suitable KD algorithms and describin workflows of KD processes. The Ontology-Based Meta-Mining of Knowledge Discovery Workflows [6] is aimed at supporting workflow construction for the discovery process. Moreover, in [14] authors propose a specific ontology to describe machine learning experiments in a standardized fashion for supporting a collaborative approach to the analysis of learning algorithms. Whereas these knowledge resources provide a way of reasoning on the semantics of data mining, our metamodel-based approach targets the automatic management and interchange of metadata on data mining experiments.

3   Knowledge Base for Enabling User-Friendly Data Mining

Following the model-driven paradigm [1], our knowledge base is created as a repository of models that conforms to a metamodel for representing the configuration and results of data mining experiments. Using models makes that knowledge base can be uniform and automatically created by using information from a set scientific workflows where data mining algorithms are applied. Once, the knowledge base is obtained the non-expert miner could use it to make informed decisions about which algorithm produces better results having into account the features of available data sets and the kind of desired results.

3.1   Metamodel

Under the model-driven umbrella, and according to [8], a model is a "description of (part of) a system written in a well-defined language, while a well-defined language is a language with well-defied form (syntax), and meaning (semantics), which is suitable for automated interpretation by a computer". Therefore, on the one hand, a model must focus on those important parts of a system, thus avoiding superfluous details. On the other hand, well defined languages can be designed by means of metamodeling [1], which provides the foundation for creating models in a meaningful, precise and consistent manner. Our metamodel contains those useful concepts for representing models with information about data mining experiments: metadata of the data source, values of data quality criteria and the results of algorithms. The idea of defining a metamodel is that in this way all the information that is collected from the experiment is homogenized, thus enabling to create models as a part of our knowledge base. Of course, this metamodel is a initial proposal that can be extended in the future.

The definition of our metamodel (see Fig. 2) is based on an analysis of several ontologies (see Section 2):

DataMiningResults. This class represents values of measures for each dataset after executing an algorithm, e.g., accuracy.

Algorithm. This class represent information about data mining algorithms. Each algorithm belongs to a specific technique. E.g., NaiveBayes, J48, RandomTree or Adaboost.

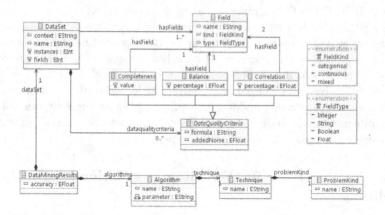

Fig. 2. Metamodel for our data mining experiments

Technique. This class defines a set of existing data mining techniques (e.g. a tree, a probability matrix, and so on)

ProblemKind. It defines the different kind of problem with which the user need is met (e.g., (classification, prediction, clustering, etc.).

DataSet. It describes the source included in the knowledge base. Each DataSet is composed of different fields with different data quality criteria. Also, the own data set has specific at quality criteria.

Field. It represents information about different columns of the DataSet.

DataQualityCriteria. This class represents the information related to the different criteria that can be presented in a DataSet or in each Field contained in this. For each data quality criteria, it is defined a formula to calculate it, and addedNoise gathers the percentage of noise included artificially for the experiment.

Balance. This class inherits from the DataQualityCriteria class and it is performed to know if the instances are uniformly distributed.

Correlation. This class inherits from the DataQualityCriteria class and represents a measure of association between two columns. By definition, it needs to be related to at least two instances of Field class.

Completeness. This class inherits from the DataQualityCriteria class and describes the grade of null structural values [4] or missing values.

FieldKind. It is an enumeration class for defining the general kind of values that the field instances may have.

FieldType. It is an enumeration class for representing the types of each Field.

3.2   Workflow Description and Experimentation

With the aim of building models belonging to our knowledge base, a set of experiments must be conducted. Scientific workflows using Taverna [7] have been proposed to assess how different data quality criteria affect behavior of different data mining techniques.

Our workflows define two steps (see Fig. 1): (i) selecting data sets and some data mining technique, and (ii) measuring certain data quality criteria on the data sets and executing data mining algorithms according to previous selected technique.

Outputs of our workflows are stored in the knowledge base and it can be used as the cornerstone of a "recommender" system that support non-expert users to select which algorithm produces better results having into account the features of available data sets and the kind of result they want (e.g. a tree, a probability matrix, and so on), thus allowing them to make informed decisions.

With the aim of checking the viability of building our knowledge base, a experimental case study based on our running example is described. Our experimentation assesses how the accuracy of classifiers varies when datasets suffer from missing values (completeness data quality criteria according to our metamodel) by means of a Taverna workflow. For this purpose, in which we have used 14 original datasets from e-learning platform logs (based on our educational context) and we have generated 42 new datasets by using a random technique to add percentages of 10%, 20% and 30% of missing values in non-class attributes. The resulting 56 datasets contain the activity carried out by students in 8 virtual courses measured in different ways, as the time spent in the courses, number of connections, number of tests answered, among others with the aim of building models to predict the students' performance.

Next, our Taverna workflow applies, to each dataset, seven of the most popular classification algorithms in data mining with their default parameters (using the Weka implementation): BayesNet, NaiveBayes, J48, RandomTree, Adaboost, OneR and Jrip. A total of 392 experiments are generated. For each experiment, a model (conformed to our metamodel) is stored in our knowledge base.

This knowledge base is the foundation of a recommender system in which, for example, a tree which can be translated as a set of rules that allows users to select the best algorithm to predict students' performance according to its accuracy. Using J48 we observed, for example, a rule that says *If numMissingValues¿0 and size¿190 then is recommended to use BayesNet with a success rate of 12/15.*

4   Conclusions

Data mining techniques could provide insights in available data but it requires a high level of expertise in both preparing data sets and selecting the right mining algorithm. Interestingly, with the advent of the open data movement, more and more data will be accessed by non-expert users and new mechanisms are required with the aim of enabling both an easy and powerfully analysis of data.

This paper intends to be a first step towards a user-friendly data mining approach in which a knowledge base is created with the aim of guiding non-expert users in obtaining reliable knowledge from data sources. Our knowledge base is described by means of outputs of Taverna scientific workflows in which the behavior of data mining algorithms is studied in presence of one or several data quality criteria. Our future work consists of conducting a wider sets of experiments (which allow us to properly extend our metamodel) and designing a data mining recommender that uses our knowledge base.

Acknowledgements. This work has been partially funded by IN.MIND project from University of Alicante (Spain), MANTRA project (GV/2011/035) from Valencia Government (Spain) and the PhD studentship program at University of Cantabria (Spain).

References

1. Bézivin, J.: On the unification power of models. Software and System Modeling 4(2), 171–188 (2005)
2. Cannataro, M., Comito, C.: A data mining ontology for grid programming. In: Proceedings of (SemPGrid 2003), pp. 113–134 (2003)
3. Diamantini, C., Potena, D., Storti, E.: Ontology-Driven KDD Process Composition. In: Adams, N.M., Robardet, C., Siebes, A., Boulicaut, J.-F. (eds.) IDA 2009. LNCS, vol. 5772, pp. 285–296. Springer, Heidelberg (2009)
4. Espinosa, R., Zubcoff, J., Mazón, J.-N.: A Set of Experiments to Consider Data Quality Criteria in Classification Techniques for Data Mining. In: Murgante, B., Gervasi, O., Iglesias, A., Taniar, D., Apduhan, B.O. (eds.) ICCSA 2011, Part II. LNCS, vol. 6783, pp. 680–694. Springer, Heidelberg (2011)
5. Fayyad, U.M., Piatetsky-Shapiro, G., Smyth, P.: The kdd process for extracting useful knowledge from volumes of data. Commun. ACM 39(11), 27–34 (1996)
6. Hilario, M., Nguyen, P., Do, H., Woznica, A., Kalousis, A.: Ontology-Based Meta-Mining of Knowledge Discovery Workflows. In: Jankowski, N., Duch, W., Grąbczewski, K. (eds.) Meta-Learning in Computational Intelligence. SCI, vol. 358, pp. 273–315. Springer, Heidelberg (2011)
7. Hull, D., Wolstencroft, K., Stevens, R., Goble, C., Pocock, M.R., Li, P., Oinn, T.: Taverna: A tool for building and running workflows of services. Nucleic Acids Research, W729–W732
8. Kleppe, A., Warmer, J., Bast, W.: MDA Explained. The Practice and Promise of The Model Driven Architecture. Addison Wesley (2003)
9. Kriegel, H.P., Borgwardt, K.M., Kröger, P., Pryakhin, A., Schubert, M., Zimek, A.: Future trends in data mining. Data Min. Knowl. Discov. 15(1), 87–97 (2007)
10. Mazón, J.N., Zubcoff, J.J., Garrigós, I., Espinosa, R., Rodríguez, R.: Open business intelligence: on the importance of data quality awareness in user-friendly data mining. In: EDBT/ICDT Workshops, pp. 144–147 (2012)
11. Nisbet, R., Elder, J., Miner, G.: Handbook of Statistical Analysis and Data Mining Applications. Academic Press (2009)
12. Panov, P., Soldatova, L.N., Džeroski, S.: Towards an Ontology of Data Mining Investigations. In: Gama, J., Costa, V.S., Jorge, A.M., Brazdil, P.B. (eds.) DS 2009. LNCS, vol. 5808, pp. 257–271. Springer, Heidelberg (2009)
13. Romero, C., Ventura, S.: Educational Data Mining: A Review of the State-of-the-Art. IEEE Tansactions on Systems, Man and Cybernetics, Part C: Applications and Reviews 40(6), 601–618 (2010)
14. Vanschoren, J., Soldatova, L.: Exposé: An ontology for data mining experiments. In: International Workshop on Third Generation Data Mining: Towards Service-oriented Knowledge Discovery (SoKD 2010), pp. 31–46 (September 2010)
15. Zorrilla, M.E., García-Saiz, D.: Mining Service to Assist Instructors involved in Virtual Education. Business Intelligence Applications and the Web: Models, Systems and Technologies (2011)

Relationships between Users, Resources and Services in Learning Object Repositories

Jordi Conesa, Julià Minguillón, and M. Elena Rodríguez

Universitat Oberta de Catalunya
Rambla Poblenou 156, 08018 Barcelona, Spain

Abstract. In this paper we describe a proposal for defining the relationships between resources, users and services in a digital repository. Nowadays, virtual learning environments are widely used but digital repositories are not fully integrated yet into the learning process. Our final goal is to provide final users with recommendation systems and reputation schemes that help them to build a true learning community around the institutional repository, taking into account their educational context (i.e. the courses they are enrolled into) and their activity (i.e. system usage by their classmates and teachers). In order to do so, we extend the basic resource concept in a traditional digital repository by adding all the educational context and other elements from end-users' profiles, thus bridging users, resources and services, and shifting from a library-centered paradigm to a learning-centered one.

Keywords: Digital repositories, Learning objects, Resources, Modeling, Recommendation systems, Reputation schemes.

1 Introduction

Learning object repositories are becoming more and more popular as more and more educational institutions are widening the scope of their institutional repositories, including not only research outcomes but also resources created during the teaching and learning processes [6]. Nevertheless, it is well known that final users (mostly teachers and learners) do not use repositories [1,6], mainly because these systems have been designed and implemented without taking into account end-users [12]. In order to become true learning spaces, learning object repositories need to attract users by creating true learning communities [9,2]. In [7] the authors describe a possible set of additional services that could be built on top of institutional repositories in order to increase their usage, pursuing also the creation of a community of learning.

A preliminary study on the UOC institutional repository (namely O2[1]), based on interviews with end-users (teachers and learners), showed that rating, tagging and finding related resources were the most valued services. Therefore, as part of the MAVSEL Project[2], we intend to extend the default set of services

---

[1] O2: http://openaccess.uoc.edu/webapps/o2/?locale=en
[2] Project MAVSEL: http://www.ieru.org/projects/mavsel/index.html

J.M. Dodero, M. Palomo-Duarte, P. Karampiperis (Eds.): MTSR 2012, CCIS 343, pp. 127–132, 2012.
© Springer-Verlag Berlin Heidelberg 2012

available in the UOC institutional repository. In order to do so, we propose to establish a conceptual model involving users, resources, additional services and their educational context. Once this initial model has been defined, a reputation scheme for both users and resources is outlined, in order to provide the basis for building a recommendation system and a service-oriented repository, taking into account user's needs and educational context.

This paper is structured as follows: Section 2 describes the main drawbacks of using digital repositories as the center of a community of learning due to their intrinsic nature. In Section 3 we propose the information architecture model involving users, resources and services. The basics of the reputation schemes and the recommendation system based on such proposal are presented in Section 4. Finally, the main results of this work are summarized in Section 5.

2   Learning Object Repositories

Digital repositories have been traditionally designed and implemented by librarians with the help of IT staff. Out-of-the-box solutions such as DSpace[3] have allowed educational institutions to build institutional repositories but from a top-down approach, without taking into account end-users' needs. Furthermore, using institutional repositories to store and share learning objects has some additional drawbacks. For instance, not all learning objects can be fully described using only author, title, publication date and some keywords. From a teacher's perspective, it is also important to contextualize every didactic resource according to the specific particularities of the teaching process. This suggests that learning objects need to be properly modeled from several related perspectives. In [8] different context categories for learning objects are identified, namely thematic context (which describes the learning objects content, i.e. domain information), pedagogical context (which deals with the knowledge and information about the teaching-learning processes where the learning objects are used), the learner context (which describes the characteristics of the students who are expected to use the learning objects), organizational context (which covers the structural composition and sequencing of learning objects) and the historical/statistical context (which captures information regarding the social patterns that are derived from the learning objects usage). The required metadata to capture all previous information mainly has, according to [10], an extrinsic nature, i.e. the values of the metadata characterizing context categories (except for the thematic context) change depending on the educational context where the learning objects are used. The problem is that available solutions to build institutional repositories mainly deal with intrinsic metadata, i.e. metadata whose values remain immutable (author and title are examples of intrinsic metadata) in all possible educational context of the learning objects. Specifically, this is the case of DSpace which uses Dublin Core as metadata schema for describing learning objects. One of the decisions made during the conceptualization of Dublin Core was precisely to avoid the definition of extrinsic metadata ([10]).

---

[3] DSpace: `http://www.dspace.org/`

3 A Model to Specify the Context of Learning Resources

As aforesaid, one of the main problems of learning object repositories is its lack of integration within the learning environment where they are used. In the context of learning, learning resources are used by human agents within a context (a subject, for instance) and for a given purpose (for giving support to an exercise, as a lecture, etc.). Relating learning resources to their learning context will facilitate the creation of services that use such contextual information to behave more intelligently. Some examples of such services may be recommendation systems or automatic evaluators. With this objective in mind, the conceptual schema in Figure 1 shows a possible contextualization of the learning domain where the learning resources are used. As can be seen in Figure 1, learning resources should be related to some concepts of the learning management system (LMS), which come from a package called LMS. Our proposal takes into account the offered curricula, the subjects each curriculum contains, the knowledge areas related to each subject, the human agents of the LMS and, in the case of learners, their enrolled and passed subjects.

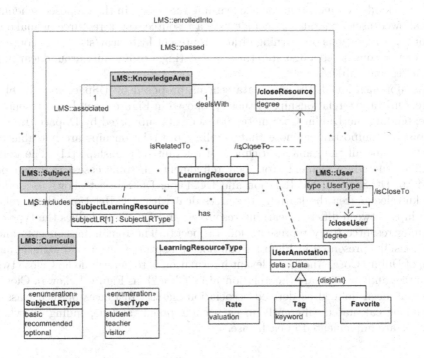

Fig. 1. Conceptualization of the learning resource context

The main element of the proposed conceptual schema is Learning Resource. This concept represents the learning resources contained in the repository. Each learning resource is related with the knowledge area it deals with, representing the thematic context of learning resources. Learning resources may also have a type, which can define their kind from a pedagogical point of view (exercise, lecture...) or their format (in this case, learning resources are described according to how they are perceived by users). In addition, learning objects can be related with other learning objects. Learning object relations are denoted in Figure 1 by means of the generic relationship *isRelatedTo*. Examples of learning object relations could be those proposed by Dublin Core and available in DSpace (e.g. *references*, *requires*, or *is version of*) as well as other relations, relevant from a pedagogical point of view (for example *exemplifies*, *deepens* or *summarizes*) that have been proposed by several authors ([3,4,5,11]). Both learning resource type characterization and relations between learning objects partially describe the pedagogical context of the learning resources. The pedagogical context of learning objects is complemented by adding the subjects where each learning object is used and through the inclusion of information that records whether the resource is mandatory, recommended or optional. This information will help to estimate the relevance of resources for each user in a given subject. On the other hand, the student context is described (at a minimum detail level) by means of the subjects that he or she has enrolled and passed. Finally, users can perform different kinds of annotations on the learning resources. In the proposed schema, the allowed user annotations include rate a resource, tag a resource or make it favorite. Annotations on learning objects represent historical/statistical context and can be considered a first step towards creating a community around learning resources and subjects.

As aforementioned, the metadata schema proposed by DSpace uses Dublin Core. Only a few relationships of those proposed in Figure 1 can be represented by extending the Dublin Core metadata elements supported by DSpace. In addition, it is important to note that Dublin Core relationships are not able to fully describe all the semantic richness of relevant relationships [11]. The non-qualified metadata elements (or their refinements in some cases) that can be used are DC.Subject, DC.Relation and DC.Type: DC Subject allows to model the knowledge area the learning resources deal with; DC.Relation relates relationships between different learning resources; and DC.Type defines the type of learning resource (only representational aspects). The remaining concepts and relationships presented in Figure 1 can not be captured given the intrinsic nature of Dublin Core. Another relevant information is to determine how close two resources and/or users are (i.e. relationship *isCloseTo* as Figure 1 shows). Closeness has been defined as derived association classes. Instances of such classes should be calculated differently in each environment and depending on what services are implemented in each case.

4   Recommendation System and Reputation Schemes

Currently now, digital repositories based on DSpace show the last five items published in the repository, which are supposed to be interesting for most users. Using the relationships aforementioned, we want to change such criterion (i.e. publication date) to other more appropriate in the context of a virtual learning environment, taking into account the activity of the community of learning. Once the proposed layer of additional services [7] will be running on top of the institutional repository, we will be able to gather the following data:

- With respect to resources: the number of times a resource has been visited, downloaded, rated (and the individual ratings given by registered users), favorited and tagged (and the individual tags).
- With respect to users: the number of resources she has downloaded, rated (and her ratings), favorited, tagged (and her tags).

With all this data we will be able to compute the following distance measures for both resources and users:

- For each resource R_i: a reputation scheme $F_R(R_i)$ used to rank resources according to their "popularity".
- For each pair of resources R_i, R_j: a distance function $d_R(R_i, R_j)$ used to find the "closest" resources.
- For each user U_i: a reputation scheme $F_U(U_i)$ used to rank users according to their "activity".
- For each pair of users U_i, U_j: a distance function $D_U(U_i, U_j)$ used to find the most "similar" users, i.e. those with the same interests.
- For each pair user/resource U_i, R_j: a distance function $D_{U,R}(U_i, R_j)$ used to find the most "relevant" resource for a given user. It can be also used to find the most "potential" users for a given resource.

The concepts of "popularity", "activity", etc. may then be tailored to the particular needs of the learning process, so learners are able to find and navigate through the most valuable resources taking into account all their needs as well as their context. For instance, at the beginning of the academic semester, some resources (i.e. preliminary readings) can be defined as more "popular" than others by just including such time concept in F_R.

5   Conclusions

In this paper we have conceptualized the relationships between users, resources and services in a digital repository, with the aim of better supporting the activities of searching and browsing learning resources, taking into account the educational context. With such proposal, the digital repository becomes more integrated into the learning process, and no longer is a mere space where thousands of resources can be found. Learners can find "close" resources according to their needs. We have also outlined the underlying reputation schemes for ranking users and resources, so the recommendation system will be able to provide users with the most tailored resources, according to their context.

Current and future work in this subject includes the development of the aforementioned services into the UOC institutional repository, gathering real usage data during one or more academic semesters. Data will be used to fine-tune both the recommendation system and the reputation schemes, the previous step before building a contextualized searching/browsing engine on top of the institutional repository giving support to the learning community.

Acknowledgements. This paper has been partially supported by Spanish Ministry of Science and Innovation funded Project MAVSEL (ref. TIN2010-21715-C02-02).

References

1. Caris, M.A.: Why don't faculty use learning object repositories? In: Cantoni, L., McLoughlin, C. (eds.) Proceedings of World Conference on Educational Multimedia, Hypermedia and Telecommunications, pp. 2838–2840. AACE, Lugano (2004), http://www.editlib.org/p/12413
2. Churchill, D., Wong, W., Law, N., Salter, D., Tai, B.: Social Bookmarking-Repository-Networking: Possibilities for Support of Teaching and Learning in Higher Education. Serials Review 35(3), 142–148 (2009)
3. Fischer, S.: Course and exercise sequencing using metadata in adaptive hypermedia learning systems. ACM Journal of Educational Resources in Computing 1(1) (2001)
4. Hamel, C.J., Ryan-Jones, D.: Towards a comprehensive learning object metadata: Incorporation of context to stipulate meaningful learning and enhance learning object reusability. International Journal of Educational Technology 3(1) (2002)
5. Lu, E.J.L., Hsieh, C.J.: A relation metadata extension for SCORM content aggregation model. Computer Standards & Interfaces 31, 1028–1035 (2009)
6. Margaryan, A., Littlejohn, A.: Repositories and communities at cross-purposes: issues in sharing and reuse of digital learning resources. Journal of Computer Assisted Learning 24(4), 333–347 (2008)
7. Minguillón, J., Rodríguez, M.E., Conesa, J.: Extending Learning Objects by Means of Social Networking. In: Luo, X., Spaniol, M., Wang, L., Li, Q., Nejdl, W., Zhang, W. (eds.) ICWL 2010. LNCS, vol. 6483, pp. 220–229. Springer, Heidelberg (2010)
8. Mohammed, P., Mohan, P.: Contextualizing learning objects using ontologies. Computational Intelligence 23(3), 339–355 (2007)
9. Monge, S., Ovelar, R., Azpeitia, I.: Repository 2.0: Social dynamics to support community building in learning object repositories. Social Dynamics 4, 191–204 (2008), http://www.ijello.org/Volume4/IJELLOv4p191-204Monge.pdf
10. Recker, M., Wiley, D.A.: A non-authoritative educational metadata ontology for filtering and recommending learning objects. Journal of interactive learning environments 9(3), 255–271 (2001)
11. Rodríguez, M.E., Conesa, J., Sicilia, M.A.: Clarifying the Semantics of Relationships between Learning Objects. In: Sartori, F., Sicilia, M.Á., Manouselis, N. (eds.) MTSR 2009. CCIS, vol. 46, pp. 35–47. Springer, Heidelberg (2009)
12. St Jean, B., Rieh, S.Y., Yakel, E., Markey, K.: Unheard Voices: Institutional Repository End-Users. College & Research Libraries 72(1), 21–42 (2011)

Towards a Semantic Segment of a Research e-Infrastructure: Necessary Information Objects, Tools and Services[*]

Sergey Parinov

Central Economics and Mathematics Institute of RAS, Moscow, Russia
sparinov@gmail.com

Abstract. Basically semantic linkage technique is used to specify in computer readable form known facts or relationships that definitely exist between information objects like people, organizations, research results, etc. Recently developers also started using it to visualize scientists' opinions or scientific hypotheses (e.g. inference/deduction, impact/usage, theoretical hierarchy, etc.) about relationships between research objects. Based on CERIF Link entity and the Semantic Layer and assuming that scientists typically re-use research objects by making relationships between them we propose a sketch of a research e-infrastructure semantic segment, which allow scientists unlimited re-use of research information systems (RIS) content. After some development a semantic linkage technique provides scientists with tools and services for semantic linking of any pair of research objects, which metadata are available within content of any RIS. This application also allows scientists a decentralized development of semantic vocabularies that guarantee a covering by this technique any new types of relationships. In the paper we discuss information objects, tools and services which are necessary for proper functioning of proposed segment of the research e-infrastructure. We also discuss a "quality control" topic which in this context is very important.

Keywords: research relationships, semantic linkages, research information system, semantic interoperability.

1 Introduction

Basically a semantic linkage technique is used to visualize known facts or obvious relationships that exist between information objects representing people, organizations, research results, scientific assertions, etc. At abstract level this technique is specified in RDF (http://www.w3.org/RDF/). It is also developed in CERIF as a specific data model with a focus on research (Jörg et al. 2012a, 2012b). Some examples of practical implementation of initial RDF Semantics specification

---

[*] The paper presents some results of a research project "A technology of decentralized interactive semantic structuring of electronic libraries contents" funded by Russian Fund of Basic Research, grant number 12-07-00518-A.

J.M. Dodero, M. Palomo-Duarte, P. Karampiperis (Eds.): MTSR 2012, CCIS 343, pp. 133–145, 2012.
© Springer-Verlag Berlin Heidelberg 2012

(http://www.w3.org/TR/2004/REC-rdf-mt-20040210/) can be found e.g. in Nano-publication approach (Groth et al. 2010). Implementation of the CERIF approach occurs in many projects; e.g. in the Semantic Linkages Open Repository (SLOR) project (Parinov 2012).

Information objects which might be semantically linked are produced by research information systems (RIS), which include a whole spectrum from Institutional Repositories (IR) to full-functional CRIS. We assume more or less homogeneous structure of information objects (e.g. CERIF compatible) and each of them has a unique identifier. We also assume that all information objects matched these requirements belong to research Data and Information Space (DIS) and we can operate with them in some standardized way.

For example, a fact that a person "A" works for organization "B" can be visualized by linking the information objects of the person and the organization existed in DIS. Person's current position "C" can be expressed as a semantic assigned to the linkage. Typically such semantic linkages are created by developers of RIS when they are designing data storage of the system. And current semantic linkage technique assumes that a linkage exists as some additional fields to metadata of one (or both) of linked objects. See examples at (Jörg et al. 2012c).

Recently appeared "nano-publication" approach (Groth et al. 2010) and "object-for-reuse" concept (Parinov 2010) demonstrate an advanced semantic linkage technique that allows a creation of semantic linkages also by scientists when they deposit their assertions/research artifacts at some repository (e.g. at ConceptWiki.org). Nanopub.org explains how scientists can create nano-publications: "Specific relations between entities ... can be thought of as specific scientific assertions. When converted to RDF, these assertions can be represented as a collection of semantic triples."[1]

In this paper we discuss the next step: how the semantic linkage technique should be developed to visualize not only scientific assertions but also professional opinions or scientific hypotheses about relationships between research objects. This approach is definitely demanded by the community since typically scientists produce not only texts (papers, articles, books, etc) but scientific relationships between existed research objects as well. And existed technique to visualize such relationships – e.g. a mechanism of citations – still is not upgraded to abilities of modern ICT.

Some new types of relationships between research outputs that scientists may want to express are: inference/deduction, impact/usage, theoretical hierarchy, and so on (Parinov 2012; Parinov and Kogalovsky 2011). In this case the semantic linkages can carry information that, e.g. a research output "D" is produced by a person "A" (in a role "author") and with a financial support of an organization "B" (in a role "funding") as the scientist's research result produced by a logical inference based on another research output "E". And at the same time, say, the research output "E" provides a broader theoretical concept then the "D".

In this example the first type of semantic relationships between "D" and "E" is the "scientific inference" with the meaning "used as a base", and the second type – the "theoretical hierarchy" with the value "broader".

---

[1] Nanopublication Guidelines v1.8, http://www.nanopub.org/guidelines/current

So now there are two cases of using semantic linkage technique: a) to visualize relationships between known facts and/or research assertions, and b) to visualize opinions and/or hypothesis. Important differences between "a" and "b":

(1) typically linkages are created: for "a" at the same time when linking information objects are created; but for "b" – when linking information objects already exist and available for scientists;

(2) a necessity to have for the case "b" something like a scientific journal's per-reviewing to provide a "quality control" over publishing semantic linkages.

The main objective of this paper is to propose an approach which responds on:

- what information objects, tools and services are needed to give scientists a simple and reliable way to visualize their opinions and hypothesis about relationships between information objects over all available content of RIS; and
- what tools and services are necessary for the scientific community to provide some kind of "quality control" over individual opinions/hypothesis and to keep the right balance of a freedom for scientific opinions/hypnotizes clashing and a respect of scientific ethic and norms.

Proposed in this paper approach should works as a universal solution covers the both cases of using semantic linkage technique. A set of tools implemented this technique has be supplemented by some services which allow scientific community to provide some quality control over published semantic linkages. Altogether these tools and services are forming a semantic segment of a research e-infrastructure.

In the next section we discuss a concept of the semantic linkage technique development according requirements listed above.

A revision of a set and templates of information objects is necessary for proper representation of new research relationship types. We propose two interrelated types of semantic objects: (1) a semantic linkage and (2) a semantic meaning. In the section "Information Objects" we discuss its templates based on CERIF and other relevant topics.

In the section "Tools and Services" we give a description of necessary instruments. One part of the instruments must be designed inside local RIS environment, and another one - outside it. This second part of tools and services can be called as a semantic segment of research e-infrastructure.

Technical realization of discussed tools, services and the whole concept are currently implemented as a part of the Socionet system (socionet.ru). But a discussion of the realization topics comes outside of this paper.

At the conclusion we summarize benefits of the proposed application.

2   A Concept of the Semantic Linkage Technique Development

When semantic linkages are carrying not only known facts but also hypotheses expressed as a personal opinion of some scientists the implementation of this technique becomes more complex. E.g. in the mentioned above example of relationships between "D" and "E" the specified semantic values have a sense if only the linkages are oriented and the orientation is: for the first - "D" -> "E"; for the second - "E" -> "D".

According our objective the semantic linkage technique has to satisfy following important requirements:

- linkages with assigned semantic meaning should be created not only by RIS developers, but also directly by scientists or their assistants with explicit indication of who is an author of the linkage and responsible for semantically expressed professional opinions or scientific hypothesis;
- a technique of semantic linkages should work at standalone mode, i.e. independently of linked objects metadata, since in many cases the semantic linkage's attributes cannot be directly included into linked objects metadata;
- semantic linkages should be deposited by their authors into DIS as a public information resource;
- since linkages are created in decentralized mode there should exist a submission procedure, which implies a moderation and validation of semantic linkages by the community before they will be publically available;
- since a set of relationship types used for semantic linkage creation cannot be completely predefined, there should exist an ability for scientists and developers to expand in some controlled way semantic vocabularies associated with types of relationship;
- the scientific community should be able to make selection by quality, impact evaluation and multiple re-use over all created semantic linkages.

Ideally any scientist should be able to establish any number of consistent and relevant research relationships in visual and computer readable form between a pair of any available research objects. And any scientist should have an opportunity to propose new types of research relationships for covering by this technique.

But at the same time the scientific community should have some kind of quality control over new semantic linkages and new types of relationships submitted by scientists for a public use. And the community should be able to evaluate impact of submitted semantic objects and re-use it in multiple forms.

Technically it means that scientists should have a personalized tool to create/manage the semantic linkages and, as well, vocabularies of semantic meanings. Such personalized tool can be a part of a Content Management System (CMS), which exist in many RIS, including repositories.

A scientist can use a CMS of some local RIS "A" for creation semantic linkages only. It means the linking objects belong, e.g. to RIS "B" and "C". In this case the linkage's attributes created by the scientist in RIS "A" cannot be directly embedded into metadata of linking objects, as it is proposed e.g. in CERIF 1.4 (Jörg et al. 2012c), because owners of the metadata are RIS "B" and "C".

To be universal the semantic linkage technique should produce linkages having a status of regular DIS information objects and so they should exist separately from the metadata of linked information objects. In such situation we have to specify a new data type "semantic linkage" and design its template which can be used by CMS of local RIS to create semantic linkages as autonomous objects.

All semantic linkages created in any RIS by this decentralized way should have unique identifiers. In the Section 4.3 we discuss how to perform this requirement.

Each semantic linkage has as an attribute a semantic meaning that belongs to some semantic vocabulary. A set of research relationship types is open for decentralized extension and development by scientists. So we should have a template to create semantic vocabulary as a collection of standardized objects of the "semantic meaning" data type, which also can be done by using CMS of local RIS.

Initial set of rendered scientific relationships built from different already existed ontologies (Parinov 2012; Parinov and Kogalovsky 2011) includes: (1) relationships between various research outputs like inference, usage, impact, comparison, etc; (2) relationships between elements of the set {scientists, organizations}; (3) relationships between research outputs on the one hand and elements of the set {scientists, organizations} on the other.

A flow of semantic linkages and/or semantic vocabularies submitted by scientists for a public use is moderated as it is typically organized for the process of research papers depositing and self-archiving.

For better utilization of created linkages and its multiple re-uses by the community all semantic objects (linkages and vocabularies) created at local RIS are aggregated at some central data storage. In more details it is discussed in the Section 4.3.

To perform necessary utilization and re-use of accumulated at the central data storage semantic objects we have to design some basic services, which is forming a research e-infrastructure semantic segment:

1. An aggregation, storage and sharing of semantic linkages and semantic vocabularies at the central data storage;
2. Maintaining of requests from local RIS to the central data storage about (a) existed ingoing and outgoing semantic linkages for specified information object and (b) available semantic vocabularies and updates of its content;
3. Interpretation of semantics, which in the general case are necessary for visualization of linkages at central data storage as multilayer networks of scientific relationships different types;
4. Navigation and searching over the objects of both types at the central data storage;
5. Monitoring service, which is tracing changes in linked objects and linkages itself. It runs a notification service and collects statistics.;
6. Notifications for authors of linked objects, for authors of linkages, for readers of linked objects;
7. Scientometrics to collect quantitative data (e.g. numbers of linkages) and qualitative data about relationship types and semantic meanings.

These listed services give the community some additional capabilities that can be characterized as better "information metabolism". It is discussed in more details in the section "Tools and services".

3   Information Objects

In this section we discuss templates of two important data types of information objects: (1) a semantic linkage and (2) a semantic meaning. A semantic linkage includes a semantic meaning as an attribute, to characterize a type of relationship between linked information objects.

To make this discussion compact we use by default CERIF terminology and specifications wherever possible, primarily the Link Entity and the Semantic Layer (Jörg et al. 2012a, 2012b).

We assume that templates proposed in this section should be implemented at local RIS: 1) to create standardized objects of both types which can be easily re-used outside local RIS; and 2) to harvest in proper way standardized semantic vocabularies from other local RIS or from the central data storage and to use it within a tool to create/edit semantic linkages.

Since we have to operate with created semantic linkages as regular information objects of DIS, which should be convenient for storing and processing, displaying for navigation across all linkages and/or across linked objects, delivering, harvesting, indexing for searching by keywords, and so on, in some cases we have to expand the initial CERIF notation of the both semantic objects. This extension of initial CERIF set of fields can look as redundancy, but it is justified in our practical implementation of this concept.

3.1   Semantic Linkage

As an initial model of information objects with the "semantic linkage" type we took the specification of CERIF Link Entity (Jörg et al. 2012a, p. 33; Jörg et al. 2012b, p. 13).

To make the semantic linkage template self-contained we add to the initial set of fields:

- more data about pair of linked objects, including clear specification of the linkage orientation (which object is a source the target one), unique IDs of linked objects, its data types and titles;
- ID and a name of selected semantic meaning and also URI and a name of parent semantic vocabulary;
- a field for comments that allows scientists to provide explanations and comments about specified semantic linkage parameters;
- a group of fields with personal, organizational data about an author of the semantic linkage and about a provider of the service;
- a title and unique ID of the linkage itself, creation and revision dates and other extra attributes if necessary.

Personal data about the linkage's creator including his/her e-mail address is used to notify the creator about a need to revise the linkage's correctness because of changes in linked objects.

A title of the semantic linkage is needed to build a table of contents and for navigation across the whole set of created semantic linkages.

We assume that semantic linkage parameters are changeable and, in principle, have a status similar to electronic publication. So it explains why we require a revision date.

More details about semantic linkage specification can be found in (Parinov 2012; Parinov and Kogalovsky 2011).

In CERIF: "... *the inherited identifiers and the date attributes build the primary key of link entities*" (Jörg et al. 2012a, p. 33). In our application this model of primary key building will not guarantee the unique identification of semantic linkages. For the same pair of objects scientists can create at the same time many semantic linkages with different authorship and/or with different types of relationship (take semantic meaning from different semantic vocabularies).

To have uniqueness of identifiers we propose to use the RePEc model of building object's ID (it is called here "Handle"). RePEc model is very useful when objects are created in decentralized mode by many people: "*The Handle: field content starts with the name of the authority (organization), for example* RePEc. *The next element is the code of the archive, then follows the code of the series and finally the number of the paper within the series. All these parts are separated by the colon character, i.e. :. Note that this field may not contain whitespace.*" (Krichel 1997).

According this model the ID of a semantic linkage looks as a text string merged of 4 domains: "orgunit_code:archive_code:collection_code:object_code".

Additionally in RePEc for three domains "orgunit_code", "archive_code", and "collection_code" exist a template, which provides information about creators, editors, etc. It is a convenient way to specify complex dependences between involved in this activity organizations, people and resources.

3.2   Semantic Meaning

According CERIF the Semantic Layer - "*supplies the means for maintaining the CERIF Semantics: types, roles, terminology, subject classifiers, or mappings. It stores the semantic values that are carried by or referred to from the link entities via the cfClassSchemId attribute references, and it assigns each semantic value to a particular classification scheme.*" (Jörg et al. 2012a, p. 33).

In our application an information object with the type "semantic meaning" exactly corresponds to cfClass. As well, a semantic vocabulary as a collection of semantic meanings representing different aspects of a specific type of research relationships corresponds with cfClassScheme. (Jörg et al. 2012b, p. 14; Jörg et al. 2012a, p. 37)

Information objects of this data type and a whole semantic vocabulary are created in our application by scientists or developers in decentralized mode. So all created objects of this type have to include a group of fields with "Authorship", which should be exactly the same as it described above for the semantic linkage data type.

And we also use RePEc model (Krichel 1997) to build ID of information objects instead of proposed in CERIF UUID model (Jörg et al. 2012a, p. 13 footnote).

4   Tools and Services

In this section we discuss two main groups of tools and services divided by its allocation: inside local RIS and outside it in a semantic segment of a research e-infrastructure.

Following tools and services are working inside of local RIS: 1) a creation, editing and managing of both types of objects and their collections; 2) a submission of created objects to make them publicly available and moderation of submitted objects; 3) an output gateway to serve requests from an aggregator of central data storage; 4) API to send requests to the central data storage to get back existed ingoing and outgoing semantic linkages for specified information objects of local RIS; 5) API to synchronize a local set of semantic vocabularies with it current content at central data storage.

Outside of local RIS should work following services: 1) an aggregator to synchronize central data sets of semantic objects with content of local RIS-provides; 2) an output gateway to give away specified objects and/or any part of central data storage on requests from local RIS; 3) a navigation and searching tools over full content of central data storage; 4) a semantic interpretation service to build proper visualization for multilayer networks of relationships; 5) a monitoring service to trace changes in the central data sets and linked objects to build data for a notification service; 6) e-mail notifications for author of linkages and linked objects; 7) a statistic service to process central data sets and build various scientometric indicators.

4.1   RIS Tools and Services to Deposit Semantic Objects

If RIS has functionality for scientists to deposit electronic publications, the same can be used for semantic objects. Typically CMS, as a tool for depositing papers at local RIS, can be configured to use additional templates for creating new types of information objects. The templates discussed above in the section "Information objects" can be used by this way.

The deposited semantic objects will be available for public utilization only if it passed through some usual quality control routine. Collections of these objects after moderation should be available at the RIS output gateway for harvesting by a central aggregation service using one of popular protocols, e.g. OAI-PMH (OAI-PMH 2008).

Only after a RIS manager will register the output gateway at some open list of providers (see the next section) and this information passed validation, the central aggregator starts everyday synchronization of the source with the central data storage.

4.2   A Registry of Semantic Objects Collections

A registry of semantic objects collections is an open catalogue of output gateways provided open access to collections of semantic linkages and semantic vocabularies. The registry can be organized by the same way as e.g. the Registry of Open Access Repositories (ROAR, http://roar.eprinst.org/). A provider of semantic objects collections (typically it is a research organization) fills in at the register an online form with parameters of the output gateways (gateway's description, URL and its protocols). This information is validated by the central data storage manager and if positive it is used by the central aggregation service to regularly synchronize a content of this provider at central data storage with its sources at local RIS.

Each semantic objects provider receives at the registry a unique ID, which can be used to build unique identifiers for all semantic objects harvested to the central data storage.

4.3   Aggregation of Semantic Objects at Central Data Storage

An aggregation service of the central data storage collects at one dataset all semantic linkages from diverse output gateways registered at the registry of semantic objects collections. Semantic vocabularies are also aggregated and stored at the central data storage to be available for using them by RIS tools for semantic linkages creation.

The central aggregator takes data from output gateways using all the most popular protocols. At least it should work as OAI-PMH harvester. Collections of semantic objects of both types at central data storage should be regularly (everyday) synchronized with its local sources.

For a situation when semantic objects IDs become not unique inside the central data storage, the provider's unique ID at the registry can be used to correct objects' ID. This correction can be made on a "fly" when semantic objects are recorded into the storage.

Central data storage also has an output gateway for giving away requested data using all popular protocols (at least OAI-PMH).

Altogether it should work just as a simple information hub. And so the central data storage has no special requirements for an authority, security, privacy and other non-functional properties.

Since in general any central data storage can be a bottleneck in a functioning system we suppose that this problem will be solved by mirroring or replication of its content, e.g. as it was implemented in RePEc system (repec.org).

4.4   Data Sharing and Embedded Software

Any local RIS is able to check presence at the central data storage already existed linkages for the local information objects. If positive, the linkages' data is transferred from the central data storage to the RIS. By this way the local RIS can visualize a network of linkages composed of articles and other information objects belong to this RIS.

Proposed application will provide some API for using within local RIS. This additional software can be integrated into RIS: (1) to visualize already accumulated at the central data storage outgoing/ingoing semantic linkages for information objects of local RIS when a user is browsing over them; and 2) to update/synchronize local set of semantic vocabularies with it current content at the central data storage.

4.5   Interpretation, Visualization and Utilization

As an end-user interface to the central data storage we propose a service of semantic meanings interpretation. It can make a specific rearranging and visualizing of linked information objects by processing of its semantic. For example, information objects connected by semantic linkages with a meaning "components of a scientific composition" can be visualized as a networked document, or as a collection of scientific artifacts, or a table of contents.

This interpretation service provides data for specific visualization of multilayer networks of various types of relationships over integrated content of research DIS.

Additionally the central data storage should have a typical navigation and searching tools over full content accumulated semantic objects.

4.6   Monitoring of Changes and Notifications of Users

Semantic linkages between a pair of research objects (e.g. between two articles) may lose their consistency if one or both of linked objects are revised by their authors. E.g. a meaning of the text fragment cited by a semantic linkage may be changed by an author of linked article, or this text fragment may disappear or move to another part of the linked article. In all such cases the author of the article that cited changeable text fragments must be informed to make reconsideration of related semantic linkages.

Scientists also can change already established semantic linkages, including: (a) a complete deletion of a linkage; (b) a redirecting of the linkage on another target object, since the new target object is better, e.g. it gives better illustration or evidence for a scientist's research output; (c) a changing of the current semantic meaning since the scientist changed his/her opinion on it.

The monitoring service has to register all such events. It stores necessary data to provide it for other services (a notification and scientometic services).

Initially designed monitoring service is processing only a flow of current changes in semantic linkages. But it can be developed to record a history of the evolution of thinking about the hypothetical relationship between DIS information objects. In this case the service also should store all previous states of semantic linkages.

A notification service uses data about changes in semantic linkages generated by the monitoring. Different types of notifications produced by this service support a scientific circulation/communication by distributing signals about semantic linkages creation/revision. To keep consistence of research DIS this service should notify:

1. the authors of objects linked by created or revised semantic linkage, just to inform them about this event, let them know about specified semantic and give them an ability to react on this event (e.g. to protest against specified semantic);
2. the author who is changing his/her object (e.g. article), if the object has linked (cited) in other objects (articles), that by this action she/he can violate have established linkages and/or its semantic;
3. the authors of semantic linkages, if there were changes in objects specified as a source and a target of the linkages, so they should reconsider their linkages and, if it necessary, correct it;
4. the users of research DIS while they are viewing some DIS object (e.g. the readers of electronic articles) that certain semantic linkages made for the displaying source object (e.g. citations in reading text) can be violated because of the target object (e.g. cited articles) was changed, and an author of the linkages has not updated suspicious linkages (e.g. citations).

If the first three types of notifications in the list above can be made by e-mail only, the last one should work as warning, that displayed on the screen when it necessary.

Thus the notification service improves scientific circulation because it immediately informs scientists about using their research outputs. And it improves research communication because authors of semantic linkages can receive a feedback on their actions from authors of linked research objects.

4.7   Collecting Statistics and Producing Scientometrics

Traditional statistical representations of changes in DIS scope and structure are well known and have had examples of good implementations (e.g. LogEc, MESUR, Socionet Stats, and other). If scientists start an intensive building of semantic linkage multilayer networks over research DIS objects it opens a new space for statistics development.

The monitoring service associated with the central data storage collects all available statistics about semantic linkages. It allows us to form a scientometric database both quantitative (number of linkages, etc.) and qualitative (semantic meanings) characteristics of scientific relationships.

Quantitative data about all accumulated semantic linkages at the central data storage includes different types of its structuring and aggregation. E.g. numbers of linkages (total and by types of scientific relationships) for selected objects, aggregated numbers of linkages for all objects of one author (total, by relationship types, by values of semantic vocabularies, etc.), and many others.

Qualitative data about relationship types accumulated at the central data storage is structured by semantic vocabularies (layers of semantic network) and then by meanings (a distribution by types). It also includes graphs of linkages with semantic meanings assigned to each edge of the graph, and so on.

This new scientometric data will give the community useful additional information for better research assessment of individual scientists and research organizations as well.

Some additional statistics about accumulated semantic linkages can be also produced by adopting to this specific case the well-known PageRank (Google page rank) algorithm.

5   Conclusion

Proposed application of the enhanced semantic linkage technique provides to the scientific community obviously benefits. It is a new type of semantic interoperability: any scientists can "interact" with any available information object of research DIS by expressing in computer readable form his/her opinion on research relationships and so re-use DIS content in some new forms. In fact, it gives scientists a new dimension for personal scientific creativity. For the community it gives better visualization of research outputs usage, improves scientific life-cycle and research communication, and supports measurements and assessment of research activity.

On one side, new tools implemented semantic linkage technique give scientists a freedom to express their professional opinions and research hypotheses. On the other side, a set of services from semantic segment of research e-infrastructure provides the scientific community with some new abilities.

The community is immediately notified about all new opinions/hypothesis expressed by individual scientist. The community can react on individual activities by expressing opinions on its correctness (from positive to negative, including a blocking). Each individual activity gets publicly available statistical portrait which accumulates both: (1) data about linkages and expressed opinions/hypotheses made by a scientist, and (2) data about reactions made by the community on activities of the scientist.

As a unified system it gives the community an ability to select opinions/hypothesis (semantic linkages) by their quality, to evaluate its impact and to re-use it in multiple forms.

References

1. Jörg, B., Jeffery, K.G., Dvorak, J., Houssos, N., Asserson, A., van Grootel, G., Gartner, R., Cox, M., Rasmussen, H., Vestdam, T., Strijbosch, L., Clements, A., Brasse, V., Zendulko-va, D., Höllrigl, T., Valkovic, L., Engfer, A., Jägerhorn, M., Mahey, M., Brennan, N., Sicilia, M.-A., Ruiz-Rube, I., Baker, D., Evans, K., Price, A., Zielinski, M.: CERIF 1.3 Full Data Model (FDM): Introduction and Specification. euroCRIS (2012a),
   `http://www.eurocris.org/Uploads/Web%20pages/`
   `CERIF-1.3/Specifications/CERIF1.3_FDM.pdf`
2. Jörg, B., Dvořák, J., Vestdam, T., van Grootel, G., Jeffery, K.G., Clements, A.: CERIF – 1.3 XML: Data Exchange Format Specification. euroCRIS (2012b),
   `http://www.eurocris.org/Uploads/Web%20pages/`
   `CERIF-1.3/Specifications/CERIF1.3_XML.pdf`
3. CERIF 1.3 Semantics: Research Vocabulary. CERIF Task Group, euroCRIS (2012),
   `http://www.eurocris.org/Uploads/Web%20pages/`
   `CERIF-1.3/Specifications/CERIF1.3_Semantics.pdf`
4. CERIF 1.3 Vocabulary. CERIF Task Group, euroCRIS (2012),
   `http://www.eurocris.org/Uploads/Web%20pages/`
   `CERIF-1.3/Semantics/CERIF1.3_Vocabulary.xls`
5. Groth, P., Gibson, A., Velterop, J.: The Anatomy of a Nano-publication. Information Services and Use 30(1/2) (2010),
   `http://iospress.metapress.com/content/ftkh21q50t521wm2/`
6. Parinov, S.: The electronic library: using technology to measure and support Open Science. In: Proceedings of the World Library and Information Congress: 76th IFLA General Conference and Assembly, Gothenburg, Sweden, August 10-15 (2010),
   `http://www.ifla.org/files/hq/papers/ifla76/`
   `155-parinov-en.pdf`
7. Parinov, S.: Open Repository of Semantic Linkages. In: Proceedings of 11th International Conference on Current Research Information Systems e-Infrastructure for Research and Innovations (CRIS 2012), Prague (2012),
   `http://socionet.ru/publication.xml?h=repec:rus:mqijxk:29`

8. Parinov, S., Kogalovsky, M.: A technology for semantic structuring of scientific digital library content. In: Proc. of the XIIIth All-Russian Scientific Conference RCDL 2011. Digital Libraries: Advanced Methods and Technologies, Digital Collections, October 19-22, pp. 94–103. Voronezh State University (2011) (in Russian),
    http://socionet.ru/publication.xml?h=repec:rus:mqijxk:28
9. Jorg, B., Dvorak, J., Vestdam, T.: Streamlining the CERIF XML Data Exchange Formats Towards CERIF 2.0. In: Proceedings of 11th International Conference on Current Research Information Systems "e-Infrastructure for Research and Innovations" (CRIS 2012), Prague, pp. 6–9 (2012c)
10. Krichel, T.: ReDIF version 1, working paper (1997),
    http://socionet.ru/publication.xml?h=repec:rpc:rdfdoc:redif
11. OAI-PMH: The Open Archives Initiative Protocol for Metadata Harvesting (2008),
    http://www.openarchives.org/OAI/openarchivesprotocol.html
12. LogEc - Access Statistics for Participating RePEc Services,
    http://logec.repec.org/
13. MESUR: MEtrics from Scholarly Usage of Resources,
    http://www.mesur.org/MESUR.html
14. Socionet Stats (in Russian), http://www.socionet.ru/stats.xml

Integrating Scholarly Publications and Research Data – Preparing for Open Science, a Case Study from High-Energy Physics with Special Emphasis on (Meta)data Models

Piotr Praczyk[1,2], Javier Nogueras-Iso[2],
Suenje Dallmeier-Tiessen[1], and Mike Whalley[3]

[1] CERN, Geneva, Switzerland
[2] Computer Science and Systems Engineering Dept.,Universidad de Zaragoza, Spain
[3] IPPP, Durham University, UK

Abstract. There is an emerging need in the research communitiy to have access to the research material beyond a publication. In an ideal scenario, scientists should have access to more than the full text: data, code, documentation and any other research output. We present here a case-study of our approach to facilitate seamless access to more than "just the paper" by integrating two complementary, heavily used, systems: Inspire and HEPData. On the one hand, Inspire, a digital library of High-Energy Physics, allows access to metadata about publications and full-text documents. On the other hand, the HEPData project has concentrated on gathering datasets behind figures and tables. We allow both systems to take advantage of a sum of their data and present a new infrastructure in Inspire making datasets equally important as publications. We also present mechanisms allowing long-term preservation of datasets and their unique identification, being an important step towards the open linked data in Inspire.

1 Introduction

Across disciplines there is a growing demand for access to scholarly materials beyond the traditional text publication [6] [4]. Such materials comprise research datasets, code, documentation, slides etc. The demand is not only triggered by the communities themselves, but also by policymakers and society as a whole who demand better preservation and access to publicly funded research. By providing access beyond the text publication, reuse of materials should be facilitated and research integrity should be secured on the long-term [1]. This is not a new demand, but has accelerated in the recent past, e.g. with the latest statement by the European Commission[1].

With the pervasiveness of the Internet, new technologies are at hand to provide seamless access to such materials and to integrate these better into digital libraries and repositories workflow and scholarly communication[2]. This facilitates

---

[1] http://europa.eu/rapid/pressReleasesAction.do?reference=IP/12/790

[2] http://oa.mpg.de/lang/en-uk/berlin-prozess/berliner-erklarung/

J.M. Dodero, M. Palomo-Duarte, P. Karampiperis (Eds.): MTSR 2012, CCIS 343, pp. 146–157, 2012.

not only the strategic preservation of such materials, but in particular enhances the discoverability for the researchers facilitiating easier reuse and reinterpretation of the existing content. This paper presents a case study from High-Energy Physics discipline. In order to provide a seamless access to the materials beyond the publications, a data repository is integrated into a large-scale digital library and its workflow and services. This paper studies the implementation and showcases which challenges needed to be overcome. In particular, an emphasis will be given to the new data preservation workflows that have been integrated alongside, such as persistent identification of objects via DOI registration. Finally, the lessons learnt from this case study will be highlighted. These could be of use for other disciplines which face similar challenges.

This case study uses Inspire, a large-scale digital library containing over a million records out of which 500,000 documents are available in Open Access. The userbase of Inspire consists of 50,000 researchers in High Energy Physics. The Inspire project arose as a collaboration of SPIRES database, created since 1970 at Stanford Linear Accelerator Center (SLAC), containing manually curated high quality records and the Invenio software platform of a digital library repository [2], developed at CERN. Invenio is a much more modern software platform supporting data exchange using the OAI-PMH[9][10] protocol and providing much wider search capabilities and higher performance than SPIRES software. The latest developments of Inspire concentrate on the creation of intelligent content-aware tools allowing automatic keywording of records, disambiguation of authors having similar names or storage and search of figures. Inspire aims at becoming a next generation digital library integrating publications and the data used during their creation. Integrating HEPData with Inspire is the first step towards providing a unified way of storing datasets.

The research datasets that are to be integrated in Inspire have been collected over 25 years as a part of the HEPData Project[3] funded by the STFC (UK Science and Technology Facilities Council). HEPData compiles and makes easily accessible a comprehensive and up-to-date database of the HEP experimental scattering data – total and differential cross sections, fragmentation functions, structure functions and polarisation spin measurements from a wide range of particle physics interactions at the colliders and the fixed target facilities worldwide. As well as a general user searchable interface to the database, HEPData also provides a variety of 'data reviews' providing indexed data on a variety of topics. Most of datasets hosted by HEPData are related to figures or tables present in the publications.

Thanks to the HEPData project, physicists specialising in HEP have access to a database of datasets, which has been manually curated by a thorough review of scholarly publications over the years. HEPData has been a standalone system, only being linked from external services like SPIRES. These links were being updated manually by the persons maintaining HEPData, which was a time consuming process leading to a higher possibility of producing errors. The body of data stored in HEPData consists of over 50.000 datasets coming from tables and

---

[3] http://www.ippp.dur.ac.uk/Research/Projects/HEPDATA.html

figures and also includes additional datasets provided by the authors. INSPIRE aims at providing seamless access to the main scholarly artifacts in HEP. Thus, the content of HEPData shall be made accessible via the INSPIRE services as well.

This paper describes the process of integration as a case study. It is structured as follows. Section 2 presents existing approaches to data integration in digital libraries. Section 3 describes the usage of the INVENIO storage model to give support for data and the workflow followed to migrate the HEP data from the Durham servers to Inspire. Then, section 4 presents how Inspire will provide access to this new functionality to access HEP data and which are the new possibilities open by this approach. Finally, this paper ends with some conclusions and outlook for future work.

2   State of the Art

There already exist several approaches to integrating data in a digital library. In this section we present several remarkable examples of digital libraries designed to also provide access to the data. In the case of Inspire and HEPData, we had to design a solution working on top of two existing systems and as such, it differs from existing approaches.

The OECD iLibrary[4] has already implemented a setup similar to ours. They have designed a digital library, in which tables and datasets are represented by individual records. Datasets are considered important and independent contributions, similar to a text publication. Records in the OECD library are also assigned persistent identifiers (DOI) and are displayed with a citation recommendation.

Several data repositories have started with enhanced preservation services for the respective user communities. UK Data Archive[5] hosts databases and corresponding services in order to enhance data preservation and access in the domain of Humanities and Social Sciences. They also use persistent identification, DOI, to reference and cite datasets. Dryad [5] is a data repository for biosciences.

DataStaR [3] is an experimental digital library developed at the Cornell university, providing users with access to datasets and allowing them to share their own results. It is also an open-source platform allowing to run a similar repository.

In the domain of geosciences, the data repository Pangaea [8] uses persistent identification for datasets and also for data collections. The users can cite the datasets with a DOI. This data repository has been working on an enhanced collaboration with publishers to facilitate data discovery beyond the data repository, so that datasets which are supplements to publications on the journal platform can be accessed by following the respective link on the publishers platform.

---

[4] http://www.oecd-ilibrary.org/
[5] http://www.data-archive.ac.uk/

3   Establishing the Interoperability between Systems

3.1   Architecture of the Integration

There exist several requirements lying at the foundation of the interoperability of Inspire and HEPData. Inspire aims at being a complete information resource for HEP and wants to provide unique identifiers of data, allowing it to be cited. HEPData provided only limited searching capabilities which could not be extended without having more extensive metadata about not only datasets but also publications.

We did not want to make one system completely replace the functionality of the other. Instead, we decided to establish a synchronisation process allowing both systems to use the same resources. At the same time we did not want to increase the amount of manual actions necessary on any of the sides to increase and we wanted to keep strict separation of responsibilities in the same state as before the integration. This means that metadata describing datasets was to be curated by the HEPData team and the metadata about publications by the Inspire team.

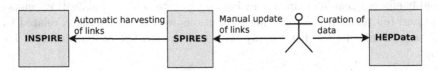

Fig. 1. Interaction between HEPData and SPIRES/Inspire before the integration

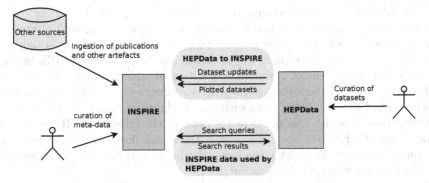

Fig. 2. Relations between the two integrated systems

This approach required us to address challenges related to maintaining both systems up to date after the data has changed in one of them. We also had to establish data exchange methods allowing to transfer datasets between Inspire and HEPData. Before the integration, there was no automatic communication between systems. Links to datasets were manually curated inside SPIRES (and subsequently, after replacing SPIRES, integrated in Inspire). The situation before the integration is depicted in Figure 1 while Figure 2 depicts interactions between Inspire and HEPData after being integrated.

The amount and the nature of information transfered in both directions is not symmetrical. We have decided to store a complete content of HEPData on the side of Inspire, which allowed us to integrate metadata in the internal search engine and by this, extend the capabilities of searching for the datasets. Having a complete copy of the data allowed us also to assign data identifiers in a persistent way. Keeping the data and publications at a single location will in the future simplify the analysis of users behaviour, which in turn can lead to the improvement of the quality of service. In addition, Inspire is under an active development which makes integration of the data inside of it easier. An alternative would be to extend HEPData with APIs allowing to manipulate and access data and making Inspire capable of using these. Such a process would be much more complicated and resource consuming.

Inspire data is not stored on the HEPData side. Instead, we have decided to exploit the Inspire search engine every time HEPData service wants to query the Inspire dataset. This has been dictated by the fact that Inspire implements a highly efficient search engine operating on separate fields of publications metadata and full text. In the following subsections we discuss decisions related to exchange of information between systems and the storage of figures inside Inspire.

3.2   The Ingestion of HEPData into Inspire

At the moment of writing, after almost 40 years of existence, the number of publications having data attached to them is close to 7000 and the rate of increase is expected to be constant because all the datasets are processed manually before being made publically available. Retrieving and processing such a number of records can be performed very quickly using modern computers, so scalability was not an issue when designing the integration of Inspire with HEPData. We have decided to implement a simplistic solution in which we always harvest a complete set of HEPData entries. In order to achieve this model of interoperability, we had to extend HEPData with the capability of exporting the list of all present datasets, which was not possible prior to the integration. If the size or growth rate of HEPData was much larger, the scalability could be achieved by designing more complicated mechanisms allowing to retrieve only data changes applied after previous synchronisation.

During the development of the integration of both systems, we have extended HEPData to store Inspire identifiers of the publications in connection with the data records. This extension has allowed HEPData users to address its content using INSPIRE identifiers as parts of the URLs. When Inspire needs to retrieve HEPData related to a particular publication record, it uses the Inspire record number to build the URL of the HEPData system representing all the data attached to a single publication. The document stored under the URL is retrieved and its content parsed to extract the described data. Harvesting of the data could have been done using a dedicated protocol similar to OAI-PMH [9][10], which is fully implemented in Invenio. However, we decided to use a much more simplistic approach by parsing the original HTML page and retrieving data from its content.

After retrieving data corresponding to every relevant Inspire record, we perform a more sophisticated merging only at the level of separate publications. Datasets retrieved from HEPData are matched with corresponding data stored in Inspire. This is done based on the content because HEPData does not have any knowledge of internal Inspire identifiers of separate datasets. We detect which datasets have changed, which have remained the same, and which have been added or removed. These changes are used to generate a minimal patch that has to be applied to existing records.

3.3   Storage of HEPData in Inspire

Artefacts managed by Inspire belong to different categories, including publications and figures. These artefacts need to be searchable and to have metadata records created for each of them.

Different auxiliary entities (like documents containing the content of publication or relations between these documents) are stored in dedicated data structures. A full model of the data managed by Inspire can be seen in Figure 3. The metadata is described in the MARC[6] format, while additional metadata which does not need to be displayed is encoded in MoreInfo structures, which are easier to process and more flexible with respect to the types of the stored data.

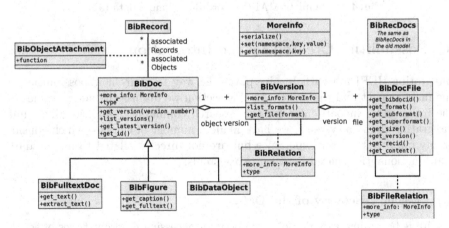

Fig. 3. Different entities in Inspire, allowing to store data outside of MARC

In order to make HEPData an integral part of the Inspire content, harvested datasets are transformed into records stored in a MARC format similar to the one

---

[6] https://twiki.cern.ch/twiki/bin/view/Inspire/DevelopmentRecordMarkup

used for regular publications, encoded with the format depicted in Figure 5. A separate MARC record is created for every data table extracted from a HEPData system and is linked to the record of the main publication using the 786 MARC field. All records describing datasets are added to a new Inspire records collection called DATA. An example of a Full MARC record describing a HEPData dataset can be seen in Figure 4.

MARC is a standard for describing metadata rather than the data itself. In the records corresponding to data tables we store only bits of information which can be considered metadata. This includes the global textual description of the dataset, headers and titles of data columns, descriptors of data and location of data inside the original publication.

The main corpus of data, with few exceptions, consists of a series of numbers that should be displayed inside a table. HEPData faciliates the reuse of the data by allowing the download in several popular formats in addition to displaying them a web-page content. The harvesting script downloads only one format ("plain text") and allows to retrieve it directly from Inspire. Rather than storing data inside a MARC record, we store the attached data using the BibDoc infrastructure.

```
001155413 001__ 1155413
001155413 245__ $$9HEPDATA$$aKEK. MEASUREMENT OF POLARIZATIONS FOR K+ N ELASTIC AND...
001155413 336__ $$tDATASET
001155413 520__ $$9HEPDATA
001155413 6531_ $$c1$$rK+ N --&gt; K+ N
001155413 6531_ $$c1$$kSQRT(S)$$v1.819 GeV
001155413 786__ $$hT 1.$$q1$$w179758
001155413 8564_ $$uhttp://inspirehep.net/record/1155413/files/Data.plain$$ydata of the table
001155413 910__ $$dCOS(THETA(RF=CM))$$n0$$t
001155413 910__ $$dPOL$$n1$$tPLAB : 1.06 GeV c^-1
001155413 980__ $$aDATA
```

Fig. 4. A complete MARC record describing a data table

4   Possibilities Created by the Integration

Integrating HEPData with Inspire paves the way to many new possibilities in the management and the search. In this section we discuss the added values of the integration, in particular for the research community. Additionally, while integrating the two systems, we have made a number of changes which considerably improve the user experience but are not directly related to having data and functionalities shared between two systems.

4.1   Easier Discovery of the Data

Inspire is becoming a single point of entry for accessing different types of scholarly content.

The storage of HEPData tables as separate MARC records allowed to index them using standard Invenio techniques. A similar approach has been followed by the OECD library[7] where books, articles and statistics are described using

---

[7] http://www.oecd.org

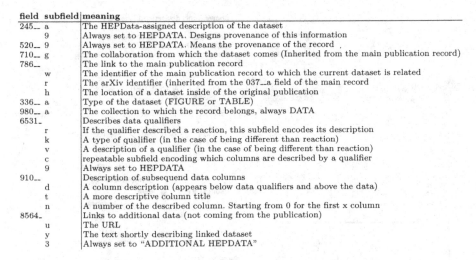

field	subfield	meaning
245__	a	The HEPData-assigned description of the dataset
	9	Always set to HEPDATA. Designs provenance of this information
520__	9	Always set to HEPDATA. Means the provenance of the record
710__	g	The collaboration from which the dataset comes (Inherited from the main publication record)
786__		The link to the main publication record
	w	The identifier of the main publication record to which the current dataset is related
	r	The arXiv identifier (inherited from the 037__a field of the main record
	h	The location of a dataset inside of the original publication
336__	a	Type of the dataset (FIGURE or TABLE)
980__	a	The collection to which the record belongs, always DATA
6531_		Describes data qualifiers
	r	If the qualifier described a reaction, this subfield encodes its description
	k	A type of qualifier (in the case of being different than reaction)
	v	A description of a qualifier (in the case of being different than reaction)
	c	repeatable subfield encoding which columns are described by a qualifier
	9	Always set to HEPDATA
910__		Description of subsequend data columns
	d	A column description (appears below data qualifiers and above the data)
	t	A more descriptive column title
	n	A number of the described column. Starting from 0 for the first x column
8564_		Links to additional data (not coming from the publication)
	u	The URL
	y	The text shortly describing linked dataset
	3	Always set to "ADDITIONAL HEPDATA"

Fig. 5. The complete syntax of MARC format used to describe HEPData entries

MARC[8] format and searchable using the central search engine. As a consequence, formulating a single search phrase in Inspire can now lead to a discovery of not only articles, but also HEPData records. This increases the visibility of HEPData and, as datasets correspond to parts of articles, also the granularity of search in Inspire.

The visibility of HEPData datasets has also increased because they are now an integral part of the standard Inspire record display. When seeing information about a publication, the user is presented with an additional tab showing related HEPData. Also when browsing figures, a link to the underlying HEPData entries can be displayed and datasets can be accessed by making only a single mouse click.

4.2   Display of Plots and Data Qualifiers

The original HEPData site provides powerful capabilities of plotting data included in tables. The functionality allows to combine in the same plot data lines coming from different tables or even publications, which makes comparing results much easier.

These capabilities have been integrated in the Inspire view of data. As can be seen in Figure 6, when displaying a data table, the user first sees only the most general descriptions of data. Two expanding options are available and they can be used to get more insight into data. The user can expand the display in the graphical direction (to the right) and to the direction of details (downwards). Being in the most general descriptions mode and expanding the graphical aspect leads to displaying a general plot containing all data lines present in the table. Expanding down allows to see the numbers and, if already being in the plotting

---

[8] http://www.oecd.org/dataoecd/37/49/48642360.pdf

Fig. 6. Comparison of how the data is displayed in Inspire and in HEPData

mode, separate plots for every data line. Hovering over a plot highlights the data
column used to generate the display. Clicking on a plot redirects to a HEPData
page which allows to modify the display parameters (like types of scales, ranges
etc...) or add/remove data lines. When the user displays the Inspire page showing
HEPData plots, the plots are generated on the fly by a Java application running on
the HEPData server. Thus, this is another example of reusing the services from
one platform (HEPData) by the other platform (Inspire).

A very important part of the description of data stored in HEPData are
the headers indicating what type of physical process is being described by the
data. Figure 6 depicts an example of these descriptors presented in the old
HEPData system. The description includes the type of a process, but also the
numerical constraints specifying the conditions under which an expersiment has
been carried. The data headers have a form of mathematical fomulæ. As can be
seen in Figure 6, the mathematical language used a special text-based notation.
Nowadays, as there are various systems allowing to display, store and process
mathematical formulæ, the text-based language becomes outdated.

As a part of the HEPData-INSPIRE integration, we developed a system for
translating formulas described in the old format to LaTeX. The translated version can be displayed in the browser using the MathJax javascript plugin.

4.3   Making Data Citeable

With the integration of HEPData with Inspire, these scholarly objects were
considered a standard record in the digital library (with an individual MARC

record). In addition, the results from the Parse.Insight survey 2007 [6] indicated that the HEP community needs a neutral preservation platform for research datasets. Moreover, there is an emerging need within the HEP community to track potential reuse of shared research data. Based on these requirements it was decided to use DOIs as an international interdisciplinary persistent identifier. DOIs will be received from the DataCite consortium[9]. By assigning a DOI to a datasets, this could be addressed uniquely and persistently, also beyond the HEP discipline. In scholarly communication as a whole, this can be considered an emerging standard in terms of research data representation (based on the existing experience with DOI for papers).

In practice, this means that selected datasets in HEPData are assigned a DOI which will be displayed along with the record/dataset. Possible (re)users of the dataset can then simply refer to the dataset by citing the DOI in their publications. It is envisioned to track such reuse, and display it on Inspire as well. That way, sharing and reuse of research data shall be facilitated.

The corpus of HEPData comes from data associated with scientific publications. Part of the data appears inside of the original papers explicitly, part is supplementary and was used to prepare plots or to derive results. Only datasets which are not explicitly present in the publications should have DOIs assigned, as the others can be uniquely identified using the parent publication identifier. HEPData stores the exact provenance of the data, which allows us to automatically identify the additional data.

As mentioned earlier, the harvesting pocedure considers situations when datasets have to be updated. This might seem to be incompatible with permanent identification, however the nature of scientific publications simplifies the situation. After an article or a book is published, it is considered to be in a final version which can not be modified. The same property is inherited by assiciated datasets. This implies that the only possible updates are corrections of mistakes related to the extraction or description of the data. As such, updated datasets describe the same data and the updating does not interfere with the DOI assignment procedure.

4.4 Linking Data and Objects

At the current state of art, the data stored in HEPData is linked to the paper from which it comes. There are also different artefacts related to a publication that are stored in Inspire or are intended to be included in the future. Figure 7 depicts some examples of scientific artefacts existing in the HEP community. An ideal preservation platform should maintain not only these objects but also relations between them. For example, a publication should be linked with its figures, tables and contained data. Additionally, it should contain references to other publications, datasets and simulations, which are not directly described or included, but were used during the preparation of the described results. Such a preservation system would be a powerful tool allowing to even better trace

---

[9] http://datacite.org/

and easier reproduce scientific results. Classical digital libraries preserve only publications and citation relations between them. Extensions of Inspire described in [7] by Praczyk et al., allow to store complicated properties of relations between arbitrary types of objects, for example figures and documents from which they have been been extracted.

HEPData records contain information about location of the dataset inside a publication. This information is represented as a short text description, for example "F 9,T 12" meaning Figure 9, Table 12, which could be parsed allowing to establish relations not only between a HEPData record and a publication but also between figure or table from which a given dataset has been extracted and the data itself.

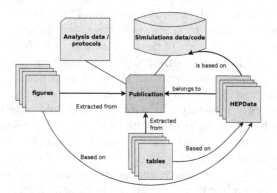

Fig. 7. Examples of elements of the information ecosystem related to a publication

5   Conclusions and Future Work

SPIRES, the predecessor of Inspire, was storing links to HEPData records as part of the publication information. The synchronisation of both systems required a great effort on the side of the human resources maintaining HEPData. Every time HEPData was updated, information about this event had to be introduced to Spires. Inspire, as a successor of SPIRES, has inherited these links and was displaying them inside bibliographic records. As the addressing of HEPData can be based on internal identifiers that can change, some of these links became obsolete with the time.

This paper has described the integration between HEPData and Inspire systems with the objective of avoiding existing problems and automating processes as much as possible. The accomplished work considerably extends the possibilities of users of both systems and improves their experience. The introduction of a completely automatic system allowing to update Inspire assets has allowed not only to reduce the number of mistakes caused by the necessity to introduce the data manually, but also to decrease the amount of the effort necessary to maintain Inspire up to date. For the research community, access to materials beyond a publication shall become more and more seamless. This work is an important step towards providing open linked data in Inspire.

However, there are still directions in which the integration and both systems could be extended. Besides data related to figures and tables in publications, HEP-Data gives access to data files provided by experiments. The nature of this data is less regular and they are currently not maintained in Inspire but it is envisioned to integrate those files as standalone objects. In addition to manual curation of publication metadata inside Inspire, an ontology of terms of HEP is being maintained. This could be used in the future to make datasets machine readable and interoperable with other repositories on a semantic level. However, this is an additional step which must be considered after the data is fully available in Inspire.

Currently, the HEPData integration has been deployed and is being used by Inspire users. The analysis of users behaviours and usage patterns will be precious for designing directions of further developments making data integrated in Inspire.

Acknowledgements. This work has been partially supported by CERN, Cátedra Logisman of Universidad de Zaragoza and Science & Technology Facilities Council (UK).

References

1. Borgman, C.L.: Research data: Who will share what, with whom, when, and why? Working Paper Series of the German Council for Social and Economic Data 161, German Council for Social and Economic Data (RatSWD) (2010)
2. Caffaro, J., Kaplun, S.: Invenio: A Modern Digital Library for Grey Literature. oai:cds.cern.ch:1312678. In: 12th. Int. Conf. on Grey Literature, Prague, Czech Republic, Geneva, p. 7 (December 2010) No. CERN-OPEN-2010-027
3. Dietrich, D.: Metadata management in a data staging repository. Journal of Library Metadata 10(2-3), 79–98 (2010)
4. Green, T.: We need publishing standards for datasets and data tables. OECD Publishing White Paper 22(4), 325–327 (2009)
5. Greenberg, J.: Theoretical Considerations of Lifecycle Modeling: An Analysis of the Dryad Repository Demonstrating Automatic Metadata Propagation, Inheritance, and Value System Adoption. Cataloging & Classification Quarterly 47(3), 380–402 (2009)
6. PARSE: First insights into digital preservation of research output in europe: interim insight report (2009),
   http://www.parse-insight.eu/downloads/
   PARSE-Insight_D3-5_InterimInsightReport_final.pdf
7. Praczyk, P., Nogueras-Iso, J., Kaplun, S., Simko, T.: A storage model for supporting figures and other artefacts in scientific libraries: the case study of invenio. In: Proc. of 4th Workshop on Very Large Digital Libraries (VLDL 2011), Berlin, Germany (2011)
8. Schindler, U., Diepenbroek, M.: Generic XML-based framework for metadata portals. Comput. Geosci. 34(12), 1947–1955 (2008)
9. de Sompel, H.V., Nelson, M.L., Lagoze, C., Warner, S.: Resource Harvesting within the OAI-PMH Framework. D-Lib Magazine 10(12) (2004)
10. Vesely, M., Baron, T., Le Meur, J.Y., Simko, T.: Creating Open Digital Library Using XML: Implementation of OAi-PMH Protocol at CERN. oai:cds.cern.ch:590906. In: Int. Conf. on Electronic Publishing, Karlovy Vary, Czech Republic, p. 7 (July 2002) No. CERN-ETT-2002-003

Reorienting Open Repositories to the Challenges of the Semantic Web: Experiences from FAO's Contribution to the Resource Processing and Discovery Cycle in Repositories in the Agricultural Domain

Imma Subirats[1], Thembani Malapela[1], Sarah Dister[1], Marcia Zeng[2], Marc Gooaverts[3], Valeria Pesce[4], Yves Jaques[1], Stefano Anibaldi[1], and Johannes Keizer[1]

[1] FAO of the UN, Italy
[2] Kent State University, USA
[3] Hasselt University Library, Belgium
[4] Global Forum on Agricultural Research, Italy

Abstract. The use of widely-used metadata standards is essential to guarantee the visibility and retrieval of documents stored in open repositories. Attention should be paid to the creation and exchange of meaningful metadata to enhance interoperability amongst repositories and provide value added services. Since 2005 the Food and Agriculture Organization of the United Nations (FAO) provides the agricultural information management community with standards, services and tools to assist open repositories in benefiting from the advantages offered by Semantic Web publishing. This paper presents the work that FAO carries out in recommending standards for the encoding and exchange of metadata while also reviewing techniques to help navigate within open repositories and services. It talks about how to improve the visibility of repository content and explains the benefits of integrating subject vocabulary tools expressed in SKOS. It concludes with a presentation of use cases integrating these recommendations into DSpace and Drupal customizations.

Keywords: Open Access, Open Repositories, Metadata, Repository Interoperability, AGROVOC, AgriOcean DSpace, AgriDrupal, WebAGRIS, LODE-BD, Linked Data, AIMS, Semantic Web, AgMES, AGRIS AP.

1   Introduction

The Open Access movement satisfies two broad intertwining goals: firstly, facilitating the online archiving of digital documents (in most cases peer reviewed post prints) and making them freely accessible through an OAI compliant repository (Green route); secondly, sustaining open access journals by depositing articles online upon publication (Gold route). The acceptance and growth of this model and its hybrids in the scholarly communication process has seen an increase in the number of open repositories available online; for instance, OpenDoar [1] reported 2,211 repositories registered by September, 2012.

J.M. Dodero, M. Palomo-Duarte, P. Karampiperis (Eds.): MTSR 2012, CCIS 343, pp. 158–167, 2012.
© Springer-Verlag Berlin Heidelberg 2012

Current technological changes especially in the Semantic Web dictates that open repositories should *not only publish local content globally,* but also offer additional *values to researchers* by harnessing participation from a broad community of data providers *(interoperability).* In this way, open repositories are poised to increase the role they play within the scholarly communication process. However, certain fundamentals have to be met if open repositories are to remain visible.

The Semantic Web has further facilitated value addition to research outputs through automatic discovery, linking and analysis. Linked Data is the set of best practices for publishing and connecting structured data on the web. Its main objective is to liberate data from silos that are framed by proprietary database schemas by following the four principles, as defined by Tim Berners-Lee [2] in 2006.

In the agricultural domain, FAO has been providing support to agricultural information communities to build and maintain open repositories that conform to recommended metadata standards. In this vein, this paper presents the role of the Agriculture Information Management Standards (AIMS) team in *re-orienting* repositories to the current demands of the Semantic Web, through (a) AIMS set of recommendations to open repositories; and (b) providing FAO's experiences and use cases in implementing these recommendations.

2   Literature Review

The major goal of digital repositories is to facilitate access to their contents. Swan and Carr aptly re-state that,

> "Repositories should be one of the institution's web based tools that take research into places that have not been reached before. One important issue … is that the primary reason for establishing a digital repository is to increase the visibility of the institution's research output by making it available on Open Access." [3]

Visibility has been defined in the context of repositories to mean the number of external links received from external sites [4], [5]. The total visits made to a repository contents by links from search engines and other databases is used to measure visibility. *The Ranking Web of World Repositories* was started with the aim to improve visibility of open repositories and to promote good practices in their publication [6]. The methodology employed by the *Ranking of the Web of World Repositories* includes the following parameters, Size; *Visibility*; Rich files and Scholar (The total number of papers in Google Scholar for a 5-year period 2007-2011)

Most repositories strive for global visibility and to fully expose their contents. [7],[8],[9]. Yet a recent study by Artlitsch and O'Brien [10] established that most repositories are invisible, for example Google Scholar had difficulty in indexing the contents of institutional repositories, and Artlitsch and O'Brien hypothesized that most repositories use Dublin core, which cannot express bibliographic citation data adequately for academic papers. During this study, experimental metadata transformation projects were implemented at Utah and were successful in achieving a greater than 90% indexing ratio. It is clear that the quality of metadata records stored in repositories assures greater visibility.

Still, when different metadata standards and schemas are used across repositories this creates challenges in achieving interoperability [11] and Haslhofer and Klas [12] proposed metadata integration to solve this. However, Park and Lu [13] discovered that even in the use of a common metadata standard there was a divergence in what local metadata guidelines contained and what they represented. This was found to be a potential hindrance to sharable metadata across repositories. Therefore, attention to the standardization of metadata at individual field level within a resource is important if the efficient retrieval of documents stored in open repository is to be achieved.

The use of vocabulary control has also been proven to be effective in retrieval of information in electronic environments [14]. In the context of the Semantic Web it has been noted [15] that the use of controlled vocabularies is useful in the retrieval and discovery of resources tagged with repository concepts. Gray *et al* [16] phrased it this way;

> "Using SKOS as a representation for a vocabulary provides a unique identifier to tag resources with, and enables vocabulary aware applications to enhance...the exploitation of relationships between concepts in the vocabulary.....vocabulary aware applications can benefit from improvements in both precision and recall, for example when searching for bibliographic or science data."

When repositories use controlled vocabularies in indexing their content great success in resource discovery improves and also facilitates easier resource sharing amongst repositories.

3   Recommendations to Open Repositories.

If repositories are to remain open and accessible in the Web of data, they must ensure that:

i.   their content is stable (browsable, searchable, discoverable, and readable by both machines and humans);

ii.   they use appropriate metadata standards to improve exchange across data silos;

iii.   they use controlled vocabularies and ensure that these are integrated within document repository management systems (essential if these vocabularies are in themselves Linked Open Data!).

Therefore, with regards to item ii. and iii. stated above, AIMS recommends that repository managers should use *Linked Open Data Enabled Bibliographic Metadata (LODE-BD) recommendations*[17] in deciding which metadata properties to use. Whereas with regards to the use of controlled vocabularies, agricultural repositories are encouraged to use the AGROVOC to describe the contents of their repositories. With the launch of the AGROVOC linked open data, repositories can simply link their resources to AGROVOC and this model has been successfully applied elsewhere

[16] and within the agricultural domain [18]. The following subsections will provide an elaborate description of this model.

3.1   The Key Step towards Semantic Interoperability: Assuring Quality in Metadata Creation

Metadata in repositories serve both an administrative role during the submission process and a technical role of resource description for resource discovery by a broad audience. If repositories are to operate across administrative and disciplinary boundaries, and are to be relevant in the Semantic Web, they should guarantee resource-level accessibility. Content description and indexing through standardized metadata, when applied to both syntax and semantics, becomes the basis of efficient visible repository to which value-added services can also be harnessed.

The AGRIS (International System for Agricultural Science and Technology) Network[19], is an international information system for sharing access to agricultural science and technology information created in 1974. It is a collaborative system which includes more than 100 national, international and intergovernmental centres with a goal to facilitate information exchange of literature dealing with all aspects of agriculture. As a result, the AGRIS Network contributes to the AGRIS Database, a content aggregator with 2.9 million bibliographical records on agricultural science and technology, maintained by FAO.

Since 2005 the AGRIS Application Profile (AP) [20] has been used as a metadata schema for the submission of agricultural information metadata to AGRIS, superseding the earlier version, AGRIN [21]. The AGRIS AP uses metadata elements from Dublin Core (DC), Australian Government Locator Service Metadata (AGLS) and Agricultural Metadata Element Set (AgMES) , developed by FAO in 2003. The AGRIS AP enforces a minimum level of quality and the use of controlled vocabularies by mandating four required elements and promoting the use of agriculture-specific thesauri such as AGROVOC [22]. The new demands of the Semantic Web and its open-world assumptions have revealed the limitations of the AGRIS AP. It seemed to be too rigid in its encoding requirements while at the same time promoting a number of properties that are too obscure for an open-world approach. It is thus not been able to guarantee interoperability among data providers and services, particularly beyond the agricultural information management community.

In 2011, FAO re-oriented its approach by providing a set of recommendations with a full range of options for metadata encoding from which bibliographic content providers could choose according to their development stages, internal data structures, and the reality of their current practices. The recommendations allow any content provider to encode bibliographic data[1] using properties from standardized namespaces, to use well-established authority data and controlled vocabularies available as linked data in agriculture and to publish data in RDF. The recommendations encourage data providers to adopt good encoding strategies to facilitate the exchange of bibliographic metadata. These recommendations are referred to as *Linked Open Data Enabled Bibliographic Metadata* [17] (LOBE-BD) version 2.0. LOBE-BD assists

---

[1] An instance of bibliographic resource includes articles, monographs, theses, paper, material presentation, research report, learning object, etc. - printed or electronic format.

repository managers in four key questions: (a)What **kinds of entities and relation-ships** are involved in bibliographic resource descriptions? (b) What **properties** should be considered for publishing meaningful/useful Linked Open Data-ready bibliograph-ic data? (c) What **metadata standards** should be used for preparing Linked Open Data-ready bibliographic data? (d) What **metadata terms** are appropriate in any giv-en property for producing Linked Open Data-ready bibliographic data from a local database?

Although LODE-BD focuses on the exchange of data, it also contains recommen-dations about the minimal set of metadata properties, and syntax encoding rules, controlled vocabularies and authority data, necessary to produce, manage and ex-change meaningful bibliographic metadata. LOBE-BD recommendations provides practical decision trees in selecting properties in its nine groups. The decision trees are arranged in a flow chart which highlights decision points and gives a step-by-step solution to a given metadata encoding. The Figure 1 below shows the example for the decision tree for Title information.

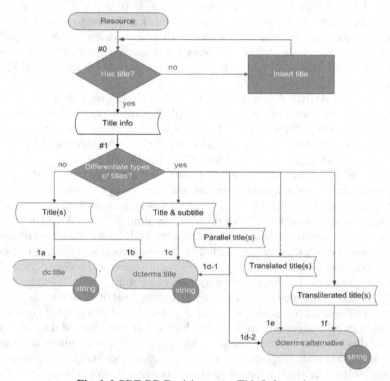

Fig. 1. LOBE-BD Decision tree – Title Information

3.2   Aids to Navigation and Visibility of Repository Contents

Most repositories have adopted the use of URLs in identifying their resources as a first step towards creating visibility of their holdings. However, differences that arise due to geographic, cultural, domain specific environments even amongst repositories with the same or similar collection scopes, still inhibit individual resource visibility.

Subject vocabularies (words or phrases taken from standardized, organised knowledge structures) should be employed to resolve indexing problems such as plurals, spelling variants, synonyms and homonyms (same spelling representing two different concepts, e.g. *blood* vessel / *fishing* vessel). In the context of Semantic Web such subject vocabularies are expressed as a concept scheme using SKOS (Simple Knowledge Organisation System) and integrated within document management or content management systems. The use of subject vocabularies guarantees meaningful metadata while also enhancing the quality of the interoperability and effectiveness of information exchange among data providers, thus facilitating the re-usage of data by other repositories/services and in the process adding value to the local researcher.

The AGROVOC [23] thesaurus contains more than 40,000 concepts in up to 22 languages covering topics related to food, nutrition, agriculture, fisheries, forestry, environment and other related domains. AGROVOC is a thesaurus expressed as a concept scheme using SKOS and this conversion from a relational database has provided added semantics value to term relationships. Therefore, current structure of AGROVOC concept scheme provides three levels of presentation. These three levels are: A) **CONCEPTS** – refers to the abstract meaning and often identified using URIs, for example maize in the sense of a cereal identified by Concept12332;B) **TERMS** - are language-specific lexical forms attached to concepts, for example maize, maïs, 玉米, ข้าวโพด, or corn, C) **TERM VARIANTS** - are the range of forms that can occur for each term such as spelling variants, singular or plural, for example organization or organisation, cow or cows.

In partnership with MIMOS Behard [24], the AGROVOC thesaurus is published as a Linked Data aligned more than ten other knowledge organization systems. The additional value that linking AGROVOC to other vocabularies provides is that *data repositories attached to those vocabularies become discoverable*. This is a very simple classic case of exposing repository contents automatically across datasets through AGROVOC indexing.

4   Use Cases in Integrating Information Management Standards in Selected Information Management (IM) Tools

Three open source management tools have been customized to facilitate the use of standards for the creation, management and exchange of metadata.

4.1   WebAGRIS

WebAGRIS [21] is an information management system for the creation and dissemination of AGRIS AP metadata based on WWW-ISIS software[25] and customized by the Institute for Computer and Information Engineering in Poland with the support of FAO [26]. Despite the obsolescence of the technology used by WebAGRIS, during the last 10 years it has been the most widely-used information management tool within the AGRIS Network. This is due to the fact that WebAGRIS does not require a complex technical infrastructure for its maintenance, a key selection point for many developing countries. WebAGRIS provides functionalities like protected access for creation and update of metadata and export of AGRIS AP records, authority data creation and maintenance (e.g. AGROVOC Thesaurus built-in), user friendly retrieval and AGROVOC Thesaurus based search. WebAGRIS can be used in a LAN or WAN, so multiple nodes may contribute to a centralized instance of WebAGRIS, simply via an IP. In 2012 the FAO AIMS team has stopped supporting new developments on WebAGRIS, and discourage new users to install it . However support to existing users will continue.

4.2   AgriOcean DSpace

DSpace is an open source and freely available software conceived for the setting up and management of open repositories. DSpace focuses on managing and preserving digital content. It is based on a solid community of DSpace users and developers. It is possible to customize it and extend it. In 2009 the FAO AIMS team, in collaboration with Hasselt University, the Institute of Biology of the Southern Seas (IBSS) and UNESCO-IOC/IODE, proceeded with a customization of DSpace, AgriOcean Dspace (AOD), based on specific information management standards widely used in the agricultural, aquatic and marine sciences.

AOD supports the use of rich metadata element set and subject vocabularies/authority control for the description of any type of information, like journal contributions, books, conference contribution, research report, working papers, theses or other like preprints.   The main features introduced by AOD are the following: i)exposure of records through the OAI-PMH protocol supporting metadata formats like AGRIS AP and MODS [27] ;ii) indexing with ASFA and AGROVOC terms; iii)authority control features for journal title; iv) submission base on type of document; v)easy to install version for Windows; vi) up-to-date lay-out: personalizable standard vii)batch import for AGRIS AP, MODS and EndNote.

AOD is based on the out-of-the-box DSpace, which its main features and functionalities are: self-archiving and submission process, different submission workflows, management of digital objects, variety of digital format and content types are supported, two levels of search, persistent identifiers (handle),long-term physical storage and OAI compliancy and RSS exposure. AOD is available in source code or with a Windows installer designed specifically to make it easy to install for organizations with limited IT support. AOD is currently used by Oceandocs [28], the Institute of Biology of the Southern Seas, Ukraine (IBSS) [29], Central and Eastern European Marine Repository (CEEMaR) [30] and the Ministry of Agriculture (Peru)[31], and is under testing by other 13 institutions.

4.3   AgriDrupal

In setting up repositories, agricultural institutions have often faced the following demands in the selection of appropriate software tools: the need to integrate a repository search and browse interface within their website, the need to implement custom content models, or custom metadata models, and,the need to be able to exchange information with other systems and participate in other networks[32].

In 2009 the FAO AIMS team initiated the project AgriDrupal [33] as a *suite of solutions* for agricultural information management and dissemination, built on the Drupal [34] platform, with special functionalities for repository management.In 2010, FAO piloted an AgriDrupal installation at the National Food Policy Capacity Strengthening Programme (NFPCSP) [35] in collaboration with the Ministry of Food and Disaster Management (MoFDM) in Bangladesh; with financial support from the European Union and the United States Agency for International Development.

The pilot made it apparent that the AgriDrupal tool was quite appropriate for managing both the electronic documentation centre and a website adopting standards that FAO had also supported [36]. AgriDupal has since been offered to agricultural information managers as an integrated solution to manage different types of information such as organizations, expert profiles, news, jobs, events, feeds, web pages, blog entries or forum topics. It has advanced features for managing Open Access document repositories in compliance with widely adopted library standards. Each AgriDrupal installation now comes with the following added-value features: i) import and export functionalities using the AGRIS-AP XML format for bibliographic records and extended RSS for other types of records; ii)ability to index any content with AGROVOC terms; iii) exposure of bibliographic records through the OAI-PMH protocol supporting two metadata formats (Dublin Core and AGRIS AP); iv) support for implementing additional metadata standards; v) all the core Drupal Content Management features for advanced management of any contents and customization of the look and feel. The AgriDrupal installation has been used also by the Ghana Agricultural Information Network System (GAINS) portal and recently by the ZAR4DIN [37] national portal in Zambia in managing their website as well as their document repositories via a single interface.

5   Conclusions

In this paper we have advocated that repositories need to strive for continuous visibility and guarantee interoperability. It has been established that most repository are invisible when searched by search engines and the semantic web threatens to render such resources further invisible in the future if they remain in their present form. In order to reorient open repositories to the demands of the semantic web, we proposed two basic interventions, the first is that repositories should adopt widely-used metadata standards for the description of information objects. Secondly, repositories should use controlled subject vocabularies which are expressed as a concept scheme and are in Simple Knowledge Organisation System (SKOS) in indexing their contents. The FAO AIMS team, therefore, recommends that AGROVOC Thesaurus as linked data is a good subject vocabulary for indexing contents for repositories in the agricultural domain. Practical examples were offered in the agricultural information management domain highlighting how the AgriOcean DSpace and AgriDrupal software(s) have integrated these recommendations ; these were also presented as open repositories use cases. Despite this model, there still remain an opportunity for further research into how open repositories can be migrated into the semantic web by having them published as Linked Open Data.

References

1. OpenDoar, http://www.opendoar.org/index.html (last accessed: July 2012)
2. Berners-Lee, T.: Linked Data (2009),
   http://www.w3.org/DesignIssues/LinkedData (last accessed: July 2012)
3. Swan, A., Carr, L.: Institutions, their repositories and the web. Serials Review 34(1),
   31–35 (2008)
4. Drewry, J.: Google Scholar, windows live academic search, and beyond: a study of new
   tools and changing habits in ARL libraries. A Master's Thesis (2007),
   http://ils.unc.edu/MSpapers/3310.pdf (last accessed September 2012)
5. Aguillo, L., Ortega, J., Ferriandez, M., Utrilla, A.: Indicators for a webometric ranking of
   open access repositories. Scientometrics 82(3), 447–486 (2010)
6. Ranking Web of Repositories website,
   http://repositories.webometrics.info/en (last accessed: September 2012)
7. Abrizah, A., Noorhidawati, A., Kiran, K.: Global visibility of Asian Universitie's Open
   Access institutional repositories. Malaysian Journal of Library and Information
   Science 15(3), 53–73 (2010)
8. Banier, J., Perciali, I.: The institutional repository rediscovered; what can a university do
   for Open Access publishing? Serials Review 34(1), 21–26 (2008)
9. Mercer, H., Koeing, J., McGeachin, R., Tucker, S.: Structure, features, and faculty content
   in ARL member repositories. The Journal of Academic Librarianship 37(40), 333–342
   (2011)
10. Arlitsch, K., O'Brien, P.S.: Invisible institutional repositories: addressing the low indexing
    ratios of IRs in Google Scholar. Library Hi Tech 30(1), 60–81 (2012)
11. Ochoa, X., Duval, E.: Automatic evaluation of metadata quality in digital repositories. In-
    ternational Journal on Digital Libraries 10(2-3), 67–91 (2009)
12. Haslhofer, B., Klas, W.: A survey of techniques for achieving metadata interoperability.
    ACM Computing Surveys 42(2), 1–37 (2010)
13. Park, J., Lu, C.: An analysis of seven metadata creation guidelines; issues and implica-
    tions. A Paper Presented at 2008 Annual Electronic Resources and Libraries Conference,
    Atlanta, Georgia, March 18-21 (2008)
14. Michael, G.: Authority control in the context of bibliographic control in the electronic en-
    vironment. Cataloguing and Classification Quartely 38(3-40), 11–22 (2004)
15. Weller, K.: Knowledge representation in the social semantic web. Walter de Gruyer, New
    York (2010)
16. Gray, A., Gray, N., Hall, C., Ounis, A.: A Finding the right term: retrieving and exploring
    semantic concepts in astronomical vocabularies. Information Processing and Manage-
    ment 46(4), 470–478 (2010)
17. Subirats, I., Zeng, M.: Linked Open Data Enabled Bibliographic Metadata (LODE-BD)
    version 2.0 (2012), http://aims.fao.org/standards/lode-bd (last accessed:
    September 2012)
18. Lukose, D.: World-wide semantic web of agriculture knowledge. Journal of Integrative
    Agriculture 11(5), 769–774 (2012)
19. Knowledge and information sharing through the AGRIS Network,
    http://agris.fao.org/knowledge-and-information-sharing-
    through-agris-network (last accessed: July 2012)

20. FAO: The AGRIS Application Profile for the international information system on agricultural sciences and technology guidelines on best practices for Information Object Description (2005), http://www.fao.org/docrep/008/ae909e/ae909e00.htm (last accessed: July 2012)

21. Onyancha, I., Weinheimer, J., Salokhe, G., Katz, S., Keizer, J.: Metadata exchange without pain: the AGRIS-AP to harvest and exchange quality metadata (2004), http://dcpapers.dublincore.org/index.php/pubs/article/download/774/770 (last accessed: July 2012)

22. Subirats, L., Onyancha, I., Salokhe, G., Keizer, J.: Towards an architecture for open archive networks in Agricultural Sciences and Technology (2008), ftp://ftp.fao.org/docrep/fao/009/ah766e/ah766e00.pdf (last accessed: July 2012)

23. AGROVOC Homepage, http://aims.fao.org/standards/agrovoc/about (last accessed: July 2012)

24. MIMOS Behard Homepage, http://www.mimos.my/ (last accessed: July 2012)

25. UNESCO. WWW/ISIS – Technical Reference Manual, v. 5.1.1 / 05-05-02, Warsaw/Rome (May 2005)

26. Rybinski, H., Kaloyanova, S., Katz, S.: WWW-ISIS: a result of a close cooperation between FAO-GIL and ICIE (2006), ftp://ftp.fao.org/docrep/fao/010/ai162e/ai162e00.pdf

27. Metadata Object Description Schema (MODS), http://www.loc.gov/standards/mods/ (last accessed: July 2012)

28. OceanDocs, http://www.oceandocs.org/ (last accessed July 2012)

29. IBSS Institutional Repository, http://repository.ibss.org.ua/dspace/ (last accessed July 2012)

30. Central and Eastern European Marine Repository, http://repository.ibss.org.ua/dspace/ (last accessed July 2012)

31. Ministry of Agriculture (Peru), http://www.minag.gob.pe/portal/ (last accessed February 2012)

32. Pesce, V., Subirats, I., Picarella, A., Keizer, K.: AgriDrupal: repository management integrated into a content management system. A Paper Presented at Open Repositories Conference, Austin (US), June 8-10 (2011)

33. AgriDrupal Homepage, http://aims.fao.org/tools/agridrupal (last accessed: July 2012)

34. Drupal Open Source Content Management System, http://drupal.org/ (last accessed: July 2012)

35. NFPCSP Homepage, http://www.nfpcsp.org/agridrupal/ (last accessed: July 2012)

36. AgriDrupal at NFPCSP, http://aims.fao.org/advice-and-capacity-development/open-access/fpmu (last accessed: July 2012)

37. ZAR4DIN Homepage, http://zar4din.org/ (last accessed: July 2012)

The Data Model of the OpenAIRE Scientific Communication e-Infrastructure

Paolo Manghi[1], Nikos Houssos[2,4], Marko Mikulicic[1], and Brigitte Jörg[3,4]

[1] ISTI - Consiglio Nazionale delle Ricerche
Via Moruzzi 1, 56124 Pisa, Italy
name.surname@isti.cnr.it
[2] National Documentation Centre / National Hellenic Research Foundation
48 Vassileos Konstantinou Avenue, 116 35, Athens, Greece
nhoussos@ekt.gr
[3] Innovation Support Center, UKOLN, University of Bath
BA2 7AY, Bath, UK
b.joerg@ukoln.ac.uk
[4] EuroCRIS
Cor van Osnabruggelaan 61, 2251 RE Voorschoten, The Netherlands

Abstract. The OpenAIREplus project aims to further develop and operate the OpenAIRE e-infrastructure, in order to provide a central entry point to Open Access and non-Open Access publications and datasets funded by the European Commission and National agencies. The infrastructure provides the services to populate, curate, and enrich an Information Space by collecting metadata descriptions relative to organizations, data sources, projects, funding programmes, persons, publications, and datasets. Stakeholders in the research process and scientific communication, such as researchers, funding agencies, organizations involved in projects, project coordinators, can here find the information to improve their research and statistics to measure the impact of Open Access and funding schemes over research. In this paper, we introduce the functional requirements to be satisfied and describe the OpenAIREplus data model entities and relationships required to represent information capable of meeting them.

Keywords: open access, data model, infrastructure, CERIF, DataCite.

1 Introduction

A fundamental requirement in scholarly communication systems is the representation of metadata about scientific publications. A typical approach for such metadata is based on variants of Dublin Core, MARC or MODS. A common underlying principle of these solutions is that metadata is represented in essentially flat, monolithic records with limited facilities (e.g. references to authority files) for capturing relationships to autonomous entities external to the publication like persons and publishers.

Emerging needs regarding capturing, publishing and preserving research output have shown limitations of these approaches. Two increasingly significant aspects can be identified that raise the bar for metadata representation techniques.

J.M. Dodero, M. Palomo-Duarte, P. Karampiperis (Eds.): MTSR 2012, CCIS 343, pp. 168–180, 2012.
© Springer-Verlag Berlin Heidelberg 2012

First, scientific output that needs to be captured is not limited to traditional publications that have the form of text documents but extends to data sets. Therefore, metadata and services that enable easy discovery and reuse of data sets are essential.

Secondly, contextual metadata about scientific output is very important for the provision of value-added services to end-users. Linking publications and data sets with specific projects, funding programmes, organisations and persons enables a range of services for monitoring and assessing research activity at various levels (e.g. organisation/research group, funding programme). Furthermore, it significantly improves common functions like discovery and browsing, since the additional contextual and provenance information can assist end users in evaluating the reuse potential of research work and ultimately in reusing it. Important requirements for contextual metadata are thus the ability to unambiguously represent the semantics of the relationships between entities (e.g. whether an organisation is a participant or a coordinator of a project) as well as the temporal aspect of relationships (e.g. date range a person has been the coordinator of the project). Another critical aspect is the constantly evolving nature of the research domain, where new types of results, tools, data sources and new semantic relationships between them ask for contextual metadata that is able to seamlessly reflect these real-world changes with minimal effort.

The OpenAIREplus project [1] needs to address both of these challenging requirements [6]. The project aims to further develop the OpenAIRE e-infrastructure, which in its current initial phase provides a central point of access to open access publications funded by the European Union Framework Programme 7 projects in a range of thematic areas. The publication metadata is harvested from institutional repositories across Europe and international thematic repositories. The next, and quite ambitious, steps evolution of the OpenAIRE infrastructure to (a) include metadata describing data sets and their semantic links to publications and to (b) incorporate research output produced all over Europe through any type of funding, thus not restricted to EU FP7, including linking of outputs and projects with funding programmes.

In order to address these important challenges (data sets and contextual metadata) the need was recognised for a substantial upgrade of the data model that had been specified and used within OpenAIRE [7]. The approach followed for the upgrade was to first take into account existing initiatives and standards that could be reused. One of them is the Common European Research Information Format (CERIF) [8][9], an EU Recommendation to Member States [1] continuously developed and maintained by euroCRIS (www.eurocris.org), a standard data model addressing representation of contextual research information, which has been adopted to cover this key aspect in the OpenAIREplus data model. CERIF inherently captures contextual metadata about data sets (e.g. semantic links of data sets to publications) and is hence used in that respect also in OpenAIREplus. Furthermore, the OpenAIRE representation of data sets information is compliant with the metadata schema of the international DataCite[2] initiative. Notably, OpenAIREplus focuses on domain-independent contextual metadata for datasets, not handling vertical, domain-specific dataset representation. In that

---

[1] CORDIS Archive: http://cordis.europa.eu/cerif/
[2] DataCite: http://www.datacite.org/

respect, the OpenAIREplus data modelling scope differs from other initiatives, such as the ENGAGE Public Sector Information datasets infrastructure, which employs a multi-level metadata architecture that handles to some extent both detailed, discipline-specific metadata, besides domain-independent contextual CERIF metadata [10]. Furthermore, the CERIF for Datasets (C4D) project aims at the representation of a detailed, discipline-specific datasets metadata standard using CERIF [11].

This article presents the results of the OpenAIREplus data modelling effort with particular emphasis on aspects related to representing semantically rich contextual metadata integrating information from many different research contexts (e.g. countries). It is structured as follows: Section 2 is an overview of the OpenAIREplus information space. Section 3 provides background information on CERIF and DataCite. Section 4 presents in detail the OpenAIREplus data model and elaborates on key aspects. Section 5 provides concrete examples of complex information representation requirements seamlessly addressed by the model through CERIF. The paper concludes with a summary of its main contributions and ideas for future directions.

2   The OpenAIREplus Information Space and Data Modelling Requirements

As mentioned in the introduction, the OpenAIRE infrastructure is conceived to support and promote modern workflows of scientific communication. In such context research datasets become as important as textual publications and Open Access policies play a major role, to be observed and measured. The main objective of the infrastructure is therefore to deliver to all actors involved in the research process and scientific communication chain an Information Space aggregating metadata descriptions and pointers to the scientific research output, together with information relative to license and research funding. To this aim, it will offer services for the registration of data sources containing metadata descriptions of research output (e.g., publications and datasets) and their contextual information (e.g., projects, funding schemes), for the collection and aggregation of such metadata, and for inferring meaningful relationships between them. Further services will provide interested actors with portals (end-users) and APIs (third-party applications) to access to the resulting aggregated Information Space. To support the effective operation of such services, the data model of the Information Space including the entities, entity properties and entity relationships must be capable of capturing the functional requirements of such actors.

End-users. In particular, end-users may belong to the following categories:

- The generic user (researcher): interested in finding publications of his/her own or other's publications and datasets and investigate on how these are interrelated with further publication and datasets, projects, other researchers, etc.;
- The data source manager: interested in observing statistics measuring how the metadata content of his/her data source is balanced and possibly connected to others; also interested to have its content visible and linked to the original data source, so as to increase its visibility;

- The project coordinator: interested in observing the research output of his/her project and its comparison with other projects in the same subject of investigation;
- The funding agency officer: interested in measuring the impact of research funding in terms of project outputs and, in some cases, in terms of Open Access vs non-Open Access production; also interested in contacting coordinators of projects which meet specific criteria, e.g., for dissemination purposes.

In order to build services meeting such demands, the information space data model should include entities such as publications, datasets, projects, licenses, persons (e.g., authors of publications and datasets and project coordinators), data sources (e.g., source of origin of the entities), and organizations (e.g., responsible of data sources, project participants), together with relationships between them.

The process of modelling such entities has "boundaries" partly imposed by the best practices and standards adopted by the data sources from which this information can be collected from. Indeed, quality information can only be found in very specific kinds of data sources, serving the needs of well-established communities, with standards data models and services. In particular, infrastructure services will collect information from four main categories of data sources: publication repositories, data repositories, CRISs, and so-called "entity registries" – entity registries are intended as sources of authoritative lists of relevant entities such as persons, e.g., ORCID[3] for researchers, projects, e.g., European Commission CORDA database[4], and data sources, e.g., OpenDOAR[5] for repositories. The architectural assumption is that the infrastructure will collect, via several standard protocols, metadata records (e.g., XML files) from such sources assuming their compatibility with the *OpenAIREplus guidelines for data source providers*[6]. The guidelines establish, for each data source typology, the metadata format to be expected from the data sources. The format consists of an XML schema and a set of vocabularies to be used for given crucial properties (paths in the XML schema).[7] The XML schemas correspond to standard formats in the given data source application domain: Dublin Core for publication repositories,[8] DataCite for data repositories, CERIF XML for CRIS systems, and arbitrary structured representations for entity registries. On the one hand, such formats suggest the entities and the relationships curated by domain experts and available to the information space, that is to the data model. On the other hand, the infrastructure includes

---

[3] ORCID, http://about.orcid.org/

[4] European Commission: COmmon Research DAta Warehouse (CORDA),
  https://webgate.ec.europa.eu/
  e-corda/resources/pdf/Confidentiality_rules_FP_data.pdf

[5] The Directory of Open Access Repositories – *Open*DOAR,
  http://www.opendoar.org/

[6] OpenAIREplus Guidelines:
  http://www.openaire.eu/en/component/attachments/download/79

[7] In general, both structure and semantics of the incoming records will be "massaged" by transformation and cleaning services, in order to ingest quality and uniform metadata records.

[8] Dublin Core will be qualified to include the representation of optional relationships with license schemes, projects, publications (e.g., citations) and datasets.

services to infer new relationships by mining the information space and therefore enrich it with content not explicitly available from any data sources. In this sense, since new inference algorithms can be added to the infrastructure at any time, hence new relationships between entities can be inferred, the data model should consider the possibility to dynamically include new semantic relationships between entities, without breaking the consistency of services operating over the information space.

Applications. Third-party applications require access to the information space through standard protocols and standard exchange formats. While the first requirement has to do with the implementation of the export services according to given API specifications, the second can impact the data model definition. In fact, the more the data model is aligned with the data models of given standard export formats, the easier and straightforward it is to map information space content onto such formats. Avoiding cumbersome structural and semantics rewriting avoids maintenance issues relative to the mappings, minimizes ambiguity and loss of information due to complex mapping rules and delivers to applications data which neatly matches the one accessible through the portal. In OpenAIREplus, this requirement will be addressed by reflecting in the information space data model the entities, the properties and the relationships identified by the standard export formats adopted by the infrastructure data sources (listed above). For example, the DataCite data model finds a straightforward mapping onto the OpenAIREplus data model. A dataset metadata record is mapped onto a set of OpenAIREplus entities and relationships: the dataset entity represented by the record with relationships to persons (e.g., dataset authors) and possibly other datasets and publications. This property allows directly exporting the subparts of the OpenAIREplus information space corresponding to dataset descriptions as DataCite records, hence to channel out incoming record formats as record export format.

3   Re-using Known Data Models

3.1   Research Information – CERIF

CERIF is a conceptual model of the research domain, typically applied in Common Research Information Systems (CRIS). It captures research results (publications, patents, products – the latter covering datasets, software and other types of output) as well as entities constituting the research context, like persons, organizations, projects, funding programmes, facilities, services. Every entity instance in CERIF is associated with a URI; the latest CERIF release allows for multiple federated identifiers.

A key feature of CERIF is the ability to represent semantic relationships (e.g. person-publication, organization-project, project-funding programme), including recursive links, e.g. connecting two project instances. Relationships in CERIF are called link entities and contain temporal information specifying the date range within which a specific semantic relationship applies, for example person A was coordinator of project X between 01-Feb-2012 to 29-Jun-2012. The semantics of each relationship instance (e.g. the role of a person in a project) and the associated vocabularies (i.e. potential values for roles) are not static components of the CERIF entity structure, but can be dynamically injected into a CERIF database. This is accomplished using the *CERIF Semantic Layer*, which enables the specification and maintenance of controlled vocabularies, called classification schemes, and their terms, called classes, as well as their association with entities. CERIF is able to represent any vocabulary structure (e.g. thesaurus) and the mapping among terms in different vocabularies. The semantic layer is also used to directly represent classifications of CERIF entities, example.g. terms from a subject classification vocabulary can be assigned to a publication, organisations can be typed. While a CERIF-based system is extensible to include any vocabulary, a set of common vocabularies is published as a separate component of the CERIF standard. The design and structure of the semantic layer facilitates the generation of Linked Open data from CERIF databases [12], which is being standardized by the Linked Open Data Task Group of euroCRIS.

The distinctive characteristics and modeling philosophy of CERIF can be briefly summarized as follows:

- The model is highly extensible and flexible, since a significant part of the information is not hard coded but specified through the semantic layer. The latter allows customization to a particular environment (e.g. research system of a country) or even the co-existence of specifics of different contexts (e.g. different European countries) in the same system, without the loss of CERIF compatibility, via the evolution of semantic definitions. This is particularly significant in the rapidly evolving research domain, where the emergence of new types of output, tools, research methods, funding schemes are commonplace. It facilitates also maintenance, since data schema evolution can be achieved to a large extent without changing the underlying database structure, since for example updating vocabularies does not require modifying table definitions in a relational database back-end.
- Entity properties can be modelled as relationships between entities with declared semantics specified within the semantic layer instead of data fields with the CERIF specification. This avoids the need for the proliferation of rigidly defined data fields. For instance, the creator property of a dataset can be a relationship of product with persons, while the creation date can be captured as temporal information in the "creator" relationship. In combination with the extensible semantic layer, this approach facilitates the generality of CERIF.
- Multi-linguality (field values in different languages) is inherently supported.

3.2   Research Dataset Modelling – DataCite

The DataCite initiative forms an international consortium addressing the challenges of making data citable in a harmonized, interoperable and persistent way. In particular DataCite supports data centers by providing persistent identifiers for datasets, workflows and standards for data publication and journal publishers by enabling research articles to be linked to the underlying data. As such, DataCite targets a wide audience and focuses on the minimal infrastructural aspects to enable cross-discipline best practices for data citation. DataCite members must assign Digital Object

Identifiers[9] (DOIs) [2] to their data sets and export metadata descriptions conforming
to the DataCite metadata format (data model) specification [3]. DataCite objects man-
datorily include the properties: title, authors, publishing year, distributor, and persistent identifier (it is a subset of the Dataverse mandatory fields [4], without the property UNF). Such properties may be structured, e.g., creators can be more than one, have
separate name separate from surname property, and may have a unique persistent
identifier. Moreover, the data model includes a rich set of optional properties. For
example, it includes properties to classify the data based on subject, format, typology,
its access rights, language, and how it is interlinked with other datasets and publications. Many data repositories are today part of DataCite and follow its directives; for
example, PANGAEA [10] (geo-referenced data from earth system research) and
DANS[11] (data for social science research), which are already liaising with the OpenAIRE infrastructure, and many others. In OpenAIRE, DataCite has been adopted as
the standard metadata to be used by data repository data sources to be able to contribute content to the infrastructure and its data model has been embedded into the information space data model, not to lose relevant information, and also to be able to
export dataset information as DataCite metadata records. Furthermore, OpenAIRE is
liaising with DataCite to exchange dataset metadata and dataset-dataset and dataset-
publication relationships.

4   The OpenAIREplus Data Model

In order to match the aforementioned requirements the OpenAIREplus data model
includes five main entities, visible as yellow boxes in see Figure 2: result (encompass-
ing publications and datasets), person, organization, project, and data source. Furthermore, the funding entity represents funding programmes. In order to support the
evolution in time of relationship-inference algorithms, the model adopts the CERIF
semantic layer approach to specify semantic-agnostic relationships between publica-
tions-datasets, publications-publications, datasets-datasets, person-results, organiza-
tions-results, projects-funding, organizations-funding, funding-funding and organiza-
tions-projects. Their intended semantics will be injected at run-time, when required,
thanks to a Class entity of a Scheme entity (see Figure 1).

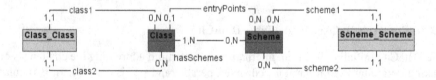

Fig. 1. E-R model: semantic layer entities

---

[9] *Digital Object Identifier System*, http://www.doi.org
[10] *PANGAEA*, http://www.pangaea.de
[11] *DANS*, http://www.dans.knaw.nl/

Similarly, whenever entities need to be classified based on a property value (e.g., nationality of a person), property and values are modeled by an association to a *Class* (e.g., *nationalityClass*) and one to the relative *Scheme* (e.g., *nationalityScheme*). The benefit of the approach is that applications can be written in such a way they cope with the dynamic addition, removal, or deletion of *Classes* and *Schemes*.

Result Entity. The *Result* entity, depicted in Figure 3, generalizes over the concept of research output and currently includes the sub-entities *datasets* and *publications*. Datasets are intended to describe any digital object that may result from a research process or be meaningful for its completion and at the same time could be useful for others to re-use or better understand research results. Examples are scientific experimental or secondary data, sensors data, proteins, but also software products. Examples of publication types are conference and journal papers, PhD theses, technical reports, project deliverables, but also emerging "enhanced publications" [5]. Other kinds of results may be added in the future to the model, as further sub-entities (e.g., patents).

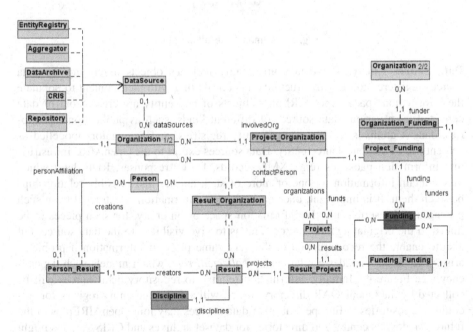

Fig. 2. E-R model: main, linked, static and structural entities

Results are also associated to a set of so-called *structural entities*, which logically describe structured properties of an entity as a hierarchy of objects "private" to a result object, i.e., not shared by other results.[12] In particular, the same result is associated to one or more *instances*. For example, the same publication may be

---

[12] An alternative conceptual representation could have been possible using the notion of structured property of an entity.

kept in two different repositories. Hence, an instance of a result is associated (relationship *hostedBy)* to one or more *web resources* relative to the sub-parts of the result and of the *data source* object from which such resources are made available.

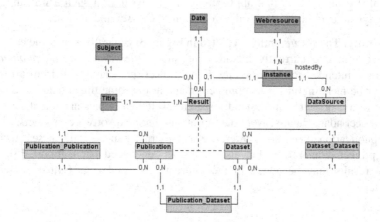

Fig. 3. E-R model: Result entities

Data Source Entity. The data source entity includes objects describing the data sources registered to the infrastructure and contributing with their content to populate the information space. OpenAIREplus objects of any entity are created out of data collected from various data sources of different kinds, such as publication repositories, dataset archives, CRIS systems, entity registries, and aggregators modelled as sub-entities of the data source entity. Data sources export to the OpenAIRE infrastructure information packages (e.g., XML records, HTTP responses, RDF data) which may contain information on one or more of such entities and possibly relationships between them. It is important, once each piece of information is extracted from such packages and inserted into the information space as an entity, for such pieces to be linked to the originating data source. This is to give visibility to the data source, but also to enable the reconstruction of the very same piece of information if problems arise. The model includes a relationship *collectedFrom*, which models such dependency (see Figure 4). Initially, information relative to repository data sources will be collected by the OpenDOAR directory, which will act as main entity registry for (literature) repositories in Europe, but other data sources may join OpenAIREplus in the future. Analogous centralized directories for dataset archives and CRIS systems might become available; meanwhile, their administrators need to provide data about them to OpenAIREplus upon registering their data sources.

Person Entity. The person entity includes all person objects describing authors or persons covering roles in project management and organizations. As such, person objects are mainly created out of data source information packages (e.g., Dublin Core records from repositories) which do not provide rich properties and unique identifiers.

OpenAIRE is liaising with ORCID, which will register as an entity registry to feed and fetch clean authoritative information. There are also plans for OpenAIRE to exchange publication-author links and license information with Mendeley.[13]

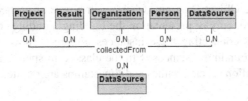

Fig. 4. E-R model: provenance relationships

Project Entity. The project entity includes objects describing funding resources (co-) granted by funding agencies, such as the European Commission or National governments. Of crucial interest to OpenAIREplus is also the identification of the funding programmes (called *funding* in Figure 2) which co-funded the projects that have led to a given result. Initially, EC FP7 programme projects data will be fetched from the authoritative EC CORDA database, together with the organizations or persons which are participants of such projects. Data relative to National funding schemes and relative projects will be instead fetched from CRIS systems, together with other entities which may be typically kept within a CRIS system (e.g., publications, datasets, etc.).

Organization Entity. The organization entity includes objects describing companies, research centers or institutions involved as project partners or as responsible of operating data sources. Information about organizations will be initially collected from the information packages collected from the entity registry of CORDA and various CRIS systems. For the future, OpenAIREplus is liaising with UK RepositoryNET+[14] to open and exchange of entity registries including organizations and authors.

5   Modelling Use Cases within OpenAIREplus

The present section provides a characteristic example of the capabilities of the OpenAIREplus data model, in particular accommodating data about national funding schemes across Europe and diverse funding programme structures from different countries, and provides links to other entities (e.g. projects, organizations). To address this, funding programmes and funding programme components are represented as instances of the Funding entity, while the recursive Funding_Funding link entity enables the representation of arbitrarily complex funding programme structures, for example hierarchies of any depth or even graphs, using an appropriate vocabulary for the classification of each instance of this relationship. The most common class term is currently "Part" upon the Funding_Funding link entity; in the CERIF vocabulary this denotes that a funding programme is a sub-programme of another one.

---

[13] Mendeley, http://www.mendeley.com/
[14] UK RepositoryNET+, http://www.repositorynet.ac.uk

As an example, Figure 5 depicts – in a highly simplified form – the representation in OpenAIREplus of a part of the European Commission Framework Programme Seven (FP7), which comprises five sub-programmes, each containing many sub-divisions. For instance, the Capacities sub programme has 6 subdivisions. It is presented as a UML Object Diagram, where each box is an instance of the Funding entity. Due to the economy of presentation the Funding_Funding entities in the figure appear only as lines connecting these instances. Figure 6 shows explicitly the link entity between two Funding instances with the class term specifying the relationship semantics (classification scheme values and timestamps are omitted for simplicity).

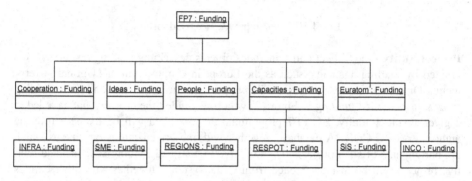

Fig. 5. OpenAIREplus data model: fragment of the FP7 funding programme structure

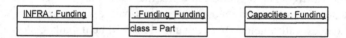

Fig. 6. Funding_Funding relationship with declared semantics (highly simplified)

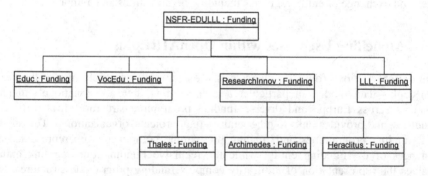

Fig. 7. OpenAIREplus *data model: fragment of the Greek EDULLL funding programme* structure

Figure 7 presents the entity instances used to represent in OpenAIREplus a Greek national funding programme, supporting education, lifelong learning and research. Lines between instances of Funding correspond also in this case to Funding_Funding

"Part" linkages. The two funding structures in Figures 5 and 7 smoothly co-exist in the OpenAIREplus data model and are linked with other entities without requiring any changes in the logical and physical model of the underlying relational database.

As an example of linking other entities to Funding, a project is connected with funding programmes through the Project_Funding link entity. Such a link is shown in Figure 8, where the OpenAIREplus project instance is related to the Research Infrastructures (INFRA) FP7 programme sub-division via two instances of the Project_Funding link entity: one stating that the INFRA programme is the FundingProgramme of OpenAIREplus (i.e. OpenAIREplus is funded by INFRA) and that OpenAIREplus, in terms of funding instrument, is a Combination of Collaborative Project and Coordination and Support Action (CPCSA). The class term may take values from a specific classification scheme that contains terms for all possible instruments. In a similar example a project X, of type CollaborativeResearch, is connected to a sub-division of the EDULLL programme called Thales.

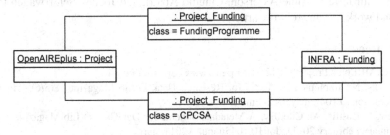

Fig. 8. Example relationships of Project to the FP7 Research Infrastructures programme

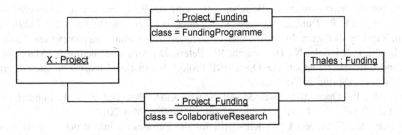

Fig. 9. Example relationships of Project to the Greek EDULLL funding programme

6   Summary and Future Work

In this paper we presented the OpenAIREplus data model, at the core of the OpenAIRE infrastructure. The intention was to focus on the informational aspects of the data model, hence on the requirements that led to the definition of its constituent parts. To this aim highlighted its modern scientific communication flavour in combination with the funding issues surrounding the research process. More, we stressed its flexibility and ability to cope with evolving requirements, in terms of entities to be modelled and relationships between them. Part of the data model, but out of the scope of this paper, is the additional scaffolding of entities, properties and relationships required to cope with data curation issues. The continuous synchronization of the information space with the data sources, removes, deletes, and updates information about one or more of the entities, as well as relationships between them. For example, some archives provide dataset metadata that also includes links to publications relevant for the dataset or vice versa. Such cross-entity and cross-sources data integration brings in data inference issues, which have mainly to do with information absence, duplication, and versioning (intended as replicas of the same entity). These issues will push into the data model a number of entities, properties, and relationships whose aim is to deliver to data curators the tools to maintain a clean, uniform, and consistent information space.

Acknowledgements. The work presented in this paper has been partly supported by the OpenAIREplus Project (Ref No: 283595) of the EU-funded FP7-INFRASTRUCTURES Programme. The authors wish to acknowledge the contribution of Keith Jeffery, Anne Asserson, Claudio Atzori, and Jochen Schirrwagen to the ideas and work presented in the article.

References

1. OpenAIREplus Project (2012), http://www.openaire.eu
2. Simons, N.: Implementing DOIs for Research Data. D-Lib Magazine 18(5/6) (May/June 2012), doi:10.1045/may2012-simons
3. Starr, J., Gastlis, A.: CitedBy: A Metadata Scheme for DataCite. D-Lib Magazine 17(1/2) (January/February 2011), doi:10.1045/january2011-starr
4. Altman, M., King, G.: A Proposed Standard for the Scholarly Citation of Quantitative Data. D-Lib Magazine (March/April 2007)
5. Woutersen-Windhouwer, S., Brandsma, R., Verhaar, P., Hogenaar, A., Hoogerwerf, M., Doorenbosch, P., Durr, E., Ludwig, J., Schmidt, B., Sierman, B.: Enhanced Publications. In: Vernooy-Gerritsen, M. (ed.) SURF Foundation. Amsterdam University Press (2009)
6. Manghi, P., Manola, N., Horstmann, W., Peters, D.: An Infrastructure for Managing EC Funded Research Output, The OpenAIRE Project. International Journal on Grey Literature (TGJ) 6(1) (Spring 2010)
7. Manghi, P.: OpenAIRE Data Model Specification. Deliverable D5.1. Funded in call INFRA-2007-1.2.1, Grant Agreement Number 246686 (May 2010)
8. Jeffery, K., Asserson, A.: CERIF-CRIS for the European e-Infrastructure. Data Science Journal 9, CRIS1–CRIS6 (2010)
9. Jörg, B.: CERIF: The Common European Research Information Format Model. Data Science Journal 9, CRIS24–CRIS31 (2010)
10. Houssos, N., Jörg, B., Matthews, B.: A multi-level metadata approach for a Public Sector Information data infrastructure. In: Proc. 11th International Conference on Current Research Information Systems (CRIS 2012), Prague, Czech Republic, June 06-09 (2012)
11. Ginty, K., Kerridge, S., Fairley, P., Henderson, R., Cramer, P., Bokma, A., Garfield, S.: CERIF for Datasets (C4D) - An Overview. In: Proc. 11th International Conference on Current Research Information Systems (CRIS 2012), Prague, Czech Republic, June 06-09 (2012)
12. Jörg, B., et al.: Connecting Closed World Research Information Systems through the Linked Open Data Web. International Journal of Software Engineering and Knowledge Engineering (IJSEKE) 22 (June 2012)

Metadata Quality Evaluation of a Repository
Based on a Sample Technique

Marc Goovaerts and Dirk Leinders

Hasselt University Library, Belgium
{marc.goovaerts,dirk.leinders}@uhasselt.be

Abstract. In this paper, we evaluate the quality of the metadata of an OAI-compliant repository based on the completeness metric proposed by X. Ochoa and E. Duval. This study focuses on the completeness of the metadata records as defined by M.A. Sicilia et al, where machine-understandability is a mandatory requirement for completeness. The goal is to use the completeness metric as a tool for harvesters and repository managers to evaluate easily the quality of the metadata of a repository. We focus on the metadata used by the communities of agriculture, aquaculture and environment from the VOA3R project. The OceanDocs repository serves as a use case. The completeness metric is used on a sample of records from the repository. The paper concludes that in the opinion of the authors quality evaluation is not a global process, but depends on the context. The completeness metric have to be used on the specific elements, relevant for the specific community.

Keywords: Metadata quality, Institutional repository, VOA3R, OceanDocs.

1   Introduction

The quality of metadata is crucial for service providers who want to develop enhanced services. VOA3R [1] is a 3-year European project launched in June 2010 and funded by the European Commission under the seventh framework ICT Policy Support Program. The VOA3R platform is a service provider who integrates existing open access repositories as well as digital libraries, sharing scientific and open access research related to Agriculture, Food, Aquaculture and Environment. VOA3R is dedicated to providing a community-oriented platform based on social networking, micro-blogging and social bookmarking. To support the quality of the harvested metadata a specific application profile was created: VOA3R AP [2]. But an application profile does not guarantee the quality of the content.

Metadata quality has not been given adequate attention in the repository community. The definition of Dublin Core as a standard for OAI-PMH [3] brought the granularity of the metadata for institutional repositories to a basic level. The Guidelines for Repository Implementers for OAI-PMH suggests that specific communities can use other standards, but in practice most of the repositories follow the standard implementation in packages like DSpace, which supports a Dublin Core qualified at maximum [4].

J.M. Dodero, M. Palomo-Duarte, P. Karampiperis (Eds.): MTSR 2012, CCIS 343, pp. 181–189, 2012.
© Springer-Verlag Berlin Heidelberg 2012

An important reason for this choice is the fact that most submitters are not information specialists. Authors do not like the administrative work of creating metadata. Therefore a minimal format seems a nice solution in an environment where authors get the responsibility to submit their papers.

The success of general search engines with simple text search made it feel superfluous to create rich metadata. In the last fifteen years, the internet has changed completely the way researchers are looking for information. Yahoo, Google and other search engines limited the search technique to a simple word search supported by a powerful ranking system. Why should people bother about rich metadata?

But rich services need better metadata. Service providers like VOA3R want to create relations between pieces of metadata automatically. Therefore you need more refined and precise metadata. Ontologies are again becoming relevant, surely if terms and concepts can be defined uniquely by an identifier or resource URI. For example, the systematic use of AGROVOC keywords makes it possible to relate research topics in AGRIS. The use of resource URIs for every AGROVOC keyword supports multilinguality.

Metadata formats guarantee the level of granularity. A full MODS, not one translated from Dublin Core qualified as in DSpace, is much more refined than Dublin Core. Specific application profiles have been developed like Agris AP [5] and VOA3R AP, as more granular formats than Dublin Core.

2   Definition of Metadata Quality

How can we define quality for metadata content? T.R. Bruce and D. Hillman [6] proposed seven parameters for metadata quality: completeness, accuracy, conformance to expectation, logical consistency, accessibility, timeliness, and provenance.

In this study we focus on completeness, as the most important parameter for the service provider, with the following definition: 'A metadata instance should describe the resource as fully as possible. Also, the metadata fields should be filled in for the majority of the resource population in order to make them useful for any kind of service'. [7] But completeness is related to granularity and precision.

Objects are described by metadata elements. Granularity defines the refinement of these elements. For example, Dublin Core has only one element for the source element (bibliographicCitation), while MODS has the possibility to split up the source description in multiple elements. The example in Fig. 1 shows part of a MODS description, where journal title, volume, start and end page are available separately.

The use of authority control, ontologies and unique identifiers defines content unequivocally. Because of its unambiguity a DOI or a handle is sometimes more relevant than a whole abstract. The use of resource URIs for author names, journal titles or thesauri terms makes these values uniquely defined. Institutional repositories are mainly based on text. Harvesters like OAIster collect structured text, but to create rich services a machine-readable approach is essential in a world with Linked Open Data. M.A. Sicilia et al. 'consider machine-understandability as a mandatory requirement for completeness of metadata records' [8].

```
<relatedItem type="host">
  <titleInfo>
    <title>Bulletin Scientifique de l'IMROP</title>
  </titleInfo>
  <part>
    <detail type="volume">
        <number>28</number>
    </detail>
    <extent  unit="page">
        <start>1</start>
        <end>31</end>
    </extent>
  </part>
</relatedItem>
```

Fig. 1. Example of a source description in MODS, specifically the reference to a journal

Granularity and precision influences our view on the completeness of the metadata. These aspects will be used in the study further on.

Traditionally, metadata quality is evaluated manually based on a questionnaire. Basically, there are many subjective aspects in this approach. It is also a work intensive job. In their article 'Automatic evaluation of metadata quality in digital repositories' [9] X. Ochoa and E. Duval describe a very complete method of automatic evaluation of the seven metadata quality parameters defined by T.R. Bruce and D. Hillman. The method does not only evaluate the metadata but also the relation to the content and the user expectations. In this article we focus only on the completeness of metadata. We used the second completeness metric of X. Ochoa and E. Duval.

3   Evaluation of Metadata Quality: OceanDocs Case

We propose a simple statistical approach using a random sample of records to evaluate the metadata quality. The completeness metrics of X. Ochoa and E. Duval are devised to analyze digital libraries and repositories with a full record set. In many cases it can be more practical to work with a limited sample. For example, when a service provider requests a sample for evaluation before harvesting the targeted repository.

While X. Ochoa and E. Duval measure the metadata quality using complete records, we focused on key elements which are machine-readable. Some elements of the metadata are difficult to evaluate because they are not always available or because they are not mandatory. For example some publications do not have an author, some journals do not have an ISSN. Every community has specific key elements, depending on their focus. The aquatic community uses for example ASFA keywords, while in agriculture AGROVOC is used. Evaluation criteria have to be adapted to the needs of the community.

The OceanDocs [10] repository, our study case, is used in the aquatic community and also harvested by VOA3R. Therefore, the ASFA and AGROVOC thesauri are relevant metadata elements for respectively the aquatic and the agricultural community.

Ex. Agrovoc term:
- Marine fisheries:
    o   with term code: c_4611
    o   with resource URI: http://aims.fao.org/aos/agrovoc/c_4611

ASFA term:
- Fisheries biology
    o   with term code: c_5839
    o   resource URI: http://aims.fao.org/aos/asfa/c_5839

Fig. 2. Example of AGROVOC and ASFA terms with their unique identifiers

The key elements analyzed were the keywords and the source description. We evaluated the precision (availability of controlled vocabulary and unique identifiers for keywords) and the granularity (source description).

The analysis went through three steps:

1. Two random samples of OceanDocs records were taken with data about keywords and source description.
2. The confidence interval was measured for each of the keyword elements and for each of the elements of the source description to check whether the sample was representative [11].
3. For both group of elements, the results were computed with Ochoa and Duval's completeness metric [12].

3.1   Creation of Samples of Metadata Records from OceanDocs

Samples were taken from the OceanDocs repository[1]. We generated the samples by applying a simple random sampling technique. Each record was included in the sample with equal probability, which was determined by the desired sample size. The first sample of 100 records gave a large confidence interval. The second sample of 300 records gave an acceptable confidence interval. Note that the size of the sample is not related to the size of the database, but to the standard deviation of the sample. Therefore, even for larger databases the technique allows to work with relatively small samples.

---

[1] The data is available in the OAI-MODS format. (ex. http://www.oceandocs.org/odin-oai/request?verb=GetRecord&metadataPrefix=mods&identifier=oai:www.oceandocs.org:18 34/1500).

From each record we collected the following elements:

- Keywords: Free keywords, ASFA term, ASFA term code, AGROVOC term, AGROVOC URI
- Source of journal contribution: journal title, volume, issue, start page, end page. Only for sample 2, we calculated the availability.

If an element is available in a record the value is 1, if unavailable 0. Table 1 shows the results.

Table 1. Availability of elements for the different samples

	Free keyword	ASFA keyword	ASFA termcode	AGROVOC keyword	AGROVOC URI
Sample 1 – 100 records					
Records with	51	71	64	51	51
Average ($\bar{x}$)	0,51	0,71	0,64	0,51	0,51
Sample 2 – 300 records					
Records with	168	211	196	161	161
Average ($\bar{x}$)	0,56	0,703	0,653	0,537	0,537

3.2   Defining the Confidence Interval of the Samples

For every keyword element of the samples, we defined the confidence interval using the formula proposed by L. Egghe and R. Rousseau. We calculated for the average $\bar{x}$ of sample size N a confidence interval with 95% certitude.

$$\left[\bar{x} - 1.96 \sqrt{\frac{\bar{x}(1-\bar{x})}{N-1}}, \bar{x} + 1.96 \sqrt{\frac{\bar{x}(1-\bar{x})}{N-1}} \right] \quad \textit{(95\% confidence interval)}$$

(1)

From L. Egghe & R. Rousseau (2001). Elementary Statistics for Effective Library and Information Service Management. London, Aslib. p. 86

The results are listed in table 2 and 3.

Table 2. Confidence interval of sample 1

Sample 1 (100 records)	Average ($\bar{x}$)	Confidence interval
Free Keywords	0,51	[0,412 ; 0,608]
ASFA keyword	0,71	[0,621 ; 0,799]
ASFA code term	0,64	[0,545 ; 0,735]
AGROVOC	0,51	[0,412 ; 0,608]
AGROVOC URI	0,51	[0,412 ; 0,608]

Table 3. Confidence interval of sample 2

Sample 2 (300 records)	Average ($\bar{x}$)	Confidence interval
Free Keywords	0,56	[0,504 ; 0,616]
ASFA keyword	0,703	[0,651 ; 0,755]
ASFA code term	0,653	[0,599 ; 0,707]
AGROVOC	0,537	[0,480 ; 0,594]
AGROVOC URI	0,537	[0,480 ; 0,594]

Sample 1 (with sample size N=100) gave a confidence interval of about 20%. Therefore we took a second sample with 300 records which had an acceptable confidence interval for our further analysis.

3.3   Evaluation of the Metadata Quality by Using a Completeness Metric

X. Ochoa and E. Duval have defined two completeness metrics. The basic completeness metric counts the number of fields in each metadata instance that contain a no-null value. In the case of multi-valued fields, the field is considered complete if at least one instance exists. They also proposes a metric with a weighting factor for the different metadata fields of the record. A higher degree of relevance of a field will be translated in a higher weighting factor. We used this weighted completeness metric.

$$Qwcomp = \frac{\sum_{i=1}^{N} \alpha_i * P(i)}{\sum_{i=1}^{N} \alpha_i}$$

(2)

From X. Ochoa & E. Duval (2009), Automatic evaluation of metadata quality in digital repositories. In Int. J. Digit. Libr., 10, (2-3), p. 71.

Note   that the maximum value for Qwcomp is 1 (all fields with importance different from 0 are non-empty) and the minimum value is 0 (all fields with importance different from 0 are empty).

As discussed above, while X. Ochoa and E. Duval measure the metadata quality using complete records, we focused on key elements of the metadata.

We evaluated the metadata quality of OceanDocs, specifically the use of keywords. We only looked at the averages of sample 2 because of their smaller confidence interval. For the aquatic community the use of the ASFA thesaurus is relevant. The agriculture community uses the AGROVOC thesaurus. Therefore we gave different weighting factors to each keyword element. Free keywords received the lowest and unique identifiers the highest weighting factor.

The quality of keyword elements for the aquatic community was measured by the use of free keywords, ASFA keywords and ASFA term codes. We gave them the following weighting factors for their relevance.

- Free keywords = 1 – ASFA keywords = 2 – ASFA term code = 3
  The completeness value from aquatic perspective:
  Qwcomp= (1*0,56 + 2*0,703+3*0,653)/(1+2+3) = 0,654

The quality of keyword elements for the agriculture community was measured by the use of free keywords, AGROVOC keywords and AGROVOC URIs with the following weighting factors.

- Free keywords = 1 - AGROVOC keywords = 2 - AGROVOC URI = 3
  The completeness value from agriculture perspective:
  Qwcomp= (1*0,56 + 2*0,537+3*0,537)/(1+2+3) = 0,540

In both cases we put a heavy weighting on the unique IDs. We believe that accuracy can be achieved mostly by using authority control and resource URIs are the most relevant exponent of it.

Based on the second sample, we also evaluated the completeness of the source description, specifically of journal contributions. From the 300 records in sample 2, 162 were journal contributions. We evaluated the source description on the existence of journal title, volume + issue, start page and end page. Volume and issue were combined - if one of both was available then it got a value - because some journals use only one of both.

The results are shown below in table 4.

Table 4. Availability of elements for publications in journals from sample 2

Sample 2	Journal title	Volume-issue	Start page	End page
Records with	146	143	142	142
Average ($\bar{x}$)	0,901	0,883	0,877	0,877

The following weighting factors were used, for:

- Journal title = 3 -   volume + issue = 2 - start page = 2 - end page=1
  The completeness value for source (journal contribution):
  Qwcomp=(3*0,901 + 2*0,883 + 2*0,877 + 1*0,877)/(3+2+2+1) = 0,888.

We have evaluated the metadata of the OceanDocs repository on the quality of the keywords and the source description, through a sample of 300 records. We obtained the following completeness values.

Table 5. Completeness values of ASFA, AGROVOC and Journal contributions

ASFA	0,654
AGROVOC	0,540
Source (Journal contribution)	0,888

The level of metadata completeness for AGROVOC was low in OceanDocs. It is an oceanographic repository, therefore we expected a higher completeness level for ASFA. In our opinion, the completeness level for ASFA is still low. What level can a service provider expect to create services with these elements ? With a result of 0,654, about 35% of the records was not accessible through the keyword elements. On the other hand the completeness level of the source description was high. It demonstrates the granularity of the OceanDocs metadata.

Other aspects of the metadata could be studied like the description of relations (DOI, URLs, versioning, ...). But the two parameters, keywords and source - ASFA and AGROVOC are similar parameters from different communities - are basic indicators of the completeness and the quality of metadata.

4   Conclusions

This contribution presents a quick and easy evaluation method of the metadata quality of institutional repositories. It evaluates the completeness and granularity of the content using a sample of records. From these records, machine-readable elements were selected to be evaluated in their context. With the completeness metric of X. Ochoa and E. Duval the quality was measured. The OceanDocs repository was used as a case study.

If harvesters want to create extra services on top of the basic search functionalities, they have to control the quality and specifically the completeness of (specific parts of) the metadata. From our test case, we see that different communities, in our case agriculture and oceanography, will have different focuses: e.g. AGROVOC against ASFA. The quality and its evaluation will depend on the standards of the community. In our opinion quality evaluation is not a global process, but depends on the context. The completeness metric will then be used on the specific fields, relevant for the specific community.

It is difficult to define the threshold values for metadata completeness based on one case study. Further studies will be necessary, but already it is clear that a high level of completeness is necessary   to create rich services on the harvester level.

Metadata quality is relevant for the services that are required and can be delivered to a community by a harvester like VOA3R. Rich metadata is for us complete, granular and precise metadata. Central in this approach is the use of authority control systems with controlled vocabularies, ontologies and ultimately the use of resource URIs as unique identifiers which guarantees the accuracy and the reusability of the metadata.

References

1. VOA3R (Virtual Open Access Agriculture & Aquaculture Repository),
   http://voa3r.eu
2. Diamantopoulos, N., Sgouropoulou, C., Kastrantas, K., Manouselis, N.: Developing a Metadata Application Profile for Sharing Agricultural Scientific and Scholarly Research Resources. In: García-Barriocanal, E., Cebeci, Z., Okur, M.C., Öztürk, A. (eds.) MTSR 2011. CCIS, vol. 240, pp. 453–466. Springer, Heidelberg (2011)

3. Guidelines for Repository Implementers: 2.1 Dublin Core and Other Metadata Formats, http://www.openarchives.org/OAI/2.0/ guidelines-repository.htm#MinimalImplementation-DC
4. DSpace, version 1.8.x. Functional Overview. Metadata, https://wiki.duraspace.org/display/DSDOC18/Functional+ Overview#FunctionalOverview-Metadata
5. The AGRIS Application Profile for the International Information System on Agricultural Sciences and Technology Guidelines on Best Practices for Information Object Description, http://www.fao.org/docrep/008/ae909e/ae909e00.htm
6. Bruce, T.R., Hillmann, D.: The Continuüm of Metadata Quality: Defining, Expressing, Exploiting. In: Metadata in Practice, pp. 238–256. ALA Editions, Chicago (2004)
7. Ochoa, X., Duval, E.: Automatic evaluation of metadata quality in digital repositories. Int. J. Digit. Libr. 10(2-3), 69 (2009)
8. Sicilia, M.A., Garcia, E., Pages, C., Martinez, J.J., Gutierrez, J.M.: Complete metadata records in learning object repositories: some evidence and requirements. Int. J. Learn. Technol. 1(4), 411–424 (2005)
9. Ochoa, X., Duval, E.: Automatic evaluation of metadata quality in digital repositories. Int. J. Digit. Libr. 10(2-3), 67–91 (2009), doi:10.1007/s00799-009-0054-4
10. OceanDocs, http://www.oceandocs.org
11. Egghe, L., Rousseau, R.: Elementary Statistics for Effective Library and Information Service Management, pp. 68–73. Aslib, London (2001)
12. Ochoa, Duval, E.: Automatic evaluation of metadata quality in digital repositories. Int. J. Digit. Libr. 10(2-3), 71 (2009)

Extending an Abstract Reference Model for Transdisciplinary Work in Cultural Heritage

Cesar Gonzalez-Perez[1], Patricia Martín-Rodilla[1], Cesar Parcero-Oubiña[1], Pastor Fábrega-Álvarez[1], and Alejandro Güimil-Fariña[2]

[1] Institute of Heritage Sciences (Incipit), Spanish National Research Council (CSIC), Santiago de Compostela, Spain
{cesar.gonzalez-perez,patricia.martin-rodilla, cesar.parcero-oubina,pastor.fabrega-alvarez} @incipit.csic.es
[2] Laboratory of Heritage, Palaeoenviroment and Landscape, University of Santiago de Compostela, Spain
alejandro.guimil.farina@usc.es

Abstract. Obtaining models of cultural heritage that guarantee information interoperability and, at the same time, maintain a high degree of fitness to the problem at hand is not a trivial quest. This paper proposes a two-step approach to attain this, where particular models for each problem at hand are derived from a common, standardised Cultural Heritage Abstract Reference Model (CHARM) by using specific rules that guarantee abstract interoperability while allowing for as much specificity as necessary. This is illustrated through a case study involving three different communities, each with a different conceptual model of cultural heritage, which still generate a seamless object model.

Keywords: abstract reference model, transdisciplinarity, conceptual modelling, cultural heritage, CHARM, ConML.

1 Introduction

A number of attempts to formally represent cultural heritage have been made in the past, with different purposes and varying degrees of success. The CIDOC Conceptual Reference Model (CRM) [3, 10], for example, is an international standard especially aimed at "the curated knowledge of museums" [2, p. i-ii]. Other models and ontologies have other purposes, such as modelling the archaeological excavation and analysis process for CIDOC CRM-EH [13]; gathering a detailed collection of heritage-related terms for [5]; or supporting interoperability for information about protected sites in relation to the INSPIRE directive for the INSPIRE SDI of [4].

All these cases, however, share a common feature: there is always tension between standardisation and customisation, between the urge to establish a common ontology that reaches as far as possible, and the need to take into account the fact that each project or endeavour has its own peculiarities and therefore cannot be subject to an all-encompassing standard. Models that are wide and deep, i.e. that aim to describe an

J.M. Dodero, M. Palomo-Duarte, P. Karampiperis (Eds.): MTSR 2012, CCIS 343, pp. 190–201, 2012.

ample scope (that of a discipline, or even the whole world) while, at the same time, specifying every detail about it, are often seen as too prescriptive and rigid, since they leave little room for the peculiarities of each individual project. On the other hand, models that are narrow and shallow, i.e. that address a limited scope (such as that of an organisation or even a particular project) and avoid detailed descriptions are easily adopted, since they are likely to be much closer to the task at hand and not as prescriptive; however, they are not as useful to guarantee conceptual and technical interoperability with others. There is a wide range of possibilities between these two extremes. CIDOC CRM, for example, aims to be quite wide in its scope and moderately deep. CIDOC CRM-EH, on the other hand, is much narrower and even deeper.

In any case, models (or ontologies) that are narrow and shallow are rarely useful, since they provide little added value; and those which are wide and deep are barely usable, since they are too prescriptive. Workable combinations are wide and shallow, or narrow and deep. Wide and shallow models are sometimes called abstract reference models or, in the ontology literature, upper ontologies. Narrow and deep models are sometimes called particular or specific models; some detailed domain ontologies also qualify as narrow and deep models.

In order to resolve the tension outlined above, a two-step solution is proposed in this paper. This solution is based on an abstract reference model from which particular models can be derived. Section 2 introduces the Cultural Heritage Abstract Reference Model (CHARM) and the extension mechanisms that are in place to create particular models. Section 3 presents and develops a comprehensive case study that illustrates how CHARM can be extended into particular models in order to carry out several related projects in a complex cultural heritage setting. Finally, Section 4 offers some conclusions.

2   The Cultural Heritage Abstract Reference Model

The Cultural Heritage Abstract Reference Model (CHARM) is a semi-formal representation of cultural heritage in the form of an abstract reference model; this means that it is wide and shallow. In other words, CHARM aims to cover as much of the social and cultural phenomenon that we know as cultural heritage as possible, but at a high level of abstraction. In contrast to CIDOC CRM, CHARM is much wider, since it does not focus only on the curated knowledge of museums but on cultural heritage in general. At the same time, it is much shallower, because of its high level of abstraction; CHARM has been designed under the assumption that extension mechanisms need to be applied before it can be used at all (see Section 2.2), whereas CIDOC CRM attempts to be an off-the-shelf solution. CHARM is expressed in ConML [6, 9], a conceptual modelling language that extends the conventional object-oriented approach with features such as temporality and subjectivity modelling.

2.1   Major Areas and Structure

CHARM comprises 175 classes that describe the following three main areas of cultural heritage:

- **Evaluable Entities.** These are entities that have been, are or may be culturally valorized. Examples include a building, a song or an archaeological site. Evaluable entities comprise the "raw matter" from which cultural heritage is socially constructed.
- **Valorizations.** These are entities of a discursive nature that add cultural value to evaluable entities through interpretive processes that have been agreed upon within a group or discipline. Examples include a technical report on a building or a feeling of attachment to a place. Valorizations are what convert evaluable entities into actual components of cultural heritage.
- **Representations.** These are entities that capture the forms, contents, characteristics and/or properties of one or more evaluable entities (called the contents) on other evaluable entities (called the medium). Examples include a document, a painting, a sound recording or a 3D architectural model.

Explaining the rationale of such a structure is beyond the scope of this paper; please see [8] for additional information. Following on this structure, Fig. 1 shows a high-level view of CHARM.

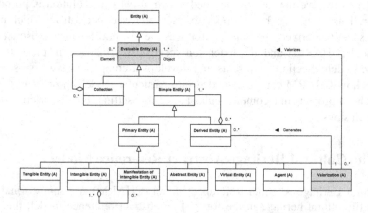

Fig. 1. High-level view of CHARM. The notation used is ConML [9]; rectangles represent classes, arrows with triangular heads depict specialisation relationships, lines with diamond-shaped terminators represent whole/part associations, and simple lines depict plain associations.

Note that evaluable entities are classified into collections and simple entities; the difference is self-explanatory. Simple entities, in turn, are classified as follows:

- A **primary entity** is one that, when perceived, is understood without the need of explicit interpretive processes. Examples include a building or a song. This definition does not mean that every agent will understand the same primary entity in the same way; it only means that the entity will be understood.
- A **derived entity**, on the contrary, is one that arises as the outcome of a valorization and, as such, is seldom understood unless mediated by an explicit interpretive process. Examples include an archaeological site or a cultural landscape.

Primary entities, in turn, are classified into a number of specific kinds depending on their nature. The following are relevant for the case study presented in further sections of this paper:

- A **tangible entity** is one that is fundamentally perceived in a direct manner and through its materiality. Examples include a building or a knife; both can be perceived straightforwardly through their materiality.
- An **intangible entity** is one that is fundamentally perceived in an indirect manner and through its particular manifestations. Examples include a song or a trade. A song is only perceived when we hear it being sung (each particular performance of the song being a manifestation of the abstract construct that we call "the song"). Similarly, a trade is perceived when we see and interact with someone performing that trade, i.e. through particular manifestations of the trade.
- A **manifestation of an intangible entity** is one that corresponds to the expression of an intangible entity at a given time and place, and which is fundamentally perceived in a direct manner through performative aspects. Examples include a song being sung or a trade being performed. As shown in Fig. 1, there is a whole/part association between Intangible Entity and Manifestation of Intangible Entity to capture the close connection between these two related but different concepts.

Fig. 2 below describes representations in CHARM.

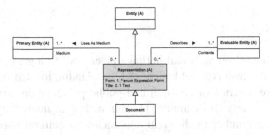

Fig. 2. Representations in CHARM. Only the Document subclass is shown for brevity; others such as Photograph, Map or Drawing exist in the complete specification.

As explained above, representations describe evaluable entities (their contents) by materializing them on a medium (one or more primary entities). Documents are one particular kind of representations that are relevant for the case study presented below.

2.2   Extension Mechanisms

CHARM is an abstract reference model, i.e. it can be hardly used for practical purposes without extension. Extending CHARM means adding extra classes, attributes and associations, as needed, in order to narrow its scope and increase its depth so as to perfectly describe the project or task at hand. The ontic and epistemic factors that determine the fitness of a model to a particular situation are complex, and have been described by works such as [7, 12]. In any case, extending CHARM always entails the production of a *particular model*, a superset of the former, so that every class in the particular model that is not in CHARM is Liskov-compatible [11] with a class in CHARM. Liskov-compatibility means that every entity represented by the particular model is also represented by CHARM, and therefore can also be treated, from a more abstract viewpoint, as an instance of the corresponding class in CHARM. This is achieved through the conventional object-oriented mechanism of type specialisation.

When a particular model is created, it is initially equivalent to CHARM, since it contains no extra elements. From that point on, the following extension mechanisms are available to extend CHARM, and can be combined as needed:

- Adding classes by specialising from one or more existing classes in the particular model.
- Removing classes in CHARM that are not linked to other classes in the particular model through a greater-than-zero cardinality.
- Adding attributes to classes in the particular model. If an attribute is added with a greater-than-zero cardinality, it cannot belong to a class in CHARM.
- Adding associations between classes in the particular model. If an association is added with an end that has a greater-than-zero cardinality, this association end cannot be attached to a class in CHARM.
- Adding enumerated types.
- Adding enumerated items.

3   Case Study

This case study is based on an actual heritage place and, to a great extent, on actual events. The site is the Iron Age settlement of Castrolandín, located in Galicia (North-West Spain), where a series of research and public presentation projects have been carried out since the early 21st century [1]. This makes an interesting case study for our purpose, since a number of different approaches to cultural heritage and agents have converged on it in a short period of time.

At the onset, the site was a simple archaeological site inventoried as such by the regional government. The site consisted of a series of ramparts and ditches on a hill-top, conforming a typical Iron Age hillfort, regionally known as a *castro*. It had been known and described since the mid-20th century by archaeologists and amateurs, and was finally included in the official inventory of heritage sites following the usual procedure: an archaeological consultancy was hired by the regional government for the recording of heritage sites within the region. A record log was assigned to the site as a heritage place, and a series of land use regulations were imposed to the area de-signed as its extent.

After that, a research project was developed on the site aimed at the anthropological documentation of the local community's perceptions and feelings about the site. This project allowed for the description and study of a traditional feast, nowadays lost, that had occurred on the site at least between the late 19th and the mid-20th centuries. Descriptions of the feast of San Xoán (St. John's) are known thanks both to some written records and the memories of local elderly people. Thanks to this project, the feast of San Xoán was brought back to life in 2003, and repeated since on an annual basis.

The interest in the place so increased and the local community promoted the development of a series of actions for the recovery of the archaeological remains and their enhancement for public visit. An archaeological project was proposed to excavate the site in order to acquire a better understanding of its structure, functions and dating, and to uncover material remains that could be enhanced and shown to a wider public. Among the results of the archaeological works, a new, more detailed knowledge of the Iron Age settlement was obtained, which included the discovery of archaeological features beyond the previously assumed boundaries of the site. A new spatial delimitation of the archaeological site was thus proposed.

Finally, and as a result of the newly acquired knowledge, the regional government extended the area that was subject to heritage protection and land use restrictions, and also declared the feast of San Xoán as an intangible heritage element.

3.1   Initial Archaeological Recording

Firstly, let us create an object model that represents the entities described by the initial archaeological recording in the case study. Fig. 3 shows a diagram of such a model.

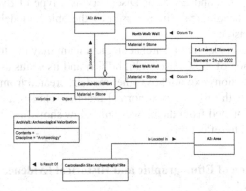

Fig. 3. Object diagram of the initial archaeological recording of the site. The names after the colon signs on the top sections of the rectangles refer to class names.

The Castrolandín hillfort appears as an object in a central position, associated to its north and west walls, which were discovered on 24-Jul-2002. The hillfort occupies an area and there is an archaeological valorization that has produced an associated archaeological site entity, located itself in its own area. Note that the area that locates the hillfort (A1 in the diagram) and the area that locates the archaeological site (A2) are not the same, since A1 pertains to the material evidence that makes up the hillfort itself (i.e. the north and west walls), whereas A2 refers to the boundaries of the archaeological site, which is an interpretive elaboration of the former.

These objects are instances of a set of given classes, as indicated in the object diagram itself. Fig. 4 depicts a class model that extends CHARM in order to generate a particular model that caters for the objects in Fig. 3.

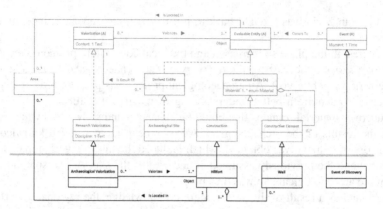

Fig. 4. CHARM extension to represent the archaeological background study of the site. The classes above the thick horizontal line are part of CHARM; the classes below it belong to the particular model.

In this particular model, Hillfort has been added as an extension class by deriving from the CHARM class Construction, and Wall has been added by deriving from Constructive Element. Archaeological Valorization has been added as a specific type of Research Valorization, and Event of Discovery as a type of Event. The CHARM classes Area and Archaeological Site are used by the object model as they are, without the need for extension.

This is a particular model that an archaeological team may use to perform a simple background description of the Castrolandín hillfort and its status as an archaeological site. The following sections explain how other models, created from different perspectives, are integrated with this. Also, in normal practice, classes are defined first, and objects are then instantiated from them. Sections below show first the class model and then the object model to reflect this.

3.2   Documentation of Ethnographic and Historical Evidence

Let us imagine that the team of anthropologists that documented the San Xoán celebrations in Castrolandín created a CHARM-derived model in order to aid with their work. Fig. 5 depicts such a model, in which the CHARM classes Social Act and Manifestation of Social Act are extended to capture the peculiarities of celebrations, and specific attributes are added to the derived classes. An Ethnographic Valorization class is also added as a subtype of Research Valorization, since this was considered to be too abstract as to be useful. However, the CHARM class Community Valorization was left "as is". Book and Letter classes were derived from Intentional Object to represent the specific material evidence that was found, and the CHARM class Document was left untouched.

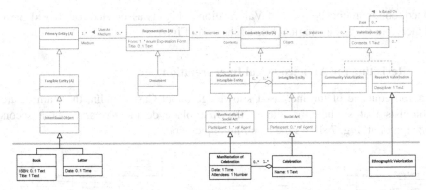

Fig. 5. CHARM extension to represent the ethnographic and historical study of the site

Fig. 6 depicts a combined object model that keeps the information of Fig. 3 and adds new objects to represent the information documented by the anthropologists using the model above.

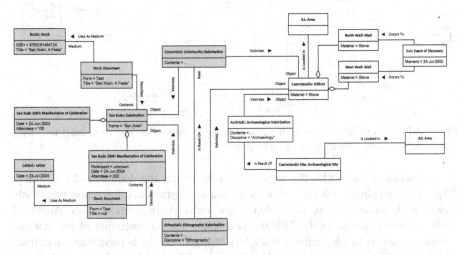

Fig. 6. Adding information about the ethnographic and historical study of the site to the previous object model (see Fig. 3). Newly added objects are shown shaded in grey.

Objects have been added to express that two manifestations of the San Xoán celebration have been documented, on 24-Jun-2003 and 24-Jun-2004, and to describe how the book and the letter describe this. Also, a community valorization on the celebration has been recorded, and an ethnographic valorization has been issued based on it.

In addition, the newly added objects, despite being based on a different particular model, can be seamlessly integrated with those of the archaeological background model because both models are derived from CHARM. Specifically, both valorizations are based on the Castrolandín hillfort (which was present in the previous object model) as well as the San Xoán celebration. This cross-model link is supported by the fact that both archaeologists and anthropologists have chosen to use a CHARM-defined, common concept, that of Valorization, which is associated to Derived Entity and therefore to Archaeological Site as shown in Fig. 4.

3.3   Revisiting the Archaeological Interpretation

As a consequence of the increased knowledge about Castrolandín, the team of archaeologists that studied the site in the first place decide to carry out a second campaign on it. Fig. 7 shows the resulting object model.

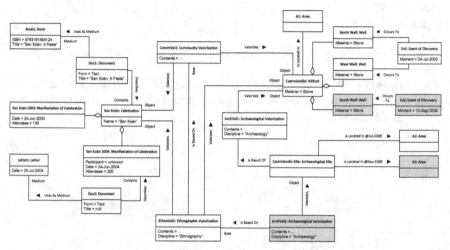

Fig. 7. Adding extra information to the previous object model (see Fig. 6) in order to convey the reinterpretation of the archaeological evidence

As a result of the works, the south wall is unearthed and documented on 13-Sep-2009. This, together with the existence of the ethnographic valorization previously issued, leads archaeologists to develop a new archaeological valorization (ArchVal2 in the diagram), based on the former. As a result, the interpretation of the material evidence as an archaeological site is slightly changed, and its boundary area redefined as A3. Note that valid times for each of the areas A2 and A3 for the site is shown in the diagram by using an "@" notation next to the corresponding links between objects.

Fig. 8 shows the necessary changes to the archaeologists' particular model in order to support these additions. Note that the only change as compared to the previous particular model used by the archaeologists (Fig. 4) is that of adding a temporal marker, indicated by a "T" in parenthesis, to the Is Located In association between Derived Entity and Area. This change adds temporal semantics to this association, which means that specific derived entities (such as archaeological sites) will be able to have different associated areas at different points in time.

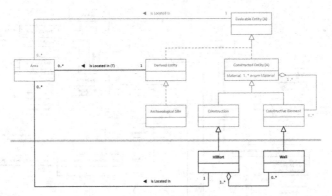

Fig. 8. CHARM extension to support the reinterpretation of the archaeological evidence

3.4   Heritage Protection and Further Consideration

As a result of the generated archaeological, anthropological and historical knowledge about Castrolandín, the regional government decides to intervene in order to apply the necessary protection schemes on both the site and the San Xoán celebration itself. Fig. 9 shows the model that the regional government uses to conceptualise their intervention.

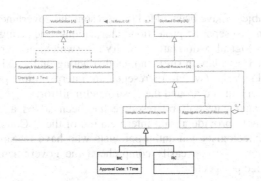

Fig. 9. CHARM extension to support heritage protection information

Only two classes are necessary as CHARM extensions: BIC stands for "Bien de Interés Cultural", Spanish for *Place of Cultural Interest*, one of the protection mechanisms for sites that are described in the heritage legislation. FIC stands for "Fiesta de Interés Cultural", Spanish for *Celebration of Cultural Interest*, another legal protection mechanism that may be applied to intangible entities. Both classes are created as subtypes of Simple Cultural Resource, since they are considered to focus on a single, well-defined entity that is constructed through a protection valorization.

The Research Valorization and Aggregate Cultural Resource classes will be used to bridge the management-research gap, as shown in Fig. 10.

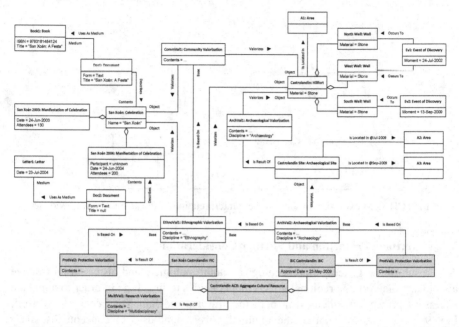

Fig. 10. Adding information about heritage protection to the previous object model (see Fig. 7)

BIC and a FIC objects have been added to represent the government-protected entities that result from two separate protection valorizations, one acting on the previously existing archaeological valorization ArchVal2 (which, in turn, represents an interpretation of the Castrolandín site), and another acting on the existing ethnographic valorization EthnoVal1 (which represents an interpretation of the San Xoán celebration that occurs on and around the Castrolandín hillfort).

In addition, an aggregate cultural resource has been added as the product of a research valorization to provide a joint interpretation of the BIC and FIC entities; by doing this, the archaeologists and anthropologists who have researched the site and the San Xoán celebrations can easily comprehend the government views on these entities from a unified perspective.

4   Conclusions

Obtaining models that guarantee information interoperability with others and, at the same time, maintain good fitness to the problem at hand is not trivial. This paper proposes a two-step approach: first, an abstract reference model is adopted, so interoperability at a high level of abstraction is guaranteed; then, a particular model for the problem at hand is derived by using rules that maintain Liskov compatibility. The Cultural Heritage Abstract Reference Model (CHARM) has been introduced as a proposal, and a case study has been used to illustrate how different teams belonging to different communities (researchers in archaeology and anthropology; the regional government) using CHARM, each working with a different particular model, can still generate a common object model and attain seamless interoperation for transdisciplinary work.

Acknowledgments. The authors thank Camila Gianotti, Charlotte Hug, Cristina Mato-Fresán, Lucía Meijueiro, Rebeca Blanco-Rotea and Rocío Varela-Pousa for their contributions to CHARM. This work has been partially funded through grants 09SEC002606PR of the INCITE Programme, Xunta de Galicia; and HAR2009-12261 of Plan Nacional de I+D+I, Ministerio de Economía y Competitividad.

References

[1] Ayán Vila, X. (ed.): Pasado e Futuro de Castrolandín (Cuntis): Unha Proposta de Recuperación e Revaloración. TAPA, IEGPS, CSIC, Santiago de Compostela, vol. 29 (2002)

[2] Crofts, N., Doerr, M., Gill, T., Stead, S., Stiff, M.: Definition of the CIDOC Conceptual Reference Model. CIDOC CRM Special Interest Group (2011)

[3] Doerr, M.: The CIDOC Conceptual Reference Module. An Ontological Approach to Semantic Interoperability of Metadata. AI Magazine 24(3), 75–92 (2003)

[4] Fernández Freire, C., del Bosque González, I., Fábrega-Álvarez, P., Fraguas Bravo, A., Parcero-Oubiña, C., Pérez Asensio, E., Uriarte González, A., Vicent García, J.M.: Cultural Heritage Application Schema: a SDI Framework within the Protected Sites INSPIRE Spatial Data Theme. In: Computer Applications and Quantitative Methods in Archaeology (CAA 2012), Southampton (2012)

[5] García Gutiérrez, A., Martín Pradas, A. (eds.): Tesauro de Patrimonio Histórico Andaluz. Instituto Andaluz de Patrimonio Histórico, Granada (1998)

[6] Gonzalez-Perez, C.: A Conceptual Modelling Language for the Humanities and Social Sciences. In: Sixth International Conference on Research Challenges in Information Science (RCIS 2012), pp. 396–401. IEEE Computer Society, Valencia (2012)

[7] Gonzalez-Perez, C.: Typeless Information Modelling to Avoid Category Bias in Archaeological Descriptions. In: Chrysanthi, A., Murrieta Flores, P., Papadopoulos, C. (eds.) Thinking Beyond the Tool: Archaeological Computing & the Interpretive Process. Archaeopress, Oxford (2012)

[8] Gonzalez-Perez, C., Parcero Oubiña, C.: A Conceptual Model for Cultural Heritage Definition and Motivation. In: Revive the Past: Proceeding of the 39th Conference on Computer Applications and Quantitative Methods in Archaeology, pp. 234–244. Amsterdam University Press, Beijing (2011)

[9] Incipit, ConML Technical Specification. ConML 1.2 (2012),
http://www.conml.org/Resources_TechSpec.aspx

[10] ISO, Information and documentation – A reference ontology for the interchange of cultural heritage information. ISO 21127:2006 (2006)

[11] Liskov, B., Wing, J.M.: A Behavioral Notion of Subtyping. ACM Transactions on Programming Languages and Systems 16(6), 1811–1841 (1994)

[12] Peterson, D. (ed.): Forms of Representation. Intellect Exeter (1996)

[13] University of Glamorgan, CIDOC CRM Implementation and the CRM-EH, web page (2011),   http://hypermedia.research.glam.ac.uk/resources/crm/ (accessed November 28, 2011)

AgRelOn – An Agent Relationship Ontology

Berenike Litz, Aenne Löhden, Jan Hannemann, and Lars Svensson

German National Library, Adickesallee 1, 60322 Frankfurt am Main, Germany
http://www.dnb.de

Abstract. In this paper we present the Agent Relationship Ontology AgRelOn. The ontology represents detailed knowledge about relations between persons and corporate bodies. Transparency of trustworthiness and provenance as well as other meta knowledge about facts is addressed in a combined n-ary modeling approach. The ontology employs existing standards in order to foster external comprehensibility, referenceability, and reusability. It is already employed in a number of Semantic Web related projects and is publicly available.

Keywords: Authority Data, Relationship Ontology, Cultural Heritage, Digital Libraries.

1 Introduction

Libraries and archives are facing the challenge of integrating new data sources and aligning them with their existing collections due to the ever-growing amount of digitized and born-digital content that is published online. This is not a trivial task, as multimedia content is inherently heterogeneous and the differing structure, quality, and reliability of the available sources makes metadata integration difficult.

The project CONTENTUS aimed at developing concepts and technologies for multimedia archives that facilitate the transition of analogue or digital media collections to searchable archives of semantically linked multimedia content. CONTENTUS [16] was a research and development project and part of the German Federal Ministry of Economy and Technology's research initiative THESEUS [7]. The CONTENTUS approach involves several interlinked processing steps, during which semantic information is extracted from media and used to link information sources and media. Among other things, named entities such as persons, places, and corporate bodies are identified in texts, audio transcripts and audiovisual media. This allows to associate content with matching authority file entries and to convert it into concepts and instances of the system's ontology and the corresponding knowledge base. The resulting knowledge network can be searched and navigated.

The relevant authority file entries are currently only manual annotations. They are formalized, but not fully connected by semantic links, and, therefore, the usability for electronic information systems is limited. Hence, this valuable knowledge needs a more semantic representation in order to be accessed and

J.M. Dodero, M. Palomo-Duarte, P. Karampiperis (Eds.): MTSR 2012, CCIS 343, pp. 202–213, 2012.
© Springer-Verlag Berlin Heidelberg 2012

utilized appropriately. For this purpose, an ontology was developed that utilizes the knowledge of the authority files, represents it in an hierarchical order and provides other semantic links. One important aspect of the ontology is the representation of relationships between persons, such as authors or public figures, as well as between persons and corporate bodies.

In this paper, we present the Agent Relationship Ontology AgRelOn. We chose the term *agent* to refer to persons and corporate bodies with a single expression. The ontology aims at utilizing existing, relevant, stable vocabulary and dataset URIs and is developed in cooperation with Semantic Web related projects. AgRelOn is an ontology module for the cultural heritage domain that can be integrated into generic ontologies.

In order to support the extension of the knowledge base by users and to maintain a high reliability of the data at the same time, a meta-ontology describes trustworthiness and provenance as well as validity period of the added facts. Reusability is an important issue in order to foster a unified view on relationships amongst cultural heritage and other content holding institutions. AgRelOn is publicly available via the Web site contentus-projekt.de and on the Web site of the German National Library (DNB, dnb.de).

The remainder of this paper is structured as follows. In Section 2, we review related work on relevant ontologies and vocabularies and discuss their influence on and differences from AgRelOn. Section 3 introduces AgRelOn in detail. We describe the CONTENTUS ontology that serves as the top level ontology for AgRelOn. The choice of relations according to the DNB authority file data is motivated, and we present a combined approach for the meta-ontology applying both reification and arity. We further present the techniques of ontology population applied in CONTENTUS. Section 4 describes how the ontology is employed in the project CONTENTUS and other projects. Finally, Section 5 contains a summary and outlook.

2   Related Work

Initially, we examined existing ontologies and vocabularies from the cultural heritage domain and for agent relationships. The reason we not only examined agent ontologies but also ontologies for the cultural heritage domain was that we expected to find modeling practices that are also relevant for our domain ontology. In general, established models help to express terminological knowledge in a widely comprehensible way. They further facilitate exchanging or linking the knowledge more easily with available assertional knowledge sources. Therefore, we planned to, at least partly, employ existing knowledge representations. However, as numerous as the related work appears, as little could we utilize for our purposes.

Notable vocabularies for the cultural heritage domain are the Europeana Data Model, Resource Description and Access and the model of the Linked Data project of the German National Library, all of which are described in the following.

Europeana Data Model (EDM, [12]) structures the data that the project Europeana aggregates and publishes. EDM includes specific formats for museums, archives and digital libraries. The format for digital libraries is the Metadata Encoding and Transmission Standard (METS, [11]) from the Library of Congress, which indicates the provenance of information of the digital objects. EDM also describes complex, structured objects and allows an event-related as well as an object-related view. EDM is more oriented towards cultural objects, for which events are relevant, as is partly the case for archives' or museums' resources. As the development is to date not finalized and EDM does so far not define agent relationships, it is not considered in our work. However, the METS format for digital libraries that is included in EDM is also employed in the CONTENTUS top-level ontology.

Resource Description and Access (RDA, [17]) comprises library regulations and an ontology. The ontology addresses metadata of cultural heritage resources and describes contents and a wide variety of media. RDA implements the Functional Requirements for Bibliographic Records (FRBR [18]) data model. Therefore, the RDA ontology differentiates Work, Expression, Manifestation and Item (group 1) and Person, Family and CorporateBody (group 2). RDA is integrated in the CONTENTUS top-level ontology. However, RDA does not specify inter-person relationships and only defines some relations with families and corporations involved. Domains and ranges are semantically fine-grained. Thus, properties are often not applicable, as they enforce the usage of the domain and range classes and exclude other domains and ranges. This affects properties for persons, families, or organizations as well as for the FRBR levels. For instance, an employer-employee relation demands a corporate body and a person. For founders of organizations there are different properties for founding families and founding persons.

The model of the Linked Data project [14] of the DNB has been initially established to publish DNB authority data about persons, corporate bodies and subject headings. By now it also includes bibliographic data and the German Dewey Decimal Classification. The development of AgRelOn incorporated the experiences made in the creation of this vocabulary. The model will, in turn, be revised in the context of the common authority file project "Gemeinsame Normdatei (GND)" of the DNB, which is the consolidation of several important German authority files [8], to successively utilize elements from AgRelOn for the representation of agent relationships.

Relevant ontologies and vocabularies describing agent relationships comprise the vocabulary for biographical information BIO, an ontology for the genealogical domain called *genont/srcont* and RELATIONSHIP, as presented in more detail in the following.

The vocabulary for biographical information BIO [1] defines biographic events for persons, including existence related, occupational, religious and personal events. Defined classes are rather state changing events such as e.g. birth, death, murder, assassination, cremation, wedding, marriage annulment than phases such as e.g. life, wedlock. Events are depicted with date, location and involved persons (e.g. witness, spectator). There are also biographic portraits and few basic relations such as child, parent and employer. As the focus of BIO is on state-changing events and for AgRelOn more on time-related connections, an integration is not possible without modifications.

Friend of a Friend (FoaF, [10]) portraits social networks and includes relations between persons and web related information about persons. FoaF defines only few relations between agents (foaf:knows, foaf:member). FoaF includes the concepts person, organization and group. The usage of properties, however, is often limited to one of these entities.

The ontology for the genealogical domain genont/srcont [20] depicts genealogical resources with embodied facts. genont models facts and srcont resources. genont defines persons and describes basic relations as properties, both gender-specific and gender-neutral. Some events such as death and wedding are modeled as concepts with date and location. srcont refers to archive resources and publications. The ontology specifies only few relations between persons. Facts are not individually associated with data sources, the resource named in a fact file seems to apply as source for all phrased facts.

RELATIONSHIP [6] is a vocabulary specifically designed to describe relationships between people. As such, it defines many properties that are also relevant for AgRelOn. The hierarchical structure of the model, however, is limited to sub-concepts of foaf:person and sub-properties of foaf:knows. Domains and ranges are limited to a certain extend, e.g. domain and range of employedBy are solely persons and not organizations. In addition, the ontology mixes properties and classes. E.g. the correlation of rel:properties with external properties via equivalentClass leads to the fact that the properties are also classes.

To summarize, ontologies and formalisms from the library and cultural heritage domain and for relations between people and corporate bodies were regarded. The vocabularies from the library and cultural heritage domains define only a few inter-person or inter-agent relationships, although the creation of the model of the DNB Linked Data service provided useful experience for the design of AgRelOn. Also, most of the vocabularies for relationships cover only a small number of relations. The RELATIONSHIP vocabulary, which provides a larger number of such relations, has not finalized its structure yet. To foster comprehensibility and reusability, an alternative to reusing existing vocabulary elements would have been to connect relationship properties of AgRelOn with similar ones in other vocabularies. While this seemed tempting indeed, the resulting ontological commitments and implications have to be paid attention to. With owl:equivalentProperty, differing, but intended domains and ranges would not be applicable. Further, rdfs:subPropertyOf is expected to result in structural issues between vocabularies.

Thus, important issues such as a rich set of person relationships, a detailed hierarchical structure, connections between relation pairs, such as symmetry, inversity and transitivity, and a pattern for creating meta-statements about relation instances suitable for CONTENTUS are still missing in existing vocabularies and are, therefore, addressed in AgRelOn.

3   The Agent Relationship Ontology AgRelOn

AgRelOn aims to enable the semantic searchability of relations between persons and corporate bodies. The design of the model was derived using two complementary approaches: a top-down approach considering the task to be completed and a bottom-up approach focusing on the available data. For the former, exemplary search scenarios were outlined, for the latter, existing data sources were examined.

AgRelOn strives for comprehensibility, citability, linkability in the continuously changing Internet. To achieve this, the ontology refers to a stable vocabulary and dataset URIs and is developed in cooperation with Semantic Web related projects. Apart from CONTENTUS, cooperating projects include ALEXANDRIA, the DNB Linked Data project, and the DNB common authority file project "Gemeinsame Normdatei (GND)" [8]. Employed dataset URIs primarily refer to DNB data records. The standard Semantic Web technologies RDF(S) and OWL are employed. Hierarchies of classes and properties are defined with RDF(S), properties are classified as symmetric, inverse, or transitive with OWL.

The ontology endeavors to indicate transparency of the information background of the contained facts regarding e.g. origin, validity, and importance of statements. When involving diverse cataloging or annotation sources to cope with the increasing volume and heterogeneity of media and metadata to be collected by the DNB, the knowledge base can contain metadata of differing quality and reliability, coming from different sources such as library experts (DNB data and the data of the DNB Linked Data project), tools (automated media analysis tools, such as employed in the CONTENTUS and ALEXANDRIA projects), and others (Web 2.0 platforms like Wikipedia, MusicBrainz). Data provenance, confidence, and also temporal validity is made transparent by meta properties with the n-ary approach as recommended by the World Wide Web Consortium (W3C), representing attributes with concepts rather than properties.

AgRelOn aims at a thorough utilization of available knowledge, meaning that heterogeneous, fragmentary data sources may also be exploited and that implicit knowledge can be retrieved. For inferable relations, like inverse or indirect relations, redundant properties are specified. The facts explicitly stated in the knowledge base can be complemented with implicit facts given by hierarchy, symmetry, inversity, transitivity, and specific connections between properties (e.g. grandparents, aunt/uncle).

In the following, AgRelOn is presented in detail. First of all, the CONTENTUS ontology is described that represents the upper level ontology for AgRelOn so far. Further, the choice of relations for modeling is motivated. Then, the n-ary approach to realizing meta-statements is introduced. Finally, the ontology population is presented.

3.1   The CONTENTUS Ontology

The CONTENTUS ontology aims to enable semantic searches of multi-media corpora and associated metadata. It primarily describes and links works, persons,

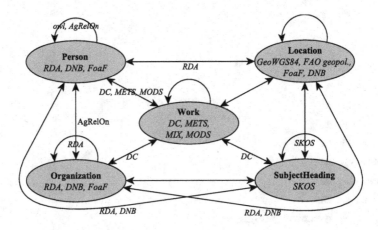

Fig. 1. Main concepts and vocabularies of the CONTENTUS top-level ontology

organizations, locations, and topics. Figure 1 shows the main concepts and the vocabularies employed for concepts and properties of the CONTENTUS ontology. The top-level ontology employs knowledge from the Resource Description and Access vocabulary (RDA), Dublin Core (DC), Simple Knowledge Organization System (SKOS), Metadata Object Description Schema (MODS) and the Metadata Encoding and Transmission Standard (METS). Most of the vocabularies are described in Section 2.

AgRelOn is a domain ontology of the CONTENTUS ontology.

3.2 Choice of Relations

AgRelOn defines almost 70 hierarchical, gender-neutral relations. The selection of relations is based on an analysis of the corresponding relation types in the person authority file (PND) of the German National Library. Since the relations in the PND are specified as free text, the relationship types had to be normalized. Most of the relations adhered to a specific gender, such as wife or husband. As this information is contained in the instances, the gender was neutralized. Further, synonym notations such as spouse and marriage partner were consolidated. Rare relations such as third cousin were subsumed under cousin and hierarchically structured. Figure 2 shows the statistics of usage of the most frequently used relations of the PND. Most frequent is the *parent* relation, followed by *spouse, child* and *sibling. Grandchild, parent-in-law, child-in-law, aunt-uncle, niece-nephew, cousin, sibling-in-law* are much less common with occurrences in the hundreds. The bars show the overall usages and are divided into the number of usages of male and female relations.

In addition to modeling common domain-independent relationships such as e.g. kinship on a detailed level, AgRelOn supports expressing relationships that are common in the library domain. For instance, the relation of a person being the muse of another. Charlotte von Stein was a famous muse, she was close

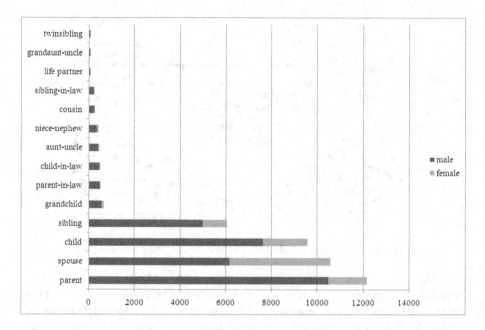

Fig. 2. Number of usages of most frequent relations in the person authority file (PND) of the German National Library. The bars show the overall usages and are divided into the number of usages of male and female relations. Date of extraction: August 2011.

friends with Goethe and Schiller and impacted Goethes works [15], so `Stein isMuseOf Goethe` and `Stein isMuseOf Schiller`.

Figure 3 shows the hierarchy of relations. The most general relations are on top and sub-relations are indicated by arrows. To give an example, child is more precise than offspring, offspring more precise than relative. The hierarchical structure has three advantages. It allows entries and searches on several abstraction levels (e.g. child, offspring, relative), and provides a better overview when many connections are given. To give one example, the DNB record of Felix Mendelssohn Bartholdy directly points to 18 other persons, the record of Bertolt Brecht to 17, the record of Richard Wagner to 13. Finally, it allows augmenting incomplete data used for population through inference.

3.3   Meta-statements and Arity

Properties of RDF and OWL are defined to be dyadic or binary, i.e. they link a subject or domain with an object or range via a predicate. However, in specific cases it makes sense to arrange for more positions in a statement. There are two reasons for creating such properties in AgRelOn. First, there is a need to valuate statements based on their trustworthiness or source. This can be seen as meta-knowledge about the facts. Second, some facts themselves are only valid for a certain time period. This knowledge is part of the facts themselves. The

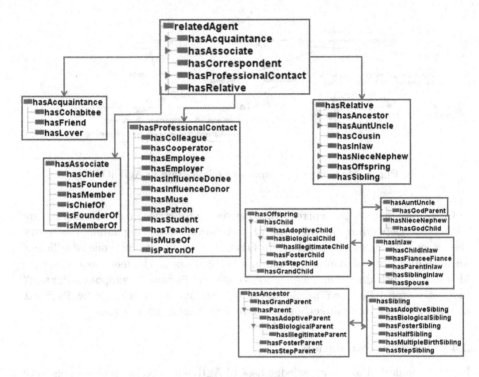

Fig. 3. The relationship hierarchy in AgRelOn

W3C recommends two ways for modeling these cases. The first one is called *RDF Reification*. RDF Reification applies the rdf:type `rdf:Statement` and the properties `rdf:subject`, `rdf:predicate` and `rdf:object`. Customized properties can be attached to the reified statement to make assertions about it. The second modeling approach is named *n-ary relations*. Here, artificial relation classes and instances substitute properties, so that meta-statements can be attached to those relation instances. The essential idea of the AgRelOn approach to modeling relations is to provide familiar representations, on the one hand, as well as to enable meta-statements, on the other hand. Therefore, a combination of classical properties and n-ary classes is needed, creating a property as well as an analogous n-ary class for relations and linking them via a `correspondsTo` connection. The knowledge that needs to be captured in AgRelOn for facts comprises: *provenance, confidence* and *validity period*.

Figure 4 depicts the modeling approach. In the dashed box on the bottom right, `LotteLenya` is connected by the `hasSpouse` relation to `KurtWeill`. The property `hasSpouse` corresponds to the n-ary class `HasSpouse`. An instance `HasSpouse_LotteLenya_KurtWeill` of the class `HasSpouse` represents a marriage between subject `LotteLenya` and object `KurtWeill`. Now, meta-statements about the marriage can be tied to the n-ary instance.

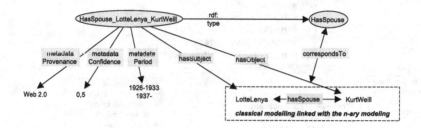

Fig. 4. Modeling of the marriage relationship in AgRelOn

Corresponding to the correlations between properties, meta-assertions are connected. Depending on the type of correlation, a varying number of n-ary classes and instances are necessary in OWL. E.g. one n-ary instance is sufficient for both directions of symmetric and inverse relations as the meta-assertions are identical in both directions, e.g., a source stating `PersonX hasSpouse PersonY` indirectly states `PersonY hasSpouse PersonX`; and a source stating `PersonX hasParent PersonY` indirectly states `PersonY hasChild PersonX`.

3.4 Ontology Population

For the population of the knowledge base of AgRelOn, several data sources were chosen as relevant. The sources can roughly be grouped into three categories based on who created them: experts from cultural heritage organizations, voluntary Internet users, and software tools automatically analyzing media.

The authority file data of the DNB constitutes the main knowledge source for AgRelOn, providing librarian knowledge via stable URIs. The PND (Personennormdatei) contains data records for individual persons and for ambiguous person names. It is Germany's largest and most complete source of structured information on persons and as such was chosen as the basis for our work. The GKD (Gemeinsame Körperschaftsdatei) provides similar data records for corporate bodies. Persons and corporate bodies are linked, the respective type of interrelation is characterized by a comment in the original authority files.

Musical information is populated with MusicBrainz [5], a Web 2.0 platform filled by volunteers with music information on artists, publications and music pieces. Artists are interrelated. The content is available via an XML web service, and the LinkedBrainz project [4] provides access to the Semantic Web.

With a platform as developed in ALEXANDRIA, Internet users can easily contribute to an ontology based knowledge source. Other than on most Web 2.0 projects, voluntary contributions are not free tags or annotations but actual ontology statements.

Software tools developed by CONTENTUS and ALEXANDRIA automatically analyze media and extract descriptive metadata about the media and identify entities relevant for semantic linking. Extracted facts can also be included in the knowledge base.

4 Application

AgRelOn is currently applied in the Semantic Multimedia Search Engine (SMMS) of CONTENTUS [19], which aims to provide semantic access to media and related information sources. AgRelOn's role in this context is to allow for the visualization and navigation of semantic relations between persons and corporate bodies. Figure 5 shows a screenshot of the SMMS. The result page is divided into three columns: A set of dynamically created filter facets on the left and right side and in the middle a result list or, in this view, the ontology and knowledge base navigation of the searched person "Bertolt Brecht". The instances shown in the relation column are references that lead to the corresponding person entry. From there it is also possible to search for the chosen person. Since CONTENTUS uses the DNB authority file for persons (PND) as part of its knowledge base, AgRelOn's relationship types are compatible to represent the relevant relations. Similarly, a subset of AgRelOn is used in ALEXANDRIA to model the relationship between persons.

The task of semantically linking these sources together is challenging for semantic web projects that utilize heterogeneous data sources. To facilitate such mappings, a web service based on AgRelOn was developed, which supports matching entity information from different sources. This service is used in several projects for semantically aggregating data, such as in CONTENTUS, the German Digital Library (DDB, [3]), and culturegraph.org [2], which aims to establish shared, persistent identifiers for cultural works.

AgRelOn is further employed in the common authority file project GND [8], a consolidation of important German authority files, such as the authority files on

Fig. 5. AgRelOn as part of the CONTENTUS Semantic Multimedia Search Engine

persons, corporate bodies, and subject headings. With the advent of the GND, relationships between persons and between persons and corporate bodies are no longer just described in textual form, but based on the relationships defined in AgRelOn. For the first stage of the GND project, a subset of AgRelOn will be used, with the intention to successively expand that subset. Codes for relations correlating to AgRelOn are determined in cooperation with the Network Development and MARC Standards Office (NDMSO) to supplement MARC. The codes will be indicated in AgRelOn.

The relationships modeled in AgRelOn also influenced the 2012 revision of the DNB Linked Data Service.

5   Conclusions and Outlook

In this paper we introduced the Agent Relationship Ontology AgRelOn that represents knowledge about relationships between persons and corporate bodies. It was developed to represent the diverse relationship types found in the authority file data of the German National Library and is inspired by known vocabularies in order to support comprehensibility, referenceability and reusability. The possibility to extend the knowledge base by users and to maintain a high reliability of the data at the same time is provided by a meta-ontology realized as an n-ary model that describes trustworthiness and provenance as well as validity period of the added facts. The novel combination of reification and arity in one n-ary approach is arguable in a strict sense. However, we chose this approach in order to maintain a low level of complexity for future users and knowledge engineers.

AgRelOn is employed in the Semantic Multimedia Search Engine of the CON-TENTUS project, adhering to established quality criteria [13,9]. Within the German Digital Library, AgRelOn is employed via the GND, which is used to provide entity information. Furthermore, the mapping web service will likely be utilized there to match information sources. The service is also integrated into the project culturegraph.org. This way, we hope to make the ontology accessible to a wide number of users and hope to receive valuable feedback by them for future work.

In order to support reusability we are providing an open source version of AgRelOn through the Web site contentus-projekt.de. We encourage the readers of this paper to download the current version and send us feedback.

Acknowledgments. The use case projects CONTENTUS and ALEXANDRIA of the THESEUS program were funded by means of the German Federal Ministry of Economy and Technology under the promotional references "01MQ07003" and "01MQ07008" respectively. We further thank Claudia Effenberger and Andreas Hess for their valuable input on earlier drafts of this paper.

References

1. BIO: A vocabulary for biographical information,
   http://vocab.org/bio/0.1/.html
2. culturegraph.org, http://www.culturegraph.org
3. Deutsche Digitale Bibliothek, http://www.deutsche-digitale-bibliothek.de
4. LinkedBrainz, http://wiki.musicbrainz.org/LinkedBrainz
5. MusicBrainz, http://wiki.musicbrainz.org/
6. RELATIONSHIP, http://vocab.org/relationship/.html
7. THESEUS, http://www.theseus-programm.de
8. Behrens-Neumann, R., Pfeifer, B.: Die Gemeinsame Normdatei - ein Kooperationsprojekt. Dialog mit Bibliotheken (1) (2011)
9. Bizer, C., Jentzsch, A., Cyganiak, R.: State of the LOD Cloud, http://www4.wiwiss.fu-berlin.de/lodcloud/state/
10. Brickley, D., Miller, L.: FOAF Vocabulary Specification 0.98, http://xmlns.com/foaf/spec/
11. Cantara, L.: METS: The Metadata Encoding and Transmission Standard. Cataloging and Classification Quarterly 40 (2005)
12. Doerr, M., Gradmann, S., Hennicke, S., Isaac, A., Meghini, C., van de Sompel, H.: The Europeana Data Model (EDM). In: Proc. of the World Library and Information Congress of the International Federation of Library Associations and Institutions (IFLA) (August 2010), http://www.ifla.org/files/hq/papers/ifla76/149-doerr-en.pdf
13. Flemming, A.: Quality Criteria for Linked Data sources, http://sourceforge.net/apps/mediawiki/trdf/index.php?title=Quality_Criteria_for_Linked_Data_sources
14. Hannemann, J., Kett, J.: Linked Data for Libraries. In: Proc. of the World Library and Information Congress of the International Federation of Library Associations and Institutions, IFLA (2010)
15. Muncker, F.: Stein, Charlotte Freifrau von. In: Allgemeine Deutsche Biographie, herausgegeben von der Historischen kommission bei der Bayerischen Akademie der Wissenschaften, Band vol. 35, pp. S.602–S.605 (1893), http://de.wikisource.org/wiki/ADB:Stein,_Charlotte_Freifrau_von
16. Nandzik, J., Heß, A., Hannemann, J., Flores-Herr, N., Bossert, K.: CONTENTUS - Towards semantic multi-media libraries. In: Proc. of 76th IFLA General Conf. and Assembly (2010)
17. Oliver, C.: Introducing RDA: a guide to the basics. ALA Editions (2010)
18. Tillett, B.: What is FRBR? A Conceptual Model for the Bibliographic Universe (2004), http://www.loc.gov/cds/FRBR.html
19. Waitelonis, J., Osterhoff, J.P., Sack, H.: More than the sum of its parts: CONTENTUS – a semantic multimodal search user interface. In: Proc. of Workshop on Visual Interfaces to the Social and Semantic Web (VISSW), Co-located with ACM IUI 2011, Palo Alto, US, February 13. CEUR Workshop Proceedings, vol. 694 (2011)
20. Zandhuis, I.: Towards a Genealogical Ontology for the Semantic Web, pp. 296–300 (2005), http://www.ahc2005.org/en/new_1/towards_a_genealogical_ontology_for_the_semantic_web/

Paths and Shortcuts in an Event-Oriented Ontology

Mark Fichtner[1] and Vincent Ribaud[2]

[1] Zoologisches Forschungsmuseum Alexander Koenig, Bonn, Germany
m.fichtner@wiss-ki.eu
[2] Lab-STICC MOCS, Université de Bretagne Occidentale, Brest, France
ribaud@univ-brest.fr

Abstract. The CIDOC CRM is an event-oriented ontology used in cultural heritage documentation. Events are temporal entities that are used as hooks for relating persistent entities. However end-users are relating persistent entities in a
direct manner (e.g. J.R.R. Tolkien wrote Bilbo the Hobbit) and skip the path
through a temporal entity. Fauconnier and Turner suggest that human conscious
thinking tends to compress complex paths into simpler relationships, despite
still knowing subconsciously about the complete paths. This paper presents two
prototypical approaches yielding compression and decompression to the end-
user, shortcuts implementation in Semantic Media Wiki and ontology path features in the WissKI system. Lessons learned yield research perspectives about
identification, names, end-user usability, and event pattern heuristics.

Keywords: CIDOC CRM, semantic association, end-user representation.

1   Introduction

"*As told in The Hobbit, there came one day to Bilbo's door the great wizard, Gandalf
the Grey, and thirteen dwarves with him [...] With them he set out [...] on a morning
of April, it being then the year 1341 [...] on the quest of a great treasure [...] The
party was assailed by Orcs in a high pass of the Misty Mountains [...] it happened
that Bilbo was lost for a while in the black orcs-mines under the mountains [...] he put
his hand on a ring, lying on the floor of a tunnel. He put it in his pocket [...] At the
bottom of the tunnel [...] lived Gollum. [...] He possessed a secret treasure [...] a ring
of gold that made its wearer invisible.*" In this excerpt from [13], J.R.R. Tolkien relates the circumstances in which Bilbo found the One Ring. Humans compress the
topic with a sentence (http://www.thehobbithole.co.uk/bilbo_page.htm) such as "*As
Bilbo groped along the dark tunnels [of the Misty Mountains], he found the Ring lying
on the ground and slipped it into his pocket. By a subterranean lake Bilbo met
Gollum, the creature who had lost the Ring.*" We might also sum up the story thus:
"Bilbo took the One Ring from Gollum in 1341 under the Misty Mountains".

Fauconnier and Turner [5] refer to the operations of representational contracting
and stretching as compression and decompression. They suggest that human conscious thinking tends to compress complex paths of relationships into simpler relationships, despite remaining subconsciously knowledgeable about the complete paths.

J.M. Dodero, M. Palomo-Duarte, P. Karampiperis (Eds.): MTSR 2012, CCIS 343, pp. 214–226, 2012.
© Springer-Verlag Berlin Heidelberg 2012

Machine processing requires a complete representation of paths. The RDF representation is a graph of nodes and arcs, where nodes are individuals (e.g. Bilbo, the Misty Mountains) or typed values (e.g. the string gold, the date 1341) and arcs are features (e.g. took place at, colour). A special feature relates an individual to its type[1].

The CIDOC Conceptual Reference Model (CRM), which is the ISO 21127 standard, is a core ontology in the cultural domain. The CRM [3] is rooted in the concept of events connecting things, concepts, people, time and place. Fig. 1 is a simplified graph of the circumstances in which Bilbo got the One Ring from Gollum. Individuals (e.g. 1341) are placed within a box labelled by type (e.g. Time-Span).

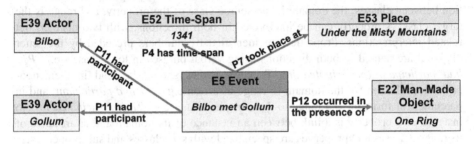

Fig. 1. Representation of the event where Bilbo met Gollum

The E5 Event "Bilbo met Gollum" is a keychain to linked entities. Talking about the One Ring discovery, humans will use a compression sentence "Bilbo found the One Ring under the Misty Mountains" that stands for paths of Fig. 1: Bilbo, an Agent, participated in an Event. The Event took place under the Misty Mountains, a Place. The Event occurred in presence of the One Ring, a Man-Made Object. To keep it simple, we have omitted the need to relate each individual to its identifier (an E41 Appellation) as well as the need to relate each appellation to its value, usually a string.

Forms facilitate data entry and retrieval and can be used to hide schema complexity from the end-user. Different instances of different classes can be presented in the same form, and any visual item can be associated with a schema property and displayed with a label that is meaningful to the end-user, e.g. replacing *P12 occurred in presence of* by *Objects used*. A semantic association [2] is a sequence of individual associations connecting two entities through intermediate entities, e.g. Bilbo and the Misty Mountains through a meeting event. Semantic associations can be discovered through schema processing or data mining techniques. Semantic associations provide the user with representational compression. Decompression aims to produce complex data behind the scenes. This paper presents two proposals for handling CRM-based compression and decompression: an extension based on Semantic MediaWiki; and WissKI, a system dedicated to cultural heritage documentation management.

---

[1] Unfortunately, there is no common agreement on concept names. In RDF, nodes refer to "things" or resources (represented by their URI reference) or constant values - called literals (represented by character strings). Arcs refer to predicates (properties). RDFS refers to types or "kinds of things" as classes, and the property rdf:type is used to indicate that a resource belongs to a class. For object oriented readers, nodes refer to instances and arcs refer to relationships. The instantiation relationship "is-a" links instances to their classes.

2   Background and Related Work

2.1   Introducing the CIDOC CRM

The CIDOC CRM is a formal ontology intended to facilitate the integration, mediation and interchange of heterogeneous cultural heritage information. The current version 5.0.4 [3] consists of a multiple inheritance hierarchy of 86 classes and 138 properties. A class (or entity) is identified by a number preceded by the letter "E" and followed by its name (e.g. E5 Event, E39 Actor). A class is a set of individuals (called class instances) that share common characteristics. A property is a binary relation between classes; the domain is the source class of the property, and range is the target class. A property can be interpreted in both directions, with two distinct, but related interpretations. Properties are identified by numbers preceded by the letter "P," and are named in both directions using verbal phrases in lower case - e.g. *P11 had participant (participated in)*. Property names should be read in their non-parenthetical form for the domain-to-range direction e.g. *P11 had participant*, and in parenthetical form for the range-to-domain direction - e.g. *P11i participated in*. An instance of a property is a link between an instance of its domain and an instance of its range. Classes and properties are specialized with sub-classes and sub-properties.

The CRM is based on a fundamental distinction [10] between persistent entities (endurants, continuants) and temporal entities (perdurants, occurrents). The CRM is rooted in four fundamental principles: endurant participation in an event, part-whole relation, reference information and classification [4] which are the most fundamental relationships connecting things, concepts, people, time and place.

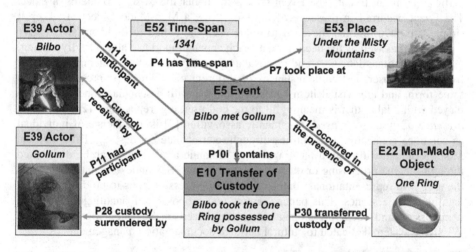

Fig. 2. Representation of a sub-event within the event in which Bilbo met Gollum

In order to provide the reader with comprehensive examples, in Fig. 2 we detail the semantic of the One Ring transfer of custody (a relevant case in cultural heritage management). The whole "Bilbo met Gollum" event *[P10i] contains* a part event, an instance of E10 Transfer of custody. Three properties specify the roles played by participants: *[P28] custody surrendered by* (Gollum's role), *[P29] custody received by* (Bilbo's role) and *[P30] transferred custody of* (One Ring role).

2.2   Semantic Associations: Paths of Knowledge

Paths between entities are semantic associations, a notion introduced by [1, 2]. Two entities e_x and e_y are semantically associated if they are semantically connected or semantically similar. A semantic connection between e_x and e_y is a sequence e_x, P_1, e_2, P_2, e_3, ... e_{n-1}, P_{n-1}, e_y where e_i, $2 \leq i < n$, are entities and P_j, $1 \leq j < n$, are properties - whereas the range of P_j is the domain of P_{j+1}. Semantic similarity is based on the existence of two semantic connections having similar properties. In this paper, semantic connectivity alone is used to find semantic associations. Semantic association discovery has been an intensive research area for ten years now. [2] states that two kinds of paths can be discovered. The first kind is paths which are obvious from the schema. The second kind is those paths that exist at data level yet are not evident at schema level. We limit our work to the former, excluding data mining techniques.

As mentioned in the introduction, there is a semantic gap: a lack of coincidence between information one can extract from the knowledge base and user interpretation. Compression/decompression techniques are helpful in reducing this gap.

The compression operation replaces a semantic association (e.g. the individual One Ring, a Man-Made Object, has custody transferred through a Transfer of Custody event, part of an Event that took place under the Misty Mountains, a Place) with a direct relationship between two individuals (e.g. the One Ring, a Man-Made Thing, was found under the Misty Mountains, a Place). The end-user proceeds with the knowledge graph from one individual (e.g. the One Ring) acting as a focal point. Any semantic association starting from this individual is meaningful to the user.

Because the end-user is building and using paths intended to compress the representation, these paths can be used to store decompressed representations. If the compressed path is used to write information (e.g. the One Ring, a Man-Made Thing, was found [by Gollum] in the Gladden Fields, a Place), it requires a decompression and the creation of the full path (e.g. the One Ring, a Man-Made Thing, has custody transferred through a Transfer of Custody event, falling within an Event that took place in The Gladden Fields, a Place). However, there are several possible decompressions, i.e. there are several paths which yield the same compression; e.g. another path might be: the One Ring was present at an Event that took place in The Gladden Fields.

We need to reuse existing paths in larger paths, a grouping feature that helps to factorize shared section of paths. Unfortunately, as stated at [8] "*if both derived and base associations are taken into account, the number of distinct semantic associations (compare to acyclic paths) between two entities may increase drastically.*"

Shortcuts. CRM addresses the problem above through shortcuts. "*A shortcut is a formally-defined single property representing a deduction or join of a data path in the CRM. [...] For each shortcut, the CRM contains in its schema the properties of the full data path explaining the shortcut.*" [3, p. 11] Shortcuts implement the compression operation, although the CRM is aware that no decompression can be guaranteed: *"An instance of the fully-articulated path always implies an instance of the short-cut property. However, the inverse may not be true; an instance of the fully-articulated path cannot always be inferred from an instance of the shortcut property."* [3, p.16]

3 Use Cases

In this section we present two approaches for compression and decompression operations and we discuss the advantages, limits and drawbacks of both approaches.

3.1 Ontology Management with SMW

Wiki (quick in Hawaiian) was defined in 1995 by its inventor, Ward Cunningham, as 'the simplest online database that could possibly work.' A wiki page is displayed according to instructions stored in the page "code" (as does HTML). For instance, linking a page to another is accomplished by surrounding the linked page name within double brackets. Semantic wikis add semantic annotations to the pages. Semantic MediaWiki (http://semantic-mediawiki.org/) is a free semantic extension for the free wiki engine MediaWiki (http://mediawiki.org/). We associate a property to a value or to another page by preceding the value or the linked page with the property name.

Fig. 3 presents the SMW code resulting from the semantization of the introductive compression sentence. It uses the CRM as the reference ontology and yields a subgraph of Fig. 1 from a focal point: an E5 Event identified by "Bilbo met Gollum".

```
As [[P11 had participant::Bilbo]] groped along the dark
tunnels of the [[P7 took place at::Misty Mountains]], he
found the [[P12 occurred in the presence of::One Ring]]
lying on the ground and slipped it into his pocket. By a
subterranean lake [[Bilbo]] met [[P11 had partici-
pant::Gollum]], the creature who had lost the [[One
Ring]].
[[Category: E5 Event]]
```

Fig. 3. Semantic MediaWiki code fragment for the E5 Event "Bilbo met Gollum"

Page names identify pages within a wiki. Each page has a URIref (Uniform Resource Identifier reference), built from a base (the wiki URL) and a relative URI (the page name). Each property or class has its own wiki page, used to build its URIref.

Any semantic annotation in the page will produce an RDF triple with the page URIref as subject, the property URIref as predicate, a literal value or an object URIref as object. Each time a page is updated, SMW regenerates that page's RDF triples.

Semantic search allows users to write queries using the same syntax as annotations; e.g. *[[E5 Event]][[P7 took place at::Misty Mountains]]* will retrieve all events located in the Misty Mountains. Semantic queries might be used to implement semantic associations, and are fairly easy for the end-user to understand. For instance, the query *P4i is time-span of.P10i contains.P30 transferred custody of. One Ring* re-trieves 1341, a Time-Span that is the time-span of [an Event] that contains [an Event] that transferred custody of [the individual identified by] One Ring.

When a page is the subject of a predicate towards another page (e.g. <Bilbo met Gollum, P11 had participant, Bilbo>, the object should be the subject of an "inverse" triple using the inverse property towards the former subject (e.g. <Bilbo, P11i partici-pated in, Bilbo met Gollum>). It requires a synchronized update of both triples. In-verse triples can be implemented with queries instead of annotations (e.g. in Bilbo's page, the query *P11 had participant::Bilbo* retrieves the page Bilbo met Gollum).

Semantic annotations require a disciplined editing process that can be supported through the use of templates. MediaWiki templates have immense value for normaliz-ing and simplifying display (such as Wikipedia Infoboxes). Semantic forms are a method for including the semantic annotations through MediaWiki templates and generated forms. Each form field is associated with a semantic property and labelled with a meaningful name. A field hosts single or multiple values or object references, according to the cardinality and type of the underlying property. Where the form is used, semantic constructs are used consistently and do not require schema knowledge.

Knowledge representation in SMW is RDF-based and is lacking in OWL charac-teristics. To benefit from inference and reasoning features, the triple set has to be exported and processed by a post-processor software. The post-processor performs URI alignment to a reference namespace, produces inverse triples and is dedicated to the processing of any operations requested to produce a sound and complete triple set. We developed a simple post-processor using XSLT for validation purposes only.

3.2   Case study: The Use of Shortcuts

Literature reports numerous cases in which semantic wikis for knowledge manage-ment are used [9, 11] with some experimentation taking place in the Cultural Heritage domain [15]. For 4 years now, we have been using CRM-based semantic wikis for labs and group projects of a semantic web course for STEM students. Each group is using SMW to build and populate a small ontology about the story of a film, book or

```
The One Ring was created by the Dark Lord [[P14 carried
out by::Sauron]] during the [[P4 has time-span::Second
Age]] in order to gain dominion over the free peoples of
Middle-earth. The Ring seemed simply to be made of [[P9
consists of::gold]], but was impervious to damage. Placed
in fire, the ring displayed an
[[P102 has title::inscription]] in the Black Speech.
Translated, the words mean:
 One ring to rule them all, one ring to find them,
 One ring to bring them all and in the darkness bind
them.
[[Category: E22 Man-Made Object]]
```

Fig. 4. End-user SMW code fragment about the One Ring

biography. Although stories are naturally event-oriented, we have observed that (i) students tend to produce Wikipedia-like pages depicting endurants rather events; (ii) students frequently misuse properties, and especially property domains. Fig. 4 shows a typical SMW code excerpt that students might produce depicting the One Ring.

End-User Representation. Typically, an end-user will relate a physical or conceptual object directly to its creator. Indeed, in CRM event-oriented ontology, going through an E12 Production or E65 Creation event is required.

As several part-whole relationships exist in the CRM, end-users might use a wrong property (e.g. linking Things with *P9 consists of*, intended for temporal entities). A user might be faced with subtle differences in part-whole relations. For instance, an E18 Physical Thing may use *P46 is composed of* to relate to its components, if they are E18 Physical Thing; but should use *P45 consists of* to relate to its E57 Material. From our experience, end-users rarely choose the right part-whole relation.

The end-user might perceive parts indissociable from the whole. She will include parts description in the page depicting the whole, where this inclusion denotes the part-whole relationship. Indeed it requires the instantiation of parts, inside their proper class, and the instantiation of the part-whole and whole-part (inverse) relationships.

CRM-Compliant Representation. Fig. 5 depicts the correct SMW code compliant with the CRM ontology. The semantic association between an object and its creator should be replaced by a path denoting the necessity of going through an E12 Production event. Indeed, the semantic association between an object and its creation date should be replaced by a path starting with the same E12 Production event, but ending with an E52 Time-span rather with an E39 Actor. This illustrates the necessity of sharing paths, so as to avoid the instantiation of two Events denoting a single event.

```
The One Ring was created by the Dark Lord [[P108B was
produced by.E12 Production.P14 carried out by::Sauron]]
during the [[P108B was produced by.E12 Production.P4 has
time-span::Second Age]] in order to gain dominion over
the free peoples of Middle-earth. The Ring seemed simply
to be made of [[P45 consists of::gold]], but was impervi-
ous to damage. Placed in fire, the ring displayed an
[[P128 carries::inscription]].

[[Category: E22 Man-Made Object]]
```
```
The inscription appearing on the [[P128i is carried
by::One Ring]] is in [[P72 has language::the Black
Speech]]...
[[Category: E33 Linguistic Object]]
```

Fig. 5. CRM-compliant SMW code fragment about instances involved in Fig. 4

Because the inscription is an E33 Linguistic Object[2], distinct from the One Ring, it should be treated as a separate part with its distinct type (due to SMW limits, the only way of doing so is to create a separate page for the inscription), and the part should be related to the whole with a special part-whole relation *P128 carries (is carried by)*. The part might have its own properties (e.g. *P72 has language*::the Black Speech).

Discussion. Clearly, semantically correct annotations cannot be produced without solid knowledge of the CRM. Contributors can be provided with well-designed forms, where paths are replaced by shortcuts and displayed with meaningful labels (e.g. creator, creation date). SMW does not offer path group management.

A drawback of this approach is that shortcuts are not handled inside SMW. When a semantic connection between entities is required, ontology managers have to create the SMW property corresponding to the shortcut with the path as a name (e.g. *P108B was produced by*.E12 Production.*P4 has time-span* to connect a Man-Made Object to its production date). Shortcuts will be processed later on by the post-processor, which will decode the full path and produce the required triples. Hence, a strong limitation of using shortcuts in SMW is that the underlying path does not exist in the triple set and that searches cannot, therefore, use the missing triples.

3.3   The WissKI Approach

WissKI [7] was a research project in the cultural heritage domain, funded by the German Research Council (DFG) from 2009 to 2012. The name "WissKI" is a German acronym for "Scientific Communication Infrastructure" (Wissenschaftliche KommunikationsInfrastruktur). The project developed a software infrastructure which enhances the Drupal CMS (http://drupal.org/) for handling ontologies and semantic data. The software is open source and available via Github (https://github.com/wisski) or the project website (http://wiss-ki.eu/). The WissKI system requires an OWL-DL compatible ontology based on description logics and therefore suitable for automatic processing by machines. Thus the system benefits from calculations performed by reasoning mechanisms, e.g. automatic calculation of inverse properties. We use an OWL-DL implementation of the CRM, available at http://erlangen-crm.org/.

In the WissKI system, data is acquired either by forms or by text annotation in free texts via a WYSIWYG editor. Both input methods store the data in the same way in a triple store backend. The system aims to provide the user with concepts and relationships close to her representation of reality. At first concepts are identified, e.g. actors, time-spans, places, events and man-made objects. Then relationships are identified. Here WissKI suggests a new approach: focusing on semantic associations between endurants and providing the user with automatic generation of event-oriented paths.

If we consider Fig. 2, from the point of view of the "One Ring" there are four basic facts related to the custody transferred through an E10 Transfer of custody event: Gollum *[P28i] surrendered custody through* [an Event] while Bilbo *[P29i] received custody through* [an Event]. The E10 Transfer of custody event *[P10] falls within* an

---

[2] Formally, the text of an E33 Linguistic Object is documented with P3 has note: E62 String.

E5 Event that *[P7] took place at* under the Misty Mountains and *[P4] has time-span* 1341. Each fact can be represented by a semantic association, e.g. relating One Ring with 1341 is the path One Ring.*P30i custody transferred through.* Bilbo took the One Ring possessed by Gollum.*P10 falls within.* Gollum met Bilbo.*P4 has time-span.*aTime-span.*P1 identified by.*anAppellation.*P3 has note.*1341. Paths are instances of constructs (called "ontology paths" in the WissKI system) which act as stencils for the data. For instance, the ontology path between One Ring and 1341 is E22.*P30i.*E10.*P10.*E5.*P4.*E53.*P1.*E41.*P3.*E62.

Fig. 6. The WYSIWYG editor in the WissKI system

Each ontology path can be attributed a name, which makes it easier for humans to read; e.g. the ontology path above could be called "Time of Transfer". A complete set of concepts and ontology paths can be defined prior to using the system, or new concepts and paths can be added on-the-fly. The semantic annotation of free text is performed within the WYSIWYG editor (see a snapshot in Fig. 6) in a two-step process. Individuals referred to in the text (e.g. One Ring) have to be tagged by the user with the right concept (e.g. Object). Then, ontology paths can be instantiated: whenever the end-user selects any tagged individual, the system offers potential ontology paths and the user is able to select the right one (e.g. One Ring had a time of transfer 1341). Ontology path use is immediately processed by the WissKI system and the triple chain is generated. Ontology paths can be used in forms instead of ontology properties, thus enabling the user to display or enter data in an endurant-centric point of view while in the backend, the full power of semantic data slumbers.

3.4   Case study: The Use of the Pathbuilder

The WissKI component called Pathbuilder is a core utility for the creation, deletion and management of ontology paths. Once an ontology (e.g. the CRM) is loaded in the system, the administrator can navigate using dropdown fields through the ontology and is thus assisted in the construction of ontology paths. Paths have attributes: names, I/O look and feel, mandatory input and disambiguation.

Individuals are identified by appellations. The CRM uses the property *P1 is identified by* (and its sub-properties) to connect an individual to one or several instances of E41 Appellation (and its sub-classes) and an appellation instance is related to its primitive datatype value: a string, a date, etc. There might therefore be several individuals associated with a single value. When referring to an individual having that value, the user might want to use an existing individual or create a homonym. This is the purpose of the disambiguation feature: the system uses the backmost part of the ontology path as a search pattern in the triple store. User input yields the search condition. Whenever a match is found in the triple store, the user is prompted as to whether she wants to use the existing instance from the triple store or whether she wants to create a new one.

The endurant-centric approach uses a set of ontology paths starting from a single concept and leading on to different concepts. The set shall be divided among subsets sharing a common path, e.g. all paths mentioned in section 3.3 share E22 Man-Made Object.*P30i custody transferred through.*E10 Transfer of Custody. The system can be instructed to use the same instances for this section of the path when it generates the path instantiation. This feature is called "grouping of ontology paths". All ontology paths which are part of a group share the same root. Path groups have attributes, e.g. names. Forms and text input in the WissKI system are automatically enabled and generated for top level groups - those which are not part of other groups.

A CRM-Compliant End-User Representation. Recall the facts about the One Ring depicted in Fig. 4 and Fig. 5. An administrator defines a set of ontology paths from which for end-users can select their annotations. Table 1 gives some examples. Each path ends with a primitive datatype to handle primitive values, which is skipped here for the sake of simplicity.

Table 1. Examples of ontology paths related to E22 Man-Made Object instances

Path name	Domain / Range	Path structure
inscription	E22 Man-Made Object / E33 Linguistic Object	E22.*P128 carries*.E33
creator	E22 Man-Made Object / E82 Actor Appellation	E22.*P108i was produced by*.E12.*P14 carried out by*.E39.*P131 is identified by*.E82
creation date	E22 Man-Made Object / E49 Time Appellation	E22.*P108i was produced by*.E12.*P4 has time-span*.E52.*P78 is identified by*.E49
language inscription	E22 Man-Made Object / E56 Language	E22.*P128 carries*.E33. *P72 has language*.E56

In Fig. 7, we use these paths to produce an annotated text corresponding to Fig. 5. CRM properties (e.g. *P128 carries*) are very simple paths (from the property domain to its range), but can be customized to have another name (e.g. inscription) or other path attributes. Paths named *creator* and *creation date* start with the same sub-path (E22.*P108i*.E12) and shall be grouped (to share the same E12 Production instance). Handling a whole and its part is performed (as in SMW) in two steps: (i) writing, annotation and storage of the text related to the whole (e.g. One Ring) that will contain part-whole instantiations to its parts (e.g. the reference to an inscription) then attributing the right types to parts (which will instantiate the parts); (ii) clicking on each part and writing, annotating and storing the text related to each part.

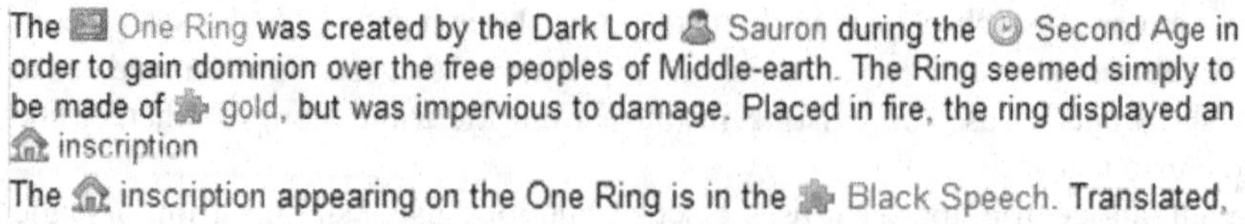

The 🖼 One Ring was created by the Dark Lord 👤 Sauron during the 🕐 Second Age in order to gain dominion over the free peoples of Middle-earth. The Ring seemed simply to be made of 🪙 gold, but was impervious to damage. Placed in fire, the ring displayed an 🏛 inscription

The 🏛 inscription appearing on the One Ring is in the 🪙 Black Speech. Translated,

Fig. 7. WissKI annotations corresponding to Fig. 5

4   Lessons Learned and Perspectives

4.1   Identifiers and Names

Typically, a (semantic) wiki uses page names as individuals' identifiers and there cannot be two pages with the same name. When several pages use the same name, a disambiguation word should be added to the name. However the CRM recognizes the fact that a distinction must be made between objects and their appellation. In WissKI, individual URIS are built from the individual's class and a generated unique identifier, e.g. E22_123 might be the relative URI of the individual identified by the appellation "One Ring", that obviously enables the use of the same name for different individuals.

This approach can be applied in a wiki, e.g. using E22_123 as a page name and the string "One Ring" as the display name. If we want to avoid each knowledge management system using its own isolated knowledge silo, we must recognize different URIs as being related to the same individual. This co-reference issue, is an active research topic. Exchanging or sharing triple sets between systems will require post-processing of the set in order to align URIs in a common agreed namespace.

4.2   End-User Usability of Instantiation, Compression and Decompression

Within SMW, the user has to create a wiki page for every individual she wants to instantiate and she has to locate the page in the right category (class). Instantiating the association between individuals is performed in the subject's page, and its inverse in the other page. In the WissKI free text editor the user has to select the type of the individual which is created if the automatic annotation process cannot find it. The user then asserts an ontology path to an individual which the text describes or refers to.

SMW templates using shortcuts or WissKI ontology paths provide the end-user with a friendly-representation of compressed paths of knowledge. WissKI uses SPARQL queries to implement ontology paths, so that the fully-articulated path and the ontology path are always synchronised. The same feature can be implemented in SMW when shortcuts are implemented using SMW queries.

When the user selects an ontology path in the WissKI editor or uses it within a form, the fully-articulated path is generated on-the-fly and stored in the triple store - whereas in SMW, decompression is performed by the post-processor after an export of the triple set (which must be re-imported if it is to be accurate).

4.3   Perspectives: Looking for Event Patterns

Almost all the shortcuts or ontology paths we encountered in our practice involve events. Following analysis of existing event models, [12] mention an agreement for six aspects and discuss a pattern for each aspect. [7] uses semantic documentation templates and an XML-based query language to create a documentation model and build flexible user interfaces for accessing and editing the documentation. In our view, whenever the end-user focuses her representation on an endurant participating in an event, this focus should be reflected by a set of semantic associations toward other endurants. When mereological relationships (part-whole) exist between events, semantic associations starting either from the part or from the whole are useful. And we could suppose that useful semantic associations can be deduced from other patterns. One perspective of this work is to use patterns and the work in [14] to generate a set of shortcuts/ontology paths for intuitive querying of CRM based repositories.

5   Conclusion

We present two prototypical approaches, SMW and WissKI, both of which aim to reduce the semantic gap between end-user representation and a complex event-based ontology. We focus on the compression and decompression of semantic associations through the use of shortcuts in the former approach, and ontology paths in the latter. Representational contracting is based on queries, and works fairly well in both approaches. Stretching end-user representation to generate fully-articulated paths is performed on-the-fly with WissKI whereas a shortcut post-processor has to be added to SMW. Considering base associations as well as derived ones is a difficult issue, as the number of possibilities may increase drastically. Thus, a skilled shortcut/ontology path design is required, to ensure end-user usability. An interesting perspective is to associate shortcut/ontology path generation with the recognition of event patterns.

References

1. Aleman-Meza, B., Halaschek, C., Arpinar, I.B., Sheth, A.: Context-aware semantic association ranking. In: Proc. of 1st Int. WS. on Semantic Web and Databases, pp. 33–50 (2003)
2. Anyanwu, K., Sheth, A.: The ρ operator: Discovering and ranking associations on the semantic web. SIGMOD Record 31, 42–47 (2002)
3. CIDOC CRM,
   http://www.cidoc-crm.org/official_release_cidoc.html
4. Doerr, M., Kritsotaki, A.: Documenting Events in Metadata. In: Proc. of 7th International Symposium on Virtual Reality, Archaeology and Cultural Heritage, pp. 1–5 (2006)
5. Fauconnier, G., Turner, M.: The Way We Think: Conceptual Blending and the Mind's Hidden Complexities. Basic Books, New York (2002)
6. Häyrinen, A.: Towards Semantic Modelling of Cultural Historical Data. In: Proc. of 12th Int. Conf. Information Modelling and Knowledge Bases, pp. 312–320 (2011)

7. Hohmann, G., Schiemann, B.: An ontology-based communication system for cultural heritage: Approach and progress of the WissKI project. In: Proc. of Scientific Computing & Cultural Heritage (2009)
8. Jämsen, J., Niemi, T., Järvelin, K.: Derived types in semantic association discovery. Journal of Intelligent Information Systems 35(2), 213–244 (2010)
9. Krötzsch, M., Vrandecic, D., Völkel, M., Haller, H., Studer, R.: Semantic Wikipedia. Journal of Web Semantics 5, 251–261 (2007)
10. Masolo, C., et al.: WonderWeb Deliverable D17. The WonderWeb Library of Foundational Ontologies and the DOLCE ontology (2002)
11. Millard, I., Jaffri, A., Glaser, H., Rodriguez-Castro, B.: Using a Semantic MediaWiki to Interact with a Knowledge Based Infrastructure. In: Proc. of 15th Int. Conf. on Knowledge Engineering and Knowledge Management (2006)
12. Scherp, A., Frantz, T., Saathoff, C., Staab, S.: A core ontology on events for representing occurrences in the real world. Multimed. Tools Appl. 58, 293–331 (2012)
13. Tolkien, J.R.R.: The Lord of the Rings - The Fellowship of the Ring. George Allen & Unwin (1954)
14. Tzompanaki, K., Doerr, M.: Fundamental Categories and Relationships for intuitive querying CIDOC-CRM based repositories. ICS-FORTH/TR-429 (2012)
15. Witte, R., Gitzinger, T., Kappler, T., Krestel, R.: A Semantic Wiki Approach to Cultural Heritage Data Management. Language Technology for Cultural Heritage Data (2008)

CULTURA: A Metadata-Rich Environment to Support the Enhanced Interrogation of Cultural Collections

Cormac Hampson[1], Seamus Lawless[1], Eoin Bailey[1], Sivan Yogev[2],
Naama Zwerdling[2], David Carmel[2], Owen Conlan[1], Alex O'Connor[1],
and Vincent Wade[1]

[1] Knowledge and Data Engineering Group, Trinity College Dublin, Ireland
{cormac.hampson,seamus.lawless,eoin.bailey,owen.conlan,
alex.oconnor,vincent.wade}@cs.tcd.ie
[2] IBM Research, Haifa, Israel
{sivany,naamaz,carmel}@il.ibm.com

Abstract. The increased digitisation of cultural collections, and their availability on the World Wide Web, has made access to these valuable documents much easier than ever before. However, despite the increased availability of access to cultural archives, curators still struggle to instigate and enhance engagement with these resources. The CULTURA project is actively addressing this issue through the development of a metadata-driven personalisation environment for navigating cultural collections and instigating collaborations. The corpus agnostic CULTURA environment also supports a full spectrum of users: ranging from professional researchers seeking patterns in the data and trying to answer complex queries; to interested members of the public who need help navigating a vast collection of resources. This paper discusses the state of the art in this area and the various innovative approaches used in the CULTURA project, with a special focus on how the underlying metadata helps facilitate its semantically rich environment.

Keywords: CULTURA, Adaptation, Personalisation, Digital Humanities, Normalisation, Social Network Analysis, Entity Extraction.

1   Introduction

The interdisciplinary field of digital humanities is concerned with the intersection of computer science, knowledge management and a wide range of humanities disciplines e.g. digital libraries, cultural heritage and digital arts. Recent large-scale digitisation initiatives have made many important cultural heritage collections available online. This makes them accessible to the global research community and interested public for the first time. However, the full value of these heritage treasures is not being realised. After digitisation, these collections are typically monolithic, difficult to navigate and can contain text which is of variable quality in terms of language, spelling, punctuation, and consistency of terminology. As a result, they often fail to attract and sustain broad user engagement leading to limited communities of interest. Thus, there

J.M. Dodero, M. Palomo-Duarte, P. Karampiperis (Eds.): MTSR 2012, CCIS 343, pp. 227–238, 2012.
© Springer-Verlag Berlin Heidelberg 2012

still remain important challenges in the presentation of new digital humanities artefacts to the end user.

Simple "one size fits all" web access is, in many cases, not appropriate in the digital humanities, due to the size and complexity of the artefacts. Furthermore, different types of users need varying levels of support, and every individual user has their own particular interests and priorities. Personalised and adaptive systems are thus necessary to help users gain optimum engagement with these new digital humanities assets.

Improved quality of access to cultural collections, especially those collections which are not exhibited physically, is a key objective of the CULTURA project [1]. Moreover, CULTURA supports a wide spectrum of users, ranging from members of the general public with specific interests, to users who may have a deep engagement with the cultural artefacts, such as professional and trainee researchers. To this end, CULTURA is delivering a corpus agnostic environment, with a suite of services to provide the necessary supports and features required for such a diverse range of users.

A central aspect of this environment is its use of rich metadata (user generated, computer generated and expert generated) coupled with natural language processing, entity extraction and social network analysis techniques, in order to support collaborative exploration, interrogation and interpretation of the underlying cultural resources. Section 2 of this paper discusses some related work in the field of digital humanities, with section 3 outlining the key challenges this research is addressing. Section 4 introduces two case studies which are central to the CULTURA project; section 5 discusses the various components and features of CULTURA's architecture; and section 6 summarises the paper and discusses the future work that remains to be undertaken.

2   Related Work

There has been substantial effort in the area of digitisation and cultural heritage preservation. Much of this work has, until recently, been focused on the creation of digital representations of cultural artefacts, and the creation of metadata and documentation associated with this. The result of this effort is that there is a vast collection of content available to digital humanists, in the form of text, images and other representations.

Textual content resources include collections arranged by theme, such as the Biodiversity Heritage Library[1], or from institutional collections, such as the Bayerische StaatsBibliothek[2] digital collections library. These collections include varying levels of metadata and some include detailed pictures which are associated with the text. It is important to note that in many cases 'textual' content actually refers to a complex cultural artefact that includes an image of the original manuscript, transcribed text associated with the content, and metadata which can describe the content, the nature of the document, and the provenance of the digital artefact. Another important type of artefact is collections of images, with detailed metadata records associated with each image.

---

[1] http://www.bhl-europe.eu/
[2] http://www.digital-collections.de/

While there have been recent attempts to use Adaptive Hypermedia techniques to support the personalised retrieval, interrogation and presentation of cultural heritage content collections, these have to-date been limited. The MultimediaN N9C Eculture project[3] aims to provide multimedia access to distributed collections of cultural heritage objects. It is an aim of the project to support the generation of various types of personalised and context-dependent presentations of cultural material. However, the current system only provides static semantic search across entities in manually annotated content collections. The CHIP project[4] aims to provide personalised presentation and navigation of the Rijksmuseum cultural resources. The *Artwork Recommender* supports the rating of artworks/topics to generate a user profile, which is then used to drive future artwork recommendations. The *Tour Wizard* is a web-based tool which uses the user profile to semi-automatically generate personalised museum tours. In the MOSAICA[5] project a mobile device-based demonstration is used to engage novice and intermediate users. The system does provide virtual visitors with access to structured descriptions of collections through a search interface, but little adaptivity is used.

The QViz[6] project has some similarities in approach to the CULTURA project in that it makes explicit recognition of the value of users as members of communities, and as contributors to digital cultural heritage collections. The focus of the QViz system is on temporal and spatial search and retrieval of archival content. While QViz is a social semantic application, facilitating user contribution and structured representation of knowledge, it does not have a personalised or adaptive aspect. Because CULTURA is producing a generalisable solution, it must be able to add value to a wide range of digital cultural heritage collections, of which there are many. One example is the Europeana project[7], which represents metadata from collections across many EU member states. While Europeana does not directly host content, it is a large repository of metadata which could be processed, alongside a specific collection's content, to seed the CULTURA environment.

3   Challenges in the Digital Humanites

The rise of 'i', 'me' and 'my' as prefixes for various web portals (e.g. iTunes[8]) and web services (e.g. MobileMe[9]) are intended to give the impression of personal tailoring of content and service to an individual user to enhance that individual's experience. Typically however, such services tend to focus on either: a) identification and ranking of relevant content or services; b) simplistic 'personalisation' of the content presentation by inclusion of the user's name, recently used resources etc.; or c) simple augmentation of screen layout.

---

[3] http://e-culture.multimedian.nl/
[4] http://www.chip-project.org/
[5] http:// www.mosaica-project.eu
[6] http://www.qviz.eu/
[7] http://www.europeana.eu/portal/
[8] http://www.itunes.com/
[9] http://www.me.com/

To effectively empower communities of researchers with personalised mechanisms which support the collaborative exploration, interrogation and interpretation of complex digital cultural artefacts, it requires the adaptivity provided in CULTURA to be more integrated and intelligent than in the portals described above. Such next generation adaptivity, as espoused by CULTURA, must support the dynamic composition and presentation of digital cultural heritage resources. However, just automated adaptivity is not enough. Ensuring that the user is in control of the personalisation process is essential. Such user-centred control is enhanced through: correlating usage patterns with self-expressed user goals; pre-defined strategies (e.g. research strategies, investigation strategies, discovery strategies, explanatory strategies etc.); and the provision of appropriate tools for users to explore and navigate large cultural heritage information spaces.

A common challenge in the humanities is that historical language hinders the accessibility of historical text documents. One solution to this problem is the use of a computational historical lexicon, supplemented by computational tools and linguistic models of variation. However, because of the absence of language standards, multiple orthographic variations of a given word or expression can be found in a collection of material, even in the same document. Hence, issues arising from the need to contend with noisy inputs, the impact noise can have on downstream applications, and the demands that noisy information places on document analysis, are addressed by CULTURA.

Social Network Analysis (SNA) can be used to analyse the people and relationships contained within humanities content collections. However, the effective application of SNA techniques to content which has major inconsistencies in the naming and identification of entities, poses a significant challenge which must be overcome. Typically digital cultural heritage collections contain complex relationships between entities which must be identified and extracted from the artefacts. This is an area CULTURA directly addresses by augmenting the existing metadata with new attributes. A second challenge for SNA is to leverage the user communities, activities, contributions and profiles to discover the rich influence network that interlinks users of these digital humanities content collections. The application of SNA to both the artefacts and the community that surrounds those artefacts, as incorporated in the CULTURA environment, is novel in the digital humanities. Such community-aware adaptivity creates an integrated, engaging experience for users of all types within the CULTURA environment.

4   Case Studies

In order to validate the CULTURA environment, two major artefacts have been selected - the *IPSA Illuminated Manuscript Collection*[10], held in the University of Padua, Italy and the *1641 Depositions*[11], held in Trinity College Dublin, Ireland. These resources, and the communities of users who work with them, are central to the

---

[10] http://www.ipsa-project.org/
[11] http://1641.tcd.ie/

design, development and evaluation of the CULTURA environment. Each are now discussed in turn.

4.1   The 1641 Depositions

The 1641 Depositions are seventeenth-century manuscripts that comprise about 8,000 witness statements, examinations and associated materials, in which Protestant men and women of all classes and from all over Ireland told of their experiences following the outbreak of the rebellion by the Catholic Irish in October 1641. This body of material is unparalleled anywhere else in early modern Europe and provides a unique source of information for the causes and events surrounding the 1641 rebellion and for the social, economic, cultural, religious, and political history of seventeenth-century Ireland, England and Scotland.

The 1641 Depositions have been digitised and transcribed and are being used to validate the techniques implemented in CULTURA. From a technological perspective, the 1641 Depositions represent a textually-rich digital humanities collection, which is characterised by noisy text, inconsistent sentence structure, grammar and spelling. The English language manuscripts contain rich metadata and descriptions of individuals, locations, events, social structures and contrasting / conflicting narratives. These artefacts have active communities of interest because of their wider social and historical implications that transcend geographical and chronological boundaries and continue to shape opinions and values to this day. The 1641 Depositions represent an ideal example of a digital humanities collection, which has deep resonance with social and cultural issues encountered throughout Europe.

4.2   The Imaginum Patavinae Scientiae Archivum

The Imaginum Patavinae Scientiae Archivum (IPSA) collection is a digital archive of illuminated medieval astrological and herbal manuscript codices dating from the 14th century with Latin, Paduan and Italian language commentaries. Herbals are manuscripts which contain hand-drawn depictions of plants, such as trees, bushes or shrubs, and their parts, such as flowers or leaves. The IPSA collection contains manuscripts written and illustrated by the Paduan School, and successive manuscripts produced in Europe under its influence. Such manuscripts have the rare characteristic of containing high quality and very realistic illustrations. IPSA is a combination of digitised images of the manuscripts and related metadata descriptions.

From a technical perspective, IPSA represents a very different kind of digital humanities collection to the 1641 depositions collection. The IPSA collection is primarily image based, with substantive metadata available. This metadata not only provides descriptive passages, but is also historically valuable as it captures the scientific processes which were prevalent during the creation of the original collection. However, the IPSA metadata is user generated which can lead to inconsistencies in terminology, spelling and grammar. The metadata contains descriptions of entities, individuals, activities and locations in multiple languages. The contrast in knowledge domain and structure of the IPSA and 1641 content collections demonstrate the broad applicability of the CULTURA methodology. Moreover, it highlights how the techniques delivered in CULTURA are not specific to an individual domain or collection but can be of benefit a wide range of digital humanities collections.

5   The CULTURA Architecture

CULTURA consists of multiple distinct services all accessed via the CULTURA portal. The services available in CULTURA are shown in figure 1 and include personalised search tools, faceted search tools, annotators, social and influencer network exploration tools, and recommenders. One of the key challenges for the CULTURA architecture is to reconcile the various models (user model, content metadata, extracted entities etc.) at runtime, in order to seamlessly provide the end user with the most appropriate content and services.

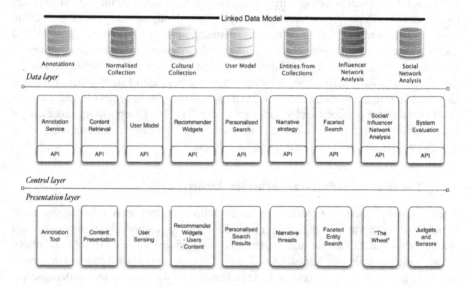

Fig. 1. CULTURA Services

A service is triggered by a user's interactions with the CULTURA portal, with requests sent from the presentation layer to the service via its API. For example, a person using CULTURA to search over the 1641 depositions triggers a series of events. First the search terms are identified and logged in the user model, which alters the areas of interest for the user. The personalised search service then normalises the search terms and identifies related entities via the linked data model. Multiple searches can now be executed using the original search terms, the normalised terms, and the related entities. Results from the searches are then merged and presented to the user. The merge process prioritises results that are related to areas that the user has an interest in, as determined by their user model.

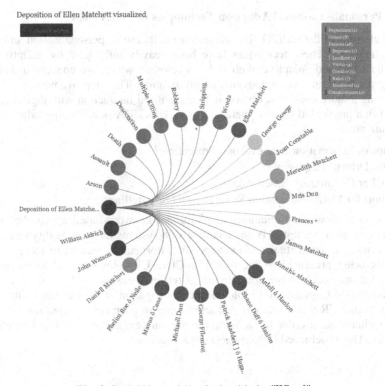

Fig. 2. Social Network Analysis with the "Wheel"

Additional tools (implemented as distinct services) can also be enabled depending on the results shown to the user. The selection of these tools is driven by modelling the correlation between a tool's affordances and the type of content to be displayed. A user's preferences in tool use, as identified by their user model, will also influence the choice of tool. When a user selects a result, the user model is again updated to reflect the preference. Additionally the system evaluation service is invoked, to inform which result the user has selected. This information can aid in evaluating the usefulness of search results, e.g. if the user rarely selects one of the top three results the ranking of results is deemed poor for that user.

The CULTURA portal utilises Drupal[12] as it provides numerous services that, while essential to CULTURA, are not core research elements, such as user authentication and system-wide logging. Drupal also has an extensible architecture that allows new modules to be developed in order to extend or replace functionality. Hence, all services developed by CULTURA are implemented as Drupal modules, and when accessed by users, the responses from these services are displayed in appropriate form e.g. social network analysis of people mentioned within the 1641 depositions can be displayed as a "wheel" as seen in figure 2.

---

[12] http://www.drupal.org

5.1   Personalisation and Adaption Techniques in CULTURA

A core element of the CULTURA architecture is its use of personalisation and adaption techniques. These techniques have been heavily influenced by Adaptive Hypermedia (AH) and Adaptive Web systems research which are concerned with improving the retrieval and composition of information. This improvement is achieved by creating a more context-sensitive and personalised interaction with digital content and is often predicated on rich metadata [4]. CULTURA is advancing adaptivity in four main areas:

- Adaptive Information Retrieval and Presentation
- Entity-Driven Adaptivity
- Social or Community-Based Adaptivity
- Support for Micro-Adaptation Strategies and Storytelling

In order to address the limitations of traditional keyword-based approaches to the retrieval of digital content, AH and adaptive web systems have the ability to enhance user queries with contextual and user-specific information, leading to more relevant materials being presented to the user [5]. CULTURA improves upon the current 'ranked list' approach to the presentation of retrieved resources, by delivering adaptively composed responses to enable deeper interrogation of the cultural heritage collections. CULTURA also extends AH approaches to adaptive presentation and navigation techniques, in order to facilitate the user in navigating across and combining resources. This is achieved by using techniques such as:

Personalised Content Recommendations

The recommendations on this page will change in response to your browsing pattern.

Place	Occupation	Person Type	Nature/Crime
Influencing Terms	**Influencing Terms**	**Influencing Terms**	**Influencing Terms**
Armagh	Captain	Deponent	killing
Levileglish	Clerk	Victim	multiple killing
Agralohoe	Colonel	Rebel	robbery
Armaghe	Farmer	Mentioned	captivity
Lurgan	Husbandman	Witness	words
onelaw	Knight	Landlord	arson
Turkharry	Wife	Proxy	stripping
Lissenesky	Esquire	Debtor	military action
Segoe	Gentleman	Apostate	death
Ballymore	Lord	Creditor	assault
Recommendations	**Recommendations**	**Recommendations**	**Recommendations**
Titlepage	Evidence against Michaell Doyne	Deposition of Lawrence Whitmore	Examination of Brian Clarke
List of losses			
Deposition of Gilbert Pemerton ex parte	Examination of Thomas Clark	Deposition of Ralphe Twyford	Examination of William Mcilduffe
Thomas and Elizabeth Powell	Examination of William Sym	Certificate of John Whitman	Information of William Beere
Deposition of Lawrence Whitmore	Examination of Valentine Blacker	Deposition of William Duffeild ex parte George Williams	Examination of Toole Mc Rory Mc Cann
Deposition of John Wisdome	Deposition of Frauncis Sacheverell	Deposition of Thomas Turke	Examination of Ralph Fester
Deposition of Thomas Turke	Deposition of William Duffeild	Examination of Grace Crowe	Examination of William Bentley

Fig. 3. An example of the personalised content displayed to users within the CULTURA portal

- dynamic hyperlinking across key sections of retrieved documents
- adaptively composing and presenting responses which combine key elements of the retrieved documents
- providing guidance for the analysis of the retrieved documents
- providing facilities to add and search digital annotations [6].

The application of these techniques helps empower experienced researchers, novice researchers and the wider community to discover, interrogate, and analyse the cultural heritage resources. Figure 3 shows one example of the recommended content shown to users who browse the 1641 depositions using CULTURA. In this example, green text links to specific depositions are listed under four headings (Place, Occupation, Person Type and Nature/Crime). These links are generated for each heading by comparing the most prominent terms in a user's browsing history (displayed under "Influencing Terms") with the metadata of all depositions, and rendering the most relevant.

5.2   Normalisation of Cultural Collections

Performing document analysis techniques (i.e. information extraction) on historical texts, which contain non-standard spelling, historical grammar and many old word forms, is a non-trivial challenge requiring normalisation of word spelling and entity extraction. The primary purpose of the normalisation process is to produce documents without historical variations on letter level. This normalised text enables better identification of entities, e.g. people, places, events, dates, as well as facilitating improved search across the collection by taking account of spelling variants of a search term. The statistical model built to automatically normalise the historical text utilised manually normalised documents. These manually normalised documents were randomly selected and accounted for approximately 6% of documents from the 1641 depositions. The Translation Model was developed on the top of the previously developed OCR correction methodology [7].

5.3   CULTURA Meta-model and Automatic Entity Detection

Data modelling is one of the crucial aspects of designing a data-centric system. In the context of digital humanities the data modelling challenge has two specific characteristics. The first requirement is to allow the incorporation of new concepts which augment the original data during the research process e.g. detection of new type of entities such as "murder" events within the 1641 depositions, which aren't explicitly encoded a priori. The other requirement is to support a layer of services that allow a range of user actions. These actions could include the manual manipulation of existing data, the user referencing of specific data elements or the interactions between sets of users.

In both cases, the system schema must evolve over time to reflect the work of researchers and others. Therefore, the data management part of the system must support easy on-the-fly modifications of the underlying schema. This requirement rules out relational databases, since modifying the columns of a populated relational database table is a costly task. However, conceptual modelling based on the Entity-Relationship model, which is commonly used in the process of relational databases schema definition, is an effective methodology for capturing data requirements. Hence, this meta-model has been chosen by CULTURA to define the digital cultural archives using its environment e.g. the IPSA collection and the 1641 depositions.

Recently, a growing number of systems which allow schema evolution have emerged, labelled under the generic term "NoSQL". There are three prominent types of NoSQL systems: Key-Value Stores, Document Stores and Graph Databases, which greatly differ in their meta-model definitions. In Key-Value Stores only pairs of key and value are allowed, thus no structure can be defined. In Document Stores the basic element is a document which contains a set of fields. In contrast, with Graph Databases, the data is managed in the form of nodes with properties, and edges (that can be labelled) connecting the nodes. In terms of these three NoSQL types, they have variable suitability for handling Entity-Relationship data. Since Key-Value Stores contain no structure, they are clearly not suitable for implementing an Entity-Relationship model over them. In contrast, Document Stores do provide a good basis for handling entities, by mapping the entities to documents and their attributes to fields. On the other hand, Graph Stores are suited to handling entities as graph nodes and relationships as edges.

Given the features of the various NoSQL types, a combination of a Document Store (to handle entity attributes) with a Graph Store (to handle relationships), appears to be an appropriate solution for digital humanities data management. However, there are a number of drawbacks to such a solution. The first issue is the weak support in Graph Databases for non-binary relationships. It is expected that digital humanities data will include complex relationships with possibly multiple entities and relationship attributes. Thus, the graph support of current Graph Databases is not sufficient. Another insufficiency is in Document Stores support of textual search, which requires the addition of a search engine to the system. Another challenge is the need to coordinate the data between the Document Store and the Graph Database during both data ingestion and query processing.

In light of these problems, a new solution has recently been proposed, which uses the open source search library Lucene[13] to index entity-relationship data, and allows expressive search capabilities ranging from simple keyword search to complex structured queries [8]. The 1641 depositions data has already been modelled and processed as part of an entity-oriented search component [9], providing a powerful exploratory search system. This entity-oriented component provides CULTURA with a powerful tool for incremental research, where results of prior analysis are accessible for search and exploration. Furthermore, it enables the improvement of existing analysis processes, and supports new insights to the collection to be discovered. The entity-oriented approach also allows researchers and other interested users to be added as entities in the system, and link them to entities identified in the data in a non-trivial manner. Such connections between the system users and the data can afterward be

---

[13] http://lucene.apache.org/core/

used to automatically define the social network of the community interested in the digital archive, and later this social network can be used to provide social-based services to the community.

5.4   Network Analysis of Cultural Collections

Normalised historical texts can then be analysed using Influencer Network Analysis (INA), a form of Social Network Analysis (SNA), which is used to identify the social structure described in the historical texts and the influential people involved in the incidents portrayed. Influential entities not only include the individuals involved within the collection, but also the issues, topics and opinions that are detailed. Entities within the historical texts are either discovered in the text through a combined manual and automatic process, or categorised as descriptive metadata that is additional to the historical text. Relationships between entities are also identified and can augment the existing metadata from the collection. These entities and relationships are graphed and shown to users allowing a user to explore the relationships between entities across multiple historical texts (see figure 2).

Network analysis also enables a tracking of entities both temporally and geographically. Due to the scale and complexity of the information held in these content collections, this has rarely been attempted by humanities researchers. Furthermore, apart from performing network analysis on the historical texts themselves, CULTURA also analyses how the community of users engaged with the collection interact. Thus it makes it easier for users to discover relevant experts, for new communities to be created based on similar activities, and for community collaboration and contribution to occur.

6   Summary and Future Work

This paper discussed the CULTURA project and outlined key challenges that it is addressing within the digital humanities field. Two contrasting cultural collections (the 1641 depositions and the IPSA collection) that have been incorporated into CULTURA were described, along with details of the service oriented architecture underpinning the environment. Three specific features of the CULTURA environment were discussed in further detail (personalisation and adaption techniques, automatic entity detection, and network analysis), with an emphasis on the importance that metadata plays in facilitating such functionality.

Further evaluation studies within the CULTURA project will take place involving both the IPSA collection and the 1641 Depositions. Moreover, all the key stakeholders in this domain (from professional researchers to members of the public) will be involved. The outcomes of these studies will help refine the implementation and underlying methodology, especially in how the various models and metadata interact. Finally, the new technologies which have been developed within CULTURA (text normalisation service, SNA and INA services, entity detection service etc.) will be fully integrated into the architecture. This will result in an end-to-end system, which encompasses all stages from the initial normalisation of cultural heritage collections, to the deployment of these resources within an online personalised portal.

Acknowledgements. The work reported has been funded by the Seventh Framework Programme of the European Commission, Area "Digital Libraries and Digital Preservation" (ICT-2009.4.1), grant agreement no. 269973.

References

1. Bailey, E., Lawless, S., O'Connor, A., Sweetnam, S., Conlan, O., Hampson, C., Wade, V.: CULTURA: Supporting Enhanced Exploration of Cultural Archives through Personalisation. In: The Proceedings of the 2nd International Conference on Humanities, Society and Culture, ICHSC 2012, Hong Kong, China, October 27-28 (in press, 2012)
2. Agichtein, E., Brill, E., Dumais, S.: Improving Web Search Ranking by Incorporating User Behaviour Information. In: Proceedings of the 29th Annual International ACM SIGIR Conference on Research and Development in Information Retrieval, Seattle, Washington, USA, pp. 19–26 (2006)
3. Ankolekar, A., Krötzsch, M., Tran, T., Vrandečić, D.: The two cultures: Mashing up Web 2.0 and the Semantic Web. In: Web Semantics: Science, Services and Agents on the World Wide Web, vol. 6(1). Elsevier Science Publishing (2008)
4. Brusilovsky, P., Kobsa, A., Nejdl, W. (eds.): Adaptive Web 2007. LNCS, vol. 4321. Springer, Heidelberg (2007)
5. Jones, G., Wade, V.: Integrated Content Presentation for Multilingual and Multimedia Information Access. In: The Proceedings of the Workshop on New Directions in Multilingual Information Access at the 29th International ACM SIGIR Conference on Research and Development in Information Retrieval, Seattle, U.S.A, pp. 49–52 (August 2006)
6. Agosti, M., Ferro, N.: A Formal Model of Annotations of Digital Content. ACM Transactions on Information Systems (TOIS), 26 (1) 26(1), 3:1–3:57 (2008)
7. Mihov, S., Mitankin, P., Gotscharek, A., Reffle, U., Schulz, K.U., Ringlstetter, C.: Tuning the Selection of Correction Candidates for Garbled Tokens using Error Dictionaries. In: Proceedings of FSTAS 2007, pp. 25–30 (2007)
8. Yogev, S., Roitman, H., Carmel, D., Zwerdling, N.: Towards expressive exploratory search over entity-relationship data. In: Proceedings of the 21st International Conference Companion on World Wide Web, pp. 83–92. ACM, New York (2012)
9. Carmel, D., Zwerdling, N., Yogev, S.: Entity oriented search and exploration for cultural heritage collections: the EU cultura project. In: Proceedings of the 21st International Conference Companion on World Wide Web, pp. 227–230. ACM, New York (2012)

Aggregative Data Infrastructures
for the Cultural Heritage

Alessia Bardi[1,2], Paolo Manghi[1], and Franco Zoppi[1]

[1] Consiglio Nazionale delle Ricerche
Istituto di Scienza e Tecnologie dell'Informazione "A. Faedo"
{name.surname}@isti.cnr.it
[2] Dipartimento di Ingegneria dell'Informazione, Università di Pisa

Abstract. Aggregative data infrastructures (ADIs) are information systems where organizations can find the tools to integrate their data sources to form uniform and richer information spaces of object metadata descriptions. Novel sustainable approaches for the realization of ADIs are based on the adoption of ADI enabling technologies which support the realization, maintenance and upgrade of ADIs and promote functionality re-use. The Cultural Heritage (CH) community is one of the most active in the realization of ADIs. Besides, the realization of ADIs for CH can be particularly complex when compared to other disciplines due to the possibly high heterogeneity of data sources involved. In this paper, we present the D-NET Software Toolkit as an ideal candidate for the realization of sustainable, extensible, scalable and dynamic ADIs for CH. To this aim we present the D-NET framework and services, and demonstrate its effectiveness in the CH scenario by describing its adoption to realize a real-case ADI for the project Heritage of the People's Europe.

Keywords: Cultural Heritage, Metadata Aggregation, Interoperability.

1 Introduction

In the last decade, the multi-disciplinary character of science and the need of researchers to gain immediate access to research material often led to the realization of so-called *aggregative data infrastructures* (ADIs). These are here intended as information systems where organizations (e.g. research centers, universities, industries) can find the tools to integrate their data sources to form uniform and richer information spaces and support their communities with enhanced access services to such content. In particular, ADIs offer functionality for (*i*) the collection and processing of metadata descriptions of files (digital objects) in order to populate a uniform aggregated information space and (*ii*) the provision of the information space to humans, via web portals, and machines, via standard APIs. On the one hand, one major challenge for ADI designers and developers is to provide tools capable of dealing with several interoperability issues derived by the mismatch between the aggregated information space and the data sources; e.g. export protocols, structure and semantics of metadata,

J.M. Dodero, M. Palomo-Duarte, P. Karampiperis (Eds.): MTSR 2012, CCIS 343, pp. 239–251, 2012.

physical representation. On the other hand, another big challenge is to realize ADI capable of coping with the dynamic and complex requirements of research communities, whose needs in terms of content, functionality, and quality of service tend to vary along time, as science evolves. Indeed, software and system refinements prove to be as expensive as necessary for the ADI to grow and be up to the challenge of its community. Therefore, the adoption of the proper enabling technology plays a crucial role for the sustainability of an ADI. Such technology should minimize the cost of design and development required to realize, operate, and modify data infrastructures. The *D-NET Software Toolkit*[1] was specifically realized to facilitate designers and developers in the realization and maintenance of ADIs. D-NET implements an open source service-oriented framework where services for the collection, processing and provision of metadata and files from a set of data sources can be customized and combined to implement the internal workflows of ADIs. As proven by the several installations[1] and adoption in a number of European projects (DRIVER, DRIVER II, OpenAIRE, OpenAIREplus, EFG, EFG1914), ADIs realized with D-NET are easily customizable, extensible, scalable, and sustainable[2].

In this work we focus on the Cultural Heritage (CH) domain, which is certainly one of the most active in the realization of ADIs[3][4]. The increased availability of CH digital content raised a natural need to realize ADIs for the integration and delivery of such content to wider research, academic, and public communities[4]; examples are the ADIs supported by Europeana[2] and its satellite projects. The realization of ADIs for CH can be particulary complex when compared to other disciplines. This is due to the high degree of heterogeneity brought in by CH communities, which are typically formed by groups of subcommunities whose research focuses may diverge but require to be connected to enable better science. In this paper, we show how the D-NET Software Toolkit can be particularly apt for the realization of ADIs for CH. Besides, we propose a two-phase metadata conversion approach to tackle with the particularly complex interoperability issues which may arise in CH scenarios featuring highly heterogeneous data sources. To this aim we present the D-NET framework and services and describe their usage to instantiate a two-phase conversion ADI in the context of The Heritage of the People's Europe (HOPE) project[3]. The HOPE project provides a unified entry point for the social and labour history from the 18th to the 21st century in Europe. It federates digital object collections from several major European institutions in the field. HOPE is an exceptionally representative scenario of CH's richness, since social and labour history covers a wide range of digital objects, such as documentaries, pictures, drawings, and archival documents, in turn described by highly heterogeneous metadata representations.

Paper Outline. Section 2 presents the evolving requirements surfacing when realizing ADIs and the sustainability issues they entail for supporting organizations. Section 3 describes the architecture and functionalities of the D-NET

---

[1] http://www.d-net.research-infrastructures.eu

[2] http://www.europeana.eu

[3] http://www.peoplesheritage.eu

Software Toolkit and explains how it minimizes the cost of addressing the evolving requirements of ADIs. Section 4 describes the HOPE real-case scenario and how D-NET has been successfully adopted to realize the HOPE ADI for CH.

2   Aggregative Data Infrastructures

In the last few years, an increasing number of research communities started federating their data sources into ADIs. A high-level functional architecture of ADIs is shown in Fig. 1: ADIs are inteded here as systems capable of collecting *metadata records* and *files* relative to objects from a set of heterogeneous *data sources* to construct an homogeneous information space of data conforming to a *common data model*. Over the resulting information space, the ADI provides community services to support advanced access to the aggregated data; e.g. cross-source search and browse, cross-source object interlinking, standard API exports, etc. ADIs typically focus on metadata aggregation and realize information spaces whose data can be used to cross-search over files which are kept at their original locations. In some cases however, files may be collected or uploaded in an ADI to offer services for digital preservation[5,6]. In the following we shall describe the two main challenges to be tackled when realizing ADIs: data interoperability and curation, and coping with evolving requirements.

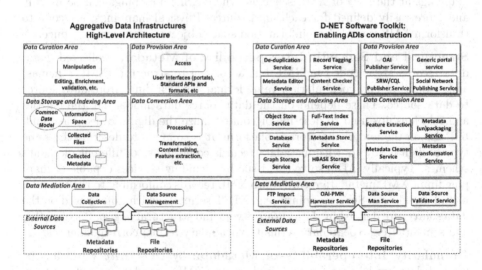

Fig. 1. Aggregative Data Infrastructures and D-NET implementation

2.1   Data Interoperability and Curation

ADIs collect from data sources, through standard APIs, files and relative metadata records. In the following we shall focus on XML metadata data sources, that is data sources exporting metadata records in XML format – the same or similar reasonings can be applied to all formats, e.g. RDF, JSON. Metadata records are on-the-wire representations of data conforming to the data source data model. The ADI information space contains data conforming to the given common data model whose physical representation may be based on several standard storage solutions, such as relational databases, graph stores, full-text indices, XML native stores, etc. ADIs must therefore provide tools to overcome two main interoperability barriers: the definition of logical mappings from data source data models onto ADI common data model and the definition of physical mappings from XML metadata records to ADI storage data representation. The design and implementation of ADIs must face the following technical challenges[2]:

Mediation Interoperability: data sources may export data according to different standard protocols. Typically, ADIs solve this issue by natively supporting standard exchange protocols, such as OAI-PMH, FTP, HTTP, and including services capable of collecting and storing data locally.

Representation Interoperability: as mentioned above collected metadata records are encoded in XML while data in the ADI information space may not necessarily be stored in the same way. Conversion software must therefore encode both logical and physical mappings from XML records onto information space objects. Typically, ADIs facilitate this task by defining a common XML schema for representing the information space data model. This leaves the logical mappings at the level of XML schemas, where XSLT mappings can be flexibly and more easily defined for each data source. Physical mappings, i.e. code to transform XML records into information space objects, is written only once.

Structural and Semantic Interoperability of Metadata: collected metadata records are encoded in XML but according to structure (XML schemas) and semantics (e.g. vocabularies, value formats) which differ from data source to data source. These depend on the data source data model, i.e. the entities and relationships used to describe or contextualize the digital objects at hand, but also on the underlying storage platform. It is common to describe the same type of digital objects with metadata records conforming to different metadata schemes. Typically, ADIs solve this issue by including services capable of mapping input XML metadata records onto XML records conforming to the common metadata schema. Such mappings (e.g. XLST scripts), which differ based on the data source, are defined by data curators who find structural (e.g. paths to paths) and semantic (e.g. vocabulary terms to vocabulary terms) correspondences.

Granularity Interoperability of Metadata: by *granularity* we mean the level of data model detail represented by one XML metadata record. In some cases each record represents one entity of the model (e.g. a Dublin Core record represents and describes one publication entity), in other cases it may represent more entities possibly with relationships between them (e.g. one ESE record can represent a set of entities, while a METS record may represent a graph of interrelated entities). Since structural and semantics mappings for XML records apply at the level of the individual entities, further services are required to *(un)package* records in order to single out the entities required for the mappings.

Manipulation of Information Spaces: the ADI common data model is typically defined to minimize information loss w.r.t. the collected data and relative data models, but also maximize the quality and richness of the generated metadata records (e.g. entity properties should rarely have missing values). In some cases, the model includes attributes whose values may be derived by extracting information from the metadata records (e.g. mining attribute values and relationships between records to infer further values or relationships) or from the files described by such records (e.g. histograms from images, keywords from text documents). Typically, ADIs solve this issues by including services capable of processing collected data to enrich the quality of records in the information space. Moreover, collecting objects from several data sources may lead to duplication of content, whenever different sources keep information about the same entities. In such cases, de-duplication actions, i.e. merge metadata records describing the same object into one, may be necessary to disambiguate the information space. To this regard, ADIs may include de-duplication services specifically devised to exploit attributes and relationships of a record to identify and (semi-)automatically merge similar records.

2.2   Coping with Evolving Requirements

Organizations willing to realize ADIs must be able to sustain the initial design and development cost, plus the refinement costs made necessary by further changes required by the operative ADIs. Indeed, ADIs are often characterized by highly evolving requirements in terms of content, functionality, and Quality of Service (QoS). On the content side examples are changes to the common metadata model, new mappings required to handle interoperability with new joining data sources, etc. On the functionality side examples are changes in the data management workflows (e.g. collection, conversion, storage, indexing workflow may turn into a collection, storage, conversion, indexing workflow, to make the index more efficiently re-generated on different mapping conversions), new services to integrate missing functionality, etc. On the QoS side, management of storage and index replicas may be required to ensure robustness and availability.

Most ADI enabling software in the literature are designed to tackle very precise data aggregation scenarios and can hardly be re-used in different contexts and domains, examples are the projects Multimatch[7], KEEP[4], MICHAEL[5], DARIAH[8] and CLARIN[9]. This is due to the overall absence of general-purpose software for ADIs, which leads organizations responsible for ADIs to face the high cost of realizing their ADIs from scratch and in a very pragmatic way. This often happens by integration of open source technologies and products, such as OAI-PMH aggregators (DLXS, Repox), full-text indices (Apache

---

[4] Keeping Emulation Environments Portable, `"http://www.keep-project.eu"`
[5] Multilingual Inventory for Cultural Heritage in Europe,
     `"http://www.michael-culture.org"`

Lucene and Solr), XML stores (Exists), etc. As a consequence, the result are ADIs which very efficiently address their initial requirements, but involve high refinement and maintenance costs whenever the dynamic requirements described above must be satisfied. In many cases, organizations must face the trade-off between refinement costs and end-user satisfaction.

3   The D-NET Software Toolkit

In the previous section we explained how the realization of ADIs is not trivial in terms of technical expertise, development and maintenance costs. The common approach to create from scratch such infrastructures, realizing functionalities for one specific community, hardly re-usable in other contexts, and re-implementing common functionalities from the bare metal up, instead of sharing them among communities turned out to be not affordable in the majority of cases. As a reaction to such drawbacks, research in the e-Infrastructure field concentrated on the realizion of software systems specifically designed to support the creation of ADIs[2,10,11]. Typically, such software systems are based on general-purpose functional patterns for data collection, processing, storage and provision in order to allow developers to realize ADIs by re-using, customizing, and pipelining functionalities into workflows to meet the specific community needs. Moreover, the underlying loosely-coupled components architectures allow developers to dynamically modify the workflows and to integrate new functionalities. Finally, a middleware with *enabling functionality* helps ADI administrator on tasks related to the QoS, such as scalability, robustness, and load balancing.

In this section we present the D-NET Software Toolkit[6] and show how it addresses the technical challenges described in Sect. 2. D-NET is an open source, general-purpose software conceived to enable the realization and operation of ADIs (initial requirements) and to facilitate their evolution in time (refinement requirements). D-NET implements a service-oriented framework based on standards, namely Web Services with SOAP and REST APIs, where ADIs can be constructed in a LEGO-like approach, by selecting, customizing, and properly combining D-NET services. The resulting ADIs are systems which can be re-customized, extended (e.g. new services can be integrated), and scale (e.g. storage and index replicas can be maintained and deployed on remote nodes to tackle multiple concurrent accesses or very-large data size) at run-time.

D-NET offers a rich and expandable set of services targeting data collection, processing, storage, indexing, curation and provision aspects. Services can be customized and combined to meet the data workflow requirements of a target user community. D-NET services can be partly or fully replicated and distributed over different servers depending on the QoS needs of the specific community. In general, multiple instances of a service increase fault tolerance, reduce the overload of each instance, and make it possible to dynamically reorganize the environment when a server is not reachable. Figure 1, presents how several D-NET

---

[6] http://www.d-net.research-infrastructures.eu

services, some of which realized in the context of the HOPE project, implement the high-level architecture and functionalities:

Data Mediation Area Services in this area are capable of managing (register and de-register) a set of available external data sources and of collecting their objects. D-NET offers services for on-demand and programmatic data collection based on the following standard protocols: OAI-PMH, FTP, FTPS (FTP over SSL/TSL), SFTP (SSH File Transfer Protocol), HTTP/HTTPS.

Data Storage and Indexing Area Services in this area manage storage and access for files and metadata records. Services offer various data storage supports, abstracting over relational databases (Postgres), file (MongoDB and file system) and graph stores (Neo4J), full-text indices (Solr), NoSQL storage (HBASE), and metadata store (abstraction on top of file storage services). Developers can configure and choose the most proper storage based on the functional requirements and the common data model of the ADI at hand.

Data Convertion Area Services in this area offer functionalities to convert XML metadata records, regardless of the structure and semantics of their schemas, and files, regardless of their storage formats. The Transformation Service can be configured to transform metadata records from one schema to another (e.g. from MARC to Dublin Core) given XSLT mappings. D-NET data managers can create, update, remove and re-use such mappings and configure the service to apply one format to a given input (e.g. a metadata store) at given time intervals. In particular, in the case of one-to-one mappings between XML records, the service provides an end-user interface for the aided-creation of mappings in the style of Repox[12] and MINT[7]. The Cleaner Service can be similarly configured to harmonise values in the records based on terms-to-terms mappings. Metadata record conversion is completed by services that solve granularity issues by (un)packaging XML records (one-to-many and many-to-one conversions). Finally, the Feature Extraction Service can perform information extraction from files according to given algorithms to produce values to be added to records (e.g. extraction of histograms from images).

Data Curation Area Services in this area offer functionalities for data curation and enrichment. The Content Checker Service provides data curators with tools to find mapping mistakes and semantic inconsistencies in records of the information space. Curators can commit content (from a given data source) as visible to the public when validation is successful. The Metadata Editor Service allows data curators to add, edit and delete metadata records, as well as to establish relationships between existing records, even if coming from different sources. The De-duplication Service[13] allows data curators to disambiguate the information space by merging duplicate records. The tool identifies the pairs of records candidate for merging based on a multi-sort version of the sorted neighbourhood algorithm and a record similarity function that is customizable by data curators. Finally, D-NET was extended in HOPE to include the Record Tagging Service,

---

[7] MINT at National Technical University of Athens, Metadata Interoperability Services. "http://mint.image.ece.ntua.gr/redmine/projects/mint/wiki"

which allows data curators to mark a group of objects in the information space according to terms of a given vocabulary.

Data Provision Area Services in this area allow third-party applications to access objects via standard APIs. D-NET currently supports the following provision protocols: OAI-PMH (enabling harvester to access metadata records), SRW, REST and WSDL/SOAP (enabling third party applications, such as portals, to perform queries on D-NET indices). Moreover, User Interface Services can be used to automatically generate templates of portals based on the common data model used across the storage services of the ADIs. Finally, in the context of HOPE we included new D-NET services for the automatic export (and removal) of videos and pictures towards social networks whenever such objects are tagged with special labels (e.g. tags by the record tagging service, values from a vocabulary). The Social Network Publishing Services are designed to be extendible to include further publishing actions and new web destinations.

4   D-NET in the Cultural Heritage: The HOPE ADI

HOPE (Heritage of the People's Europe, FP7 EU eContentplus, grant agreement: 250549)[8] is a "Best Practice Network" for archives, libraries, museums and institutions operating in the fields of social and union history. The goal of the project is providing a unified access to materials about the European social and labour history from the 18th to 21st centuries, proposing guidelines and tools for the management, aggregation, harmonisation, curation and provision of digital CH content. Institutions joining the HOPE network benefit of an advanced, distributed ADI instantiated and maintained by ISTI-CNR (Pisa, Italy). The ADI enables them to enhance the quality and the visibility of the digital cultural objects they preserve. Moreover, the project also delivers a Shared Object Repository, external to the ADI and realized and managed by IISG in Amsterdam, Netherlands. The repository deals with the management (storage, access, and conversion) of digital files for HOPE partners who cannot afford the cost of a local object file store. It allows institutions to deposit their files and it automatically applies conversion algorithms to create files in standard formats and with sizes suitable for web dissemination.

The HOPE ADI is implemented using the D-NET Software Toolkit, by extending it to include new services such as the Record Tagging Service and the Social Network Publishing Services (as presented in the previous section) and to adopt a two-phase approach to metadata record conversion. In the following sections we shall introduce the requirements of the HOPE infrastructure, as exemplary of the CH domain, and describe how the D-NET software is today used to implement them in an efficient and sustainable way.

4.1   The HOPE Aggregative Data Infrastructure

The project HOPE includes an initial set of content provider institutions whose common need is the realization of an ADI. The community is willing to make

---

[8] http://www.peoplesheritage.eu

objects files from all data sources accessible from an aggregated information space whose metadata records obey to the same HOPE common data model. The aim is to group and interlink such objects in order to establish opportunities for a new cross-country, cross-institution social history background. The ADI should be able to handle a varying number of content providers, which may be in turn deliver several data sources, each dedicated to storage of metadata records and files relative to different object typologies; e.g. an institution may offer two data sources, relative to an archive and a library. Indeed, as it often happens in the CH domain, content providers may deliver data sources whose objects belong to diverse sub-communities (in HOPE referred to as *profiles*), which in HOPE are: *library, archive, visual, audio video*. Although a profile marks a data source as including material of the same "semantic domain", distinct data sources may store objects of different formats (e.g. images, videos, audio, text material) and different descriptive data models and relative metadata formats. For example, librarians and archivists typically model their digital objects according to different data models and schemata (e.g. Dublin Core for libraries, and EAD for archivists), but each of them may have a variety of ways to describe their objects (e.g. libraries may also use MARC). Furthermore, data sources may export their content via several standard protocols, such as OAI-PMH, FTP, etc.

The information space is populated by collecting and converting metadata records from HOPE content providers, and curated by HOPE data curators, who can edit/correct metadata records and tag objects in order to : (i) classify them, based on a vocabulary of historical themes (defined as part of the HOPE data model), or (ii) establish which social networks they should be sent to, based on a list of social networks. Finally, the information space is searchable and browsable by end-users from the project web portal (IALHI[9] portal) and made available to Europeana and other interested service consumers via OAI-PMH APIs.

Based on the four HOPE domain profiles, the HOPE consortium defined a common metadata model and its corresponding XML schema. In order to capture the commonalities of diverse object domains and formats, the model has been defined by studying the characteristics of the four profiles from the perspective of well-established standard format in the respective field: MARCXML for libraries, EAD for archives, EN 15907 for audio video, and LIDO for visual.

As depicted in Fig. 2, seven class of entities resulted from this process. Descriptive units represent digital objects and include descriptive information about the real world object (e.g. date of creation, type of material, title). According to the identified profiles, the descriptive unit class has four subclasses containing properties that are peculiar to one specific domain. Cross-domain properties are instead defined in the descriptive unit super class. Descriptive units are related with each other via containment and sequential relationships so that it is possible to represents hierarchies of objects (for example a book with miniatures, where there is a description of the whole book - the container - and a description of each miniatures in it). A digital resource contains technical information about a digital representation of the object (e.g. the picture of one side of a coin,

---

the digitised page of a book) and it is linked to the corresponding descriptive unit. Digital resources related to the same descriptive units can express sequential relationships, thus establishing a "reading path". Agents, places, concepts, events, and themes contextualize the object and are linked to descriptive units via relationships whose names describe the semantics of the association.

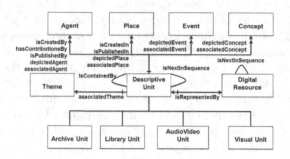

Fig. 2. HOPE common metadata model: main entities and relationships

4.2 D-NET and HOPE ADI: Two-Phase Approach

As pointed out by Haslhofer and Klas in [14], the use of cross-walks (or mappings) solves structural and semantic heterogeneities of metadata records, enabling the realization of homogeneous information spaces where curators and automatic services can operate on. The typical approach is that of defining a common metadata format and establishing a mappings from each input format to the common one. In the case of HOPE, this process was complicated by the high degree of heterogeneity. As described above, since the objects and metadata records collected from the content providers may belong to sub-communities of the overall ADI, the HOPE common metadata model tends to abstract over all of such communities and therefore the mapping from data source data models into the common data model is not straightforward. For those reasons, instead of adopting a "classic" cross-walk from one input metadata format to one target metadata format, HOPE ADIs adopts a "two-phase approach". The first phase solves intra-profile structural and semantic heterogeneities, while the second phase solves inter-profile heterogeneities. The first phase is realized by mapping the metadata records of all data sources of the same profile onto metadata records conforming to a given standard data model for such profile; i.e. MAR-CXML (library), EAD (archive), EN 15907 (audio video), and LIDO (visual). The second phase is accomplished by providing stable mappings from such standard metadata records onto records of the HOPE data model. The approach brings two main benefits: it is easier for data source managers to map their formats into a standard format in their community (in some cases they are adopting the very same standards); and the ADI can export data source content through standard formats without further data processing. On the other side, the adoption of standards can be a drawback for data richness in cases where

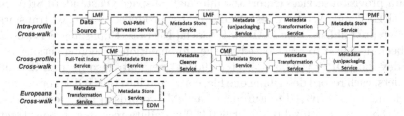

Fig. 3. The HOPE aggregation workflow

the input format is richer than the adopted standard. For example, multilingual descriptions may be lost when mapping onto MARCXML.

The whole aggregation workflow (Fig. 3) starts from data collection and processing and ends up to enrichment and provision. D-NET services from different functional areas are configured and combined by data managers to realize the flow, which is automatically orchestrated by the system.

Data mediation services have been configured to handle the (de-)registration and management of a variable set of data sources belonging to different content providers (organizations), each data source associated to one of the four HOPE profiles. Services can collect UTF-8 encoded XML metadata records via OAI-PMH, FTP, SFTP, HTTP and HTTPS. There are no requirements on the structure or content of records apart from one stable identifier for each record.

Data Conversion services have been combined and customized to realize the "two-phase transformation" and to deliver records to Europeana. One Tranformator Service instance is created for each data source to transform input records based on mappings defined with the help of the content provider. Once records are transformed into the profile standard format (PMF) they are further processed by another Transformator Service instance configured with the cross-walk from the PMF to the HOPE common metadata format (CMF). At this point, the flow goes to the Cleaner Service which applies the semantic transformation of values (provider vocabulary terms to common vocabulary terms). Cleaned records are delivered to the index (for use of the portal) and transformed into the Europeana Data Model[10] (EDM) to be OAI-PMH harvested by Europeana.

The HOPE information space is handled in the form of XML files, stored in Metadata Store Services and accessible via Full-text Index Services. Data curation and enrichment services, i.e. the Content Checker service and the Record Tagging Service, have also been deployed. These allow data curators to: (*i*) search and browse for records in the information space in order to check the correct implementation of the cross-walks, identify records with insufficient information, check the effectiveness of the cleansing phase, and identify records that need to be updated; and (*ii*) create new virtual, cross-data source collections by tagging records with historical themes or social network publishing tags, e.g. objects tagged with "YouTube" are automatically exported to that social site.

---

[10] http://pro.europeana.eu/edm-documentation

Data provision services export the information space via standard SRW/SRU APIs (REST and Web Services). EDM records produced in the last transformation step are published via OAI-PMH. Social Network Publishing Services have also been deployed to react based on the aforementioned tagging actions.

Today the HOPE ADI has collected 190.000 metadata records from 12 content providers, each record describing one file, converted into the HOPE common data model, and then delivered to Europeana as XML records in EDM format. At the end of the project, a total of about 900.000 metadata records will be extracted, describing around 3.000.000 files in the CH domain. HOPE digital objects will be available from the IAHLI portal and Europeana.

5   Conclusion

We highlighted the need for aggregative data infrastructures (ADIs) in the Cultural Heritage (CH) domain and described the important role of enabling software for ADIs. We argued that the realization of ADIs with a from scratch approach is not affordable in terms of re-usability, scalability and dinamicity required to satisfy the evolving functional and architectural requirements of modern user communities. On this regard, we presented the D-NET Software Toolkit, which is specifically designed to support developers of ADIs to address the above issues with a generic and effective approach, providing ready-to-use services that can be configured, extended and composed in workflows to meet the specific community's needs. We demonstrated the effectiveness of D-NET in the CH domain by describing how it has been adopted in the context of the HOPE project for the realization of an ADI implementing a two-phase approach to metadata record conversion.

References

1. Manghi, P., Mikulicic, M., Candela, L., Artini, M., Bardi, A.: General-Purpose Digital Library Content Laboratory Systems. In: Lalmas, M., Jose, J., Rauber, A., Sebastiani, F., Frommholz, I. (eds.) ECDL 2010. LNCS, vol. 6273, pp. 14–21. Springer, Heidelberg (2010)
2. Manghi, P., Mikulicic, M., Candela, L., Castelli, D., Pagano, P.: Realizing and maintaining aggregative digital library systems: D-net software toolkit and oaister system. D-Lib Magazine 16(3/4) (2010)
3. Blanke, T.: From tools and services to e-infrastructure for the arts and humanities. In: Lin, S.C., Yen, E. (eds.) Production Grids in Asia, pp. 117–127. Springer US (2010)
4. Loebbecke, C., Thaller, M.: Digitization as an it response to the preservation of europe's cultural heritage. In: Carugati, A., Rossignoli, C. (eds.) Emerging Themes in Information Systems and Organization Studies, pp. 359–372. Physica-Verlag HD (2011)
5. Cramer, T., Kott, K.: Designing and implementing second generation digital preservation services: A scalable model for the stanford digital repository. D-Lib Magazine 16(9/10) (2010)

6. Li, Y., Banach, M.: Institutional repositories and digital preservation: Assessing current practices at research libraries. D-Lib Magazine 17(5/6) (2011)
7. Amato, G., Debole, F., Peters, C., Savino, P.: Multimatch: Multilingual/multimedia access to cultural heritage. In: Agosti, M., Esposito, F., Thanos, C. (eds.) IRCDL, DELOS: an Association for Digital Libraries / Department of Information Engineering of the University of Padua, pp. 162–165 (2009)
8. Blanke, T., Hedges, M.: Providing linked-up access to cultural heritage data. In: Proceedings of the ECDL 2008 Workshop on Information Access to Cultural Heritage, Aarhus, Denmark (2008)
9. Váradi, T., Krauwer, S., Wittenburg, P., Wynne, M., Koskenniemi, K.: Clarin: Common language resources and technology infrastructure. In: Calzolari, N., Choukri, K., Maegaard, B., Mariani, J., Odjik, J., Piperidis, S., Tapias, D. (eds.) Proceedings of the Sixth International Conference on Language Resources and Evaluation (LREC'08), Marrakech, Morocco. European Language Resources Association, ELRA (2008), http://www.lrec-conf.org/proceedings/lrec2008/
10. Simeoni, F., Candela, L., Lievens, D., Pagano, P., Simi, M.: Functional Adaptivity for Digital Library Services in e-Infrastructures: The gCube Approach. In: Agosti, M., Borbinha, J., Kapidakis, S., Papatheodorou, C., Tsakonas, G. (eds.) ECDL 2009. LNCS, vol. 5714, pp. 51–62. Springer, Heidelberg (2009)
11. Calanducci, A., Sevilla, J., Barbera, R., Andronico, G., Saso, M., De Filippo, A., Iannizzotto, S., Vicinanza, D., De Mattia, F.: Cultural Heritage Digital Libraries on Data Grids. In: Agosti, M., Borbinha, J., Kapidakis, S., Papatheodorou, C., Tsakonas, G. (eds.) ECDL 2009. LNCS, vol. 5714, pp. 469–472. Springer, Heidelberg (2009)
12. Reis, D., Freire, N., Manguinhas, H., Pedrosa, G.: REPOX – A Framework for Metadata Interchange. In: Agosti, M., Borbinha, J., Kapidakis, S., Papatheodorou, C., Tsakonas, G. (eds.) ECDL 2009. LNCS, vol. 5714, pp. 479–480. Springer, Heidelberg (2009)
13. Manghi, P., Mikulicic, M.: PACE: A General-Purpose Tool for Authority Control. In: García-Barriocanal, E., Cebeci, Z., Okur, M.C., Öztürk, A. (eds.) MTSR 2011. CCIS, vol. 240, pp. 80–92. Springer, Heidelberg (2011)
14. Haslhofer, B., Klas, W.: A survey of techniques for achieving metadata interoperability. ACM Comput. Surv. 42, 7:1–7:37 (2010)

Poisonous India or the Importance of a Semantic and Multilingual Enrichment Strategy

Marlies Olensky, Juliane Stiller, and Evelyn Dröge

Humboldt-Universität zu Berlin, Berlin School of Library and Information Science
Dorotheenstr. 26, 10117 Berlin, Germany
{marlies.olensky,juliane.stiller,evelyn.droege}@ibi.hu-berlin.de
http://www.ibi.hu-berlin.de

Abstract. Cultural heritage information systems offer access to objects coming from museums, archives and libraries. To enhance retrieval performance and access across languages, metadata is enriched with controlled vocabularies or other datasets with structured information. During this process many pitfalls occur which lead to wrong or poor enrichments thus decreasing the user experience. Taking the use case of Europeana, this paper investigates the extent of enrichment flaws and their causes. A categorization of these deficiencies is proposed as well as a strategy to avoid common enrichment mistakes.

Keywords: Semantic and multilingual enrichment, problem diagnosis, enrichment strategy, Europeana.

1 Introduction

When a user in Europeana[1], the single access point to European cultural heritage, searches for *poison* in the collections provided by Swiss institutions, she will find photographs from India and Indian movie covers. The relevance of the retrieved documents to the query is not comprehensible. A deeper investigation reveals that retrieved objects were automatically enriched with the term *poison* and its multilingual equivalents. In Latvian *poison* means *Inde* which is the same keyword the French-speaking domain expert gave the objects to describe its content: India. This striking example shows one of the potential pitfalls in semantic and multilingual enrichments if no strategy is applied.

Semantic and multilingual enrichment of information objects is a process with the goal to enhance the retrieval experience for the user. Digital libraries like Europeana aggregate a vast amount of cultural heritage information objects from different countries and in different languages; semantic and multilingual enrichment of metadata supports disambiguation in such multilingual environments. Synonyms, homonyms and cross-lingual ambiguities are the main reasons for improper search results and consequentially a poor user experience. Enrichment of metadata with structured information resources can support the disambiguation on the one hand and the enhancement of multilingual search results on

---

[1] http://europeana.eu/

J.M. Dodero, M. Palomo-Duarte, P. Karampiperis (Eds.): MTSR 2012, CCIS 343, pp. 252–263, 2012.

the other hand. However, the question is: what makes enrichments usable and valuable and how can we ensure that enrichments are correct? In this paper, we show the importance of applying a semantic and multilingual enrichment strategy. We identify the influencing factors that lead to successful, correct and in the best case useful enrichments. Europeana serves as use case. From the investigated enrichments we derive a set of factors and rules that should constitute an enrichment strategy which can be applied across domains.

The paper is structured as follows: section 2 elaborates on related work on semantic and multilingual enrichment and its evaluation; section 3 describes the use case Europeana and the applied methodology; section 4 presents the diagnosis of enrichment problems, section 5 derives a generalized strategy from the findings and section 6 concludes the paper.

2   Background

The paper focuses on semantic and multilingual enrichment which can also be referred to as semantic and multilingual tagging [1]. The Europeana Data Enrichment Requirements [2] define data enrichment as the overall process of enrichment, cleaning and normalization of collections with insufficiently rich metadata to be carried out by the data ingestion team. This includes de-duplicating objects across collections, adding string-valued fields to metadata records and linking objects to other internal or external knowledge sources and or to other objects. We define the term semantic and multilingual enrichment as the process of identifying concepts, places, agents and time periods in the metadata of a cultural heritage object (CHO) and linking them to a knowledge resource (such as ontologies, thesauri or other controlled vocabularies) by adding the respective labels and URIs from these vocabularies to the CHO. For example, a CHO might hold the term *London, UK* as a value in its metadata field coverage and enriching this object would mean finding the place *London* in the UK in an appropriate vocabulary (a suitable one would be GeoNames[2]); adding the label / URI of the correct *London* to the metadata would be a semantically correct and valuable enrichment, adding labels in other languages would be a multilingually correct and valuable enrichment.

Semantic enrichment experiments have been carried out in the Europeana-Connect project[3] where the Free University of Amsterdam (VUA) used their Amalgame tool[4] to enrich metadata values by mapping them to existing vocabularies. The Amalgame tool is basically a vocabulary alignment tool; to use it as enrichment tool they created a temporary vocabulary from the metadata values and in a second step mapped this vocabulary to existing ones. In principle, the alignment and the enrichment processes are quite similar to each other, as they both involve a matching process, and therefore might use similar quality evaluation methods. Tordai et al. [3] checked all alignments manually in order

---

[2] http://www.geonames.org/
[3] http://www.europeanaconnect.eu
[4] http://semanticweb.cs.vu.nl/amalgame/

to evaluate their quality. As a manual check is not feasible for large vocabularies, they developed a disambiguation technique to improve the precision of alignments where the parent and/or the child match of the respective term is taken into account. Even though this will increase the quality, it still does not provide a method to evaluate the quality of the alignments. To align vocabularies semantically, the project EuropeanaConnect [4] identifies six characteristics that influence the mapping of vocabularies and that also need to be considered during the enrichment process: lexical variance of the labels, use of preferred/alternative labels, number of labels, use of diacritics, nature of hierarchy and multilinguality. Furthermore, it points out that thesauri or controlled vocabularies for alignments should be chosen according to their institutional and collection adequacy, in terms of scope and uptake [5]. With regard to vocabulary evaluation, a lot of research has been conducted recently, with the main focus to find categories which allow for comparison of knowledge organization systems or other controlled vocabularies. Approaches of Vrandecic [6] in measuring ontology quality or of Mader [7] for choosing SKOS quality criteria are more elaborated as both have additionally identified evaluation criteria regarding the completeness or consistency of vocabularies, among others. Still, even if the result of the evaluation suggests that one vocabulary suits best for the enrichment task, this may not be the case in a specific context. If, for example, a vocabulary is too general it may not be as appropriate as a vocabulary that is less linked to other vocabularies but more precise than the first one.

3   Use Case - Europeana

Europeana is a single access point to digitized cultural heritage coming from libraries, archives, museums and audio-visual archives. Currently, Europeana provides access to over 23.5 million objects (images, textual objects, sound and audiovisual files). More than 2,200 institutions based in 33 different countries contributed to the aggregated content representing the diverse and heterogeneous cultural objects of Europe. This poses a challenge as each record has two multilingual dimensions: the language of the object and the language of the metadata, both not necessarily matching. The goal of Europeana is to provide access to this material in different languages and to unlock the cultural heritage. A means to reach this objective is the semantic and multilingual enrichment of Europeana's content carried out by the Europeana Office. Table 1 shows the enriched metadata fields and the datasets[5] used for the enrichment. All of them are linked open data resources which can be either described as controlled vocabularies or datasets representing structured information (e.g. DBpedia). At the time of writing this paper over 16 million records were enriched with either one or more of these labels.

---

[5] Two of the datasets, DBpedia and GeoNames, were analyzed by [8] with the qSKOS tool: DBpedia concepts are never documented, 77,062 concepts (~10%) have no associative or hierarchical relationships and 3,058 concepts (~0.4%) are not labeled. GeoNames concepts have no semantic relations at all. Both vocabularies are nevertheless used for enrichments.

Table 1. Controlled vocabularies and datasets with structured information used to enrich Europeana's metadata fields

Vocabulary	Tag type	Enriched metadata fields
GEMET Thesaurus[6]	Concept	dc:subject dc:type dcterms:alternative
DBpedia[7]	Agent	dc:contributor dc:creator
Semium Time Ontology[8]	Period	dc:date dc:coverage dcterms:temporal
GeoNames[9]	Place	dc:coverage dcterms:spatial

The AnnoCultor Tagger has been used to enrich objects in Europeana[10]. In terms of quality control, enrichments were applied to certain sets of metadata fields to avoid mislabeling. For example, a geographic location occurring as a subject keyword was not enriched with GeoNames. Furthermore, the tagging tool only applied the European subset of cities in GeoNames to avoid ambiguous matches with cities outside of Europe. In general, the enrichment rules are not documented but can be extracted from the actual source code[11]. Although Europeana requirements [1,2] point out the need to evaluate the enrichment results before they are included in the Europeana metadata base, this requirement was disregarded during the enrichment process.

To get an overview of the areas of concern for semantic and multilingual enrichment, a purposeful sample of 200 records enriched with controlled vocabularies was pulled from Europeana. The goal was not the selection of a statistical representative sample but the aggregation of insightful and diverse enrichments across providers, languages and metadata fields. For each of the four tag types, 50 metadata records were analyzed and the enrichment process reproduced. Of value here are the so-called information-rich cases offering insights into the pit-

---

[6] http://www.eionet.europa.eu/gemet/

[7] http://dbpedia.org/

[8] http://semium.org/time.html

[9] http://www.geonames.org

[10] A thorough explanation of the enrichment process can be found here: http://europeanalabs.eu/wiki/EDMPrototypingTask21Annocultor which is a copy of the following blog post: http://borys.name/blog/semantic_tagging_of_europeana_data.html

[11] http://europeanalabs.eu/browser/europeana/trunk/tools/trunk/annocultor/src/main/java/eu/annocultor/converters/solr/BuiltinSolrDocumentTagger.java

falls which can occur during enrichments [9, p. 230]. The analysis was performed with focus on executed enrichments and missed ones were touched peripherally. Deducing causes for missed enrichments is mostly impossible and reasons can be multifaceted. Therefore, we refrained from a deeper analysis, acknowledging that omitted enrichments can decrease retrieval performance and user experience.

4   Enrichments - Problem Diagnosis

In this section, different reasons for the error-proneness of enrichments[12] in the presented use case Europeana will be listed, grouped in categories and described.

4.1   Incorrect Metadata

When an object is enriched, it can introduce semantic errors, simply because its metadata is incorrect. This includes mapping errors at ingestion time, i.e. mapping provider metadata fields to wrong Europeana metadata fields, typographical mistakes that were made at indexing time or in the worst case wrong metadata assigned at indexing time. Irrespective of the reason for incorrect metadata, the insufficient metadata quality is the basis for wrong, and in most cases absurd enrichments and can also lead to omission of potential enrichments. A measure to avoid these enrichments is to have a data cleaning process installed at ingestion time. This corresponds to the functional requirements of data enrichment where the need for data cleaning is emphasized [2].

4.2   Inconsistent Structure of Metadata

Related to incorrect metadata is the inconsistent structure of metadata in Europeana, which causes major problems at enrichment time. The following three aspects of inconsistent metadata structure, again, correspond to the functional requirements of data enrichment which state the need for data normalization [2].

Inconsistent Name Structure. We found incorrect enrichments caused by the names of creators and contributors not being structured as last / middle / first names or identified as named entities. For example, the tagging tool enriched any value in a name field with a matching agent in DBpedia. Therefore, the *[Copy of request and confirmation of special dispensation granted to the friars of the Irish Franciscan province in 1663.]*[13] by *Bongiorno, Michelangelo, Fr* and *Docherty, Anthony, Fr* was enriched with the "wrong" *Michelangelo*[14] *(Buonarrotti)*. Defining a consistent structure for names would increase the enrichment precision of agents enormously. The structure could follow common

---

bibliographic conventions, like *Last_name, first_name middle_name*. First and middle names could optionally be abbreviated by the respective initial(s). Multiple agents should be distinguished by a semicolon. As Europeana does not have such a structure implemented, the safest way to enrich agents would be to use exact matches only, which would lead to a decrease in the amount of enrichments but also to an increase in quality.

Inconsistent Date Structure. Our investigation showed that the date enrichment with the time vocabulary caused the least problems. However, we did find objects that were not enriched or not fully enriched due to inconsistent date structure. Dates and time periods can have different formats (numeric, numeric and literal or literal characters only). The inconsistent date structure is similar to the structure of names. A standardized format for dates, e.g. YYYY-MM-DD, should be used. Also, a clear structure for dates BC and AD as well as time durations need to be agreed on. Multiple values in one field must be clearly indicated. One interesting example, where no time labels were enriched although the object holds a valid date and historical period, is *Fragment eines ionisches Kapitells*[15] with the date *285 - 280 v. Chr.* and the time period *Hellenistisch*. A correct and valid enrichment would have added the label for the first millenium BC[16]. An additional benefit would be the label for the *hellenistic period*[17], if German labels were available in the Time Vocabulary.

Inconsistent Field Structure / Refinements. In the specification for the Europeana Semantic Elements [10], the current metadata model in Europeana, the field *dc:coverage* should be used to describe "the spatial or temporal topic of the resource, the spatial applicability of the resource, or the jurisdiction under which the resource is relevant". It therefore comprises a temporal or a spatial aspect and should be refined to *dcterms:temporal* or *dcterms:spatial* where applicable. We found objects that held the values about their temporal and spatial coverage in the same field (*dc:coverage*) instead of splitting these data to the correct refined elements. These inconsistencies can lead again to missing out on potential enrichments, as additional values in the same field are disregarded by the enrichment tool. Additionally, it is important to get the structure of the fields and their refinements straight, in order to choose the correct fields to enrich with a certain vocabulary. For example, our investigation showed that the video *Akten werden hinausgeworfen*[18] holds *Wien* and *20. Jahrhundert* in the field *dc:coverage*. Had this coverage been distinguished into the temporal and the spatial aspect, the tagging tool could have identified *20. Jahrhundert* (20th century) as time period as well as *Wien* as place and enriched them with the

---

[15] http://europeana.eu/portal/record/15502/
     AEED91B8CF6FCF1D3C81EB71E471108BD82D83F6.html
[16] http://semium.org/time/BC1xxx
[17] http://semium.org/time/greek_hellenistic
[18] http://europeana.eu/portal/record/00901/
     57525CB2B138706A9094714E76C38D7C2B41FF5D.html

respective labels. Here, a consistency check at ingestion time should be carried out in order to ensure that metadata is accurately refined and represented in appropriate granularity.

4.3 Context Disregarded

Another reason for erroneous enrichments is the syntactically correct but semantically incorrect matching of labels. The video with the title *Renault*[19] holds a contributor *Daniel Richter*. In this case, *Daniel Richter* is a French trade unionist and not the German artist who was found as matching DBpedia label for *Daniel Richter*[20]. Another example is the incorrect matching of places that exist in more than one country, e.g. *Córdoba* in Spain and Argentina or *Guadalajara* in Spain and Mexico. As noted in the description of the use case, Europeana intentionally only included the European subset of GeoNames in order to avoid mismatches with ambiguous places outside of Europe. Yet, we found two objects[21], where exactly this restriction caused incorrect enrichments. All three examples prove that if the enrichment tool had considered the context of objects, i.e. other metadata and broader or narrower labels, in the matching processes, the persons or places could have been disambiguated and correct enrichments could have been made.

4.4 Choice of Enrichment Fields

The decision on the enrichment fields and the corresponding vocabularies depends on quality control and on considerations what value a vocabulary can add to a certain metadata field. It is debatable if *dc:type* is a good choice for concept enrichment, as *dc:type* does not describe the concept an object is about. We found objects that are of type *book, photo, video, map, patent,* etc. and were enriched with the respective labels from the GEMET thesaurus. These enrichments add multilingual labels and therefore enhance the multilingual retrieval experience for the user. Yet, they do not add value in terms of semantics. Therefore, these enrichments optimize recall but also create a lot of noise.

4.5 Non-domain Specific Vocabulary

Choosing the right enrichment vocabulary is not a trivial task. Especially across domains, terms occur to be ambiguous and the problem rises exponentially in a multilingual environment. For example, in German the term for *print* is *Druck*.

---

[19] http://europeana.eu/portal/record/04802/
F51D452365426ECD303C40F87134A383B91D89C3.html

[20] http://dbpedia.org/page/Daniel_Richter

[21] http://europeana.eu/portal/record/10102/
BA5342F824A2CF7EAD1F7130FC5EDFFFBB2BD2E2.html
http://europeana.eu/portal/record/00901/
7D1F2919B80CE8BF070CE1695BF304473FE07419.html

In physical science, *Druck* also means *pressure* and is therefore one of the many homonyms in the German language. In Europeana, this ambiguity leads to poor enrichments as many records are indexed with the term *Druck* and then wrongly enriched with the term *pressure* in the GEMET thesaurus[22]. Domain-specific vocabulary introduces certain implications even if the term as such is not ambiguous. An example is the term *paper* which, in cultural heritage, is a type of material used for printing and drawing. In environmental science, *paper* is mainly understood to be an industrial product with the emphasis on the production of this resource[23]. Enrichment flaws like this can be avoided by choosing a domain-related vocabulary.

4.6   Named Entity Treatment

Named entities always require special treatment as they carry particular characteristics such as being predominantly language-agnostic or at least require specific translations. Therefore, in retrieval and natural language processing, the first step is to identify these named entities. In the cultural heritage domain, named entities relate to geographic locations, names or time periods but also work titles of books or performances. The dimension of named entities in this domain needs to be considered to avoid deficient enrichments.

4.7   Cross-lingual Ambiguity

When dealing with cross-lingual collections and records, the issue of multilingual ambiguity needs to be addressed. With a growing number of languages, the potential for having the same term with totally different meanings in different languages rises. This is a pitfall for enrichments which do not acknowledge the language of the metadata. Terms which are the same across languages but with completely different meaning are sometimes referred to as "false friends" in language learning and this term is very suited to be applied here. One example are German records dealing with *power* (in German: *Strom*) erroneously enriched with the term *tree*[24]. The explanation is the Czech word for *tree*: *strom*. In German, this term means *power*, the enrichment presumed that *strom* is a Czech word meaning *tree*. This example might appear like a one-off but in a portal with records in more than 23 different languages, this is an area of concern. Avoiding this means to identify the language of the metadata and map only terms with the appropriate language.

4.8   Weighting of Enrichments

It is obvious that the enrichment of terms makes the associated documents much more retrievable across languages. An enriched term has a lot of influence on the

---

[22] http://europeana.eu/portal/record/92060/
2B66D3FACA9A0047916E51E0C0556BECF9259142.html
[23] http://www.eionet.europa.eu/gemet/concept?cp=6023&langcode=en&ns=1
[24] http://europeana.eu/portal/record/92063/
B1CD66B8D6FB2FF6CC33B0279C81571572F2F90B.html

retrievability of documents. If an object has many keywords, choosing only one of them for enrichment can be counter-productive. One example is the enrichment of the word *history* for a record which has very specific keywords attached to it in Estonian and its English translations[25]. It is disputable whether such an enrichment is useful. In total, almost 80,000 records[26] were enriched with *history* and its translation equivalents. This is adding to the pool of records which are retrieved as they have *history* somewhere in their metadata. In general, every record in Europeana is related to history. In particular, if *history* is only one aspect of the resource, the danger is to decrease precision in the search results and thus create noise. Nevertheless, such an enrichment might still be relevant in minor languages with few objects. Anyway, enrichments should be weighted according to their significance for the record.

4.9 Workflow

Most of the items listed above are also of concern with regard to the enrichment workflow. The workflow summarizes the rules and strategies in place to balance out poor metadata quality and vocabulary restrictions. Additionally, the choice of the mapping or enrichment tool is crucial as it should be able to handle special cases.

5 Framework of Strategies for Semantic and Multilingual Enrichments

By generalizing the findings from our case study, we found that the consequences of these problem areas are always the same: enrichments are semantically or multilingually wrong, objects have not been enriched with the most useful labels or objects were not enriched at all. The areas of concern that influence an enrichment strategy can be divided into three different levels: metadata, vocabulary and workflow (Table 2).

On the metadata level, the quality and structure of the underlying metadata is crucial. When deciding on an enrichment strategy, one needs to be aware of the metadata quality. A data cleaning and standardization process should be applied at ingestion time and ideally, metadata quality is assessed and measured by a score. Afterwards, a minimum level of quality can be defined and only records above this score will be enriched. In the standardization process, syntactic rules on how to format values within metadata fields are defined, thus ensuring a common structure.

On the vocabulary level, an enrichment strategy needs to specify what collections to enrich by what vocabularies. In the cultural heritage domain, you will

---

[25] http://europeana.eu/portal/record/92067/
    28296EA118D9DF7E307F3B51E3C552F5A2D3E1F1.html
[26] http://europeana.eu/portal/search.html?
    query=enrichment_concept_label:histoire

Table 2. Framework of strategies for semantic and multilingual enrichments

Level	Areas of concern	Strategic execution
Metadata	Metadata quality	Quality score for metadata, no enrichments below the score, data cleaning process
Metadata	Structure of metadata	Data normalization e.g. surname forename, rules for syntax, validate fields against a schema, consistency check for field refinements
Vocabulary	Choice of vocabulary	Choose domain-specific vocabulary or a subset of a vocabulary, exclusion of parts of the vocabulary
Vocabulary	Scope of enrichment	Choose fields to be enriched with a specific vocabulary or even limit enrichment to subsets or specific collections
Workflow	Semantics	Disambiguate metadata values and use context
Workflow	Named entities	Apply automatic named entity recognition
Workflow	Cross-lingual ambiguities	Metadata records and enrichment term need to have the same language
Workflow	Weighting of enrichments	If multiple values in one metadata field are enriched, they should be weighted according to their relevance
Workflow	Matching rules	Use exact matches, include variants from the controlled vocabulary, rule on how to enrich multiple values in a field
Workflow	Quality assurance	Quality checks (automatically or manually) before enrichments go live
Workflow	Quality assessment	Assess the scope of the enrichments with regard to their occurrence in search results

hardly find a thesaurus or controlled vocabulary that can be applied for any collection available. Yet, in order to make most of the enrichments, one has to ensure that the right vocabulary is chosen for the right purpose. The pros and cons of selecting a domain-specific vocabulary versus a non-domain specific one must be weighted. A non-domain specific vocabulary might be available in more languages with a broader coverage; however, it probably will hold more ambiguous terms. The choice of the vocabulary also influences the enrichment workflow.

On the workflow level, several aspects need to be taken into account. The semantics of metadata fields as well as the semantics of the actual values should be considered for enrichment. For example, a birth date or place of birth could be leveraged to identify the correct match for agents carrying the same name. Applying automatic named entity recognition, especially for agents and titles, will avoid enriching named entities with wrong tags which match only parts of the term. To avoid cross-lingual ambiguities, one should only allow enrichments of objects where the language of the metadata and the enriching labels are the same. If a metadata field holds multiple values, a weighting of these must be carried out according to their relevance for the object.

Decisions made on the metadata and the vocabulary level influence the enrichment workflow. The better the underlying metadata quality is and the better it is standardized, the less strict the matching rules can be. For example, the better structured the metadata is, the less important it is to use exact matches; the less structured the metadata is, the more important it is to include (spelling) variants from the vocabulary. Furthermore, the choice of vocabularies and the limitations one sets to the fields / objects / collections to be enriched influence the grade of complexity of the matching rules. For example, explicit rules must define how to enrich multiple values in a field. Applied quality assurance (manual, automatic or semi-automatic in order to check whether the enrichments are correct) can also influence the matching rules. It is obvious that without any quality checks, the matching rules must be as conservative as possible. This implies decreasing the number of enrichments, but at the same time increasing the quality of the actual enrichments. Finally, the scope of the enrichments with regards to their occurrence in search results should be assessed to know what the influence of erroneous enrichments might be for the user.

6   Conclusion

When implementing a strategy for semantic and multilingual enrichments, one needs to be aware of the different aspects which impact the quality of the enrichment result. The development of such a strategy implies determining deficiencies in the metadata quality. In addition, certain circumstances, such as access restrictions, can limit the vocabulary choices. To keep the impact of these two factors small and redeem certain shortcomings, workflow and enrichment tools need to be developed. The quality of the metadata and the adequacy of the vocabulary on the one hand and the elaborateness of the workflow and enrichment rules on the other hand tend to be inversely correlated. The more precise and targeted the enrichment rules are, the less impact the flaws in metadata quality and the vocabulary choice have. Thus, lack of quality in the records and the vocabulary can be balanced out with a reasonable workflow strategy and enrichment rules.

In future work, it needs to be determined to which degree the different areas of concern influence the enrichment and consequently the retrieval results. Recall and precision as the common measures of retrieval effectiveness are means to determine the impact of enrichments. Poor enrichments will influence both figures negatively. Either relevant documents cannot be identified anymore among the enlarged pool of retrieved records or none of the retrieved documents are relevant, both resulting in a bad user experience. Furthermore, poor enrichments impact search results in different degrees. A relevant document hidden among less significant ones is much to a provider's regret but might not attract the user's attention in a negative way. Whereas, if an inappropriate document is found based on a semantically wrong enrichment, the mistake is more severe which leads to consequences that are counterproductive to the goal of a cultural institution to carefully curate cultural heritage content. It is beneficial to set priorities in the enrichment strategy to ensure the impact of poor enrichments is as small as possible.

To measure the visibility and impact of poor enrichments not only their number is crucial but additionally, the frequency of the documents occurring in the search results based on these deficient enrichments needs to be included. An enrichment approach based on the quantity of enriched terms is like shooting oneself in the foot, as it increases the potential impact of poor enrichments. To avoid this, quality should outweigh the quantity in an enrichment strategy and an assessment of the process is inevitable. In severe cases, an omitted enrichment can be the better choice.

Acknowledgements. We are very grateful to Antoine Isaac for his feedback. This research was partly financed by the projects Europeana v2.0[27] and DM2E[28] under the ICT PSP Work Programme.

References

1. Isaac, A.: EDM Prototyping, 2.1. Enrichment of EDM data (2011), http://www.europeanalabs.eu/wiki/EDMPrototypingTask21
2. Isaac, A.: Functional Requirements: Data Enrichment (2010), http://europeanalabs.eu/wiki/SpecificationsDanubeRequirementsEDMDataEnrichment
3. Tordai, A., van Ossenbruggen, J., Schreiber, G.: Combining Vocabulary Alignment Techniques. In: Proceedings of the 5th Int. Conf. on Knowledge Capture, K-CAP 2009, pp. 25–32. ACM, New York (2009)
4. EuropeanaConnect: Milestone 1.2.1: Specification of preferred terms identification methodology (Internal document) (2010)
5. EuropeanaConnect: D2.3.1 Multilingual mapping of schemes and vocabularies (Internal document) (2010)
6. Vrandecic, D.: Ontology Evaluation. KIT, Karlsruhe (2010), http://digbib.ubka.uni-karlsruhe.de/volltexte/1000018419
7. Mader, C.: Quality Assurance in Collaboratively Created Web Vocabularies. In: Simperl, E., Cimiano, P., Polleres, A., Corcho, O., Presutti, V. (eds.) ESWC 2012. LNCS, vol. 7295, pp. 870–874. Springer, Heidelberg (2012)
8. Mader, C., Haslhofer, B., Isaac, A.: Finding Quality Issues in SKOS Vocabularies. In: Zaphiris, P., Buchanan, G., Rasmussen, E., Loizides, F. (eds.) TPDL 2012. LNCS, vol. 7489, pp. 222–233. Springer, Heidelberg (2012)
9. Patton, M.Q.: Qualitative Research and Evaluation Methods. Sage Publications (2002)
10. Europeana: ESE specifications 3.4.1. (2012), http://pro.europeana.eu/documents/900548/dc80802e-6efb-4127-a98e-c27c95396d57

---

[27] http://pro.europeana.eu/web/europeana-v2.0
[28] http://dm2e.eu/

Automatic Generation of Crosswalks through CIDOC CRM*

Panorea Gaitanou, Lina Bountouri, and Manolis Gergatsoulis

Database & Information Systems Group (DBIS),
Laboratory on Digital Libraries and Electronic Publishing,
Department of Archives and Library Science, Ionian University,
Ioannou Theotoki 72, 49100 Corfu, Greece
{rgaitanou,boudouri,manolis}@ionio.gr

Abstract. In this paper, we propose an algorithm that automatically generates crosswalks between metadata schemas. The algorithm exploits the mappings between the schemas and the CIDOC Conceptual Reference Model (CRM), defined as part of an ontology-based integration architecture proposed by our research team. These mappings are expressed in a rule-based path oriented language, named Mapping Description Language (MDL). The algorithm is evaluated by producing a crosswalk from Encoded Archival Description (EAD) to VRA Core 4.0.

Keywords: Metadata interoperability, Crosswalks, Encoded Archival Description, VRA Core 4.0, CIDOC CRM.

1 Introduction

Archives, libraries, museums and other cultural heritage institutions manage collections with heterogeneous material, often described by different metadata schemas. Managing these schemas as an integrated set of objects is vital for information retrieval and (meta)data exchange. To achieve this, interoperability techniques have been proposed, such as the *crosswalks*.

A *crosswalk* defines the semantic mapping of the fields of a source metadata schema to the fields of a target metadata schema, so as to semantically translate the description of sources encoded in different schemas. A crosswalk is expressed through a table that shows the equivalent metadata fields of the metadata schemas involved. Specific policies and tools have been developed, on the purpose of converting metadata records using crosswalks. As mentioned in [9], the main reason that leads to the definition and implementation of crosswalks is the need to locate material in heterogeneous collections (see [11]). The

---

* This research has been co-financed by the European Union (European Social Fund ESF) and Greek national funds through the Operational Program "Education and Lifelong Learning" of the National Strategic Reference Framework (NSRF) Research Funding Program: Heracleitus II. Investing in knowledge society through the European Social Fund.

J.M. Dodero, M. Palomo-Duarte, P. Karampiperis (Eds.): MTSR 2012, CCIS 343, pp. 264–275, 2012.
© Springer-Verlag Berlin Heidelberg 2012

crosswalk method is adequate, when the case is to define semantic mappings between a limited number of metadata schemas. In a different case, where multiple schemas are implemented, defining crosswalks requires a lot of effort, since a growing number of mappings is needed, depending on the number of the schemas involved; hence, other metadata interoperability techniques have been developed to deal with these cases, such as the *ontology-based integration*.

Our research team has proposed an ontology-based integration architecture [1,6], based on the use of the *CIDOC Conceptual Reference Model (CRM)*. CIDOC CRM [15] is a semantically rich model used to conceptualize the cultural heritage domain. As part of this architecture, mappings have been defined between the metadata schemas of the participating sources and CIDOC CRM that acts as the mediator, promoting the interoperability between the sources and the mediator. The mappings are expressed in a rule-based path oriented language named *Mapping Description Language (MDL)* [6,5]. In this paper, we propose an algorithm that automatically generates crosswalks between metadata schemas. The algorithm exploits the mappings between these schemas and the CIDOC CRM. The algorithm is evaluated by producing a crosswalk between the Encoded Archival Description (EAD) and the Visual Resources Association Core (VRA Core 4.0).

2 Preliminaries

In this section, we briefly present our ontology-based integration architecture. We also present the EAD and VRA Core 4.0 to CIDOC CRM mappings, which are part of the architecture and are used to explain the algorithm in Section 3.

2.1 CIDOC-CRM Based Integration Architecture

The architecture promotes interoperability between a set of local sources, encoded in XML schemas, such as EAD [12], VRA Core 4.0 [14], Dublin Core (DC) [4], Metadata Object Description Schema (MODS) [13], etc. It (see Figure 1) consists of the following components: a) *Local XML data sources*, b) *Mediator*, and c) *Mappings*. The proposed architecture uses the CIDOC CRM as the mediated schema, so as to integrate these sources. CIDOC CRM is chosen to act as the mediator, given that it is a semantically rich model that uses 86 classes and 138 properties to conceptualize the cultural heritage domain. The mappings are defined in order to map: a) the metadata schema of a local XML data source to the ontology, b) the ontology to a metadata schema of a local XML data source, and c) the metadata schema of a local XML data source to the metadata schema of another local XML data source. As part of this architecture, we have proposed the Mapping Description Language (MDL) to express the mappings in the form of rules. MDL is path-oriented, given that both XML metadata schemas and CIDOC CRM follow a path-based syntax. A MDL rule consists of two parts: the left part ("Left"), which represents an *enriched XPath location path*, and the right part ("Right"), which represents an *enriched CIDOC CRM path* to which

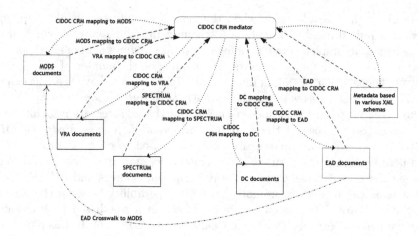

Fig. 1. A CIDOC CRM ontology-based integration architecture

the XPath described in the left part of the rule is mapped. More details about this architecture can be found in [1,6].

2.2   EAD to CIDOC CRM Mappings

EAD is an XML metadata schema used to encode archival descriptions, expressed in the form of *finding aids*. An EAD document starts from the ead root element and consists of three elements: the eadheader (including the meta- metadata); the frontmatter (carrying information for the printed finding aid); and the archdesc (providing information on the archives content and context). The characteristics of an archival description, expressed in EAD, are: 1) the multi-level hierarchical structure representing the archive and its components (encoded in the dsc subelement of archdesc through the component elements c01-c12, and c), and 2) the inheritance of information from the higher levels of description (i.e. fonds) to the lower levels (i.e. subfonds, series etc.).

The first step taken to map EAD to CIDOC CRM is to define the main concepts of the archive and its components, as well as of the archival description. Based on this analysis, we concluded that a finding aid (and/or an EAD document) and the archive described in it are represented by a a set of four isomorphic CIDOC CRM semantic hierarchies (trees) (see Figure 2):

a the *hierarchy of documentation elements and attributes (HDEA)*, where the ead, eadheader, frontmatter, archdesc, c01-c12 and c elements are mapped to instances of the E31 Document class, linked between them through the P106 is composed of property,

b the *hierarchy of physical objects (HPO)*, where the archive and its components, namely archdesc, c01-c12 and c, are considered as physical objects and are mapped to instances of the E22 Man-Made Object class and linked between them via the P46 is composed of property, c the *hierarchy of information objects (HIO)*, where the archive and its components are considered as information objects and are mapped to instances of the E73 Information Object class, linked between them via the P106 is composed of property, and

d the *hierarchy of linguistic objects (HLO)*, where the archive and its components as linguistic objects are mapped to instances of the E33 Linguistic Object class, linked between them via the P106 is composed of property.

These hierarchies refer to the same object (the archive), documented by the finding aid (the EAD document), for this they are semantically related to each other in CIDOC CRM through the following path:

E31 Document→P106 is composed of→E31 Document→P70 documents→E22 Man-Made Object→P128 carries→E73 Information Object→P67 refers to→E33 Linguistic Object

This path declares that an EAD document (E31 Document) includes (P106 is composed of) the archival description (E31 Document), which is the documentation (P70 documents) of a physical object that has been created by human activity (E22 Man-Made Object) and that carries (P128 carries) information, which is immaterial and can be carried by any physical medium (E73 Information Object). Finally, the information carried by the archive can be expressed (P67 refers to) in one or more languages (E33 Linguistic Object). The afore-mentioned path expresses in CIDOC CRM the semantic views for every archival component. MDL has been used to express these horizontal relationships for each component. To formally express the vertical relationships between the hierarchy trees HDEA, HPO, HIO, and HLO, that is, to connect the nodes (instances) of the classes E31 Document, E22 Man-Made Object, E73 Information Object, and E33 Linguistic Object respectively, we used the *Semantic Web Rule Language (SWRL)* [16].

The mapping of an EAD document to the four semantic hierarchies in CIDOC CRM is depicted in Figure 2. In the right hand side of the figure, the CIDOC CRM graph obtained by applying both MDL and SWRL rules, is shown. This graph consists of the four semantic hierarchies along with the (horizontal and vertical) relations between their nodes.

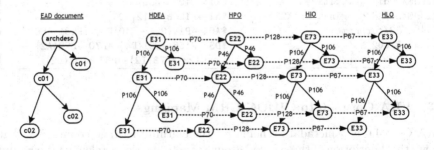

Fig. 2. Semantic hierarchies and their relationships

Having defined the EAD semantic hierarchies and their associations, we have to define the mappings for the EAD descriptive fields that provide the detailed information for the content and context of the archive and associate them with the appropriate (nodes of) semantic hierarchy(ies). This is done in three steps: a) based on the semantics of an EAD node (i.e. element/attribute), choose the appropriate hierarchy(ies) to which this node is related, b) select an appropriate CIDOC CRM class to map the node, and, c) associate the selected class with the proper semantic hierarchy(ies) through appropriate CIDOC CRM paths.

Part of the EAD to CIDOC CRM mapping appears in Table 1. Rules R1, R2, R19 and R29 express the horizontal relationships between the semantic hierarchies, while the rest of the rules express the mapping of several descriptive elements/attributes. More information about the mapping appears in [3].

Table 1. MDL rules expressing part of the EAD to CIDOC CRM mapping

Rule	Left part (EAD)	Right part (CIDOC CRM)
R1:	/ead{X0}	E31{D0}
R2:	$X0/archdesc{X2}	$D0→P106→E31{D2}→P70→E22{A0}→ P128→E73{I0}→P67→E33{L0}
R3:	$X2/@level*{Y10}	$D2→P2→E55{D01}
R4:	$Y10{Y20}	$D01→P71B→E32{=''level''}
R5:	$X2/@relatedencoding*{Y30}	$D2→P2→E55{D02}
R6:	$Y30{Y40}	$D02→P71B→E32{=''relatedencoding''}
R7:	$X2/did/unitid*	$I0→P1→E42
R8:	$X2/did/unittitle*	$I0→P102→E35
R9:	$X2/did/origination{X22}	$A0→P108B→E12{A03}
R10:	$X22/corpname*	$A03→P14{C1}→E40{F1}→P131→E82
R11:	$X2/did/physloc*	$A0→P53→E53
R12:	$X2/did/unitdate*	$A03→P4→E52→P78→E50
R13:	$X2/did/langmaterial/language*	$L0→P72→E56
R14:	$X2/controlaccess/subject*	$I0→P67→E28
R15:	$X2/controlaccess/persname*	$I0→P67→E21→P1→E41
R19:	$X2/dsc/c01{X3}	$D2→P106→E31{D3}→P70→E22{A1}→ P128→E73{I1}→P67→E33{L1}
R20:	$X3/@level*{Y31}	$D3→P2→E55{D301}
R21:	$Y31{Y32}	$D301→P71B→E32{=''level''}
R22:	$X3/did/unittitle*	$I1→P102→E35
R23:	$X3/did/origination{X23}	$A1→P108B→E12{A04}
R24:	$X23/corpname*	$A04→P14{C3}→E40{F3}→P131→E82
R29:	$X3/c02{X4}	$D3→P106→E31{D4}→P70→E22{A2}→ P128→E73{I2}→P67→E33{L2}

2.3 VRA Core 4.0 to CIDOC CRM Mappings

VRA Core 4.0 is a metadata schema for the cultural heritage community that allows the description of three broad groups of entities: *works* (element work) and *collections* (element collection) of visual culture, as well as *images* (element image) that document them. A work is a physical entity that exists, existed in the past, or may exist in the future. It might be an artistic creation (painting, sculpture etc.), a performance, a building or other construction, etc. An image is a visual representation of a work that may come in a wide range of formats (such as JPEG, GIF, TIFF) or physical photographs, slides, etc. Finally, a collection is an aggregation of works or images.

VRA Core 4.0 offers a set of top level elements (agent, culturalContext, date, description, inscription, location, material, measurements, rights, relation, source, stateEdition, stylePeriod, subject, technique, textref, title and worktype), and several optional global attributes (dataDate, extent, href, pref, refid, rules, source, vocab, xml:lang), which are applied to any element or subelement. An essential feature of VRA Core 4.0 is the mechanisms to define hierarchical relationships between its records, through the relation element and its type attribute with the value partOf.

The VRA Core 4.0 to CIDOC CRM mapping focuses on the restricted version of the schema, which imposes controlled vocabularies and type lists as values of the XML nodes of the schema. As a consequence, each attribute assigned to an element of the metadata schema may lead to the generation of different semantic paths in the ontology, depending on the values of that attribute, and produces a plethora of conceptual expressions corresponding to the same element. Furthermore, the use of several global attributes provided by the schema makes the mapping procedure even more complicated, by generating additional semantic paths in the ontology. In the VRA to CIDOC CRM mapping, the work element is associated with an instance of the class E24 Physical Man-Made Thing, which comprises all persistent physical items that are purposely created by human activity. The class E24 was selected since it is considered as a semantically broad class that comprises other more specialized classes, like E22 Man-Made Object or E25 Man-Made Feature. Part of the VRA Core 4.0 to CIDOC CRM mapping is presented in Table 2. A detailed description can be found in [5].

3 A Crosswalk Generation Algorithm

In this section, we present an algorithm, which automatically generates crosswalks between XML metadata schemas using the mappings defined between the schemas and CIDOC CRM. The algorithm is based on the following assumption:

Assumption 1. *The algorithm applies to pairs of metadata schemas (source and target schema), provided that the mapping of each participating schema maps a resource described using the schema to a single class instance in CIDOC CRM.* Notice that, as an EAD document (see Subsection 2.2) maps to four different class instances, EAD violates Assumption 1. However, in Section 4, we propose an extension of the algorithm that also applies to EAD. The algorithm proceeds in two phases:

Phase 1 of the Algorithm: Phase 1 is based on a *Path_construction_procedure*, whose input is the mapping of a metadata schema to CIDOC CRM (expressed in

Table 2. Part of the VRA to CIDOC CRM mapping in MDL (work level)

Rule	Left part (VRA Core 4.0)	Right part (CIDOC CRM)
R1:	/vra/work{X1}	E24{C1}
R2:	$X1/agentSet{Y1}	$C1→P108B→E12{J1}
R3:	$Y1/agent[name/@type="personal"]{Y5}	$J1→P14{S2}→E21{J5}
R4:	$Y1/agent[name/@type="corporate"]{Y10}	$J1→P14{S3}→E40{J10}
R5:	$Y1/agent[name/@type="family"]{Y15}	$J1→P14{S4}→E74{J15}
R6:	$Y5|$Y10|$Y15/name*	$J5|$J10|$J15→P131→E82
R7:	$Y5|$Y10|$Y15/culture*	$J5|$J10|$J15→P107B→E74
R8:	$Y5|$Y10|$Y15/role*	$S2|$S3|$S4→P14.1→E55
R9:	$Y5/dates[@type="life"]/earliestDate*	$J5→P98→E67→P4→E52→ P78→E50
R10:	$Y5/dates[@type="life"]/latestDate*	$J5→P100B→E69→P4→E52→ P78→E50
R17:	$X1/materialSet/material*{T1}	$C1→P45→E57{A1}
R18:	$T1/@type*	$A1→P2→E55
R22:	$X1/titleSet/title*{Q1}	$C1→P102{S1}→E35
R23:	$Q1/@type*	$S1→P102.1→E55
R29:	$X1/techniqueSet/technique*	$C1→P108B→E12→P32→E55
R30:	$X1/descriptionSet/description*{V1}	$C1→P3→E62{H1}
R31:	$V1/@source*	$H1→P67B→E73
R32:	$X1/locationSet/location{O1}	$C1→P53→E53{I1}
R33:	$O1/@type*	$I1→P2→E55
R34:	$O1/name*{O4}	$I1→P87→E44{I4}
R35:	$O4/@type*	$I4→P2→E55
R36:	$O1/refid*{O7}	$I1→P48→E42{I7}
R37:	$O7/@type*	$I7→P2→E55
R38:	$X1/@id*	$C1→P48→E42
R39:	$X1/worktypeSet/worktype*	$C1→P2→E55

MDL) and whose output is a two column table, called *Schema2CRM_Path_Table*, which contains all possible source schema paths, stored in its first column, and the corresponding CIDOC CRM paths stored in the second column.

To construct a *Schema2CRM_Path_Table* the *Path_construction_procedure* starts from the mapping rule R defining the mapping of the root element of the schema (e.g. the Rule R1 of Table 2 in the VRA Core 4.0 to CIDOC CRM mapping), and proceeds by combining this rule with the rules whose left part starts with the variable appearing in the end of the left part of rule R. In this way, the MDL rules are combined, and the XPath fragments appearing on the left side of the rules (resp. CIDOC CRM path fragments appearing on the right sides of the rules) are merged, constructing in this way more complex XPath (resp. CIDOC CRM) paths. The schema paths and the corresponding CIDOC CRM paths are then added to the *Schema2CRM_Path_Table*.

Example 1. Starting with the Rule R1 of Table 2, we get the following pair of corresponding paths (between VRA Core 4.0 and CIDOC CRM):

(/vra/work, E24)

Now, combining Rule $R1$ with Rule $R22$ we get the pair:

(/vra/work/titleSet/title, E24 → P102 → E35)

Notice that the variables on both sides of a MDL rule are used to link the path fragments contained in different rules, so as to construct longer paths. More pairs obtained by applying the *Path_construction_procedure* to the VRA to CIDOC CRM mapping appear in Table 3.

Table 3. Part of the *VRA2CRM_Path_Table*

VRA Core 4.0 path	CIDOC CRM path
/vra/work	E24
/vra/work/agentSet/agent [name/@type="corporate"]	E24→P108B→E12→P14→E40
/vra/work/agentSet/agent [name/@type="corporate"]/name	E24→P108B→E12→P14→E40→ P131→E82
/vra/work/titleSet/title	E24→P102→E35
/vra/work/descriptionSet/description	E24→P3→E62
/vra/work/locationSet/location	E24→P53→E53
/vra/work/worktypeSet/worktype	E24→P2→E55
/vra/work/@id	E24→P48→E42

It should be noted that for each application of the proposed algorithm the *Path_construction_procedure* is executed twice. It applies to the source schema S to produce a *Source2CRM_Path_Table* and to the target schema T to produce a *Target2CRM_Path_Table*. Both tables are then used in Phase 2.

Phase 2 of the Algorithm: The input of Phase 2 is *Source2CRM_Path_Table* and *Target2CRM_Path_Table*, as well as the CIDOC CRM classes and properties' hierarchy. The output of this phase is the source to target schema crosswalk. Before presenting Phase 2, we define the following:

Definition 1. *A* CIDOC CRM path *is a sequence of the form:*
$$C_0 \rightarrow P_1 \rightarrow C_1 \rightarrow \ldots \rightarrow P_n \rightarrow C_n$$
with $n \geq 0$, such that C_i, with $0 \leq i \leq n$, are CIDOC CRM classes and P_i, with $1 \leq i \leq n$, are CIDOC CRM properties.

Definition 2. *Let A, B be two CIDOC CRM paths where A is of the form $C_0 \rightarrow P_1 \rightarrow C_1 \rightarrow \ldots \rightarrow P_n \rightarrow C_n$, and B is of the form $C_0' \rightarrow P_1' \rightarrow C_1' \rightarrow \ldots \rightarrow P_n' \rightarrow C_n'$, with $n \geq 0$. We say that A isa-subsumes B if for each i with $0 \leq i \leq n$, C_i is either the same class or a subclass of C_i' and for each j with $1 \leq j \leq n$, P_j is either the same property or a subproperty of P_j'.*

Example 2. Consider the CIDOC CRM paths A and B where
A : E24 → P108B → E12 → P14 → E21 → P131 → E82, and
B : E24 → P108B → E12 → P14 → E39 → P1 → E41.

Given that the class E21 Person is a subclass of E39 Actor, P131 is identified by is a subproperty of P1 is identified by and E82 Actor Appellation is a subclass of E41 Appellation, we conclude that the path A isa-subsumes the path B.

To construct the crosswalk, Phase 2 proceeds as follows: for each pair (S, C) in the $Source2CRM\_Path\_Table$ (obtained in Phase 1) the algorithm checks if there is a pair (S, C') in the $Target2CRM\_Path\_Table$ such that the CIDOC CRM path C isa-subsumes C'. If such a pair exists, then the pair (S, S') is added to the crosswalk table. Otherwise, no pair is added to the crosswalk corresponding to the source schema path S appearing in the pair (S, C).

4   Considering Metadata Schemas Describing Objects Mapped to More Than One CIDOC CRM Classes

The proposed algorithm applies to metadata schemas that obey Assumption 1. However, EAD violates this assumption as each archival object (the archive and its components) is mapped to four semantic hierarchies in CIDOC CRM. Besides, its descriptive fields are mapped to CIDOC CRM paths that are associated with one or more of these hierarchies, according to their semantics. Therefore, EAD cannot be used by the present form of the algorithm. Nevertheless, EAD is one of the most widely used metadata schema in (digital) archival collections; hence, it would be of great importance to extend the algorithm to apply also to EAD. We present an appropriate extension that is based on a preprocessing phase in which EAD (and, in general, metadata schemas that violate Assumption 1), is transformed into a form which can be used by the algorithm. The main idea behind this preprocessing is to construct a single hierarchy tree by merging the four semantic trees on which an EAD document is mapped. Besides, the isa-subsumption definition used by the algorithm is slightly modified.

To explain the preprocessing phase, consider the rule $R2$ in Table 1, which corresponds to the mapping of the archive (archdesc subelement of the ead root element). The right part of this rule:

$\$D0 \rightarrow P106 \rightarrow E31\{D2\} \rightarrow P70 \rightarrow E22\{A0\} \rightarrow P128 \rightarrow E73\{I0\} \rightarrow P67 \rightarrow E33\{L0\}$

describes the horizontal relationship between the corresponding nodes of the hierarchy trees that semantically represent the archive's description. These nodes are assigned to the variables $D2$, $A0$, $I0$ and $L0$. To merge these nodes into a single node, we follow two steps. Firstly, we replace $R2$ by a new rule:

$R2'$: $\$X0/\texttt{archdesc}\{X2\} - -\$D0 \rightarrow P106 \rightarrow \{E31, E22, E73, E33\}\{V_{new}\}$

where $\{E31, E22, E73, E33\}$ represents a new "virtual" class whose instances are supposed to share all properties of the constituent classes, and V_{new} is a fresh variable. Secondly, the occurrences of the variables $D2$, $A0$, $I0$ and $L0$ in all MDL rules representing the EAD to CIDOC CRM mapping, are replaced by the variable V_{new}. Some of the rules obtained by applying this preprocessing to the EAD to CIDOC CRM mapping (Table 1) are depicted in Table 4.

Notice that combining rules $R1'$ and $R2'$ in Table 4 we get a CIDOC CRM path with prefix E31 $\rightarrow$ P106 $\rightarrow$ which expresses the hierarchy of the EAD document and does not relate to the semantics of the archival object (given by the

Table 4. Preprocessing EAD to CIDOC CRM mapping

Rule n	Left part (EAD)	Right part (CIDOC CRM)
R1':	/ead{X0}	E31{D0}
R2':	$X0/archdesc{X2}	$D0→P106→{E31,E22,E73,E33}{V_{new}}
R7':	$X2/did/unitid*	V_{new}→P1→E42
R8':	$X2/did/unittitle*	V_{new}→P102→E35
R9':	$X2/did/origination{X22}	V_{new}→P108B→E12{A03}
R10':	$X22/corpname*	$A03→P14{C1}→E40{F1}→P131→E82
R11':	$X2/did/physloc*	V_{new}→P53→E53
R13':	$X2/did/langmaterial/language*	V_{new}→P72→E56

mapping of archdesc). For this, in the preprocessing phase, we remove, from the right part of each rule mapping an archival object, the (sub)path (i.e. the prefix) that encodes the archival structure. In this way, $R1'$ and $R2'$ are replaced by the rule:

$R1\&2'$: /ead/archdesc{X2} $-$ $-${E31,E22,E73,E33}{V_{new}}

Also, we slightly refine the notion of isa-subsumption as follows:

Definition 3. *Let A, B be two CIDOC CRM paths where A is of the form $C_0 \to P_1 \to C_1 \to \ldots \to P_n \to C_n$, and B is of the form $C'_0 \to P'_1 \to C'_1 \to \ldots \to P'_n \to C'_n$, with $n \geq 0$. Assume that some classes participating in these paths are virtual, represented as sets of conventional CIDOC CRM classes. Assume also that every conventional CIDOC CRM class C can also be seen as a virtual class represented by the singleton $\{C\}$. We say that A isa-subsumes B if for each i with $0 \leq i \leq n$, C_i is a v-subclass of C'_i and for each j with $1 \leq j \leq n$, P_j is either the same property or a subproperty of P'_j. We say that a virtual class C is a v-subclass of a virtual class C' if there is a class $c \in C$ and a class $c' \in C'$, such that c is either the same class or a subclass c'.*

5 An Example: Constructing an EAD to VRA Crosswalk

In this section, we apply the modified algorithm (of Section 4) to construct an EAD to VRA Core 4.0 crosswalk. The algorithm proceeds as follows:

Step 1: the EAD to CIDOC CRM mapping rules are preprocessed.

Step 2: Phase 1 of the algorithm is applied to both: 1) the VRA Core 4.0 to CIDOC CRM mapping rules, and 2) the simplified rules of EAD to CIDOC CRM mapping, obtained by the preprocessing applied in Step 1.

Part of the *VRA2CRM_Path_Table* obtained in Phase 1 is depicted in Table 3, while Table 5 shows the result of applying Phase 1 to the simplified rules (expressing the EAD to CIDOC CRM mapping), which was obtained in Step 1.

Step 3: Phase 2 is applied on the tables obtained in Step 2. The output is the EAD to VRA crosswalk. A sample of this crosswalk appears in Table 6.

Our algorithm applies to every archival object described in EAD. The mappings for component elements are similar to those of the corresponding elements

Table 5. Part of the *EAD2CRM_Path_Table*

EAD path	CIDOC CRM path
/ead/archdesc	{E31,E22,E73,E33}
/ead/archdesc/did/unitid	{E31,E22,E73,E33}→P1→E42
/ead/archdesc/did/unittitle	{E31,E22,E73,E33}→P102→E35
/ead/archdesc/did/origination	{E31,E22,E73,E33}→P108B→E12→ P14→E40
/ead/archdesc/did/origination/corpname	{E31,E22,E73,E33}→P108B→E12 →P14→E40→P131→E82
/ead/archdesc/did/physloc	{E31,E22,E73,E33}→P53→E53

Table 6. EAD to VRA Core 4.0 crosswalk table

EAD path	VRA Core 4.0 path
/ead/archdesc	/vra/work
/ead/archdesc/did/unitid	/vra/work/@id
/ead/archdesc/did/unittitle	/vra/work/titleSet/title
/ead/archdesc/did/origination	/vra/work/agentSet/agent
/ead/archdesc/did/origination/corpname	/vra/work/agentSet/agent [name/@type="corporate"]/name
/ead/archdesc/did/physloc	/vra/work/locationSet/location

appearing in Table 6. However, the archival components are linked through a multi-level hierarchical relationship. VRA Core 4.0 provides the necessary nodes to express such relations between VRA records representing the archival objects. Extending the algorithm to express EAD's multi-level archival structure in VRA is within our plans for future work (see [2] for a similar work).

6   Conclusion and Related Work

In this paper, we proposed an algorithm that automatically generates crosswalks between metadata schemas by exploiting mappings between the schemas and CIDOC CRM. To evaluate the algorithm, we constructed a crosswalk from EAD to VRA, two schemas that describe resources with different substance and structure. In this case, as EAD is a richer metadata schema than VRA, the generation of the crosswalk takes advantage of the isa-subsumption relationship, through which it becomes feasible to express relations from the specialized CIDOC CRM paths (obtained by the EAD to CIDOC CRM mapping) to broader CIDOC CRM paths (obtained by the VRA to CIDOC CRM mapping).

Several research efforts related to crosswalks appear in the literature. In [8] a translation service between metadata schemas using crosswalks is proposed. This work differs from ours, as it focuses mostly on the translation of bibliographic metadata records and does not use an ontology as part of its translation mechanism. In [7] a METS model for crosswalks is proposed, which associates the crosswalk, the source metadata schema, and the target metadata schema. The crosswalks are made available to a repository for processing by search engines, OAI harvesters, and custom-designed Web services. Again, this approach does not involve the participation of an ontology in the translation mechanism, but a metadata schema (the METS). Both pre-mentioned approaches do not deal with metadata schemas that have a complex structure such as the EAD. Finally, it is important to mention that an EAD to VRA crosswalk has been proposed in [10]. Nonetheless, this crosswalk differs from the crosswalk proposed in this paper, since it proposes the mappings for a limited number of metadata fields and does not deal with the hierarchical structure of the archival description.

References

1. Bountouri, L.: Interoperability between Metadata Schemas. PhD thesis, Department of Archives and Library Science, Ionian University, Corfu, Greece (2012) (in Greek)
2. Bountouri, L., Gergatsoulis, M.: Interoperability between archival and bibliographic metadata: an EAD to MODS crosswalk. Journal of Library Metadata 9(1-2), 98–133 (2009)
3. Bountouri, L., Gergatsoulis, M.: The Semantic Mapping of Archival Metadata to the CIDOC CRM Ontology. Journal of Archival Organization 9(3&4), 174–207 (2011)
4. DCMI. Dublin Core Metadata Element Set, Version 1.1 (2008),
   http://dublincore.org/documents/dces/
5. Gaitanou, P., Gergatsoulis, M.: Defining a semantic mapping of VRA Core 4.0 to the CIDOC Conceptual Reference Model. International Journal of Metadata, Semantics and Ontologies (to appear)
6. Gergatsoulis, M., Bountouri, L., Gaitanou, P., Papatheodorou, C.: Query Transformation in a CIDOC CRM Based Cultural Metadata Integration Environment. In: Lalmas, M., Jose, J., Rauber, A., Sebastiani, F., Frommholz, I. (eds.) ECDL 2010. LNCS, vol. 6273, pp. 38–45. Springer, Heidelberg (2010)
7. Godby, C.J., Smith, D., Childress, E.: Two Paths to Interoperable Metadata. In: Proceedings of DC 2003, Seattle, Washington, USA (2003)
8. Godby, C.J., Smith, D., Childress, E.: Toward element-level interoperability in bibliographic metadata. The Code4Lib Journal (2) (March 2008)
9. Godby, C.J., Young, J.A., Childress, E.: A Repository of Metadata Crosswalks. D-Lib 10(12) (December 2004)
10. Getty Research Institute. Metadata standards crosswalk (research at the getty),
    http://www.getty.edu/research/publications/
    electronic_publications/intrometadata/crosswalks.pdf
11. Li, J., Gao, J., Dong, J., Wu, W., Hou, Y.: A metadata registry for metadata interoperability. Data Science Journal 6, 379–384 (2007)
12. Library of Congress. EAD 2002 Schema (2002),
    http://www.loc.gov/ead/eadschema.html
13. Library of Congress. Metadata Object Description Schema, MODS (2010),
    http://www.loc.gov/standards/mods/
14. Library of Congress. VRA CORE - a data standard for the description of works of visual culture: Official Web Site (Library of Congress) (2011),
    http://www.loc.gov/standards/vracore/
15. ICOM/CIDOC CRM SIG. Definition of the CIDOC Conceptual Reference Model, Version 5.0.4. (November 2011), http://www.cidoc-crm.org
16. W3C. SWRL: A Semantic Web Rule Language Combining OWL and RuleML (May 2004), http://www.w3.org/Submission/SWRL/

Preliminary Exploration of Using RDF for Annotating DITA Topics on Agroforestry

Thomas Zschocke[1] and Sissi Closs[2,3]

[1] World Agroforestry Centre, PO Box 30677, Nairobi 00100, Kenya
t.zschocke@cgiar.org
[2] Karlsruhe University of Applied Sciences, Postfach 2440, 76012 Karlsruhe, Germany
[3] Comet Computer GmbH, Rückertstrasse 5, 80336 München, Germany
closs@comet.de

Abstract. Collections of topics composed with the Darwin Information Typing Architecture (DITA) depend on annotations for improved search and retrieval. Through a set of metadata capabilities embedded in the DITA markup authors can define controlled values to identify and classify the subject matter of the content as well as to express the hierarchy and relationships between DITA elements and non-DITA resources. However, while these mechanisms typically provide both structural and semantic markup of DITA topics, it is difficult to manage, extend, and integrate a growing volume of DITA-based content and make them available for more intelligent Semantic Web services. Rather, the search and retrieval of DITA topics can benefit if combined with annotations captured in the Resource Description Framework (RDF). The paper addresses the issue of making the semantics of DITA XML documents explicit by using RDF for annotating existing documents. It reviews options for lifting DITA XML data into RDF for ease of processing. The paper shows that enriching DITA topics with semantic annotations helps to make DITA content more comprehensible and accessible, and improves the semantic interoperability among DITA topic instances. It concludes with general observations and an outlook on future work on exploiting the mapping and linking of DITA topics with RDF for improved sharing of data across collections as well as Linked Data.

Keywords: DITA XML, RDF, semantic annotation, metadata, AGROVOC.

1 Introduction

The Semantic Web envisions enhanced structure to a Web of data and information of shared semantics and data integration through well-defined meaning based on a "ladder of authority" as a sequence of specifications of Web standards [28]. Two of the important components for developing the Semantic Web are the eXtensible Markup Language (XML) and the Resource Description Framework (RDF) [4]. XML allows authors to use tags (or labels) to annotate Web pages or sections of text on a page, but without a fixed vocabulary. RDF represents a

J.M. Dodero, M. Palomo-Duarte, P. Karampiperis (Eds.): MTSR 2012, CCIS 343, pp. 276–288, 2012.

minimalist knowledge representation for the Web in terms of making assertions about objects with certain properties and values [9].

In general, RDF was designed to standardize the definition and use of metadata in terms of a basic object-attribute-value data model. Metadata is important for both resource discovery to locate and access resources as well as for resource management to facilitate the effective use of structured documents. In the context of XML, metadata can be both captured within the XML markup as well as or stored in XML-encoded documents [23]. RDF, instead, can express meaning encoded in a set of triples, which in turn can be written using XML tags. In addition, RDF provides more appropriate mechanisms for knowledge representation on the Web by applying ontology representation languages [4]. When expressed in the RDF/XML format, resources can be described in various alternative ways, which is especially relevant when the discovery and understanding of these resources would benefit from additional interrelated descriptive information. RDF enables the encoding, exchange, and reuse of structured metadata, which can be defined as needed, and supports metadata interoperability.

Even though XML as a format for metadata can also enhance the interoperability of metadata resources, RDF is more suitable for semantic interoperability by better defining mappings between terms with the data and making them understandable. Semantic interoperability is defined as the ability of different agents, services, and applications to exchange data, information and knowledge as a prerequisite to manage, share, and retrieve such information effectively in an networked environment [36]. While XML only aims at the document and does not provide a general interpretation of a document's data, RDF's object-attribute structure provides the natural semantics because all objects are treated as independent entities. They can be more easily mapped between two RDF transcriptions without additional translation steps that would be needed in XML. The advantage of RDF for semantic interoperability is that its object-attribute structure provides semantic units that can be used to constitute a domain model for data interchange, which increases the level of potential reuse of components [4].

The Darwin Information Typing Architecture (DITA) is an XML markup language designed for generating topic-oriented, information-typed content that can be reused and single-sourced in a variety of ways [7], [22]. DITA supports metadata in its basic building blocks, that is, topics and maps. The semantic markup in DITA provides intelligence about its content. However, these common textual annotations about the content of the documents are limited in scope and mostly intended for content creators. Instead, viewing DITA documents as "intelligent documents" [32] would be more beneficial by annotating document content based on well-defined semantics from domain ontologies to identify concepts and relations between concepts in documents. Semantic annotations provide enhanced information retrieval through the improved ability to perform searches, and increased interoperability, for instance, by providing a framework based on a common ontology to integrate information from different sources in different formats that do not easily interact.

When considering a large store of DITA topics, it becomes expensive to search the entire store sequentially to locate the content information needed. While DITA embeds metadata to describe its content in the sense of semantic hinting, it would be more beneficial to make this information explicit through semantic lifting, that is, by extracting the knowledge in terms of semantic annotation from the stored content [8]. By aggregating descriptions from both metadata and the XML markup through RDF, new documents can be created to indicate the component elements as well as the possibilities of combining and recombining relations for the original or new resources, which would lead to more consistency and enhanced interoperability. The advantage of utilizing markup languages such as DITA and metadata description frameworks like RDF allows the development of more robust mechanisms for linking many different document instances in a particular collection into a complex associated web [29], [35]. This issue is particularly important when considering that DITA documents are composed of single topics that can be aggregated to larger entities and collected in an even larger pool.

This paper explores the notion of semantic annotation as applied to DITA topics. The first section presents a general overview of handling metadata in DITA. Then, the paper introduces the notion of semantic annotation and semantic lifting to RDF. In the fifth section it illustrates the lifting of semantic information from DITA to RDF using a set of DITA topics on agroforestry. The final section provides some concluding remarks and an outlook of future work.

2   Metadata Handling in DITA

In general, metadata contains information to describe, provide context, indicate the quality, or to document other relevant characteristics of any document or object in both digital and conventional formats [10]. In DITA, metadata is embedded into the markup and can be applied through the <metadata> element in both DITA topics (<prolog> elements) and DITA maps (<topicmeta> element). DITA also provides support for learning metadata, <lcLom>, based on a subset of the IEEE standard for learning object metadata (LOM) [11]. DITA supports the three broad functional categories metadata, that is, descriptive, structural, and administrative [19] (see Table 1). Elements inside of <metadata> provide information about the content subject of a topic (descriptive metadata); prolog elements outside of <metadata> provide lifecylce information for the content unit (administrative or provenance metadata, including rights management metadata and preservation metadata).

DITA contains additional elements that correspond with Dublin Core, but are not strictly handled as metadata. For instance, the DITA <desc> contains the description of the current element. Similarly, the short description (<shortdesc>) element represents the purpose or theme of the topic. This is similar to the DC.description element. Or, the DITA <title> element contains a heading or label for the main part of a topic; it can also be used to provide a title for a map. This is similar to the DC.title element. The @xml:lang metadata

Table 1. Examples of metadata types, DITA metadata elements, and equivalent Dublin Core elements

Metadata types	Function	DITA metadata elements	Dublin Core elements
Descriptive metadata	*Resource discovery and identification*		
		author	DC.creator
		publisher	DC.publisher
		coverage	DC.coverage
			DC.subject
Administrative metadata	*Resource management (Preservation)*		
Technical metadata	*Processing*		
Provenance metadata	*Lifecyle management*	author	DC.creator
		critdates	DC.date
		resourceid	DC.identifier
Rights management metadata	*Use and access control*	copyright permissions	DC.rights
Structural metadata	*Storage and presentation of resources (composition)*		
		critdates	DC.date
		subject scheme map	DC.relation
		classification domain elements	

attribute corresponds with the DC.language element to indicate the language of the resource.

The DC.relation element defines an unambiguous reference to a related resource within a given context with the following qualifiers: IsPartOf, IsFormatOf, IsVersionOf, References, IsBasedOn, and Requires. The most flexible facility to manage relationships in DITA are the classification elements implemented through (1) a subject scheme and (2) the subject classification domain. The specialized DITA map, <subjectScheme>, is used to create custom controlled values and to manage metadata attribute values. A subject scheme can be enhanced to form a taxonomy using the same core elements and specify a binding between a category and its subject that enumerates the values of a metadata attribute. Similar to the DC.relation qualifiers, the <hasNarrower>, <hasPart>, <hasInstance>, <hasKind>, and <hasRelated> elements specify the kind of relationship in a hierarchy between a container subject and its contained subject. The classification domain elements are used to identify the subject matter of content that is referenced in a map. The subjects must be elements defined in a subject scheme map.

3   Managing Semantic Annotations

In general, metadata can be associated with a resource by either locating the embedded metadata within the markup of the resource or by coupling the associated metadata in a separate file that is closely coupled with the resource [6]. While both types of associating metadata can be harvested, the advantage of associated metadata is that the metadata files can be managed without modifying the content of resource files. Semantic annotation implies that descriptive data is attached to some other data in the sense of associated metadata. It entails the transformation of documents into computer-understandable descriptions of resources by augmenting them with metadata that describe their meaning and allow for new or extended ways to access information [13].

In a comparative study Schönberg & Freitag [25] analyzed the performance of different graph-based RDF querying models based on technical documentation, and contrasted the results with standard path-based technologies like XQuery on XML serializations. Even though the RDF framework outperformed the XQuery approached, one of their datasets based on a collection of DITA topics showed that RDF frameworks could not effectively take advantage of the simplified structures. However, in a subsequent study on an improved framework for verifying technical documentation, including DITA [26], the authors were able to demonstrate that the information extraction of content fragments and the mapping of metadata and structural data on a RDF graph of the document model resulted in the anticipated performance results.

In a related study [18], an ontology-driven approach was used for the semantic annotation, indexing and retrieval of document units. The authors applied a novel semantic document model, which was modeled on DITA. By utilizing DITA's ability to divide content into small, self-contained topics for reuse in different deliverables, the authors used their model to create office-like document units with unique IDs, semantic annotations based on concepts from annotation ontologies as RDF graphs, and the ability for generating links across a pool of documents. The results showed that their semantic document model achieved the improved performance over simple syntactic matching.

Other corresponding studies on managing collections of technical documentation [31], [34] applied controlled vocabulary of faceted classifications for the semantic specification of modular content elements rather than RDF/OWL triples. However, while this novel approach helps in the structured decomposition of documents in constituent elements, it does not appear to show the same flexibility for semantic annotations as can be achieved with RDF/OWL.

4   Lifting XML Markup to RDF

RDF represent statements about resources in the form of triples of subject-predicate-object, which can be rendered as graphs. The literature documents different approaches to lift XML markup to RDF. For instance, Patel-Schneider & Siméon [20] address the issue that these two distinct models, along with specific processing steps for XML and for RDF, amount to additional efforts in processing information both at the data level and at the semantic level, including duplication of work due to the similarity of processing in both cases. The authors developed a unified XQuery and XPath data model for both XML and

RDF that integrates XML processing before moving to semantic processing of RDF in order to avoid these duplications.

Sperberg-McQueen & Miller [30] address the same problem of mapping XML into RDF. Their approach associates the mappings with the vocabulary using the `xsd:annotation` mechanism of XML Schema. RDF allows to make more explicit some of the assumptions embedded in XML vocabularies, and, more importantly, to make the data available for greater reuse and improved understanding by larger user communities.

In a related approach [14], the proposed procedure applies an ontology to specify relevant concepts, their relationships, and properties. The conversion process begins by changing the document into an active resource, that is, the URI of the document will serve as the subject of the first statement. Then, all the elements of the XML document are traversed before mapping each element with the corresponding property, class definition or text element in the describing ontology. The goal of this process is to transform ambiguous XML data into more useful RDF statements.

A similar approach of XML to RDF conversion [33] integrates the XML Schema with the accompanying XML data, an OWL ontology, and the mapping document. The latter describes the link between an XML data and an OWL ontology. The result of this procedure are RDF instances based on the XML data, which are compliant with the applied OWL ontology.

In another example [21] bibliographic metadata was combined with non-bibliographic data from different sources by lifting and mapping the former to RDF triples based on a Dublin Core XML representation. This process begins with a lossy mapping from a few pre-identified ontologies. Then, the triples are supplemented by incorporating relevant data from external sources in order to reveal the relationships among data elements. After that, those relationships are considered that could benefit from RDF graph representations. Finally, the collection is made available for further exploration by end-users. The goal was to integrate digital library content with data from non-library sources, and to provide semantically enhanced services to end-users to explore such collections more effectively.

In the example of a system for semantic annotations and search in virtual collections of cultural-heritage objects [27] the procedure begins by translating thesauri into RDF/OWL in order to make the controlled vocabularies interoperable. In a second step, the metadata schema is aligned by mapping it to Dublin Core. Then, the collection metadata is enriched through a basic transformation to RDF/OWL triples. Finally, the controlled vocabularies are aligned using owl:sameAs and skos:exactMatch relations. The result of this harvesting process leads to a graph representing a connected network of objects and thesauri entries that serve as the background knowledge of the collection.

In a corresponding example of a document management architecture [17] annotations serve as external remarks that can be attached to a document or a subsection of a document. As annotations reside outside, the document can be annotated as a whole or in part without actually having to modify its content or structure. At the same time the annotations are used to enhance query requests to access all the annotations for a particular document as well as to access the metadata property of specific annotations.

5   Case Example: Annotating DITA Topics

The following example has been produced to illustrate the application of semantic annotation of DITA topics derived from material on agroforestry. The following code snippet is a DITA concept on tree nurseries, one of the key practices in the work of the World Agroforestry Centre:

```
<?xml version="1.0" encoding="UTF-8"?>
<!DOCTYPE concept PUBLIC "-//OASIS//DTD DITA Concept//EN"
"concept.dtd">
<concept id="concept_nursery_res">
 <title>Tree nurseries</title>
 <shortdesc>Nurseries managed by research units.</shortdesc>
 <prolog>
  <author>James M. Roshetko</author>
  <publisher>World Agroforestry Centre, Winrock International
  </publisher>
  <copyright>
   <copyryear year="2010"/>
   <copyrholder>World Agroforestry Centre</copyrholder>
  </copyright>
  <metadata>
   <audience type="user" job="using" experiencelevel="novice"/>
   <keywords>
    <keyword keyref="plantnurseries">
    plant nurseries
    </keyword>
   </keywords>
  </metadata>
 </prolog>
 <conbody xml:lang="en">
  <p>A tree nursery is a managed site, designed to produce
  tree seedlings grown under favorable conditions until they
  are ready for planting.</p>
 </conbody>
</concept>
```

The example produces the definition of the concept "tree nursery" along with some metadata descriptions contained in the <prolog> and the corresponding <metadata> element. Noticing that many metadata elements in DITA map to Dublin Core, the topic can be expressed in RDF as follows:

```
<?xml version="1.0" encoding="utf-8"?>
<rdf:RDF xmlns:rdf="http://www.w3.org/1999/02/22-rdf-syntax-ns#"
         xmlns:dc="http://purl.org/dc/elements/1.1/">
  <rdf:Description rdf:about="http://mydita.com/concept#
  concept_tree_nursery">
    <dc:title xml:lang="en">Tree nurseries</dc:title>
  </rdf:Description>
      <ex:editor>
      <rdf:Description ex:fullName="James M. Roshetko">
      </rdf:Description>
    </ex:editor>
  </rdf:Description>
</rdf:RDF>
```

The concept "tree nurseries" can now be expressed in RDF as follows (using the Turtle syntax for RDF):

```
ex:tree nurseries rdf:type skos:Concept;
  skos:prefLabel "tree nurseries"@en.
```

Following the procedure of [14] the following interpretation of the meaning of some of this data can be produced based on the tag names of the DITA markup (using pseudo syntax):

```
Class prolog
Class copyryear
Property copyright
Property year
 - rdfs:domain copyryear
```

Assuming that the URI to identify the document is http://mydita.com/concept#concept_tree_nursery, the following sample RDF triples can be produced:

subject	predicate	object
http://mydita.com/concept# concept_tree_nursery	rdfx:describes	anon_1
anon_1	rdf:type	onto:prolog
anon_1	onto:copyright	anon_2
anon_2	rdf:type	onto:copyryear
anon_2	onto:year	"2010"

The elements inside of <metadata> in the example above provide information about the content and subject of the topic. One of the elements is a keyword related to the concept retrieved from AGROVOC. However, the relationship is not indicated. Instead, a <subjectScheme> is referenced in which the keyword is listed within a collection of controlled values:

```
<?xml version="1.0" encoding="UTF-8"?>
<!DOCTYPE subjectScheme PUBLIC "-//OASIS//DTD DITA
Subject Scheme Map//EN" "map.dtd">
<subjectScheme>
    <subjectdef href="http://aims.fao.org/aos/agrovoc/
    data/c_5973" format="rdf+xml"
        keys="plantnurseries" navtitle="Plant nurseries">
        <hasNarrower keys="ornamentaltreenurseries" navtitle=
        "Ornamental tree nurseries"/>
        <hasNarrower keys="forestnurseries" navtitle="Forest
        nurseries"/>
        <hasNarrower keys="fruittreenurseries" navtitle="Fruit
        tree nurseries"/>
        <hasRelated keys="seedbeds" navtitle="Seedbads"/>
        <hasRelated keys="plantingstock" navtitle="Planting
        stock"/>
        <hasRelated keys="fruittreenurseries" navtitle="Fruit
        tree nurseries"/>
    </subjectdef>
</subjectScheme>
```

The controlled vocabulary has been retrieved from AGROVOC. Noticing the similarity in expressing the semantic relationship in DITA with the SKOS, the DITA <subjectScheme> map can easily be transformed to the skos:ConceptScheme class in SKOS/RDF:

```
ex:plant nurseries rdf:type skos:Concept;
    skos:inScheme ex:agroforestryThesaurus.
ex:ornamental forest nurseries rdf:type skos:Concept;
    skos:broader ex:plant nurseries;
    skos:inScheme ex:animalThesaurus.
ex:Forest nurseries rdf:type skos:Concept;
    skos:broader ex:plant nurseries;
    skos:inScheme ex:agroforestryThesaurus.
```

These few examples provide a brief glimpse into the issue of expressing topics and relationships authored in DITA by lifting DITA XML to RDF. The use of controlled vocabularies on agroforestry in the semantic annotation in the above examples retrieved from the AGROVOC thesaurus provides an additional mechanism to enhance the discovery of these topics in both the original DITA markup and in RDF. However, while these terms are embedded in the markup, it would be more beneficial to utilize AGROVOC published as Linked Data [1], [16]. The relevant terms can be linked by pulling content to the referencing element using DITA's addressing attributes @conref or @href, as indicated above, especially when handling non-DITA XML resources. At the same time, DITA could be exposed as Linked Data by pushing content using its @id attribute (for topics or elements) or its URI-based (direct) addressing mechanism.

6   Conclusion

Studies have shown that DITA is cost-effective in integrating the management of technical documentation and training materials for increased reusability [15]. Semantic annotations provide the flexibility to make more explicit the topic-oriented structure of DITA and corresponding aggregates in larger stores of DITA topics for improved searches by adding more valuable background knowledge. Novel graph-based RDF querying models for managing large data stores seem equally effective for DITA topics (see [26]). However, more testing is needed with respect to the transformation of DITA XML files into RDF by exploring and adapting existing generic XSLT transformations (e.g., [2]). We also intend to continue developing a thesaurus on agroforestry to be integrated as controlled vocabulary into DITA topics (see [37]), making it available as linked data while benefiting from mappings of existing thesauri with AGROVOC [16]. Using DITA's topic-based structure, we intend to experiment with services based on these components and semantic annotations to couple DITA topics with potential user actions as Linked Data. For instance, this could enhance DITA-based online help [3] towards micro-applications that are joined together using automated assistance for more unified and rich user interaction (for a related example, see [5]).

References

1. Baker, T., Keizer, J.: Linked Data for fighting global hunger: Experiences in setting standards for agricultural information management. In: Wood, D. (ed.) Linking Enterprise Data, pp. 177–201. Springer, Heidelberg (2010)
2. Breitling, F.: A standard transformation from XML to RDF via XSLT. Astron Nachr. 330, 755–760 (2009)
3. Closs, S.: Single Source Publishing. Modularer Content für EPUB & Co (Single source publishing. Modular content for EPUB & co). entwickler.press, Frankfurt/M (2011)
4. Decker, S., Meinik, S., Van Hermelen, F., Fensel, D., Klein, M., Broekstra, J., Erdmann, M., Horrocks, I.: Semantic Web: The Roles of XML and RDF. IEEE Internet Comput. Mag. 4, 63–74 (2000)
5. Dix, A., Lepouras, G., Katifori, A., Vassilakisc, C., Catarci, T., Poggie, A., Ioannidis, Y., Mora, M., Daradimos, I., Md. Akima, N., Humayoun, S.K., Terella, F.: From the web of data to a world of action. Web Semant Sci. Serv. Agents World Wide Web 8, 394–408 (2010)
6. Duval, E., Hodgins, W., Sutton, S., Weibel, S.L.: Metadata Principles and Practicalities. D-Lib Mag. 8, http://dlib.org/dlib/april02/weibel/04weibel.html (retrieved September 16, 2012)
7. Eberlein, K.J., Anderson, R.D., Joseph, G. (eds.): Darwin Information Typing Architecture (DITA) Version 1.2. Organization for the Advancement of Structured Information Standards (OASIS), Burlington, MA (December 2010), http://docs.oasis-open.org/dita/v1.2/spec/DITA1.2-spec.html (retrieved September 16, 2012)

8. Ferdinand, M., Zirpins, C., Trastour, D.: Lifting XML Schema to OWL. In: Koch, N., Fraternali, P., Wirsing, M. (eds.) ICWE 2004. LNCS, vol. 3140, pp. 354–358. Springer, Heidelberg (2004)

9. Gibbins, N., Shadbolt, N.: Resource Description Framework (RDF). In: Bates, M.J., Maack, M.N. (eds.) Encyclopedia of Library and Information Science, 3rd edn., vol. 5, pp. 4539–4547. CRC Press, Boca Raton (2010)

10. Greenberg, J.: Metadata and Digital Information. In: Bates, M.J., Maack, M.N. (eds.) Encyclopedia of Library and Information Science, 3rd edn., vol. 6, pp. 3610–3623. CRC Press, Boca Raton (2010)

11. IEEE Std 1484.12.1™-2002:IEEE Standard for Learning Object Metadata. Institute of Electrical and Electronics Engineers (IEEE), New York, NY (June 2002)

12. ISO 15836:2009: Information and Documentation—The Dublin Core Metadata Element Set (2nd ed.). International Organization for Standardization (ISO), Geneva (February 15, 2009)

13. Kiryakov, A., Popov, B., Terziev, I., Manov, D., Ognyanoff, D.: Semantic annotation, indexing, and retrieval. Web Semant. Sci. Serv. Agents World Wide Web 2, 49–79 (2004)

14. Klein, M.: Using RDF Schema to interpret XML documents meaningfully. In: Handschuh, S., Staab, S. (eds.) Annotation for the Semantic Web, pp. 79–89. IOS Press, Amsterdam (2003)

15. Levine, D.B.: Cost-benefit analysis of a bridge to integrate the management of technical information for producing technical manuals and training courses. Institute for Defense Analyses, Alexandria (2010),
    http://oai.dtic.mil/oai/oai?verb=
    getRecord&metadataPrefix=html&identifier=ADA542429
    (retrieved September 16, 2012)

16. Morshed, A., Caracciolo, C., Johannsen, G., Keizer, J.: Thesaurus alignment for Linked Data publishing. In: Proceedings of the International Conference on Dublin Core and Metadata Applications (DC 2011), pp. 37–46. Dublin Core Metadata Initiative (DCMI), Dublin (2011),
    http://dcevents.dublincore.org/index.php/IntConf/dc-2011/paper/view/59
    (retrieved September 16, 2012)

17. Meena, E., Kumar, A., Romary, L.: An extensible framework for efficient document management using RDF and OWL. In: Ide, N., Romary, L. (eds.) Workshop on NLP and XML (NLPXML-2004): RDF/RDFS and OWL in Language Technology (NLPXML 2004), pp. 51–58. Association for Computational Linguistic, Stroudsburg (2004), http://acl.ldc.upenn.edu/acl2004/nlpxml/pdf/meena-etal.pdf (retrieved September 16, 2012)

18. Nešić, S., Jazayeri, M., Crestani, F., Gaševic: Concept-based semantic annotation, indexing and retrieval of office-like document units. Technical report, USI-INF-TR-2010-1, Faculty of Informatics, Università della Svizzeria italiana (2010), http://www.inf.usi.ch/research_publication.htm?id=56 (retrieved September 16, 2012)

19. NISO: Understanding Metadata. National Information Standards Organization (NISO) Press, Bethesda, MD (2004), http://www.niso.org/ (retrieved September 16, 2012)

20. Patel-Schneider, P.F., Simeon, A.: The Yin/Yang Web: a unified model for XML syntax and RDF semantics. IEEE Trans. Knowl. Data Eng. 15, 797–812 (2003)

21. Powell, J.E., Collins, L.M., Martinez, M.L.B.: Semantically enhancing collections of library and non-library content. D-Lib Magazine 16 (2010), http://www.dlib.org/dlib/july10/powell/07powell.html (retrieved September 16, 2012)
22. Priestley, M., Hargis, G., Carpenter, S.: DITA: An XML-based Technical Documentation Authoring and Publishing Architecture. Tech. Comm. 48, 352–367 (2001)
23. Salminen, A., Tompa, F.: Communicating with XML. Springer, Heidelberg (2011)
24. Sánchez-Alonso, S., Sicilia, M.-Á.: Using an AGROVOC-based ontology for the description of learning resources on organic agriculture. In: Sicilia, M.-Á., Lytras, M.D. (eds.) Metadata and Semantics, pp. 481–492. Springer, Heidelberg (2009)
25. Schönberg, C., Freitag, B.: Evaluating RDF querying frameworks for document metadata. Technical report, MIP-0903, Fakultät für Informatik und Mathematik, Universität Passau (2003), http://www.fim.uni-passau.de/wissenschaftler/ forschungsberichte/mip-0903.html (retrieved September 16, 2012)
26. Schönberg, C., Weitl, F., Freitag, B.: Verifying the consistency of web-based technical documentation. J. Symbolic Comput. 46, 183–206 (2011)
27. Schreiber, G., Amin, A., Aroyo, L., van Assem, M., de Boer, V., Hardman, L., Hildebrand, M., Omelayenko, B., van Osenbruggen, J., Tordai, A., Wielemaker, J., Wielinga, B.: Semantic annotation and search of cultural-heritage collections: The MultimediaN E-Culture demonstrator. Web Semant. Sci. Serv. Agents World Wide Web 6, 243–249 (2008)
28. Shadboldt, N., Berners-Lee, T., Hall, W.: The Semantic Web revisited. IEEE Intell. Syst. 21, 96–101 (2006)
29. Shreve, G.M., Zeng, M.L.: Integrating resource metadata and domain markup in an NSDL collection. In: Proceedings of the International Conference on Dublin Core and Metadata Applications (DC 2003), pp. 223–229. Dublin Core Metadata Initiative (DCMI), Dublin (2003), http://dcpapers.dublincore.org/ojs/pubs/article/viewArticle/750 (retrieved September 16, 2012)
30. Sperberg-McQueen, C.M., Miller E.: On mapping from colloquial XML to RDF using XSLT. In: Extreme Markup Languages 2004 (2004), http://conferences.idealliance.org/extreme/html/ 2004/Sperberg-McQueen01/EML2004Sperberg-McQueen01.html (retrieved September 16, 2012)
31. Streich, R.: Techniques for managing collections of interrelated text modules. Markup Languages: Theory and Practice 1, 77–94 (1999)
32. Uren, V., Cimiano, P., Iria, J., Handschuh, S., Vargas-Vera, M., Motta, E., Ciravegna, F.: Semantic annotation for knowledge management: Requirements and a survey of the state of the art. Web Semant. Sci. Serv. Agents World Wide Web 4, 14–28 (2006)
33. Van Deursen, D., Poppe, C., Martens, G., Mannens, E., Walle, R.: XML to RDF conversion: A generic approach. In: Nesi, P., Ng, K., Delgado, J. (eds.) International Conference on Automated Solutions for Cross Media Content and Multi-Channel Distribution (AXMEDIS 2008), pp. 138–144. University of Florence, Florence (2008)
34. Wild, P.J., Giess, M.D., McMahon, C.A.: Describing engineering documents with faceted approaches. J. Doc. 66, 420–445 (2009)

35. Zeng, M.L.: Domain-specific markup languages and descriptive metadata: Their
    functions in scientific resource discovery. Revista Eletrônica de Biblioteconomia e
    Ciência da Informação 15, 164–176 (2010),
    http://www.periodicos.ufsc.br/index.php/eb/article/view/16890
    (retrieved September 16, 2012)
36. Zeng, M.L., Chan, L.M.: Semantic Interoperability. In: Bates, M.J., Maack, N.
    (eds.) Encyclopedia of Library and Information Sciences, 3rd edn., vol. 6, pp. 4645–
    4662. CRC Press, Boca Raton (2010)
37. Zschocke, T.: Resolving controlled vocabulary in DITA markup: A case example
    in agroforestry. Program. 46, 321–340 (2012)

ATOL: The Multi-species Livestock Trait Ontology

Wiktoria Golik[1], Olivier Dameron[2], Jérôme Bugeon[3], Alice Fatet[4],
Isabelle Hue[1], Catherine Hurtaud[5], Matthieu Reichstadt[6],
Marie-Christine Salaün[5], Jean Vernet[6], Léa Joret[3], Frédéric Papazian[1],
Claire Nédellec[1], and Pierre-Yves Le Bail[3]

[1] INRA, UR1077 Jouy-en-Josas, France
[2] INSERM, UMR936 Université de Rennes1, France
[3] INRA, UR1037 Rennes, France
[4] INRA-CNRS, UMR0085 Université F. Rabelais, Tours, France
[5] INRA, UMR1348 Agrocampus Ouest, Rennes, France
[6] INRA, UMR1213 VetAgro Sup, Clermont-Ferrand, France

Abstract. This paper presents the multi-species Animal Trait Ontology
for Livestock (ATOL) and the methodology used for its design. ATOL
has been designed as a reference source for indexing phenotype databases
and scientific papers. It covers five major topics related to animal pro-
ductions: growth and meat quality, animal nutrition, milk production,
reproduction and welfare. It is composed of species-independent concepts
subsuming species-specific ones so that cross-species and species-specific
reasoning can be performed consistently. In order to ensure a large consensus, three complementary approaches have successively been applied
to its design: reuse of existing ontologies, integration of production-
specific livestock traits by a large team of domain experts and curators
and terminology analysis of scientific papers. It resulted in a detailed taxonomy of 1,654 traits that is available at http://www.atol-ontology.com

Keywords: animal trait, livestock, ontology, terminological analysis.

1 Introduction

A phenotype is a set of values of the observable traits that characterize the
animal at the molecular, physiological, anatomical, morphological or ethologi-
cal levels. For example, an organism has the phenotype "blue" associated with
the trait "eye color". Phenotypes are determined by multiple factors: simple
genotypes determine eye color and complex genotypes interacting with environmental conditions determine size or behaviors. Observations and analysis of
phenotypes are essential for both the understanding by physiologists of the conditions that produce phenotypes of interest and the selection effort conducted
by geneticists. Animal selection has been performed empirically since domes-
tication, and more rigorously since Mendel. It consists of improving a race by
limiting the breeding to animals with the desired phenotypes. One of the major

J.M. Dodero, M. Palomo-Duarte, P. Karampiperis (Eds.): MTSR 2012, CCIS 343, pp. 289–300, 2012.
© Springer-Verlag Berlin Heidelberg 2012

stakes for life sciences to become integrative and predictive is the ability to uniformly describe the traits (markers and effectors) that determine the phenotypes of interest. The evolution of life sciences over the last two decades generated a deluge of data [1] that concerns many levels of biology that have potential implications for phenotypes [2] (particularly genomics, epigenomics, transcriptomics, proteomics and metabolomics). Bio-ontologies are an essential part of information systems because they support data integration and analysis across multiple levels of biology [3]. In this paper, we describe the ATOL multi-species livestock trait ontology, the motivation and its design method.

2   Background

In this section, we identify the main challenges to the integration of livestock production traits data and we survey previous efforts based on ontologies.

2.1   Data Integration

Phenotype-related data is scattered across multiple databases, which makes their integration and their processing difficult. They are produced in numerous organizations, and each of these organizations is likely to harbor heterogeneous data structures. The databases typically have different models even when they refer to the same kind of information, different field names and different representations. For example, a first database can contain a column "weight" representing the weight in kilograms of a trout at three months, whereas a second database would contain a column "mass", a column "species" and a column "age" representing the weight in grams of animals from several species of different ages. Both databases fit the requirements of the daily internal activity of their producers, but their integration or their reuse in another context requires *ad-hoc* domain specific handling, independently of the unit conversion issues. The underexploitation of the phenotype data is the consequence of the lack of interoperability. It also hinders the progress of phenotype-related activities.

In practice, the conversion of all the existing databases into a unifying framework is impossible, assuming that such a framework would be unique. The classical solution for addressing heterogeneity consists of annotating data with metadata, i.e. describing them explicitly using a common formal framework [4]. In our previous example, this would mean that metadata indicate that the "weight" column from the first database and the "mass" column from the second database refer to the same entity and similarly it would normalize species and units. Metadata use offers a lightweight and flexible solution that does not require the modification of existing data to achieve at least partial interoperability. The first step consists of considering the existing databases for the definition of a common schema of metadata, then of defining an identifier for each notion of interest and finally of using these identifiers to describe the existing data. Each identifier can be associated to preferred terms and synonyms, possibly in multiple languages. This approach has been successfully used in the biomedical domain. In addition to a common framework for annotating data, it is also necessary to represent explicitly the generality relations between the annotations in order to reconcile and process automatically information with different levels of precision.

2.2   Ontologies

The explicit and formal description of livestock production traits and the relations between some of these traits constitute an ontology [5]. Several trait and phenotype ontologies are under active development. For phenotype measurement ontologies, see the review by Shimoyama et al. [6]. The Mammalian Phenotype Ontology (MPO) [7] is an OBO ontology describing phenotypes in a context of mutation and QTL studies in mammalian model species and human pathologies. It is mainly used for describing mouse and rat phenotypes. The Animal Trait Ontology (ATO) [8] is an ontology of traits for livestock and not of phenotypes. ATO provides a uniform vocabulary within one species as well as between species and it is used to annotate genomic data (for example QTL or SNP). The Vertebrate Trait Ontology (VT) [9] was created to provide a standardized vocabulary to facilitate the comparison of trait data within and across vertebrate species. It aims to describe vertebrate traits, defined as "measurable or observable characteristics", pertaining to the morphology, physiology, or development of an organism or its substructures. None of these ontologies fulfills the need for a reference source of metadata in the domain of multi-species livestock traits. ATO and VT partly covers the scope of ATOL. They are further detailed in sections 3.1 and 4.1.

2.3   Knowledge Acquisition

The various methods applied to ontology modeling in specific domains mainly belong to three classes: reuse of existing ontologies, knowledge acquisition from experts and corpus-based acquisition [10]. The reuse ensures consistency and interoperability. Experts complement existing ontologies in order to fully cover the target scope. Document collections, i.e corpus, are also recognized as a rich source of knowledge as they provide terms that denote concepts, candidate to belong to the ontology. Corpus terms ensure a large coverage of the domain. They are also a source of alternative labels for naming the concepts. Term extractors automatically generate candidate terms when applied to a relevant set of documents. Among term extractors, BioYateA [11] is efficient [12] and well-adapted to the design of scientific ontologies. Despite the recent advances in term extraction and ontology learning, term candidates still need manual treatment. Termino-ontology editors support the construction of the ontology based on the terminology in a user-friendly way [11], [13]. TyDI fitted ATOL design needs because it supports expert collaborative work and direct expert interaction [11].

3   Methods

ATOL was developed in OWL format by a group of curators and domains experts using Protégé-4.1 and the WebProtégé collaborative environmentThe workgroup was composed of a leader, a biomedical ontology expert, five curators and about 50 domain experts. Each curator was in charge of one of the five topics according to his/her domain of expertise. He/she managed a subgroup of domain experts. Special care was devoted to mix competencies in the subgroups and to balance expertise according to their scientific interest, fields and livestock species. INRA experts were motivated by the normalization effort to overcome their various laboratories and experimental farms specificities. Moreover, comparative physiology researchers conduct several collaborative programs on different species that needed to uniform definitions of phenotypic traits. We followed a three-step approach, (1) the reuse of ATO and VT, (2) the extension with livestock production specific traits (Section 3.1) and (3) the revision based on Animal Journal analysis (Section 3.2 and 3.3). Each step was done in close collaboration with James Reecy's group from Iowa University in order to maintain compatibility with the two ontologies, ATO and VT.

3.1   Construction of the Initial Version by the Curators

First, each curator performed an extraction of the potentially relevant subtrees of the March 6, 2009 version of ATO and VT. Then, the curators and their respective experts subgroups selected the relevant concepts in the extraction and reviewed their definitions. This review phase was carried out in coordination with the ATO and VT team. For the sake of interoperability, references to the original concepts were preserved. Therefore, ATOL is aligned with ATO and VT by construction. Finally, the curators and their experts subgroups enriched the ontology by adding new concepts and by organizing them in a sound taxonomy. ATOL is composed of species-independent concepts subsuming species-specific ones. Each expert subgroup determined which species each concept could be associated with.

3.2   Analysis of Corpus Coverage by ATOL

Ontology modeling based on expertise has been usefully complemented by the study of a corpus of scientific international papers published in the animal trait domain conducted by a terminologist. The motivation was first to validate the terms chosen by experts as concept labels by checking their use in the literature. We chose the *Animal journal* because its scope includes all ATOL topics and beyond. We used the v1.0 early version of ATOL (April 2010) in order to evaluate the benefit of the corpus-based approach for the design of the next versions. This version contained 1,373 labels. The Animal corpus consists of 697 papers. The mapping of the concepts to the corpus was done by a straightforward projection of the concept labels to the corpus strings. 570 (42%) ATOL labels were found in the corpus. The high percentage of the matched terms was unfortunately due to many short and ambiguous labels that were too general (e.g. "performance", "approach") or incomplete (e.g. "pH"). They had to be rewritten and specialized accordingly. For instance, "pH" as descendant of "meat quality" should become "meat pH". Conversely, the terminologist identifies syntactic flaws that were easy to correct without involving deep expertise, including typographic errors, translation errors, unnecessary conjunction of coordination (e.g. "and") and frequent non-alphabetic characters that prevented the occurrence of ATOL labels in the corpus that were unnecessary in most of the case. This first analysis of ATOL labels led to a systematic correction reported in (Section 4.2).

3.3 Linguistic Approach

A deeper linguistic terminological analysis was needed for suggesting further revisions of the ATOL labels that were not found in the corpus. It compared ATOL concept labels to the terms extracted from Animal journal papers.

Improvement of Concept Labels by Linguistic Variation. Among the 2,550 labels and synonyms found in ATOL version 3.5.8, only 922 occurred in scientific papers as measured by using Google Scholar hits. The manual examination of a subset of labels with 0 or rare occurrences showed that a major source of discrepancy was the choice of rare forms as concept labels over alternative names actually preferred by the authors of papers. Hopefuly many synonyms in the corpus were direct morpho-syntactic and semantic variations of the concept labels, such as "consumption of water" versus "water intake". In this example, "water intake" is obtained by the permutation of the nouns of "consumption of water" and the replacement of "consumption" by its synonym "intake. We used FastR [14] for automatically computing such variations from ATOL labels with the goal of discovering relevant variants. Section 4.3 details the result of the application of FastR and its use for ATOL improvement.

Terminological Analysis of the Significance of ATOL Labels. The variants of most of the long labels over 3 words were out of reach of FastR variations. We wanted then to discover new terms in the corpus that were synonym of the concept labels but not direct variations. We performed an extensive term extraction on the Animal corpus that provided many candidate terms for renaming these concepts among which the experts had to select the relevant ones.

We used BioYateA [11] for term extraction, after syntactic analysis by AlvisNLP [15]. BioYateA was provided with ATOL as source of certified terms. The extraction yielded 144,928 candidate terms. TyDI (Terminology Design Interface)) [11] assisted the manual exploration of the candidate terms and their matching to ATOL labels. For each label that was absent from the corpus, TyDI displayed the corpus terms that shared common features with the label and that could possibly be synonyms. The selection of the relevant features is done interactively. For instance, "withdrawal reflex" label had no match in the corpus and no FastR variant. The user enters queries such as "withdrawal" as term argument into TyDI interface. It displays 7 terms among which "withdrawal response" and "withdrawal reaction" are relevant related synonyms. The number of occurrences and the context help to select the most relevant and less ambiguous (see [11] for more details). The new term is then added as the preferred name for the concept in the ontology displayed by TyDI. The results of the use of BioYateA and TyDY for ATOL design is detailed in section 4.3.

ATOL Extension by Corpus-Based Term Extraction. The lexical corpus-based approach supported by term extraction has also been applied to populate ATOL with new concepts. It differed from the previous case in that the experts used corpus term extraction from the beginning to design a whole ontology sub-tree, instead of using it for *a posteriori* revision. They looked for terms denoting new concepts on a given subject starting from representative words searched by TyDI. This work aimed at evaluating TyDI usability by a domain expert without the assistance of a knowledge engineer. Section 4.3 details the results.

4   Results

4.1   Initial Version Construction by the Curators

The design of ATOL started with the reuse of existing ontologies, in particular ATO and VT. The 06 March 2009 version of ATO and VT was composed of 4,182 concepts, 3,692 (88 %) of which had a textual definition. Each curator and subgroup of experts selected the subtree of potential relevance for their domain of interest. Next, they manually enriched and organized their branch of interest. During these three steps, the ATO and VT parallel evolutions were monitored so that their changes could be propagated to ATOL. Conversely, the concepts added to ATOL by the experts were proposed for review to the ATO and VT experts. Figure 1 presents the composition and overlap of the five topics during the automatic extraction of concept from ATO and VT, the manual selection of the relevant ones and the addition of new concepts in version 4.4 of ATOL. The decreasing number of concepts of the growth and meat quality topics along the three steps can be explained by the fact that many concepts from ATO and VT were related to a specific muscle and sometimes to non edible muscle (eye muscle for example). They were first automatically extracted, but the focus of ATOL led us to manually exclude them. On the contrary, only few concepts related to milk production were present in the initial extraction and this topic was then notably extended in ATOL.

During the enrichment phase, a particular effort was devoted to organizing the ATOL ontology as a sound taxonomy, i.e. each class is formally a kind of its parents. For example, "adipose tissue fatty acid content" (atol:0074) and "adipose tissue lipid oxydation" (atol:0075) are two siblings subclasses of "adipose tissue lipid quality" (atol:0073). Thus, the superclass features logically hold for each of its subclasses and the subclasses of the subclasses by inference. Heritage allowed us to simplify modeling by factoring common features. It supports automatic reasoning so that if given data is annotated by a concept, one can infer that it is also annotated by all the ancestors of this concept since they are more general. This is used to reconcile data with different levels of precision. Whenever necessary, we also used multiple inheritance by assigning more than one superclass to a class. For example, "body weight" (atol:0351) is a subclass of both "animal performance trait" (atol:1516) and "growth trait" (atol:0855). Table 1 presents the distribution of the concepts among topics and their overlap.

Fig. 1. Composition and overlap of the five branches of ATOL: meat growth and quality (red, top left), milk (light green, left), nutrition (dark green, bottom left), reproduction (blue, bottom right) and welfare (purple, top right) at the three stages of ATOL design, (1) extraction from ATO and VT, (2) manual selection of relevant concepts and (3) ATOL v4.4 after enrichment

Table 1. Concept distribution by topic after manual enrichment of ATOL version 4.4

?	Repro	Milk	Meat	Welfare	Nutrition
Repro	274	0	0	67	0
Milk	0	420	0	5	0
Meat	0	0	228	15	2
Welfare	67	5	15	331	6
Nutrition	0	0	2	6	462

The structuring phase resulted in concepts previously shared between welfare and nutrition being assigned to either of the two domains (6 shared concepts), whereas the concepts shared between welfare and reproduction (67 concepts) remained common. During the selection and the enrichment phases, the experts determined for each concept the list of species they were relevant for. Figure 2 shows the distribution of shared concepts between cow and sheep (left, 93 % of common traits) and cow and trout (right, 51 % of common traits) for each ATOL topic. Not suprisingly cows and sheep globally share the same traits. Cows and trout share the meat quality traits and are less similar otherwise. Obviously, milk-related traits are cow-related and have no counterparts in trout. This illustrates the genericity of ATOL traits among species.

4.2   Analysis of Corpus Coverage by ATOL

The extensive shallow analysis of ATOL labels with respect to the Animal Journal yielded 156 new concepts or synonyms in ATOL 1.0 (10% increase) and among them, 27 were present in the corpus. This work led to clear guidelines about the form of the labels that curators should apply to the future versions of ATOL. We then measured the improvement of label quality in version 3.5.8 of ATOL (Dec. 2011) that followed the guidelines and included many new traits. Only 2% of the 2,550 labels had typographic errors. The measure of their occurrence in the literature reached 43%, a much higher rate than previously, which demonstrates the benefit of a corpus-based evaluation of the ontology.

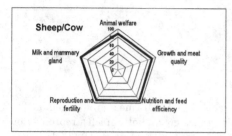 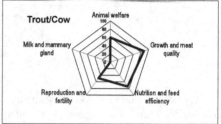

Fig. 2. Number of common traits between cow and sheep (left) and cow and trout (right) traits for the five subtree of ATOL

4.3   Linguistic Approach

Improvement of Concept Labels by Linguistic Variation. Compared to straightforward coverage analysis, the application of FastR led to many revisions based on morpho-syntactic analysis. All 1,605 ATOL labels without any occurrence in the corpus were given to FastR together with the corpus of 697 papers and WordNet as a source of semantic variations [16]. Table 2 gives the most frequent variants with their frequency. It is noticeable that in many cases, the variant was the most frequent form but not necessarily the less ambiguous as "slaughter age" instead of "age at slaughter". The table illustrates the diversity of the lexical relations between the labels and their variants. They are not all synonyms but also hyper- or hyponyms that may be relevant to ATOL.

Table 2. ATOL original terms and most frequent variants proposed by FastR

ATOL label	#occ	Corpus variant	#occ
milk yield	1192	milk production	1485
energy expenditure	48	energy intake	291
meat trait	10	meat quality trait	194
age at slaughter	52	slaughter age	133
parental behaviour	0	maternal behaviour	104
milk yield	1192	milk fat yield	85
water intake	147	water consumption	76
feeding behaviour	0	feeding behavior	71

FastR computed the label variants from corpus terms by applying variation rules that performed insertion, permutation and replacement of words by WordNet synset members. It yielded 1,190 pairs of ATOL labels – variants for 218 different labels. Among them a knowledge engineer validated 541 synonymy pairs for 171 different labels, excluding specializations and other relevant terms that were not strict synonyms. Semantic variation that is due to WordNet is involved in 60% of the positive pairs (50% of the total) demonstrating the clear benefit of semantic variation and the use of external resource. Among the 1,605 labels without any occurrence in the corpus, FastR then automatically found relevant alternative names for 10% (171) of them. The computation of term variants by linguistic analysis appeared as a valuable solution for improving concept names especially short names. Their inclusion in ATOL is in progress.

Terminological Analysis of the Significance of ATOL Labels. After synonym computation, 1,434 ATOL labels still remained with 0 occurrences in the corpus. We used BioYateA and TyDI to analyze the reasons why so many long ATOL labels are absent from the corpus. The lessons from this first terminological study are various. (1) The paper corpus should be extended to journals other than Animal in order to explore a larger set of candidate terms. The *Journal of Animal Science* and *Livestock Science* are obvious candidates relevant to the scope of ATOL. (2) Some synsets are missing in WordNet that are very relevant to the Animal domain. Providing FastR with them would enable it to compute many additional relevant synonym variants. Among the most frequent related synonyms, "content"/"concentration" occurs in 857 of the 0–occurrence labels and "meat"/"flesh" in 31. This would enable to compute for instance "adipose tissue vitamin content"$_L$ / "vitamin concentrations in adipose tissue"$_T$ or "flesh physicochemical trait"$_L$ / "physicochemical properties of meat"T_T . Such frequent synonyms in ATOL should be considered in order to improve WordNet power. (3) The animal product is always mentioned in the trait label, e.g. "Meat" and "Milk" frequently occurred in 263 of the missing labels. Automatically removing the product name from the labels yielded many hits in TyDI; thus proving the relevance of those labels although the matched terms were not synonym. For instance, "milk color redness" is not synonym of "meat color redness", but the presence of "color redness" in the text is a good indicator of the use of the redness concept. (4) Animal names are frequently inserted in corpus terms, as in "average daily gain"$_L$ / "average pigs daily gains"$_T$ preventing the label from being found. However, the occurrence of such more specific terms confirms the relevance of the label. The matching process can be automated, first by using the list of animals associated to the concepts in the ontology in the form of subsets, then by designing an extensive list of their variant names. The remaining cases are due to paraphrases: the concept is not expressed by a term but by a more complex construction. Corpus term analysis combined with the semantic search engine AlvisIR [17] helps in finding these paraphrases but their association to ATOL labels cannot be fully automated.

Example. "Seasonality of female sexual activity"$_L$ / "Decreasing photoperiod plays an important role in activating sexual activity in seasonal breeders"$_T$.

The terminological analysis of terms that are close to ATOL labels yielded promising new directions for automatically identifying ATOL concepts in the corpus. Their relevance will be assessed in the future by quantitative measures of ATOL label occurrences in a larger corpus.

ATOL Extension by Corpus-Based Term Extraction. We experimented with the corpus-based approach described in section 3.3 for creating new concepts in the feed domain. An expert was taught how to use TyDI. He measured the relevance of the terms proposed by TyDI, according to their frequency and decided accordingly wether to create the corresponding concept or not. The words "nutrition", "feed" and "flux" that are representative of the topic were first searched through TyDI interface. It yielded 847 terms among which a subset has been used to design the nutrition subtree. Then synonyms of these concepts have been searched and added to ATOL. TyDI was then particularly useful to evaluate which of the forms is the most popular, e.g. "nitrogen content in feed" versus "nitrogen content of feed". It was then used for enriching the ontology by systematically looking for all specific arguments of a given concept. For instance, digestibility is a main concepts in nutrition. TyDI supported the search for all nutriments to which digestibility applies, (e.g. nitrogen, phosphorus, fiber). It yielded about thirty words. The search for the organs where the digestibility is measured (e.g. rumen, intestinal tract, cloacae) yielded 16 new concepts. This experiment confirmed that TyDI tool as a valuable solution for supporting corpus-based terminological analysis for ontology design.

5   Discussion

The current version 4.6.8 of ATOL defines 1,656 concepts among which 1,186 are specific to ATOL. 545 concepts are shared with VT and 341 VT concepts were annotated by the ATOL group. ATOL fills a gap in the domain of trait and phenotype ontologies such as ATO and VT that have different scopes. Their structure was not compatible with ATOL requirements preventing extension to livestock. ATO recently evolved towards a consortium of ontologies on products (PT), Animal breed ontology on species, and VT. Originally, VT was intended to describe model species traits like those of mice and rats. Its organization follows an academic point of view (e.g. morphology, functions) without reference to species. Its further extension to livestock species via ATO retained this hierarchical perspective. Moreover, VT only considers directly measurable traits (called simple traits). It excludes complex traits that are defined from other simple or complex traits such as gonado-somatic ratio or body mass index. ATOL focuses on the different kinds of animal products (quantity and quality of meat, milk and eggs) or of breeding (alimentary efficiency, fertility, welfare). These domains rely on numerous complex traits used by both breeding professionals and researchers. However, the VT, ATO and ATOL leaders agreed to shared as many traits as possible using explicit cross-references. This solution both preserves the specific traits and organization of ontologies, and maximizes interoperability. In the current version of ATOL, the traits are organized in a is-a hierarchy. We plan to include additional relations such as part_of to represent composition, as well as is_an_indicator_of and is_a_standardization-of to take into account the connection between a trait of interest and the different modes of observation of this trait. Human effort made by INRA for the specific development of ATOL and its sustainability over time is part of its strategy to develop operational integrative and predictive biology approaches for the systemic management of livestock in France and Europe. Since the project start in 2009, ATOL development is estimated at 62 man-months. The second phase of maintenance and evolution of ATOL is estimated at 3 man-months that will be spread over a group of 10 persons from INRA. Among the programs in which ATOL is used, AQUAEXCEL [18] is an example in which the fish-related part of ATOL is reused for resource sharing and normalization among partners, notably for fish models and experimental methods. Conversely, improvements suggested by AQUAEXCEL are propagated into ATOL. User feedback through the ATOL website is welcome. As ATOL gains acceptance, it will be important to follow international standard for ontology design and description

The design of ATOL has shown that the terminological analysis was more efficient when used during the design of the ontology as done for nutrition, than *a posteriori*. This is the consequence of both methodological reasons and expert motivation. When the experts considered the design achieved, the terminological analysis appeared more as a corrector that revealed flaws than as a useful support for finding new concepts or the best way to express them. For the development of the new parts of ATOL, such as environmental factors, the terminology-based approach will be used from the very beginning and fully integrated into the methodology. The addition of synonyms to ATOL from the corpus opened new perspectives: it made ATOL usable for full-text indexing of the Animal journal by the semantic search engine AlvisIR. A preliminary public version is available at [18]. Semantic search fully takes advantage of the hierarchical structure of ATOL. For instance, the query "milk composition trait" retrieves 77 articles that mention specific traits such as "milk fat concentration". The query on Google Scholar does not retrieve any answer. The Google Scholar query "milk composition" without "trait" retrieves only 24 papers from the same collection. The query "meat quality" yields 318 hits in AlvisIR, 71 in Google Scholar. These two examples illustrate the added value of ATOL for semantic search. In the near future, the extension of ATOL by the terminology level will be achieved, thus making the *Animal search engine* fully operational.

6   Conclusion

This paper has presented ATOL, a multi-species livestock trait ontology. It has been designed as a reference source for phenotype databases and scientific papers metadata. ATOL covers five major topics related to animal product: growth and meat quality, animal nutrition, milk production, reproduction and welfare. The initial design phase relied on groups of experts and curators. This ensured a general coverage of each five topics and that concepts were organized in a sound taxonomy. A terminological analysis of the Animal Journal was then conducted in order to identify and rename irrelevant concept labels and to identify new concepts. It improved ATOL at different levels of conceptualization. In addition the terminological analysis validated the relevance of ATOL as a resource for the automatic semantic indexing of literature.

References

1. Blake, J., Bult, C.: Beyond the data deluge: Data integration and bio-ontologies. Journal of Biomedical Informatics 39(3), 314–320 (2006)
2. Hocquette, J.-F., Capel, C., David, V., Guéméné, D., Bidanel, J., Ponsart, C., Gastinel, P.-L., Le Bail, P.-Y., Monget, P., Mormède, P., Barbezant, M., Guillou, F., Peyraud, J.-L.: Objectives and applications of phenotyping network setup for livestock. Animal Science Journal 83, 517–528 (2012)
3. Cimino, J.J., Zhu, X.: The practical impact of ontologies on biomedical informatics. Methods of Information in Medicine (2006)
4. Shah, N.H., Jonquet, C., Chiang, A.P., Butte, A.J., Chen, R., Musen, M.A.: Ontology-driven indexing of public datasets for translational bioinformatics. BMC Bioinformatics 10(suppl. 2), S1 (2009)
5. Bard, J.B.L., Rhee, S.Y.: Ontologies in biology: design, applications and future challenges. Nature Reviews. Genetics 5(3), 213–222 (2004)
6. Shimoyama, M., Nigam, R., Sanders McIntosh, L., Nagarajan, R., Rice, T., Rao, D.C., Dwinell, M.R.: Three ontologies to define phenotype measurement data. Frontiers in Genetics 3, 87 (2012)
7. Smith, C.L., Goldsmith, C.-A.W., Eppig, J.T.: The mammalian phenotype ontology as a tool for annotating, analyzing and comparing phenotypic information. Genome Biology 6(1), 7 (2004)
8. Hughes, L.M., Bao, J., Hu, Z.-L., Honavar, V., Reecy, J.M.: Animal trait ontology: The importance and usefulness of a unified trait vocabulary for animal species. Journal of Animal Science 86(6), 1485–1491 (2008)
9. Park, C., Bello, S., Smith, C., Hu, Z.-L., Munzenmaier, D., Shimoyama, M., Eppig, J., Reecy, J.: The vertebrate trait ontology: A controlled vocabulary to facilitate cross-species comparison of trait data. In: Proceedings of the 20th Conference on Plant and Animal Genomes, San Diego, CA (2012)
10. Uschold, M., King, M.: Towards a methodology for building ontologies. In: IJCAI 1995 Workshop on Basic Ontological Issues in Knowledge Sharing (1995)
11. Nédellec, C., Golik, W., Aubin, S., Bossy, R.: Building Large Lexicalized Ontologies from Text: A Use Case in Automatic Indexing of Biotechnology Patents. In: Cimiano, P., Pinto, H.S. (eds.) EKAW 2010. LNCS, vol. 6317, pp. 514–523. Springer, Heidelberg (2010)
12. Mondary, T., Nazarenko, A., Zargayouna, H., Barreaux, S.: The quaero evaluation campaign on term extraction. In: Proceedings of the Eighth International Conference on Language Resources and Evaluation, LREC (2012)
13. Aussenac-Gilles, N., Després, S., Szulman, S.: The terminae method and platform for ontology engineering from texts. In: Bridging the Gap between Text and Knowledge - Selected Contributions to Ontology Learning and Population from Text, pp. 199–223 (2008)
14. Jacquemin, C.: A Symbolic and Surgical Acquisition of Terms Through Variation. In: Wermter, S., Scheler, G., Riloff, E. (eds.) IJCAI-WS 1995. LNCS, vol. 1040, pp. 425–438. Springer, Heidelberg (1996)
15. Nédellec, C., Nazarenko, A., Bossy, R.: Information Extraction. In: Ontology Handbook, pp. 663–686. Springer (2008)
16. Miller, G.A., Beckwith, R., Fellbaum, C.D., Gross, D., Miller, K.: WordNet: An online lexical database. Int. J. Lexicograph. 3(4), 235–244 (1990)
17. Bossy, R., Kotoujansky, A., Golik, W., Aubin, S., Nédellec, C.: Close integration of ML and NLP tools in BioAlvis for semantic search in bacteriology. In: Proc. of the Workshop on Semantic Web Applications and Tools for Life Sciences (2008)
18. AlvisIR for ANIMAL, http://bibliome.jouy.inra.fr/test/alvisir/animal/

Data-Driven Schema Matching in Agricultural Learning Object Repositories

Antonis Koukourikos[1,4], Giannis Stoitsis[2,3], and Pythagoras Karampiperis[4]

[1] University of Piraeus, Department of Digital Systems. 80,
Karaoli and Dimitriou Str, Piraeus, Greece, 18534
[2] Agro-Know Technologies, Grammou 17, Vrilissia, Athens, Greece, 15235
[3] Universidad de Alcalá, Pza. San Diego, s/n - 28801 Alcalá de Henares, Madrid, Spain
[4] Software and Knowledge Engineering Laboratory,
Institute of Informatics and Telecommunications, National Center for Scientific Research
"Demokritos"Agia Paraskevi Attikis, P.O. Box 60228, 15310 Athens, Greece

Abstract. As the wealth of structured repositories of educational content for agricultural object is increasing, the problem of heterogeneity between them on a semantic level is becoming more prominent. Ontology matching is a technique that helps to identify the correspondences on the description schemas of different sources and provide the basis for interesting applications that exploit the information in a linked fashion. The present paper presents a data-driven approach for discovering matches between different classification schemas. The approach is based on content analysis and linguistic processing in order to extract information in the form of relation tuples, use the extracted information to associate the content of different repositories and match their underlying classification schemas based on the degree of content similarity. The preliminary results verified the validity of the approach, as both experiments produced a semantically valid matching in 68% of the examined classes. The results also exposed the need for refinements on the linguistic processing of the available textual information and on the definition of relation similarity, as well as, the need to exploit structural information in order to move from discovering semantically valid matches to effectively handling class specializations and generalizations.

Keywords: ontology matching, classification schemas, educational content, agricultural objects.

1   Introduction

The progress on the availability and structuring of online information has made available huge amounts of disjoint information for multiple domains. The usability and effectiveness of this information is greatly increased if the contributions of different content providers is associated and used in liaison with each other. Therefore, the problem of managing the heterogeneity between various information resources in order to integrate seamlessly and efficiently the underlying knowledge is of particular interest.

J.M. Dodero, M. Palomo-Duarte, P. Karampiperis (Eds.): MTSR 2012, CCIS 343, pp. 301–312, 2012.
© Springer-Verlag Berlin Heidelberg 2012

In the context of the Semantic Web, ontologies are a common medium for describing the domain of interest and providing a contextualization of the different terms used for specifying the characteristics of the involved entities. Ontology matching is one of the prominent technologies used for integrating such descriptions on the conceptual level However, information and knowledge resources are not always associated with an ontology. Classifications of different complexity and formalization are employed in different repositories. Some of them do deploy full-fledged ontologies, usually expressed in OWL or RDFS, while others use less complex solutions, like XML schemas or simple categorization.

The present paper builds on the ideas from the fields of ontology matching and discusses a data-driven approach towards the consolidation of the schemas describing different repositories. Our approach is based on the notion that documents from different repositories that discuss similar subjects are likely to have corresponding classifications in their respective schemas. Therefore, by extracting and comparing relations from these documents we are able to identify alignments between the schemas. Furthermore, additional restrictions can be posed after taking into account the hierarchical structure of the compared classifications. We formalized the above hypothesis and tested its application using repositories of educational content for agricultural objects.

The rest of the paper is structured as follows: We present some of the popular techniques of ontology alignment and relevant systems. Afterwards, a description of our method and the data collections that we used is provided. Next, the obtained results for the examined datasets are presented. We conclude with an indication of rooms for improvement and report future steps for calibrating and expanding on the existing infrastructure.

2   Related Work

The purpose of ontology matching is, in a broad context, to define correspondences and mappings between concepts, as the latter are expressed in different conceptualization schemas. Several formalizations of the above statement have been proposed [1, 2, 3]. In [4] it is stated:

Let O1 and O2 distinct ontologies. An alignment between these ontologies is a set of correspondences between entities belonging to the two ontologies. A correspondence is a quadruple of the form:<id,e1,e2,r>, where:

- id is a unique identifier for the correspondence
- e1 is an entity of the first ontology O1
- e2 is an entity of the second ontology O2
- r is the type of relation between e1 and e2

The relation between the matched entities can be equivalence, generalisation/specialisation and others, depending on the nature of the problem that is being examined.

There are various techniques used for performing ontology matching. A common method is the application of linguistic analysis within the ontology in order to compute similarities on the textual level. Another strategy for ontology matching is the examination of structural properties of the ontologies to be merged. The graph structure derived from the ontology, commonly via is-a/ part-of relationships between concepts, provides a means for examining the similarity between two ontologies based on the connections between their concepts. Instance-based approaches, where the objects described by the ontologies are available and annotated with ontological terms, are also of particular interest. Similarity between instances can lead to suggestion of similarities between the underlying concepts. Finally, external knowledge information, such as thesauri, dictionaries and taxonomies, are frequently employed in ontology matching in order to provide further information about the semantics of the concepts and relations in the ontologies to be matched.

In practice, these approaches are not mutually exclusive, as ontology alignment systems can use combinations of them or employ selection strategies to invoke a matcher based on features specific to the matching task at hand. Some prominent recent alignment systems and their approaches are described below.

SAMBO [5] is used for matching (and merging) biomedical ontologies. It supports the merging of ontologies expressed in OWL format. The system combines different matchers, each one computing a similarity value in the [0, 1] space. The terminological matcher examines similarities between the textual descriptions of concepts and restrictions of the ontologies, using the n-gram and edit distance metrics and a linguistic algorithm that compares the lists of words of which the descriptions terms are composed and discovers the common words. A structural matcher relies on the position of concepts relative to already aligned concepts and iteratively aligns additional entities based on their structural association (is-a/part-of connections with entities aligned during a previous iteration). SAMBO also examines the similarity of terms in the ontologies with an external domain-specific resource (UMLS) and employs a learning matcher that classifies documents with respect to their relation with ontology concepts and associates the entities that encapsulated the same documents.

RiMOM [6] uses a multi-strategy ontology matching approach. The matching methods that are employed are (a) linguistic similarity and (b) structural similarity. The linguistic similarity adopts the edit distance and vector instance metrics, while the structural similarity is examined by a modified similarity flooding [7] implementation. For each matching task, RiMOM quantifies the similarity characteristics between the examined ontologies and dynamically selects the suitable strategy for performing the task.

The ASMOV [8] system handles pairs of ontologies expressed in OWL. The process employed by ASMOV includes two distinct phases. The similarity calculation phase activates linguistic, structural and extensional matchers in order to iteratively compute similarity measures for each pair of entities comprised by the elements of the ontologies to be matched. The measures are then aggregated into a single, weighted average value. From this phase, a preliminary alignment is produced by selecting the maximum similarity value for each entity. During the semantic verification phase, this alignment is iteratively refined via the elimination of the correspondences that are not verified by assertions in the ontologies.

BLOOMS [9] is an alignment system that discovers schema-level links between Linked Open Data datasets by bootstrapping already present information from the LOD cloud. After a light-weight linguistic processing, it feeds the textual descriptions of concepts in two ontologies to the Wikipedia search Web Service. The Wikipedia categories to which the search results belong to are inserted into a tree structure that is expanded with the subcategories of the aforementioned categories, until the tree reaches the fourth level. The trees belonging to the "forests" of the two input ontologies are compared in pairs and an overlap value is assigned to each tree pair. Based on this value, BLOOMS defines equivalence and specialization relations between the concepts of the ontologies.

The aforementioned systems have produced significant results in the context of classification schema matching. However, they mostly handle schemas expressed in a specific format (e.g. OWL ontologies), so they require a certain level of conformance in order to perform the matching task. Repositories of learning content for agriculture, however, use a wide variety of different formalizations for classifying their content and their metadata. The amount of different approaches [10, 11] and the variability on the methodologies and lexicalization [12, 13] pose several interesting issues for the efforts of ensuring that the crucial need for interoperability is met. Our approach aims to exploit the strategies employed in ontology alignment in order to develop a system that is able to match classification schemas expressed in different ways. In order to remedy the inability of direct comparison of the schemas due to their different formats, we consider the examination of the underlying actual data as a means for discovering the semantic associations behind the different classifications.

3   Methodology

Our approach focuses on the analysis of the actual educational objects described by the classification schemas to be merged. The specific goal of our experiments was to match each of two distinct description schemas with a third one, that is, to perform two independent, one-to-one matching tasks. The base schema for our experiments was the one use by the Organic.Edunet Web portal. In the first run, we applied our method for the base schema and the schema of OER Commons Green. For the second run, we matched the Organic.Edunet ontology and the taxonomy of Organic Eprints.

The following subsections describe (a) The datasets that we used and their description schemas, (b) the process of extracting information from the datasets and (c) the execution of the matching task.

3.1   Datasets

The schema that was used in both runs of our experiment was the ontology of the Organic.Edunet Web portal (http://www.organic-edunet.eu). The Organic.Edunet Web portal for agricultural and sustainable education was launched in 2010. Its aim has been to facilitate access, usage and exploitation of digital educational content related to Organic Agriculture (OA) and Agroecology (AE). In order to achieve this aim, it networked existing collections with educational content on relevant topics from various content providers, into a large federation where content resources are described according to standard-complying metadata. The underlying description schema, the Organic.Edunet organic ontology, is expressed in OWL. An example of a metadata record from the Organic.Edunet repository is depicted in Figure 1.

```
<lom xmlns="http://ltsc.ieee.org/xsd/LOM">
<general>
    <identifier></identifier>
    <title><string language="en">Insulating livestock and other farm build-
ings</string></title>
</general>
<technical>
    <format>text/html</format>
    <location>http://www.ces.purdue.edu/extmedia/AE/AE-95.html</location>
</technical>
<taxonPath>
    <source>
      <string language="en">Organic.Edunet Ontology</string>
    </source>
    <taxon>
      <id>http://www.cc.uah.es/ie/ont/OE-
Predicates#ProvidesNewInformationOn    ::    http://www.cc.uah.es/ie/ont/OE-
OAAE#LivestockHousing</id>
      <entry>
        <string>ProvidesNewInformationOn :: LivestockHousing</string>
      </entry>
    </taxon>
</taxonPath>
</lom>
```

Fig. 1. Snippet of a metadata entry from Organic.Edunet

On the first run of the system, the second input classification schema was the one of the OER Commons Green repository (http://www.oercommons.org/green). OER Commons Green is part of OER Commons, which was created by ISKME (http://www.iskme.org/) as a way to provide support for and build a knowledge base around the use and reuse of open educational resources. From the content available via OER Commons Green, there are currently 3157 documents organized by subject in a 2-tier hierarchy.

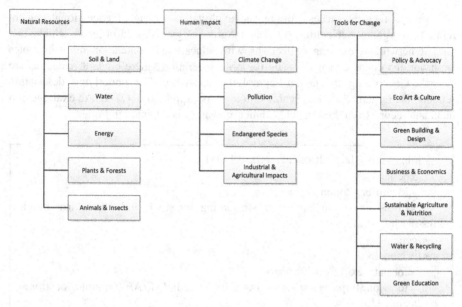

Fig. 2. The Green OER classification of educational content by subject

The XML metadata descriptions of the educational objects included in the Green OER Commons repository use external classification methods to provide additional taxonomical information for each object. Since our goal is to match the central taxonomy of Green OER Commons to that of the Organic.Edunet portal, we did not take into account these associations. Instead, we produced an augmented version of the original XML file with an added <goer_subject> element for each document, based on its classification at the Green OER Commons site. For adding the new element, we parsed the web page dedicatied to the document in order to extract the classification lexicals. Then, we manipulated the DOM of the XML file using the standard Java libraries for the task, inserted a new node for the element with the Green OER classification as its value and serialized the final DOM into the final XML document.

```
<record>
<header>
<identifier>oai:orgprints.org:122</identifier>
</header>
<metadata>
<dc:subject> Crop combinations and interactions</dc:subject>
<dc:subject> Cereals, pulses and oilseeds</dc:subject>

</metadata>
</record>
```

Fig. 3. Snippet of an object description in the Organic Eprints record list

The second experiment aimed to match the classification of Organic.Edunet with that of Organic Eprints (http://www.orgprints.org/). The Organic Eprints archive has been developed by the International Centre for Research in Organic Food Systems (http://www.icrofs.org/) and its main goal is to facilitate the communication and dissemination of research objects in the domain of organic agriculture. Its classification system is based on subject definition for the included material. The maximum depth of the classification is 4; however, most categories reach level 2 at most. The subjects of each object are declared in its metadata description via one or more dc:subject elements.

3.2   Information Extraction

The first step on the implementation of our system is to extract a relation set from the documents within the datasets. At this stage, we take into account educational content solely in the English language and we handle documents in the DOC, PDF and HTML formats. Using the metadata descriptions for the records in each repository, we selected 500 entries from each one. The XML file for each record set was parsed and the record entries were stored as objects in a linked list. We selected random indexes from the lists and, as long as the format and language of the corresponding document were suitable and we had not reached the amount limit, we retrieved the actual resource for further processing.

Before performing the information extraction task some pre-processing of the ontological elements and the examined documents was necessary. We applied some lightweight linguistic processing to the textual descriptions of the classification schemas, in order to obtain proper terms and capitalization. For the documents retrieved in HTML format, we applied a boilerplate removal module in order to exclude formative content (tags, scripting snippets) and content irrelevant to the interesting content (menus, advertisements, comments etc.). The module was built on top of the boilerpipe library (http://code.google.com/p/boilerpipe). A step that was deemed necessary was the resolution of co-references within the text. The absence of such an analysis led to the production of numerous relations that were not useful since they associated entities that could not be resolved. Use of pronouns and generic terms, like "the band", "the group" do not allow the direct expansion of the relation set for an entity. To overcome this issue, we use the co-reference resolution module of the OpenNLP Tools (http://opennlp.apache.org/).

For the information extraction process, we used the REVERB system [14], which follows the Open Information Extraction paradigm, building on the methodology of previous systems, like TEXTRUNNER [15]. TEXTRUNNER returns a set of relation tuples by executing a single pass over the entire input corpus and assigns a probability to each tuple based on the probabilistic model of redundancy in text proposed by [16]. REVERB expands this method and introduces a constraint enforcement mechanism in order to improve on the accuracy of the produced relation set. A syntactic constraint eliminates incoherent and uninformative extractions, while a lexical constraint rejects overly specific - and thus not useful - relations by examining the amount of distinct arguments presented in the corpus for the relation. The relation tuples produced by

REVERB include three components. That is, they have the form (Arg1, Rel, Arg2), where Arg1 is an entity connected unidirectionally via the relation Rel with Arg2.

The use of an open information extraction module, as opposed to a domain-aware system, can be somewhat detrimental to the precision of the results set; however, it constitutes the system adaptable to radically different content and allows its usage for educational objects of different domains.

We ran the information extraction system for each document in the three collections. The results are presented in Table 1.

Table 1. Amount of relations obtained from each document collection

Dataset	Retrieved Relations
Organic.Edunet	28,620
OER Commons Green	21,462
Organic Eprints	30,583

3.3   Alignment

We define the following cases for pairs of relation triples that are likely to have some semantic relevance between them:

- Relations triples with similar Rel fields but different Arg fields
- Relation triples with similar Arg fields but different Rel fields
- Relation triples with all three fields similar

At this version of the system, we use a pure linguistic approach for deciding on the similarity between the fields of a triple. First, the corresponding fields are stemmed and possible secondary terms (prepositions, auxiliary verbs etc.) are eliminated. Then, we retrieve the senses to which the resulted terms belong according to WordNet (http://wordnet.princeton.edu/). If the terms under comparison shared a common WordNet sense, we consider the terms similar. The notion of "sense" includes the case of synonyms and to some extend covers related terms, though domain-specific relations are not always discovered.

The next step is the calculation of a similarity score for each pair of documents from the educational repositories. The relations retrieved from each document are compared and a similarity score is generated for each document pair. The score is calculated following the formula

$$RelSim(d1, d2) = \sum_{i=1}^{N} \sum_{j=1}^{M} Comp(t_i, t_j)$$

where d1 and d2 are the compared documents and ti, tj are relation triples retrieved from d1 and d2 respectively. The function for determining the similarity between triples was straight-forward for this implementation of our method. We assigned a value of 1 when all fields were similar, a value of 0.66 when the argument fields were similar and a value of 0.33 when only the relation field was similar between the triples.

The aforementioned process produces a similarity score matrix for the examined documents. The document similarity scores are then transferred to the classification similarity by associating the documents with their already existing categorizations. Let C1 be a class of the first classification schema and C2 a class of the second classification schema. The system (a) locates the documents that are classified under C1 and those that are classified under C2, (b) retrieves the similarity scores of each pair constructed from these subsets of documents and (c) adds their similarity scores. Formally,

$$ClassSim(C1, C2) = \sum_{i=1}^{N} \sum_{j=1}^{M} RelSim(d_i, d_j)$$

where di is classified under C1 and dj is classified under C2. A bigger ClassSim score indicates a higher probability that C2 is a classification equivalent to C1.

4   Results

In this section we will present the results of the described system for two distinct matching tasks. The first run aimed to match the classification schema of OER Commons Green with that of Organic.Edunet. The second execution matched the classification schema of Organic Eprints against the Organic.Edunet schema. For each task, we provide the amount of similar relation tuples between the two document collections employed, the average RelSim scores produced. The results were compared to the manual matching between the used classification schemas.

4.1   Matching between Organic.Edunet and OER Commons Green

As mentioned, the REVERB system returned 28,620 relations for the Organic.Edunet document collection and 21,462 for the OER Commons Green document collection. The similarities on the relation tuple level are summarized in Table 2.

Table 2. Related relation tuples between the Organic.Edunet and OER Commons Green document collections

Relation Similarity Case	Total Amount	Average	Average RelSim
All fields similar	768	1.536	
Argument fields similar	2,167	4.334	9.285
Relation fields similar	7,407	14.814	

From the 19 subjects included in the OER Commons Green classification, 6 were deemed equivalent to the appropriate Organic.Edunet class. 7 of the subjects were associated with a class that should be its generalization as opposed to its equivalent. Finally, 6 of the OER Commons Green subjects were not matched to the most suitable Organic.Edunet class. In the latter case, the ClassSim score for the most appropriate was the third larger in the two worst cases and the second larger in the remaining four cases. Overall, the matching was semantically correct in 68.4% of the examined classes.

4.2   Matching between Organic.Edunet and Organic Eprints

The comparison of the 28,620 relations derived from Organic.Edunet and the 30,583 relations derived for Organic.Eprints produced the results presented in Table 3.

Table 3. Related relation tuples between the Organic.Edunet and Organic Eprints document collections

Relation Similarity Case	Total Amount	Average	Average RelSim
All fields similar	814	1.628	
Argument fields similar	2,416	4.832	9.042
Relation fields similar	6,402	12.804	

The Organic Eprints classification system includes 66 topics and subtopics. 13 of the subjects were associated with the appropriate Organic.Edunet class by the matching system. 32 were deemed equivalent to an Organic.Edunet class that is semantically their specialization or generalization, while 21 subjects were matched erroneously. Similarly to the Green OER Commons case, 68.1% of the classes were matched correctly with respect to their semantics.

5   Conclusions and Future Work

The preliminary results of our experiment indicate that there are adequate reasons to further investigate the described approach. However, there is significant work that needs to be done in order to improve on the system. The calculation of relation triple similarity seems to be the most detrimental aspect for the accuracy of the system. The simple textual analysis that was employed for determining similar fields in the triples does not produce a reliable response in all cases, as it is both imprecise and incomplete. Specifically, it seems that a common relation field is not a good indicator of a semantic association per se, so its contribution to the similarity score should be reduced. We will examine the use of external information, like the AgroVoc vocabulary (http://aims.fao.org/website/AGROVOC-Thesaurus/sub) for the specific use case, and more elaborate techniques like entity matching on the argument fields of the relations in order to improve the efficiency of this step. Furthermore, we will observe the impact of introducing domain knowledge on the precision of the information extraction process. The need to retain the open, domain-independent nature of the information extraction process is important to us; however, approaches like the ones proposed by [17] and [18] allow the unobtrusive inclusion of domain-specific information.

An important issue that has not been addressed adequately by the current method is distinguishing between equivalence and specialization relations between the compared classes. An important step is to combine our metrics with the existing structural information in the classification schemas so as to identify the exact type of association between two classes.

An interesting outcome from the examination of our results is that there is a significant amount of relations that deal with objects relevant to the domain but do not seem to be covered by the existing classifications. In the future, we will examine in more detail the abilities of our approach in terms of automatically enriching and populating the classification schemas of the repositories, leading to a more accurate and fine-grained description for the specific domain.

Acknowledgments. The research leading to these results has received funding from the European Union Seventh Frame-work Programme, in the context of the Sema-Grow (ICT-318497) project.

This paper also includes research results from work that has been funded with support of the European Commission, and more specifically the project CIP-ICT-PSP-270999 "Organic.Lingua: Demonstrating the potential of a multilingual Web portal for Sustainable Agricultural & Environmental Education" of the ICT Policy Support Programme (ICT PSP).

References

1. Kalfoglou, Y., Schorlemmer, M.: Ontology mapping: the state of the art. The Knowledge Engineering Review 18(1), 1–31 (2003)
2. Shvaiko, P., Euzenat, J.: A Survey of Schema-Based Matching Approaches. In: Spaccapietra, S. (ed.) Journal on Data Semantics IV. LNCS, vol. 3730, pp. 146–171. Springer, Heidelberg (2005)
3. Zimmermann, A., Krötzsch, M., Euzenat, J., Hitzler, P.: Formalizing ontology alignment and its operations with category theory. In: Proceedings of the 4th International Conference on Formal Ontology in Information Systems (FOIS), pp. 277–288 (2006)
4. Euzenat, J., Shvaiko, P.: Ontology Matching. Springer (2007)
5. Lambrix, P., Tan, H.: SAMBO – a system for aligning and merging biomedical ontologies. Journal of Web Semantics 49(1), 196–206 (2006)
6. Li, J., Tang, J., Li, Y., Luo, Q.: Rimom: A dynamic multistrategy ontology alignment framework. IEEE Transactions on Knowledge and Data Engineering 21(8), 1218–1232 (2009)
7. Melnik, S., Garcia-Molina, H., Rahm, E.: Similarity flooding: a versatile graph matching algorithm. In: Proceedings of the 18th International Conference on Data Engineering (ICDE), pp. 117–128 (2002)
8. Jean-Mary, Y.R., Shironoshita, E.P., Kabuka, M.R.: Ontology matching with semantic verification. Journal of Web Semantics 7(3), 235–251 (2009)
9. Jain, P., Hitzler, P., Sheth, A.P., Verma, K., Yeh, P.Z.: Ontology Alignment for Linked Open Data. In: Patel-Schneider, P.F., Pan, Y., Hitzler, P., Mika, P., Zhang, L., Pan, J.Z., Horrocks, I., Glimm, B. (eds.) ISWC 2010, Part I. LNCS, vol. 6496, pp. 402–417. Springer, Heidelberg (2010)

10. Palavitsinis, N., Manouselis, N.: A Survey of Knowledge Organization Systems in Environmental Sciences. In: Athanasiadis, I.N., Mitkas, P.A., Rizzoli, A.E., Marx-Gómez, J. (eds.) Proceedings of the 4th International ICSC Symposium on Information Technologies in Environmental Engineering. Springer, Heidelberg (2009)
11. Palavitsinis, N., Manouselis, N.: Agricultural Knowledge Organisation Systems: An Analysis of an Indicative Sample. In: Sicilia, M.-A. (ed.) Handbook of Metadata, Semantics and Ontologies. World Scientific Publishing Co. (in press)
12. Manouselis, N., Najjar, J., Kastrantas, K., Salokhe, G., Stracke, C.M., Duval, E.: Metadata interoperability in agricultural learning repositories: An analysis. Computers and Electronics in Agriculture 70(2), 302–320 (2010)
13. Manolis, N., Kastrantas, K., Manouselis, N.: Revisiting an Analysis of Agricultural Learning Repository Metadata: Preliminary Results. In: Dodero, J.M., Palomo-Duarte, M., Karampiperis, P. (eds.) MTSR 2012. CCIS, vol. 343, pp. 325–335. Springer, Heidelberg (2012)
14. Etzioni, O., Fader, A., Christensen, J., Soderland, S., Mausam.: Open Information Extraction: the Second Generation. In: International Joint Conference on Artificial Intelligence (2011)
15. Yates, A., Cafarella, M., Banko, M., Etzioni, O., Broadhead, M., Soderland, S.: TextRunner: Open Information Extraction on the Web. Computational Linguistics 42 (2007)
16. Downey, D., Etzioni, O., Soderland, S.: A probabilistic model of redundancy in information extraction. In: Proceedings of International Joint Conferences on Artificial Intelligence (IJCAI 2005), pp. 1034–1041 (2005)
17. Soderland, S., Roof, B., Qin, B., Xu, S., Mausam, Etzioni, O.: Adapting open information extraction to domain-specific relations. AI Magazine 31(3), 93–102 (2010)
18. Wu, F., Weld, D.S.: Open Information Extraction using Wikipedia. In: Proceedings of the 48th Annual Meeting of the Association for Computational Linguistics (ACL 2010), pp. 118–127 (2010)

The Use of Metadata in the Description of e-Learning Content for Organic Agriculture

Maria Toader[1], Gheorghe Valentin Roman[1], and Vassilis Protonotarios[2,3]

[1] University of Agronomic Sciences and Veterinary Medicine Bucharest
mirelatoadervali@yahoo.com, romangv@agro-bucuresti.ro
[2] Agro-Know Technologies, Athens, Greece
[3] Greek Research & Technology Network, Athens, Greece
vprot@agroknow.gr

Abstract. Currently there is a number of EU-funded projects that include the development of an agriculture-related training curriculum as one of their core activities, as well as an additional number of such projects that have already developed related content collections. However, in most cases, this content is not easily available through any mean of access, such as a portal, a course management platform or a website. This paper presents the development of the Organic.Balkanet training curriculum, describing the use of metadata for the annotation of the training material through the use of a course management platform. It also provides an overview on the issues that were met during the metadata annotation process, including the manual translation of these metadata in the languages of the project.

Keywords: Organic.Balkanet, e-learning, organic agriculture, vocational education, educational metadata, training curriculum, training scenarios, metadata issues.

1 Introduction

1.1 Vocational Education and Training in Organic Agriculture

The European Commission (EC) actively supports the vocational education and training (VET) activities and projects under the Leonardo da Vinci programme of the Lifelong Learning Program (LLP) [1]. During the last years, there have been a number of EU projects in this framework that aimed to contribute to the vocational training of stakeholders in the area of organic agriculture (OA), such as OA advisors and trainers, as well as agronomists who are involved in OA. In those countries whose competency certification and training systems are in an advanced stage of development, the training on offer already incorporates a competency-based approach, whereas in other countries this objective has yet to be achieved. In the case that an established system of competency standards is not available, then a competence-based training is more difficult to achieve despite the fact that a clear identification of competencies is required in most cases and is now considered as a

J.M. Dodero, M. Palomo-Duarte, P. Karampiperis (Eds.): MTSR 2012, CCIS 343, pp. 313–324, 2012.
© Springer-Verlag Berlin Heidelberg 2012

prerequisite. In this direction, the EC supports the integration of such standards for the development of harmonized training curricula and the precise identification of the competencies acquired during certified trainings related to organic agriculture, such as the European Qualifications Framework (EQF) [2]. Such standards are also used in other related sectors of training; for example the European water sector, by initiatives and projects also supported by the EC [3].

One of the aforementioned projects related to organic agriculture is the CerOrganic Development of Innovation LdV project (www.cerorganic.eu), which took place between 2009-2011 and focused on the development of a quality assurance methodology based on EU standards that should be applied to all related training events in order to achieve a common level of quality in the trainings and the ability to provide a certificate for that. In addition, during the application of the outcomes of this project, a prototype training curriculum was developed by the content providers of the project. As a validation of this curriculum and quality assurance methodology, a 7-day training school which applied this curriculum and methodology took place in the context of the project, including as trainees both project partners and external stakeholders.

Another example of these projects is Organic.Mednet (www.organic-mednet.eu), a 24-month Transfer of Innovation LdV project (2009-2011), which aimed to enhance the skills and knowledge of stakeholders from Mediterranean countries (such as Spain, Greece and Turkey) involved in the area of OA by providing them with new tools and methodology, as well as with updated information on OA. The project focused on the use of training scenarios as an alternative approach to the traditional training techniques, as well as the use of ICT tools in the training context [4].

1.2   The Contribution of the Organic.Balkanet Project

Organic.Balkanet (www.organic-balkanet.eu) was a 24-month EU project which started in December 2009 and successfully ended in December 2011, partially funded by the LdV LLP programme of the European Commission. The project consortium consisted of seven project partners coming from five countries (Romania, Slovenia, Bulgaria, Greece and Spain). The representation of these countries in the project aimed to facilitate the implementation and transfer of innovation, good practices and expertise among them. More specifically, the consortium included higher educational institutes (Agricultural Universities of Romania, Slovenia and Bulgaria), farmers' organizations (Association for Organic Agriculture Northeast of Slovenia and Biomold Association, Romania) as well as technical partners (Greek Research & Technology Network and University of Alcala - Information Engineering Research Unit). As a result, there was a close cooperation between research and academic organizations with expertise in learning technologies, enterprises that are active in rural areas and public bodies for the development and application of a training program for VET trainers of rural SMEs. With the combined actions of these organizations, the project aimed to meet the raising demands for OA trainers and familiarize them with new related ICT and training tools, in order to improve their knowledge and market competitiveness [5].

The project was based on the fact that despite the importance and rapid growth of OA in Europe, both in academic and professional level, in Balkan countries the uptake of OA practices and techniques is still developing. This is shown by a variety of data sources, such as the Organic Europe database [6]. One of the reasons that cause delays in these countries is the lack of a sufficient number of courses related to OA topics in both academic and vocational educational systems, which could potentially contribute to the education of OA-related professionals.

2   The Organic.Balkanet Training Curriculum

2.1   The Organic.Balkanet Training Curriculum Rationale

Vocational education and training (VET) opportunities are seen more and more as important instruments which in the medium to longer term are indispensable to contribute significantly to the management of present global crisis. They generate human capital with relevant skills and improve competiveness and adaption to new demands. Vocational education and training has a crucial role to play in Europe's efforts to raise the skills of its citizens [7].

The learning outcomes used in Organic.Balkanet courses were based on the definition used in the EQF. The proposed training course for acquiring the professional competences for Organic.Balkanet was based on the fact that "there is a necessity of new knowledge", on the requirements that the agricultural production should meet in order to be certified as "eco-produce", as well as on practical skills for implementation of "ecologically-friendly technologies". The application of the EU standards of training contributes to the achievement and recognition of professional competences and the transparence of qualifications of the end users of Organic.Balkanet project [8].

The profile of the Organic.Balkanet trainers was the following: a degree in agricultural sciences; basic knowledge in Agriculture/Organic Agriculture; 2 years field experience, practical skills and competences in Organic Agriculture; knowledge in agriculture sciences – agronomist. Based on the need analysis of knowledge and skills during the survey of farmers, specialists, managers and as a result of a wide discussion among the partners from the three end-users Balkans countries, Level 4 was proposed for organic advisors. Organic.Balkanet training are categorized in three groups: Competences related to management, production the use of Information & Communication Technologies (ICT) [8].

2.2   Development of the Organic.Balkanet Training Curriculum

The Organic.Balkanet project aimed to develop the skills of Organic Agriculture (OA) trainers in the Balkan countries by developing a training curriculum which consisted of a number of courses on the use of ICT tools and methodology for the training of OA trainers, advisors and other stakeholders.

As a first step, the user requirements for training agricultural professionals in the participating countries (Bulgaria, Romania and Slovenia), were identified in specialized workshops organized by each partner of the project, in order to identify the farmers' participation in each country. These requirements were collected, analyzed and used for the elaboration of specialized curricula, one for each participating country, which acted complementarily to a main core of training courses that were common for all partners, including the ones on ICT and methodology. Feedback on farmer's needs and production problems was part of each training course [5].The courses that focused on the integration of ICT in the training context included courses on metadata, focusing on their importance and usage, the use of web portals as means for retrieval of related resources and the use of a course management platform for organizing training content and delivering online courses.

The training curriculum developed by Organic.Balkanet was structured in eight (8) training modules (in the form of training scenarios), including topics on pedagogy/training methodology, the use of ICT tools and various topics on OA. For developing a complete training module, the trainers should include the basic three modules about pedagogy, technology and training and then include or develop the training modules on OA according to their interest [7]. In total, twenty-six (26) training units were developed by the project partners responsible for the content development. The topics included in the training curriculum of the Organic.Balkanet program were specialized according to the needs of each participating user organization and the competences that the Organic.Balkanet trainers should acquire [8]. The content was mainly available in the form of documents (such as handbooks, guides, basic literature etc.) and presentations and included a number of interactive sessions, which encouraged the active participation of the trainees. It was developed by the project partners assigned to this task according to their expertise, based on quality criteria and with the absolute responsibility of the author / owner. The OA and Agroecology content came exclusively from Balkan countries (Romania, Slovenia and Bulgaria) [9].

This content was further supported by additional related material coming from various sources, such us the institutional collections of the participating universities, the libraries of the farmers' associations as well as related material that was carefully selected according to its usefulness and quality from online sources. In general, the project provided the trainees not only with high quality and evaluated content in order to inform and educate farmers and advisors and improve the educational procedures that are followed by school and university teachers [9].

The training sessions for advisors combined the traditional teaching methods with self-paced learning based on the training resources that are published in the Organic.Balkanet version of the MOLE portal (http://ob.moleportal.eu), which will be described in the following section. The training curriculum followed a blended learning approach and combined traditional presentations and lectures, demonstrations with informal discussions and opportunities to try out new knowledge and skills in the field, such as case-study visits.

3   Course Management Platform and Metadata

3.1   Course Management Platform

After the Organic.Balkanet curriculum was prepared, each training unit was uploaded in a course management platform, which was an adapted version of the MOLE (Multimedia Open Learning Environment) portal. The MOLE portal (http://ob.moleportal.eu) enables the organization of courses in a curriculum using a user-friendly interface while at the same time providing detailed information about the course, the tutors. It also provides space for the uploading of supporting material, description of assignments and collection of reports, provides access to a wealth of communication tools at course level, such as private chat, forum and instant messages, all of which facilitate the communication between the trainer and the trainees as well as among the trainees [10].

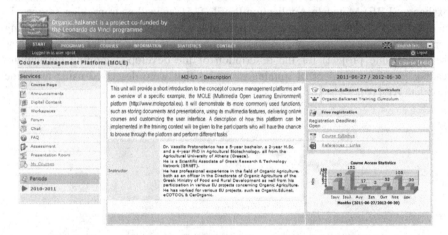

Fig. 1. A course page in the Organic.Balkanet version of the MOLE portal

The MOLE feature to record a presentation as a video file and then deliver the presentation/course at a different time, as well as the option to playback the slides and make a distance presentation to a remote audience were crucial for the deployment of the Organic.Balkanet courses, since the audience could consist of participants from different places, geographically remote, and their physical presence in e.g. a classroom where a face-to-face training would take place could not be achieved [10].

In addition, the MOLE portal provided an easy way for the translation of the user interface of the portal in additional languages, through the use of an online form. In this direction, and towards the localization of the portal in the user countries' languages (Bulgarian, Romanian and Slovenian), user partners were asked to provide the corresponding translations of the MOLE's user interface in their languages, in order to facilitate its usage by those who would feel more comfortable with a localized version of the platform. It is worth mentioning that in the case of training farmers, who in most cases were not speaking English, the localized version of the

portal along with the translated training material was used, showing the flexibility of
the Organic.Balkanet training curriculum.

3.2   Metadata

The Organic.Balkanet instance of the MOLE portal featured a metadata-editing
environment, which allowed the users to describe the material uploaded in their
course pages with metadata, for easier retrieval [11]. For the description of the
learning material, the Organic.Edunet metadata application profile (AP), an adapted
version of the IEEE LOM (Learning Object Metadata) AP was integrated in the
Organic.Balkanet instance of the MOLE portal and used by the project partners [12].
This AP has been developed during the Organic.Edunet eContentPlus project
(http://project.organic-edunet.eu), for the description of learning resources in the
context of organic agriculture and agroecology [13-14]. Apart from the LOM
vocabularies, the AP also contains vocabularies from the Learning Resource
Exchange (LRE) Metadata Application Profile [15], as well as from other sources, in
an effort to better meet the specific purpose of the description of agricultural learning
content. The same AP has been used by a number of other relevant initiatives (such as
the CerOrganic project) for the description of the developed training curriculum,
leading to a large number of training resources that were described using the same
metadata AP [16].

Fig. 2. The metadata editing interface of the MOLE portal

The selection of the specific AP was based on the fact that it was developed and
widely used by a closely related project for the description of agricultural learning
resources [17]. In addition, a number of the partners involved in the development of
this AP were also participating in the Organic.Balkanet project, providing direct
access to technical support. Last but not least, the metadata records would be exposed
through an OAI-PMH (Open Archives Initiative - Protocol for Metadata Harvesting)

target and would be harvested at a later stage by the Organic.Edunet Harvester, so to become available through the Organic.Edunet Web portal (www.organic-edunet.eu), as a part of its vocational education section. The Organic.Edunet Web portal is seamlessly connected to the Organic.Edunet AP and also provides a multilingual user interface as well as the option to display and retrieve multilingual metadata, including the languages of the Organic.Balkanet project [13], [18].

All training material that was uploaded in the Organic.Balkanet instance of the MOLE portal was first described in English and the native language of the user who uploaded the material (i.e. Bulgarian, Greek, Romanian & Slovenian) by completing the information for the mandatory elements of the Organic.Edunet metadata AP (Title, Description, Keywords, Language and Copyright/Cost), and in addition as much information as possible in the recommended metadata fields. The next step included additional translations of the metadata records, which were provided by the rest of the partners in the languages of the project (Bulgarian, Greek, Romanian and Slovenian). A handbook including step-by-step information about the annotation and translation process was developed in order to support the partners involved in this task and was translated in all languages of the project.

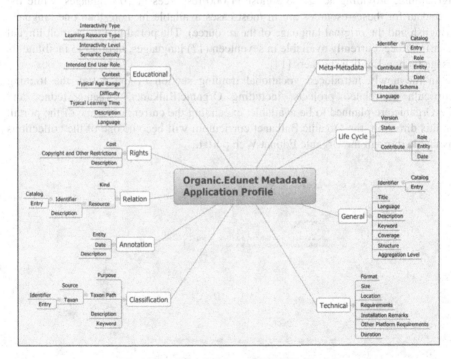

Fig. 3. The Organic.Edunet IEE LOM AP v2.0

The translation of these metadata records proved to be a time-consuming task, since domain experts had to be trained in the use of the metadata editing interface in order to provide the translation of domain-specific terms and work closely with the content providers and the metadata experts of each team, in order to ensure the correct translations of the metadata records. In addition, since the tool did not allow simultaneous access to a record from more than one user, a translation plan had to be made and followed by all partners so that each resource was only translated in one language at a time. Last but not least, the translation of the metadata proved to be error-prone, mostly due to the lack of fluent English-speaking domain experts, which caused errors in the translation from the native language to English. This resulted in delays, as the next domain expert assigned with the translation in another language of the project had to consult the previous expert and identify the exact term in English before he could proceed with the translation of the problematic term from English to his own native language.

3.3   The Organic.Balkanet Collection in the Organic.Edunet Web Portal

The metadata describing the Organic.Balkanet training curriculum will be exposed through the OAI-PMH target of the Organic.Balkanet instance of the MOLE platform and will be made available through the Organic.Edunet Web portal. The portal is considered as a single point of access to quality material related to organic agriculture, providing access to almost 11,000 resources in 10 languages, while the metadata for these resources are in most cases available in more than one language (English and the original language of the resource). The portal features a multilingual user interface, currently available in seventeen (17) languages, in order to facilitate its usage by non-English speakers [14].

In the newly introduced vocational training section of the portal, the training curricula of related projects, including Organic.Balkanet, Organic.Mednet and CerOrganic are planned to be available, expanding the current coverage of the portal. In this direction, the Organic.Balkanet curriculum will become one of the collections available through the Organic.Edunet Web portal.

Fig. 4. Display of metadata through the Organic.Edunet Web portal

The contribution of the Organic.Balkanet project to the Organic.Edunet Web portal is summarized in Table 1, which also provides a comparison with the current status of the content available through the portal.

Table 1. The contribution of the Organic.Balkanet collection in Organic.Edunet

	Number of resources	Content Languages	Metadata Languages	Metadata completeness
Organic.Edunet Web portal	11,000	10	10	≈ 80%
Organic.Balkanet collection	81	4	4	≈ 25%

As regards the completeness of the metadata records, the low percentage for the Organic.Balkanet collection could be partially explained due to the fact that the content providers/metadata editors of the consortium were only asked to provide information for the mandatory elements of the Organic.Edunet IEEE LOM AP, while they were also asked to provide any additional information in the recommended fields as well. Table 2 provides an indicative list of the completeness of specific metadata elements in the Organic.Balkanet collection, excluding the mandatory ones, which were completed in a high degree (reaching 100%).

Table 2. Metadata completeness in the Organic.Balkanet collection. Asterisk denotes the automatic completion of the element by the system.

Metadata element	Completeness
General.Identifier	81/81 (100%)*
Meta.Metadata	81/81 (100%)*
Technical.Location	81/81 (100%)*
Technical.Size	72/81 (88,9%)*
General.Coverage	67/81 (82,7%)
General.Structure	29/81 (35,8%)
LifeCycle.Version	3/81 (3,7%)
LifeCycle.Status	2/81 (2,5%)
LifeCycle.Contribute.Role/Entity/Date	2/81 (2,5%)

The data of the previous table shows that the only elements to be completed in all metadata records, apart from the mandatory ones, are the ones automatically completed by the system. In the rest of the cases, only two elements may be considered as completed (General.Coverage and General.Structure), while the completeness of the rest of the elements was in the best of the cases was less than 3%.

4 Discussion

During the two years of its operation, the Organic.Balkanet project followed a well-defined process in order to achieve its aims and objectives: An overview of the current status of the training initiatives and material in the context of organic agriculture was combined with the user needs analysis in each one of the participating countries in order to develop the training curriculum of the project and support it with quality material from public sources. The training curriculum was applied to a number of seminars in the participating countries, where a selected number of participants were trained so that they could also train in turn other OA advisors or farmers using the same or adapted curriculum and methodology. The results were more than encouraging, as the participants of the training events found both the methodology and the content to be proper for the specific purpose, and they adapted rather quickly to the use of the course management platform.

Despite the fact that the project was more content- than technologically-oriented, it used a number of tools, such as a course management platform, in order to support the blended learning approach of the training curriculum and at the same time to enable a distant delivery of courses, so that remotely located stakeholders could also participate in the trainings. In addition, in order for the training curriculum to reach a wider audience, the project described all digital training material with metadata using the Organic.Edunet AP, so that these metadata records could be exposed to a number of related portals, such as the Organic.Edunet Web portal, using the OAI-PMH functionality supported by the Organic.Balkanet instance of the MOLE portal. In addition, the metadata for each training material were manually translated in the languages of the participating countries, using the metadata editing interface of the MOLE portal. Even though the initial resources were adequately described with metadata by the project partners, at least regarding the mandatory elements, additional material uploaded to the course management platform by the trained participants was either incompletely or incorrectly described with metadata. A discussion with these trainers about this issue at a later stage showed that the importance of the metadata records for their resources was not clear to them. In addition, since this was their first experience with metadata, they also lacked the required experience to successfully complete this task, despite the fact that only a minimum number of metadata records were required.

Another metadata-related issue identified during the Organic.Balkanet project was the reluctance of the metadata editors of the project in providing information in the metadata elements other than the mandatory ones, which was identified through the analysis of the metadata completeness. This seems to be a more general issue, not focused in the Organic.Balkanet project, and may also be explained due to the fact that the annotation of the resources with metadata was not the primary focus of the content development tasks of the project and in addition the specific task was in several cases undertaken by people not experienced in the use of metadata. The solution to this issue is the enrichment and validation of the metadata records, a task currently in progress, which will enable the full and correct description of the actual resources and their exposure to a wider audience through the Organic.Edunet Web portal.

Additional issues that were identified in the annotation and translation of metadata records (such as the time needed and the possibility of errors in translations) are used as a basis for other EU projects, like the Organic.Lingua ICT-PSP project (www.organic-lingua.eu), which focus their efforts towards the achievement of high-quality automated translation of both metadata and documents in the agricultural sector. In the Organic.Lingua project, a consortium consisting of agronomists with experience in related efforts, metadata experts and technical partners are working together on the development and training of machine translation tools, using agricultural-related terminology and documents. The outcomes of this project will benefit projects similar to Organic.Balkanet, which use metadata and semantics not as the core of their activities, but as a tool for further exploitation and exposure of their outcomes. In this way, a significant amount of effort could be re-allocated from metadata-related tasks to more content-related activities, which belong to the core of such projects.

The main outcome of this was the interoperability achieved between two EU-funded projects, the LdV Organic.Balkanet and the eContentPlus Organic.Edunet. This interoperability was achieved through the use of the Organic.Edunet metadata AP for the annotation of the content developed by Organic.Balkanet, the use of a platform (Organic.Balkanet instance of MOLE) that supported the exposure of these metadata through an OAI-PMH target, so that these metadata records will eventually become available through the Organic.Edunet Web portal, contributing to the vocational training section of the portal. Similar efforts are expected to take place in the future as well, networking collections of educational and training material developed by other projects in the context of agriculture, agroecology and related green topics.

Acknowledgements. The work presented in this paper is funded with support by the European Commission, and more specifically the project CIP-ICT-PSP-270999 "Organic.Lingua: Demonstrating the potential of a multilingual Web portal for Sustainable Agricultural & Environmental Education" of the ICT Policy Support Programme (ICT PSP). This work was also supported by the Leonardo da Vinci project "Organic.Balkanet - Developing the skills of Organic Agriculture Trainers for the Balkans" of the European Commission, No 2009-1-RO1-LEO05-03584 LLP-LdV-TOI-2009-RO-008.

This publication reflects the views only of the authors, and the Commission cannot be held responsible for any use which may be made of the information contained therein. Authors thank all the consortium partners for their contribution in the design and realization of the requirements analysis.

References

1. European Commission: Education, Audiovisual and Culture Executive Agency, EACEA (2012),
   http://eacea.ec.europa.eu/llp/leonardo/
   leonardo_da_vinci_en.php
2. European Commission: European Qualifications Framework, EQF (2012),
   http://ec.europa.eu/education/
   lifelong-learning-policy/doc44_en.htm
3. Thanopoulos, C., Stracke, C., Rátky, É., Sgouropoulou, C.: Requirements for competence modelling in professional learning: experience from the water sector. Agrárinformatika/Agricultural Informatics 1(2), 42–57 (2010)

4. Wannop, C., Timmers, B., Sanchez-Alonso, S.: Training Scenarios Design. Organic.Mednet LdV EU project Deliverable D2.1 (2011)
5. Roman, G.V., Toader, M., Palavitsinis, N.: Organic.Balkanet project – a support for innovative training practices and e-learning content about organic agriculture in Balkan region. Scientific papers. Series A. Agronomy. USAMV Bucharest (2010)
6. Organic Europe: European section of the Organic World Website (2010), http://www.organic-europe.net
7. European Centre for the Development of Vocational Training (CEDEFOP): Continuity, consolidation and change Towards a European era of vocational education and training. CEDEFOP Reference series 73 Luxembourg: Office for Official Publications of the European Communities (2009) ISBN 978-92-896-0585-4
8. Roman, G.V., Toader, M.: Training Scenarios Design. Organic.Balkanet LdV EU project Deliverable D2.1 (2010)
9. Protonotarios, V., Palavitsinis, N., Papakonstantinou, K., Roman, G.V., Toader, M.: Identifying the Training Content Needs in Vocational Education & Training Projects: The Organic.Balkanet Case. In: EFITA/VOA3R 2011 Workshop on Open Access Agriculture & Aquaculture Repositories, Prague, Czech Republic, July 11-14 (2011)
10. Pappas, N., Arapi, P., Moumoutzis, N., Mylonakis, M., Christodoulakis, S.: The Multimedia Open Learning Environment (MOLE). In: EDEN Open Classroom 2011 Conference, Athens, Greece, October 27-29 (2011)
11. Mylonakis, M., Arapi, P., Pappas, N., Moumoutzis, N., Christodoulakis, S.: Metadata Management and Sharing in Multimedia Open Learning Environment (MOLE). In: García-Barriocanal, E., Cebeci, Z., Okur, M.C., Öztürk, A. (eds.) MTSR 2011. CCIS, vol. 240, pp. 275–286. Springer, Heidelberg (2011)
12. Institute of Electrical and Electronics Engineers (IEEE): Learning Object Metadata Standard (2002), http://ltsc.ieee.org/wg12/20020612-Final-LOM-Draft.html
13. Palavitsinis, N., Manouselis, N., Sanchez Alonso, S.: Evaluation of a Metadata Application Profile for Learning Resources on Organic Agriculture. In: Sartori, F., Sicilia, M.Á., Manouselis, N. (eds.) MTSR 2009. CCIS, vol. 46, pp. 270–281. Springer, Heidelberg (2009)
14. Palavitsinis, N., Ebner, H., Manouselis, N., Sanchez-Alonso, S.: Using e-learning technologies and standards to make educational content available: the Organic. Edunet approach. Journal of Information Technology in Agriculture 4(1) (2011)
15. Massart, D., Shulman, E.: Learning Resource Exchange Metadata Application Profile version 4.7. European Schoolnet, EUN (2011)
16. Manouselis, N., Najjar, J., Kastrantas, K., Salokhe, G., Stracke, C.M., Duval, E.: Metadata Interoperability in Agricultural Learning Repositories: An Analysis. Computers and Electronics in Agriculture, Special Issue on Information and Communication Technologies in Biological and Earth Sciences 70(2), 302–320 (2010)
17. Manolis, N., Kastrantas, K., Manouselis, N.: Revisiting an Analysis of Agricultural Learning Repository Metadata: Preliminary Results. In: Dodero, J.M., Palomo-Duarte, M., Karampiperis, P. (eds.) MTSR 2012. CCIS, vol. 343, pp. 325–335. Springer, Heidelberg (2012)
18. Palavitsinis, N., Manouselis, N., Sanchez-Alonso, S.: Metadata Quality in Learning Object Repositories: a Case Study. The Electronic Library, TEL (in press, 2012)
19. Palavitsinis, N., Ebner, H., Manouselis, N., Sanchez, S. and Naeve, A.: Evaluating Metadata Application Profiles Based on Usage Data. In Proc. of the International Conference on Digital Libraries and the Semantic Web (ICSD 2009), Trento, Italy, LNCS. Springer (2009)

Revisiting an Analysis of Agricultural Learning Repository Metadata: Preliminary Results

Nikos Manolis, Kostas Kastrantas, and Nikos Manouselis

Agro-Know Technologies, 17 Grammou St., 15235 Athens, Greece
{Manolisn,kkastrad}@agroknow.gr,
nikosm@ieee.org

Abstract. Agricultural learning repositories can provide new opportunities for sharing, searching, accessing and using learning resources. In order to facilitate the exchange of information between such repositories, the issue of metadata interoperability is crucial. In this paper, we present preliminary results of a revised analysis aiming at the review of implementations of metadata standards in agricultural learning repositories. The results of this study can be beneficial to the achievement of interoperability across agricultural learning repositories and useful for designers and developers in this application field.

Keywords: Learning repository, Application Profile, Metadata, Agriculture.

1   Introduction

The rapid evolution of Information and Communication Technologies (ICT) creates new opportunities for providing new services for education and training. Also, it is observed that the amount of digitally available learning resources is growing exponentially.

In order learning resources to be easily accessed, retrieved, used and reused they are very often organized in databases that are called learning repositories (LRs), which are systems for the storage, location and retrieval of the content. In LRs, resources are being described using appropriate metadata that helps the users to discover them online.

Regarding the agricultural domain a number of agricultural learning repositories (AgLR) have been developed and deployed during the last few years [10]. However, recent studies have indicated that the implementation of such systems in the agricultural domain is taking place in a widely dispersed manner [9], [10]. Therefore, metadata interoperability is a crucial issue that has to be addressed in order to facilitate the exchange of information between such repositories [7].

In this paper we revisit the analysis of agricultural learning repositories presented in [7]. Moreover, some new agricultural learning repositories and the applied metadata application profiles (APs) are analysed.

In a nutshell, the contribution of this paper lies in (a) testing the current status of the development and implementation of metadata application profiles studied in [7],

J.M. Dodero, M. Palomo-Duarte, P. Karampiperis (Eds.): MTSR 2012, CCIS 343, pp. 325–335, 2012.

(b) extending the set of the analysed AgLR systems, (c) checking the analysed APs for conformance against the base schema(s), identifying their weak points and proposing some solutions, (d) identifying the elements often used in most of the studied APs to provide an indication of the basic elements which all agricultural APs should include.

2   Related Studies

There have been several studies investigating the usage and the implementation of metadata application profiles in various learning repositories. Some studies focus on the learning repositories' users and usage [11] while other studies examine how learning repositories are deployed and implemented [12], [13].

Moreover, there are studies that focus on the way metadata APs are implemented in learning repositories of a particular domain and examine metadata interoperability. For instance, in [6] the most frequently used elements of 11 architecture repositories are identified and summarized into groups according to their usage. Moreover, authors of [5] examine the metadata elements sets used by 10 Canadian academic institutional repositories to describe their electronic theses and dissertations. Variations in metadata usage and associated issues related to interoperability across institutional repositories are being discussed. Metadata interoperability in institutional repositories has also been studied in [14]. Finally, AIMS team[1] has recently published a report[2] with a set of recommendations for the usage of common properties for describing bibliographic resources.

As regards related studies in the agricultural domain, [8] partially covers the implementations of metadata standards in AgLRs and in [9] two particular implementations of metadata APs in AgLRs have been compared. A more systematic analysis and comparison of the way metadata standards are implemented in AgLRs has been presented in [7]. More specifically, 9 AgLRs have been examined and 6 application profiles have been analyzed in depth. Finally, that work reports on the compliance of the developed APs with their base schemas and makes some initial recommendations regarding both the design and the implementation of such APs.

3   Analysis of AgLR APs

3.1   Methodology

This section provides an overview of the methodology that has been followed for the analysis of the AgLR APs. We have followed a set of principles and practicalities that have been defined by the Workshop on Learning Technologies (WS-LT) of the European Standardization Committee CEN [3]. Additionally, based on the guidelines and recommendations of CEN WS-LT [3] and Najjar et al [2], a number of analysis

---

[1] http://aims.fao.org/
[2] http://aims.fao.org/lode/bd

dimensions have been incorporated into an appropriate analysis tool. This aimed at supporting the analysis of the agricultural APs, through a template that has been developed as an Excel file that included the following components:

- An overall overview of the analysed AP, which includes general information (such as title, description, and producer), information about existing documentation (such as a conceptual model and data bindings), information about its scope and purpose (such as clear scope definition and use cases), and an overview of the results of the mapping of the AP into its base schema (particularly focusing on allowed and non-allowed modifications).
- A detailed mapping of the analysed AP onto its base schema(s), i.e. IEEE LOM [16], DC [17], or both.

We have followed this methodology to test the current status of the APs previously analysed in [7], namely: (i) FAO Agricultural Learning Resources AP, (ii) CGIAR LOM Core AP (CG LOM Core), (iii) BIAGRO LOM AP, (iv) Biosci Education Network (BEN) AP, (v) Sustainable Agriculture and Natural Resource Management Collaborative Research Support Program (SANREM CRSP) AP, (vi) Rural-eGov IEEE LOM AP (ReGov LOM). Since the previous analysis there have not been any changes regarding the metadata APs and consequently the same conclusions are still valid for the APs (i)-(v). The only case for which we have identified changes is ReGov LOM, that has been renamed as *Rural Inclusion Digital Training Object AP* and it is analyzed in the following section.

By following this methodology, we also aimed to analyse the applied metadata application profiles in the following agricultural repositories: (i) Organic.Balkanet MOLE, (ii) Organic.Mednet MOLE, (iii) CerOrganic MOLE, (iv) Digital Green, (v) ProdInra, (vi) OERAfrica, (vii) AbioDoc and (viii) GreenOER Commons. As regards the first 4 repositories in the previous list the applied application profile is the same, namely Organic Edunet AP.

Therefore, the set of the agricultural APs we have studied complementary to the analysis in [7] is comprised by: (i) Organic.Edunet, (ii) Rural Inclusion Digital Training Object (DTO), (iii) ProdInra, (iv) GreenOER Commons, (v) OER Africa, (vi) ABioDoc.

3.2   Analysis of Agricultural Application Profiles

3.2.1 Organic.Edunet
The Organic.Edunet AP is an IEEE-LOM based AP that has been designed and developed for describing learning resources related to Organic Agriculture and Agroecology. The Organic.Edunet AP is supported by the Organic.Edunet web portal[3] and the "Multimedia Open Learning Environment" educational web portal[4]. The

---

[3] http://portal.organic-edunet.eu/
[4] http://www.moleportal.eu/

Organic.Edunet AP has been published on 20 May 2009 in the context of the Organic.Edunet project.

Within its documentation the conceptual data model of the Organic.Edunet AP has been thoroughly presented. Additionally, a clear purpose statement of the Organic.Edunet AP and examples of usage are being provided within its documentation.

This application profile contains all elements from the IEEE LOM standard and it can be considered as a conforming IEEE LOM AP. Contrary to the IEEE LOM Standard where the use of all of its elements is optional the Organic.Edunet AP defines 29 mandatory elements. Regarding the value space of this AP, it adapts certain vocabularies and recommendations from the Learning Resource Exchange (LRE) Metadata AP[5] developed by the European Schoolnet (EUN) Consortium [2]. Overall, our analysis has shown that there have not been any non-allowed modifications.

3.2.2 Rural Inclusion Digital Training Object (DTO)

Rural Inclusion DTO AP is an IEEE LOM-based AP that has been developed to facilitate the description and categorization of learning resources that have been developed to support the training on rural and agricultural small and medium enterprises on topics related to the use of e-government.

Within its documentation basic information of the conceptual data model of the Rural Inclusion DTO AP has been presented. Also, no technical binding of the conceptual data model has been provided.

This application profile contains some of the IEEE LOM standard's elements. More specifically, from a total of 77 elements it uses 45 elements. Therefore, it can be considered as a subset AP of IEEE LOM.

Contrary to the IEEE LOM Standard where the use of all of its elements is optional this application profile defines 30 mandatory elements (from which 15 have default values). Additionally, it reduces the size of some elements to one, contrary to LOM that defines their size as multiple, e.g. *1.1:General.Identifier* and *1.4:General.Desctiption*. As regards the used value spaces, for some elements references to another standard have been used, e.g the value space of the element *8.2.1: Source* is defined from *NACE Codes of Economy Activity: Subject Categories Vocabulary* (while in LOM this is *ISO/IEC 10646-1:2000*).

This application profile has changed the datatype of the following elements: *1.3: General.Language, 4.1: Technical.Format* from 'CharString' to 'Vocabulary'. Also the datatype of the elements *3.4:Meta-metadata.Language, 9.2.1 :Classification.Source, 9.2.2.1:Classification.TaxonPath.Id, 9.2.2.2 :Classification.TaxonPath.Entry* has been changed from 'Langstring' to 'Vocabulary'. The last modification is non-allowed according to the CWA 1555 guidelines. It could be suggested to the developers of the AP to keep the datatype as 'LangString', and to provide as a recommendation to the implementers that they allow only the desired text values in the metadata input interface.

---

[5] http://lreforschools.eun.org/web/guest/metadata

3.2.3 ProdInra

ProdInra AP is applied in the bibliographic database listing the publications of INRA results of researchers in the areas of agriculture, food and environment.

The ProdInra AP contains elements from IEEE LOM standard and some additional local elements. In specific, from a total of 77 LOM elements it uses 35 elements and 4 elements have been added for storing language ISO codes. Therefore, it can be considered as a mixture of a *subset AP* and an *ad hoc AP* of IEEE LOM. Due to insufficient documentation, a further analysis of the AP was not possible.

3.2.4 GreenOER Commons

GreenOER Commons AP is dedicated to the description of environmental and sustainability-related open educational resources. This AP has been developed to support the description of resources in the OER Commons web portal[6].

Within its documentation the conceptual data model of this application profile has been presented. However, a clear purpose statement is not included. Also, no technical binding of the conceptual data model is being provided.

Green OER Commons AP is conformant to the simple DCMES and it defines 14 mandatory elements, namely *CR_Title, CR_URL, CR_Subject, CR_Material_Type, CR_Media_Formats, CR_Level, CR_Sub_Level, CR_Grade, CR_Typical_Age_Range, CR_Typical_Age_Range,   CR_Keywords,   CR_Institution,   CR_COU_URL, CR_COU_Description*. Overall, this application profile can be considered as a *subset AP*.

A vocabulary set has been defined for describing the elements *CR_Level, CR_SubLevel, CR_Grade, CR_Subject, CR_Media_Formats and CR_Material_Type*. However, this modification does not conform to the CWA 1555 guidelines since this value space is not referenced by any other known standard or specification nor they were published in a public namespace. It is suggested that the developers of the schema make their new value spaces available in a public namespace.

3.2.5 OER Africa

The OER Africa AP is an application profile that has been developed to support the description/annotation of open educational resources collected in the OER Africa web portal[7].

The OER Africa AP is conformant to the simple DCMES and it defines 11 elements. Therefore it can be considered as a *subset AP* of DCMES. No additional modifications have been made to the value space of the base schema. Due to insufficient documentation, further analysis as regards the obligation status of the elements was not possible.

3.2.6 ABioDoc

AbioDoc[8] is a National Resource Centre for Organic Agriculture that provides information and documentation concerning the technical, economic and regulatory aspects in organic farming and sustainable agriculture.

---

[6] www.oercommons.org/green/
[7] http://www.oerafrica.org/
[8] http://www.abiodoc.com/

The ABioDoc metadata application profile is conformant to the simple DCMES and it can be considered as a *subset AP* of DCMES. The ABioDoc AP defines 6 elements of DCMES, namely *Title, Subject, Creator, Description, Publisher, Contributor, Language, Identifier.* Due to insufficient documentation, a further analysis was not possible.

3.3   Outcomes

3.3.1   General Observations

Based on the analysis of which elements are selected from the base schema and following the method proposed in [2], we have concluded in the following classification of the analysed APs:

- Complete APs, two of them. These are Organic.Edunet and ProdInra.
- Subset APs, five of them. These are Rural Inclusion DTO, GreenOER Commons, OER Africa and ABioDoc.

Moreover, regarding the obligation of the elements in the examined sample:

- Two APs require more than 25 mandatory elements: Organic.Edunet (29), Rural Inclusion DTO (30).
- One AP requires less than 15 mandatory elements: Green OER Commons (14).

For ProdInra, OERAfrica and ABioDoc, information about the obligation status of elements was not available.

3.3.2   Elaboration of Mappings

An outcome of the analysis was the elaboration of mappings of all studied APs against the metadata standards they have been based on (either IEEE LOM or DCMES). An example of how these mappings have been carried out is presented in Table 1, where some of the LOM-based APs are mapped against the elements of the LOM standard. In a similar way, the DC-based APs were mapped against the DC element set.

The total number of APs we have studied is 12, including the 6 APs described in the section 3.2 and the following 6 APs analysed in [7]: (i) FAO Agricultural Learning Resources AP, (ii) CGIAR LOM Core AP (CG LOM Core) [15], (iii) BIAGRO LOM AP, (iv) Biosci Education Network (BEN) AP, (v) Sustainable Agriculture and Natural Resource Management Collaborative Research Support Program (SANREM CRSP) AP, (vi) Traglor AP.

Table 1. A sample of elements of LOM-based APs mapped to LOM standard's elements

IEEE LOM	Organic.Edunet AP		Rural Inclusion LOM	
1. General	**1. General**	M	**1. General**	M
1.1 Identifier	*1.1 Identifier*	M	*1.1 Identifier*	M
1.1.1 Catalog	*1.1.1 Catalog*	M	*1.1.1 Catalog*	M
1.1.2 Entry	*1.1.2 Entry*	M	*1.1.2 Entry*	M
1.2 Title	*1.2 Title*	M	*1.2 Title*	M
1.3 Language	*1.3 Language*	M	*1.3 Language*	M
1.4 Description	*1.4 Description*	M	*1.4 Description*	M
1.5 Keyword	*1.5 Keyword*	R	*1.5 Keyword*	O
1.6 Coverage	*1.6 Coverage*	R	*1.6 Coverage*	O
1.7 Structure	*1.7 Structure*	R	*1.7 Structure*	M
1.8 Aggregation Level	*1.8 Aggregation Level*	O	*1.8 Aggregation Level*	M

In order to conclude to some observations about the occurrence of elements in the examined agricultural APs, a number of steps have been followed:

i) We treated the set of IEEE LOM elements as the reference ones and mapped the elements of each individual AP upon them, either the AP is based on IEEE LOM or upon DCMES. In order to make the meta-mapping among a DC-based application profile to LOM we have followed the mapping proposed by the IEEE LOM standard[9]. Table 2 presents these meta-mappings for some DC-based APs.

ii) The number of times that a LOM element appears in the examined APs has been counted. This has been denoted as the metric *Count*.

iii) We have counted whether an element has been defined as mandatory, recommended or optional in an AP in order to give an indication of an element's importance. For this purpose we have used a metric denoted as *Weighted*: this weights the occurrence of an element depending on if it is mandatory (where it is weighted with 1.5), recommended (where it is weighted with 1), or optional (where it is weighted with 0.5). In case the AP does not define a particular obligation status, then its occurrence is weighted with 1.

Table 3 gives an overview of the results of this analysis. More specifically, for the IEEE LOM elements that appear in more than the half of the studied APs, it shows how many times exactly they appear and the gives the *Weighted* metric. The presentation of elements follows the IEEE LOM categorization of elements.

From this analysis the most interesting observations are the following:

• All the APs are using some element (*identifier*) to store information regarding the **identification of the resource**. In some cases (e.g in SANREM KB AP) this is only a URL.

• As far as the rest of the **general characteristics** of the resource are concerned, the following information is usually captured: i) Title, ii) Language, iii) Description, iv) Keyword, v) Coverage.

---

[9] http://ltsc.ieee.org/wg12/files/
LOM_1484_12_1_v1_Final_Draft.pdf

Table 2. A sample of elements of DC-based APs mapped to LOM standard's elements

DC METADATA ELEMENT SET		IEEE LOM	SANREM KB AP	OER Africa	GreenOER Commons
Element (dc:)	Qualifiers (dcterms:)				
Title		1.2:General.Title	Title		Title
	Alternative		Alternate title		
Identifier		1.1.2:General.Identifier. Entry	i)Identifier, ii) URL	Identifier	
Creator			Creator (author)	Creator	Author_Name
Subject		1.5:General.Keyword or 9:Classification with 9.1:Classification.Purpos e equals "Discipline" or "Idea"	i) Restricted keywords, ii) Unrestrictre d keywords		i) Subject, ii) Keywords
Descripti on		1.4:General.Description	Description	Descripti on	Description

- As far as the **life cycle** of the resource is concerned, the following information is usually stored: i) Role of the entities that have contributed to the resource, ii) Information about these entities, iii) Date of contribution/production/publication.
- As far as the **technical characteristics** of the resource are concerned, the following information is usually captured: i) Technical format, ii) Size, iii) Technical location, iv) Some technical requirements for its viewing/execution.
- As far as the **educational characteristics** of the resource are concerned, the following information is usually captured: i) Type of the learning resource, ii) Educational context/level, iii) Intended end user role.
- As far as the **copyrights of the resource** are concerned, the following information is usually captured: i) Cost, ii) Copyrights and restriction in use, iii) Description of use.
- As far as the **relationship characteristics** of the resource are concerned, the following information is usually captured: i) Description of the target learning object.

Table 3. Overview of the most common IEEE LOM elements in agricultural application profiles

Element	Category	Count	Weighted
1.1 Identifier	General	12	13.5
1.2 Title	General	11	15.5
1.3 Language	General	12	19
1.4 Description	General	12	16
1.5 Keyword	General	11	12
1.6 Coverage	General	7	5
2.3.1 Role	Life Cycle	12	8.5
2.3.2 Entity	Life Cycle	12	14.5
2.3.3 Date	Life Cycle	11	8.5
4.1 Format	Technical	11	12.5
4.2 Size	Technical	7	5
4.3 Location	Technical	7	7
4.6 Other Platform Requirements	Technical	7	4.5
5.2 Learning Resource Type	Educational	11	14.5
5.5 Intended End User Role	Educational	7	7.5
5.6 Context	Educational	7	8
6.1 Cost	Rights	7	9
6.2 Copyrigths and Other Restrictions	Rights	7	9.5
6.3 Description	Rights	10	10

Moreover, by taking under consideration the *Weighted* metric and by examining the elements for which the value of this metric is over 10 we conclude that the elements presented in Table 4 are the most important ones.

Table 4. Overview of the most important IEEE LOM elements in agricultural application profiles

Element	Category
1.1 Identifier	General
1.2 Title	General
1.3 Language	General
1.4 Description	General
1.5 Keyword	General
2.3.2 Entity	Life Cycle
4.1 Format	Technical
5.2 Learning Resource Type	Educational

4   Conclusions

In this paper, we present preliminary results of a revised analysis of existing implementations of metadata APs in agricultural learning repositories.

Apart from complying with the conformance rules of the base schemas, we aimed to identify elements often used in most of the studied agricultural application profiles and to rank their importance. The resulting element set could be used as an indication of the basic elements which all agricultural APs should include. However, these results would be more valuable if they were combined with empirical studies on how the elements are being populated in practice.

Moreover, the identification of well-accepted element sets is of great importance for building guidelines and recommendations for describing resources of a particular domain in order to enhance the quality of the interoperability and effectiveness of information exchange. Our future work focuses on complementing this study with such kind of recommendations for the agricultural domain.

Acknowledgements. This work is funded with the support by European Commission, and more specifically the FP7 project agINFRA "A data infrastructure to support agricultural scientific communities" (http://aginfra.eu/), which is funded by the schema "Combination of Collaborative Project and Coordination and Support Action: Integrated Infrastructure Initiative (I3)" under the work programme topic "INFRA-2011-1.2.2: data infrastructures for e-Science". This publication reflects the views only of the authors, and the Commission cannot be held responsible for any use which may be made of the information contained therein. The authors would like to thank all the consortium partners for their contribution in the analysis of the metadata used to describe agricultural data sources and collections.

References

1. Begg, I., Erhel, C., Mortensen, J.: Medium-term Employment Challenges. Centre for European Policy Studies Special Report (2010) ISBN: 978-92-9079-977-1

2. EUN Consortium. The EUN Learning Resource Exchange Metadata AP, version 3 (2007), `http://insight.eun.org/intern/shared/data/insight/lre/AppProfilev3p0.pdf` (retrieved)
3. CEN Workshop on Learning Technologies (CEN WSLT): CWA 15555:2006 Guidelines and Support for Building Application Profiles in E-Learning (2006), `ftp://ftp.cenorm.be/PUBLIC/CWAs/e-Europe/WS-LT/cwa15555-00-2006-Jun`
4. Najjar, J., Ternier, S., Duval, E.: Interoperability of Learning ObjectRepositories:Complications and Guidelines. IADIS International Journal of WWW/Internet (2004), `http://www.cs.kuleuven.ac.be/~najjar/papers/IadiswwwJournal.pdf`
5. Park, E.G., Richard, M.: Metadata assessment in e-theses and dissertations of Canadian institutional repositories. The Electronic Library 29(3), 394–407 (2011)
6. Park, E.G.: Building interoperable Canadian architecture collections: initial metadata assessment. The Electronic Library 25(2), 207–218 (2007)
7. Manouselis, N., Najjar, J., Kastrantas, K., Salokhe, G., Stracke, C.M., Duval, E.: Metadata interoperability in agricultural learning repositories: An analysis. Computers and Electronics in Agriculture 70(2), 302–320 (2010)
8. Tzikopoulos, A., Manouselis, N., Costopoulou, C., Yialouris, C.P., Sideridis, A.B.: "Investigating Digital Learning Repositories" Coverage of Agriculture-related Topics". In: Proc. of the International Congress on Information Technologies in Agriculture, Food and Environment (ITAFE 2005), Adana, Turkey (October 2005)
9. Manouselis, N., Salokhe, G. (eds.): Agricultural Learning Repositories (AgLR 2008) EConference: Summary Report, Agricultural Learning Repositories Task Force (AgLR-TF) (June 2008), `http://aglr.aua.gr/files/AgLR2008.pdf`
10. Manouselis, N., Salokhe, G., Keizer, J.: Comparing Different Metadata Application Profiles for Agricultural Learning Repositories. In: Sicilia, M.-A., Lytras, M. (eds.) Metadata and Semantics, Metadata and Semantics, pp. 469–479. Springer (January 2009) ISBN-978-0-387-77744-3
11. Najjar, J., Ternier, S., Duval, E.: The actual use of metadata in ARIADNE: an empirical analysis. In: Proceedings of the 3rd Annual Ariadne Conference, pp. 1–6
12. Tzikopoulos, A., Manouselis, N., Vuorikari, R.: An Overview of Learning Object Repositories. In: Northrup, P. (ed.) Learning Objects for Instruction: Design and Evaluation, pp. 29–55. Idea Group Inc., New York (2007)
13. Ochoa, X., Duval, E.: Quantitative Analysis of Learning Object Repositories. In: Luca, J., Weippl, E. (eds.) Proceedings of World Conference on Educational Multimedia, Hypermedia and Telecommunications 2008 (2008)
14. Bueno-de-la-Fuente, G., Hernández-Pérez, T., Rodríguez-Mateos, D., Méndez-Rodríguez, E.M., Martín-Galán, B.: Study on the use of metadata for digital learning objects in institutional university repositories (MODERI). Cataloging and Classification, Special Issue on Metadata and Repositories 47(3/4), 262–285 (2009)
15. Zschocke, T., Beniest, J., Paisley, C., Najjar, J., Duval, E.: The LOM application profile for agricultural learning resources of the CGIAR. Int. J. Metadata, Semantics and Ontologies 4, 13–23 (2009)
16. IEEE LOM, Draft Standard for Learning Object Metadata. IEEE Learning Technology Standards Committee, IEEE 1484.12.1-2002 (July 15, 2002), `http://ltsc.ieee.org/wg12/files/LOM_1484_12_1_v1_Final_Draft.pdf`
17. Dublin Core Metadata Element Set, Version 1.1: Reference Description (2004), `http://dublincore.org/documents/2004/12/20/dces/`

The CEREALAB Database:
Ongoing Research and Future Challenges

Domenico Beneventano[1], Sonia Bergamaschi[2], Abdul Rahman Dannaoui[1,2],
Justyna Milc[2], Nicola Pecchioni[2], and Serena Sorrentino[1]

[1] Department of Engineering "Enzo Ferrari" - via Vignolese 905, 41125 - Modena
[2] Department of Life Sciences, via Giuseppe Campi 287, 41125 - Modena
University of Modena and Reggio Emilia - Italy
`firstname.lastname@unimore.it`

Abstract. The objective of the CEREALAB database is to help the breeders in choosing molecular markers associated to the most important traits. Phenotypic and genotypic data obtained from the integration of open source databases with the data obtained by the CEREALAB project are made available to the users. The first version of the CEREALAB database has been extensively used within the frame of the CEREALAB project. This paper presents the main achievements and the ongoing research related to the CEREALAB database. First, as a result of the extensive use of the CEREALAB database, several extensions and improvements to the web application user interface were introduced. Second, always derived from end-user needs, the notion of provenance was introduced and partially implemented in the context of the CEREALAB database. Third, we describe some preliminary ideas to annotate the CEREALAB database and to publish it in the Linking Open Data network.

1 Introduction

The CEREALAB database [14] is a tool realized to help the breeders in choosing molecular markers associated to the most important economically phenotypic traits. The CEREALAB database can help breeders and geneticists to unravel the genetics of economically important phenotypic traits, to identify and to choose molecular markers associated to key traits, and finally to choose the desired parentals for breeding programs. The CEREALAB database development was one of the objectives of the CEREALAB projects and of the BIOGEST-SITEIA laboratory[1] funded by Emilia-Romagna (Italy) regional government, aiming to increase the competitiveness of Regional seed companies through the use of modern selection technologies such as the Marker-Assisted Selection (MAS).

The key feature of the CEREALAB database is that phenotypic and genotypic data are obtained from the integration of open source databases with the data obtained by the CEREALAB project. Data integration is obtained by using the MOMIS[2] system (Mediator envirOnment for Multiple Information Sources), a framework to perform integration of structured and semi-structured data sources [2,5]. MOMIS is characterized

---

[1] `www.biogest-siteia.unimore.it`
[2] `http://www.dbgroup.unimore.it/Momis/`

J.M. Dodero, M. Palomo-Duarte, P. Karampiperis (Eds.): MTSR 2012, CCIS 343, pp. 336–341, 2012.
© Springer-Verlag Berlin Heidelberg 2012

by a classical wrapper/mediator architecture: the local data sources contain the real data, while a Global Schema (GS) provides a *reconciled, integrated, read-only view* of the underlying sources. The GS and the mappings between the GS and the local sources are semi-automatically defined at design time by the Integration Designer component of the system [2]. After GS creation end-users can pose queries over this GS in a transparent way w.r.t. the local sources. An open source version of the MOMIS system is delivered and maintained by the academic spin-off DataRiver[3].

As a result of the extensive use of the first version of the CEREALAB database (which was accessible through a Java Web Start Application) within the frame of the CEREALAB project, several extensions and improvements to the graphical user interface were introduced (see Section 2). In Section 3 we present the ongoing research on the design and development of a Provenance Management component, PM_{MOMIS}, for the MOMIS System. PM_{MOMIS} functionalities have been studied and partially implemented in the domain of genotypic and phenotypic cereal-data management within the CEREALAB Database. In Section 4, we describe some preliminary ideas to annotate the CEREALAB database (in particular w.r.t. agricultural ontologies, such as AGROVOC[4]) and to publish it in the Linking Open Data network.

2 A Web-Based GUI for the CEREALAB Database

In the first version of the CEREALAB database, a Graphical User Interface (GUI) was available as a Java Web Start application [14]. A significant extension to this first version, derived from real needs of the end-user, was the development of a web-based, user-friendly GUI, in order to improve and simplify the access to the database (www.cerealab.org). New functionalities and additional tools were realized for better accessibility of the available information. The achieved extensions identify a second phase of the research activity focused on the construction of the CEREALAB database. Such improvements led to the release of its v 2.0, that is being published [10].

The new GUI, realized using the PHP programming language, gives to the final user the possibility to perform a simple/complex query, browse the data and save the final result. The interface is very user-friendly and contains a guideline on how to use each of the sections and the meaning of each value presented in the forms to help users in formulating queries and analysing the results. The results are given as simple structured reports containing information about the searched object (Gene, Marker, Germplasm, etc.) that can be exported by the final users on their local machine. The requirements of the new GUI were mainly derived from the experience in the use of the database in the CEREALAB project and from the interviews/feedbacks with its industrial partners, breeders and private seed companies.

Another extension to the first version, was the development of a data entry module, implemented for the CEREALAB local source, in order to give to the CEREALAB project members the possibility to insert the new data resulting from new experiments. With the virtual approach offered by MOMIS system, the new inserted data are immediately available at the level of the CEREALAB database; in fact, queries are executed

---

[3] http://www.datariver.it

[4] http://aims.fao.org/standards/agrovoc/about

directly on the data sources that are integrated in the CEREALAB database, thus providing always up-to-date information. Finally, end-user feedbacks were taken into account also for a tuning of the Global Schema: some global classes, automatically generated in the integration phase, were modified by the integration designer; in particular, some global classes omitted in the initial integration phase were added to the Global Schema.

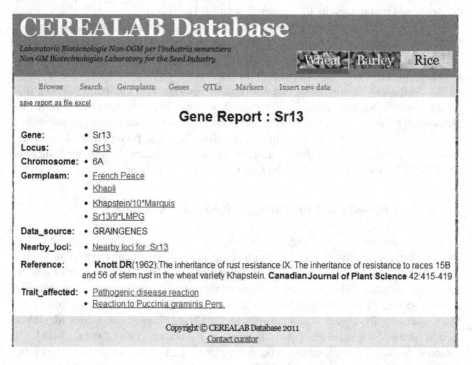

Fig. 1. Structured report with all available information present in the database for the Sr13 Gene of resistance to a wheat pathology. Each report contains results that can be queried singularly to obtain more detailed informations, and each report can be saved as MS Excel file.

3   Provenance of Cereal Genotypic and Phenotypic Data

A requirement emerging from CEREALAB database users was that in many cases they would prefer to give a look at the data coming from the local sources, i.e. they need *provenance*. *Lineage*, or *provenance*, in its most general definition, describes where data came from, how it was derived and how it was modified over time. Lineage provides valuable information that can be exploited for many purposes, ranging from simple statistical resumes presented to the end-user to more complex applications, such as, managing data uncertainty or identifying and correcting data errors.

In [4], we discussed the ongoing effort on the design and development of a Provenance Management component, PM$_{MOMIS}$, for the MOMIS System; PM$_{MOMIS}$ provides the provenance management techniques supported by the most relevant data provenance systems, the *Perm* [11] and *Trio* [1]. systems and extends them by including the data fusion and conflict resolution techniques provided by MOMIS. PM_{MOMIS} functionalities have been studied and partially implemented in the domain of genotypic and phenotypic cereal-data management within the CEREALAB project.

In [3] we introduced the notion of provenance into MOMIS, by defining the provenance for the *full outerjoin-merge operator*; this definition is based on the concept of *PI-CS*-provenance (Perm Influence Contribution Semantics) proposed in *Perm* (Provenance Extension of the Relational Model) [11] to produce more precise provenance information for outerjoins. Another important reason behind the choice of using the *PI-CS*-provenance, was that it is fully implemented in an open-source provenance management system that is capable of computing, storing and querying provenance for relational databases. At present, we are using the *Perm* system as the SQL engine of MOMIS, so that to obtain the provenance in our CEREALAB Application. The main problems we foresee in transferring existing solutions developed for provenance in data warehouse systems to our context is the presence of particular operators, such as outerjoins and complex resolution functions.

The need to support detailed data provenance is one of the main requirements of biological data management identified in [12]. Our focus is the provenance in a context of data fusion which involves the resolution of possible conflicts among data, a crucial aspects when integrating a large number of independent data set. In [4] we showed how the provenance is a useful metadata to query conflicting data, by providing the user with different *search strategies* for querying the Global Integrated Schema.

4   Annotate CEREALAB for Linking Open Data

The *Linked Open Data* (LOD) project is a community effort (founded by the W3C Semantic Web Education and Outreach (SWEO) group[5]) which aims to extend the Web with data by publishing various open data sets as RDF on the Web and by setting RDF links between data items from different data sources[8]. Nowadays, LOD includes more than 300 data sets from different domains of knowledge: among them, we recall general domain data sets like Wikipedia[6] and WordNet[7], and agriculture data sets like AGROVOC[8] and NALT[9]. The great majority of agricultural resources is typically accessed only by closed communities and even when they are make available on the Web, they look more as a sets of disconnected information units than as an integrated information space [15]. As a consequence, our goal is to publish and link CEREALAB to the LOD cloud in order to facilitate breeders and geneticists in searching and exploiting linked agricultural resources.

However, even if the LOD community is constantly growing, there is still a few applications making use of its data sets. This is mainly due to the reasons that links

---

[5] http://www.w3.org/wiki/SweoIG/TaskForces/
CommunityProjects/LinkingOpenData
[6] http://it.wikipedia.org/
[7] http://wordnet.princeton.edu/
[8] http://aims.fao.org/standards/agrovoc/about
[9] http://agclass.nal.usda.gov/

between LOD data sets are almost exclusively on the instance level, while schema level information is almost ignored [13]. Moreover, integrating LOD data sets from different organizations can yield high value information [9]; in particular, schema-level integration of LOD data sets is an issue which has been pointed out in [8] as a core challenge. In this context, "semantic annotation", i.e. the explicit association of the "meaning" to a schema element with respect to reference knowledge sources is a key tool; in particular, starting from semantic annotations, it is possible to discover schema mappings, i.e. semantic correspondences at the schema-level.

To publish and annotate CEREALAB in the LOD network, first of all, we need to translate the relational CEREALAB database into an RDF database (this process is called *RDF-ization* [16]). Secondly, to annotate the CEREALAB schema with respect to a reference knowledge source, we analyzed the database element names, and we compared two main ontologies in the agricultural domain: AGROVOC and the Plant Ontology[10]. We decided to use AGROVOC as it covers the great majority of the CERE-LAB names (indicatively a 80%) while the Plant Ontology only contains the 60% of the names. However, CEREALAB also contains several names that are not specific of the agricultural domain and thus are not present in both the ontologies (e.g. "index" and "ratio"). For these terms, we decided to employ in association with AGROVOC the WordNet general domain thesaurus. Since WordNet terms may have more than one possible meaning (e.g., the term "index" may mean a numerical scale or the finger next to the thumb), a Word Sense Disambiguation algorithm is needed; we are using our CWSD (Combined Word Sense Disambiguation) algorithm [7]; however, other WSD algorithms might be applied. The main problem we foresee in the application of WSD algorithms to our context is the presence in CEREALAB of several compound names (i.e., names composed by more than one term, e.g., "Septoria Tritici"). To annotate these names we could employ the normalization tool described in [17] which allows to annotate compound names by considering the whole meaning of its constituent terms.

Finally, we need to link the RDF CEREALAB data set to the other LOD resources in the agriculture domain (as AGROVOC itself and NALT). To semi-automatically perform this step, we might exploit the instance mapping techniques implemented in the RELEVANT approach and described in [6].

5 Conclusion and Future Work

This paper presented the main achievements and the ongoing research (web-based GUI, Provenance and Annotation for Linking Open Data) related to the CEREALAB database. As future works provenance and annotation will be used to enrich the GUI functionalities; in particular, the use of semantic annotation techniques might help users in querying CEREALAB through the GUI. In particular, we can associate each GUI label with a description about its meaning and with is-a relationships with other terms, thus helping also less skilled users to understand the meaning of the specific agricultural terms used in the CEREALAB database.

---

[10] http://www.plantontology.org/

Acknowledgements. This work is partially supported by the BIOGEST-SITEIA laboratory (www.biogest-siteia.unimore.it), funded by Emilia-Romagna (Italy) regional government.

References

1. Agrawal, P., Benjelloun, O., Sarma, A.D., Hayworth, C., Nabar, S., Sugihara, T., Widom, J.: Trio: a system for data, uncertainty, and lineage. In: VLDB 2006, pp. 1151–1154 (2006)
2. Beneventano, D., Bergamaschi, S., Guerra, F., Vincini, M.: Synthesizing an integrated ontology. IEEE Internet Computing 7(5), 42–51 (2003)
3. Beneventano, D., Dannaoui, A.R., Sala, A.: Data lineage in the momis data fusion system. In: ICDE-Workshops, Hannover, Germany, April 11-16, pp. 53–58 (2011)
4. Beneventano, D., Dannoui, A.R., Sala, A.: Integration and provenance of cereals genotypic and phenotypic data. In: SEBD 2011, Proceedings of the 20th Italian Symposium on Advanced Database Systems, Venice, Italy, June 24-27, pp. 84–94 (2012); poster presented at the Data Integration in the Life Sciences Conference, June 28-29, Maryland (2012)
5. Bergamaschi, S., Beneventano, D., Guerra, F., Orsini, M.: Data integration. In: Handbook of Conceptual Modeling: Theory, Practice and Research Challenges. Springer (2011)
6. Bergamaschi, S., Guerra, F., Orsini, M., Sartori, C., Vincini, M.: A semantic approach to etl technologies. Data Knowl. Eng. 70(8), 717–731 (2011)
7. Bergamaschi, S., Po, L., Sorrentino, S.: Automatic Annotation in Data Integration Systems. In: Meersman, R., Tari, Z., Herrero, P. (eds.) OTM-WS 2007, Part I. LNCS, vol. 4805, pp. 27–28. Springer, Heidelberg (2007)
8. Bizer, C., Heath, T., Berners-Lee, T.: Linked data - the story so far. Int. J. Semantic Web Inf. Syst. 5(3), 1–22 (2009)
9. Coletta, R., Castanier, E., Valduriez, P., Frisch, C., Ngo, D., Bellahsene, Z.: Public data integration with websmatch. CoRR abs/1205.2555 (2012)
10. Dannaoui, A.R., Sala, A., Beneventano, D., Milc, J., Caffagni, A., Pecchioni, N.: Release of the cerealab database v 2.0. submitted to DATABASE (2012)
11. Glavic, B., Alonso, G.: Perm: Processing provenance and data on the same data model through query rewriting. In: ICDE 2009, pp. 174–185 (2009)
12. Jagadish, H.V., Olken, F.: Database management for life sciences research. SIGMOD Rec. 33, 15–20 (2004), http://doi.acm.org/10.1145/1024694.1024697
13. Jain, P., Hitzler, P., Sheth, A.P., Verma, K., Yeh, P.Z.: Ontology Alignment for Linked Open Data. In: Patel-Schneider, P.F., Pan, Y., Hitzler, P., Mika, P., Zhang, L., Pan, J.Z., Horrocks, I., Glimm, B. (eds.) ISWC 2010, Part I. LNCS, vol. 6496, pp. 402–417. Springer, Heidelberg (2010)
14. Milc, J., Sala, A., Bergamaschi, S., Pecchioni, N.: A genotypic and phenotypic information source for marker-assisted selection of cereals: the cerealab database. Database (2011)
15. Nešić, S., Rizzoli, A.E., Athanasiadis, I.N.: Publishing and Linking Semantically Annotated Agro-environmental Resources to LOD with AGROPub. In: García-Barriocanal, E., Cebeci, Z., Okur, M.C., Öztürk, A. (eds.) MTSR 2011. CCIS, vol. 240, pp. 478–488. Springer, Heidelberg (2011)
16. Nolin, M.A., Corbeil, J., Lamontagne, L., Dumontier, M.: Bio2rdf: Convert, provide and reuse. In: Biocuration Meeting 2010, Tokyo, Japan (October 11, 2010)
17. Sorrentino, S., Bergamaschi, S., Gawinecki, M.: NORMS: An automatic tool to perform schema label normalization. In: Abiteboul, S., Böhm, K., Koch, C., Tan, K.L. (eds.) ICDE, pp. 1344–1347. IEEE Computer Society (2011)

Consortium for e-Resources in Agriculture – An Effective Tool for the Agriculture Researchers: A Case Study

Maltesh Motebennur

Librarian, Rajiv Gandhi University, Rono-Hills, Itanagar, Aruanchal Pradesh, India
maltesh.motebennur@gmail.com

Abstract. The present paper highlights the CeRA (Consortium for e-resources in Agriculture) which is an ambitious initiative from IARI (Indian Agriculture Research Institute) aiming to provide scholarly information in the broad spectrum of Agricultural Sciences to foster academic quality research amongst its institutes and other Agricultural Universities. Group of more than 280 students who opted the course Library and Information Services PGS-501 (Post Graduate Studies-Course 501) were interviewed with short structured questionnaire and analyses was done on the effective tool for the Agricultural Researchers on the CeRA. It is a case study, the outcome and findings are very positive and effective. The subject disciplines covered under CeRA are broad to cover. There by meet the academic and research needs of faculty, research scholars and students across these disciplines.

Keywords: CeRA, Consortium, e-resources, Research, National Agricultural Innovation Project, Indian Agricultural Research Institute.

1 Introduction

As a part of the initiative in creating user awareness programme for UASD on CeRA awareness training w a s organised in the University Library of Agricultural Sciences, Dharwad on November 8, 2010. The programme had an overwhelming response from faculty members of various disciplines. More than 200 post graduate students, and research scholars attended and benefited by the programme. "Information is a powerful tool for the development of society". It is a valuable commodity required for the planning, directing, controlling, decision-making, motivating, forecasting, research and development activities to ensure productive and gainful operation [2].

Across all civilizations oral communication has been an integral part of people in interaction. With the advancement of science and technology, the process of communication has expanded over the years to cover print and other modes like computer, mobile phone and associated gadgets. India is predominantly an agrarian country, and the growth of agriculture is reflected in the good yields of different crops that depend on various factors-natural and man-made. Agricultural research,

J.M. Dodero, M. Palomo-Duarte, P. Karampiperis (Eds.): MTSR 2012, CCIS 343, pp. 342–347, 2012.
© Springer-Verlag Berlin Heidelberg 2012

the backbone of agricultural growth in the country, demands timely dissemination of knowledge being generated and updated across the globe from time to time. Research and Development institutions have been procuring print versions of journals and literature in aid of science and technology.

With the rapid growth of internet facilities and advancement of web technology, almost all reputed international journals are available on- line and can easily be accessed by researchers over the network. Since Indian Council of Agriculture Research (ICAR) is having network connectivity across institutes and state agricultural universities, selected journals are available over the network for the use of scientific community. Accordingly, the (NAIP) National Agricultural Innovation Project has funded for establishing the Consortium for e-Resources in Agriculture (CeRA) at the Indian Agricultural Research Institute (IARI), Delhi in November 2007. Duration of the project is five years, from 2007-08 to 2011-12. Total cost of the project is Rs. 938.542 lakhs, to facilitate accessibility of scientific journals to all researchers/teachers in the National Agricultural research system by providing access to information specially through online journals which is crucial for having excellence in research.

In India there are many similar consortia such as UGC-INFONET (University Grants Commission- Information Network), Ahmadabad, INDEST (Indian National Digital Library in Engineering Science and Technology), Delhi. With resource crunch and escalation of prices of e-resource it is very difficult to start any consortium in India. Despite the constraints, the consortiums mentioned above are doing very well.

UASD's CeRA can be accessed via the World Wide Web directly linked to the end users' through UASD's website at www.uasd.edu. Commercial search engines can also guide to access CeRA in the campus. Now Wi-Fi (Wireless Fidelity) connectivity facilitates to access CeRA, even in the hostels, canteens and departments. UASD is a member of the NAIP and Networked Digital Library of CeRA consortium, which is at the forefront of the digital library movement. The CeRA usage is aimed at improving post graduate education by ensuring that students learn about publication issues and about using digital libraries. At the same time, the e-journal full text is helping to develop an important digital library that ultimately will include millions of full-text or even hyper thermal documents. Researchers can search and browse more than 2000 CeRA Collection, as well as the full text or abstract or pdf or html format, through on-line 24X 7 availability It enhances increased level of scientific activity/output.

1.1   Objectives of CeRA

  ➢ To expand the existing R & D information resource base of ICAR
    Institutions/Universities, etc., comparable to leading institutions/organizations
    of the world.
  ➢ To nucleate e-access culture among scientists/teachers in ICAR Institutes
    /Agricultural Universities.

- Development of Science Citation Index Facility at IARI for evaluation of scientific publications.
- Impact analysis of CeRA based on the level of research publications measured through SCI.
- Constitution of National Steering Committee comprising members from select beneficiary institutions/disciplines under the Chairmanship of the Director, IARI.
- IARI, New Delhi will be the co-ordination unit of the Consortium.
- Access to E-Resources will be given to 126 libraries (All SAUs and select libraries of ICAR) in the first place.
- Negotiations with publishers will be made by the E-Journal Consortium Negotiation Committee constituted by the O&MPC for procurement of various e-resources.
- The publishers provide direct access for all selected journals subscribed to the user libraries.
- Arrangements will be made for sending the reprints / documents which is not available on line by cost after downloading the same at IARI.
- Organize awareness programmes (workshops/trainings) from time to time for Scientists, Research scholars and others
- Monitor and compile usage reports
- Carry out impact analysis of CeRA on scientific output.

1.1.1 Expected Output/ Impact/ Deliverables
- Establishment of CeRA Co-ordination cell.
- Installation and commissioning of a dedicated server for consortium.
- On-line availability of e- journals & e-resources 24 x 7.
- Increased level of scientific activity/output.
- Enhanced scientific temper and competence of scientific staff.

Fig. 1. Print screen of CeRA main menu

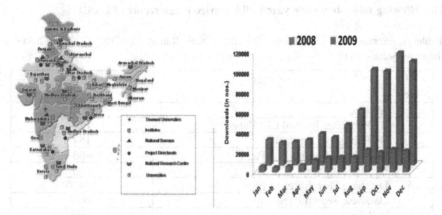

Fig. 2. Map showing institutions NARS availing CeRA facility. (Source: [1])

Fig. 3. Graph shows scientific articles downloaded in CeRA during 2008-2009 (Source: [1])

2   Methodology

This preliminary study concentrates on the CeRA service usage by the PG, research students, faculty members and scientists in the UASD. The research method used in this study is the structured short questionnaire served to two hundred eighty post graduate and research students in the class PGS 501 Library and Information Services and during one day awareness programme of JCCC@CeRA (J-Gate Custom Content for Consortium). It is basically users' study. In the short structure questionnaire, main focus was emphasized on how CeRA consortium can be an effective research tool.

2.1   Analysis of Short Questionnaire

A short questionnaire was designed to prove CeRA as an effective and comprehensive scientific research tool. Around two hundred eighty post graduates and research students were personally interviewed by using short structured questionnaire in the class PGS 501 Library and Information Services, and the result was positive. More than two hundred and fifty post graduates and research students agreed that the CeRA in the University of Agriculture Sciences Dharwad, Karnataka is a very effective tool in their research. Twenty students are not taking help of CeRA. The rest one hundred ten are using some other open source and different search engines. Majority of them are of the opinion that CeRA consortium of NAIP (National Agriculture Innovative Project) helps them to get full text peer reviewed e- journal articles for their research work. They agreed that CeRA consortium saves a lot of their valuable time.

The following table shows one year CeRA service usage report of UASD

Table 1. Service Usage Report for the Date Range: 12/7/2009 and 12/30/2010 (http://www.uasd.edu)

Sl No	Service	Hits
1	Abstract	2473
2	By Publisher Journal List Page	121
3	By Publisher List Page	154
4	By Subject Journal List Page	463
5	By Subject Page	289
6	Database Search Result Page	12420
7	Database Search Page	6814
8	Full Text	7016
9	Hard Copy	1273
10	Journal List Page	3529
11	Lateral Search	98
12	Latest Updates	52
13	Supplementary URL	6
14	Table of Contents Archive Page	883
15	Table of Contents Page	2659
16	User Login	4956

2.1.1 Result

This small study showed very positive result. The CeRA usage among the young scientist in the field of Agriculture and allied Sciences is common in all state and central agricultural Universities and Agricultural Research Stations in India. It enhances scientific temper and competence of the scientific staff.

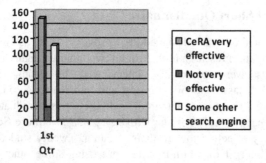

Fig. 4. CeRA how effective as a research tool

3   Conclusion

The greatest advantages of CeRA consortia are online accessibility of all important journals related to agriculture and allied sciences to researchers and students of the Consortium members. Quick access to R & D information as available worldw i d e along with permanent archive of the subscribed e-databases, improvement in the quality of scientific publications, teaching and research guidance, Avoiding duplication in research work, ensuring quick retrieval of information, promoting resource sharing, and providing a permanent solution to the problem of space are some of other advantages of CeRA. The establishment of CeRA under NAIP is a part of the ongoing activities of the Unit of Simulation and Informatics (USI) setup since November 2003 by merging the Unit of Applications System Simulation (UASS), the Bioinformatics Centre and Internet Facilities. As compared to other consortium in India and other parts of the world, CeRA consortium is no doubt helping quality research and improving crop yields, and thereby indirectly helping grass root level workers i.e. farmers.

References

[1] About CeRA.pdf,
     http://www.cera.jccc.in/about/AboutCeRA.pdf (retrieved)
[2] Chandel, S.S.: Information management in academic libraries, p. 1. Rawat Publications, Jaipur (2003)
[3] Jadhav, S., Jange, S.: Library and Information: sources and services, pp. 19–21. Daya Publishing, New Delhi (2012)

Author Index